The Temple of Culture

The Temple of Culture

*Assimilation and Anti-Semitism
in Literary Anglo-America*

Jonathan Freedman

OXFORD

UNIVERSITY PRESS

2000

OXFORD
UNIVERSITY PRESS

Oxford   New York
Athens   Auckland   Bangkok   Bogotá   Buenos Aires   Calcutta
Cape Town   Chennai   Dar es Salaam   Delhi   Florence   Hong Kong   Istanbul
Karachi   Kuala Lumpur   Madrid   Melbourne   Mexico City   Mumbai
Nairobi   Paris   São Paulo   Singapore   Taipei   Tokyo   Toronto   Warsaw

and associated companies in
Berlin   Ibadan

Copyright © 2000 by Jonathan Freedman

Published by Oxford University Press, Inc.
198 Madison Avenue, New York, New York 10016

Oxford is a registered trademark of Oxford University Press.

Library of Congress Cataloging-in-Publication Data
Freedman, Jonathan, 1954–
The temple of culture : assimiliation and anti-Semitism
in literary Anglo-America / Jonathan Freedman.
p.   cm.
Includes bibliographical references and index.
ISBN 0-19-513157-6
1. Jews—United States—Intellectual life. 2. Jews—Cultural assimilation—
United States. 3. American literature—Jewish authors—History and criticism.
4. Jews—England—Intellectual life. 5. Jews—Cultural assimilation—
England. 6. English literature—Jewish authors—History and criticism.
7. James, Henry, 1843–1916—Criticism and interpretation.
8. Antisemitism in literature. I. title.

E184.35.F74   1999
305.8924073—dc21   99-054306

1 3 5 7 9 8 6 4 2

Printed in the United States of America
on acid-free paper

Acknowledgments

THIS PROJECT HAS BEEN in the works for some time, and over that period its author has moved in four or five separate academic life-worlds—a somewhat diasporic existence, indeed, but not an unpleasant one. Indeed, to the contrary, I have been lucky to have been enriched by comments, suggestions, and examples from colleagues at many different institutions and discursive communities. From my years at Yale, where this project began, I want to record with special warmth the aid and counsel of Lynn Wardley (who first helped me see that I had a topic when it was just a one-page conference proposal), Sara Suleri, Kevin Dunn, and Richard Brodhead. Hugh Baxter, Bernardine Connelly, Blakey Vermeule, Jodie Greene, and Danny Hack all contributed more than they knew. During my summers at Bread Loaf, I profited from advice and inspiration from Jim Maddox (who kept "having me back" to try out ideas that wormed their ways into these pages), Isobel Armstrong, Dare Clubb, Elly Eisenberg, Susanne Wofford, Kate Greenebaum, Jacques Lezra, Anne Marshall, Dianne Sadoff, and Michael Wood. Dixie Goswami is so powerful an inspiration that she deserves a sentence of her own. During a year at the National Humanities Center, Helmut Müller-Sievers cannily answered questions about German philosophy and the metaphysics of (his) Cadillac ownership; Sarah Beckwith offered major inspiration in the weight room of the Imperial Health Center as well as her abilities as a reader of academical prose; Toril Moi provided incentive to run faster and think harder, often both at the same time. In addition, conversations with Robert Ferguson, Priscilla Ferguson, Kent Mullikin, and Luise White helped make my project clearer to myself, if not always to them.

At the University of Michigan, colleagues and pals alike have provided both intellectual and moral support. Anne Gere, Sandra Gunning, Linda Gregerson, George Sanchez, Mike Schoenfeldt, and David Scobey will recognize ideas I have tried out in conversation—or lifted from them; June Howard, John Kucich, Anita Norich, and Tobin Siebers added their skills as readers to their friendship. Anita lent help in things Jewish; she is to be absolved of my persistent misunderstandings of her very clear explanations. Other Ann Arborites, past or present—Leonard Barkan, Liz Barnes, Phil Blumberg, Nick Delbanco, Susan Douglas, Linda Eggert, Geoff Eley, Chris Flint, Ari Roth, Gina Morantz-Sanchez, and Athera Urettos, are chief among them—created in various ways the kind of community that makes work possible, as on a spectacular level did Bob Weisbuch before he left Ann Arbor to save American education. Finally, graduate students patient enough to work or run with me—David Anthony, Maria Bergstrom, Susan Rosenbaum, and Misha Tepper are just a few of many who should be acknowledged here—contributed more than they know. What they will not recognize, but should, are all the ways, small and large, in which their friendship and faith in me have allowed me to keep going despite the occasional blast of cold Michigan wind.

Friends at the University of Virginia may recognize much the same; this is the place to single out Alison Booth, Pat Spacks, David Levin, Eric Lott, Susan Fraiman, Teju Olaniwan, and Clare Kinney, for their extraordinary graciousness and generosity, intellectual and otherwise. I want also to register the warmth and support offered by my friends and colleagues at the California Institute of Technology, especially Kevin Gilmartin, Cathy Jurca, Mac Pigman, and Cindy Weinstein. Indeed, without Cindy's lending library (and our frequent visits to Peet's), this book would never have been completed. Sammy and Sara Weinstein deserve a special nod. So does LA tour guide extraordinaire, Valerie Karno—though we have yet to find the corner of Rockingham and Bundy. None of the above, needless to say, should be held responsible for the opinions or mistakes of the author.

I need to thank two wonderful organizations, the National Humanities Center and the John Simon Guggenheim Foundation, for providing the support necessary to begin and complete (respectively) this project. Portions of this book have appeared in the *Henry James Review* and *American Literary History*; I thank both for permission to reprint. T. Susan Chang had faith in this project and helped speed it toward completion; since her acceptance came at a very propitious moment, she is due special thanks.

This book is for my family, in its ever-ramifying sense. Ralph, Lila, Mark, Kate, Weli, Mishka, and Jemia gave me life, encouragement, delight, instruction, and amusement along with the usual amounts of German-Jewish angst and Russian-Jewish *tsuris*. The Blairs—Lillian, Koren, Joe, Kitra, Eva, and Bill—have taught me more Yiddishkeit than they know. Benjamin Blair Freedman reminds me of what's important on a daily basis (usually about 5:30 A.M.). Sara Blair read every single word of this manuscript and improved most of them, while writing, teaching, childbearing, and being a wonderful partner. That she makes it all look so easy and does it with such love only adds to the miracle.

Contents

The Temple of Culture

Introduction

Every day during my fourteen years in New Haven—six in graduate school, eight on the faculty—I trudged across a large thoroughfare on my way from breakfast at Naples Pizza to Linsly-Chittenden Hall, home of Yale's famous English department. On Fridays, the corner was occupied—there is no other word—by a group of Lubavitcher Hasidim who sought out Jewish-looking folk like myself, walked up to us, and shouted in our ears, "Excuse me, sir, are you Jewish?" Needless to say, they presented me with something of a dilemma. Had I answered yes—I never did—they would have escorted me into the back of their mitzvah-mobile, taught me a prayer or two, and helped me on the path toward Jewish enlightenment. I had no interest in this, since my own Jewishness consists of a passionate belief in voting the straight Democratic ticket, fasting on Yom Kippur, eating bagels and lox—and doing no more. Had I answered no, however, I would have been disavowing not only my own Jewishness but also that of my family who after all, certain Europeans had tried to stick in ovens a generation earlier and who had only escaped their fates by a series of flukes too fortuitous to be believable. So I just hurried by, envying my friend the ex-kibbutznik Lewis, who took to responding in Hebrew, *"Hishtagata!"* which he translated as: "Go to hell, you jerks."

There was another way into work, through the aptly named Old Campus, one that led me an extra block or so to a portal through that walled enclave called Phelps Gate before leading me to my office. A few years later, I came to learn a bit more about the figure after whom Phelps Gate was named. William Lyon "Billy" Phelps was a popularizing Yale English professor who helped to bring about the middle-class enthusiasm for highbrow literature that is the subject of much of this book. Phelps, I also learned, was a genteel anti-Semite in the mode of many of his generation; according to Dan Oren's fine history of Jews at Yale, *Joining the Club*, Phelps expressed in his private correspondence the opinion that, while it might be fine for Jews to teach other subjects, English literature needed

3

to remain off-limits to them. How could a Jew, a non-Christian, successfully teach Robert Browning's *Christmas-Eve* and *Easter-Day*?¹

This, then, was my ambulatory choice: to be classed as a kind of Jew that I did not wish to be, or to pass through the portals of anti-Semitic high culture as a tweed-wearing, briefcase-bearing literatus (albeit one who purchased both at the Hadassah Thrift Shop). In many ways, this book is not so much an attempt to figure out a solution to this problematic—which luckily is much less of a problem than it used to be, for a number of reasons that I detail later—as a way of historicizing it, thinking about its intellectual roots and cultural ramifications. For my own situation came very much at the end of that of two generations of American Jews who sought in the academy that sine qua non of the middle classes, the career open to talent, and who both transformed and were transformed by that career in general. My German-born father, for example, had been more or less forced by his own father to become an academic rather than a freelance writer some thirty years before I was dodging Tough Moral Choices on the streets of New Haven. My mother of Russian Jewish descent—her father was born in Kiev but found a career for himself in America as a dental equipment salesman—had escaped Brooklyn and the Katherine Gibbs Secretarial School by pursuing an advanced degree in English; her career had taken her to such enclaves of the postwar education boom as the University of North Carolina and the University of Wisconsin before she discovered her vocation as a demoniacally blue-penciling editor of a course catalog at the very institution where I was dodging importunate Hasidim. For both of them, and for many other members of my family, the literary academy provided financial security and social status in a postwar world that was opening itself up to Jews in fits and starts and that, by the time I came along, seemed to be so accepting as to make the entire matter an irrelevancy.

Since my own career has been marked by one job crunch after another, this career path seems to me more of a historical anomaly than the historical inevitability it no doubt appeared to be to my parents. But what has struck me not only about them but about the entire world in which I was raised was the emphasis that was placed on the idea and the ideal of culture. Growing up in Iowa, for example, I only realized how anomalous we were when I visited my friends' houses and saw that every kid didn't have Picasso and Degas prints from the Metropolitan Museum plastered on their bedroom wall. And during my parents' acrimonious divorce in Princeton, New Jersey, I remember patiently explaining to an uncomprehending friend that a major issue in contention was whether my brother and I would continue to read Jane Austen—a synecdoche, in my mother's eyes, for retaining what vestiges of civility our fascination with the New York Knicks was leaching out of us. I didn't truly understand the motives for the wall hangings or Austen idolatry until I read about Lionel Trilling's own Brooklyn-bred mother, who read him Dickens and who interceded with his Columbia admissions officer to explain away Lionel's poor scores on science tests. Nor did I understand why my father, who wouldn't buy a Volkswagen because of its Nazi origins, nevertheless taught German Romantic literature until I read more about the experience of cultivated German Jews who truly believed that they, and not the benighted Nazi-infatuated *Volk*, were the true heirs of the culture of Goethe and Schiller, of Kant and Hegel.

In many ways, then, this book is an attempt to make some sense out of my relation to this milieu—the *habitus*, in Pierre Bourdieu's resonant and well-nigh indefinable term in which my fundamental dispositions and doxa were formed and contested. But my predominant aim here is not autobiographical (indeed, these are just about the last autobiographical notes the reader of this book will hear struck). The story of culture-making has been at the center of most interesting scholarly work in both American and British venues in the past fifty years. Raymond Williams argued for the constitutive powers of the split between "culture" and "society" some forty years ago, and his insight may in some sense—methodologically, if nothing else—be said to serve as the origin of the new discipline of so-called cultural studies.[2] Separately, Americanists of the past two or three generations—Neil Harris, Lawrence Levine, Richard Ohmann, Richard Brodhead, Joan Shelley Rubin, and Janice Radway are prime among them—have been delineating the social work that the organization of "high culture" did on these shores, particularly as that notion arose in relation to the exfoliation of mass culture in the late nineteenth and early twentieth centuries. Meanwhile, under the impetus of critics like Jonathan and Daniel Boyarin, David Biale, Sander Gilman, Michael Ragussis, Bryan Cheyette, Elaine Marks, James Shapiro, and a host of others, the critical study of Jewishness has been transformed. These scholars and literary critics have brought contemporary theoretical discourses on gender, race, nation, and identity to bear on the question of Jewishness, revising our understanding both of Jewishness and of the ways in which the matter of Jewry entered into the philosophical, literary, and ideological traditions of the West. As a result, the terms in which we have traditionally thought about Jewishness in the modern world and the archetypal, if not clichéd, issues that follow from it—the much vexed questions of Jewish identity, assimilation, the conflict between religion and secularism, the nature of historical memory, and so on—have gotten immensely more complicated. Indeed, the paradigm-shifting power of this work has been so great that many are proclaiming the rise of an entirely new field, Jewish cultural studies.[3]

Perhaps such a new field will develop, although I myself doubt that the moniker "cultural studies" will mean anything much more in this context than it has proven to in any other. What I undertake here, however, is more focused. I want here to bring together these two broad currents of thought—the new ways in which we have come to think about this mysterious entity we call culture, the odd things the Western imagination has done when it comes into contact with Jews—in such a way as to illuminate each other, or to at least trace out new patterns of complication. For to bring the spectacularly anomalous example of Jewishness to bear on the central questions of our own critical moment is to thicken the terms in which those questions have been posed just as fully as bringing the new forms of discourse to bear on the matter of Jewishness has changed the ways we think about Jews, Judaism, and Jewishness.

I should stress that my aim in exploring the resultant nest of complexities is not to install Jewish difference as yet another participant in the parade of alterities that critics have focused on in recent years. There are indeed interesting parallels between the Jewish experience in the West and those of other racial minorities, of women, and of the sexually transgressive. But out of respect both for the distinctive histories of these groups and for the idiosyncrasy of Jews—as well as a wariness of recapitulating dominant culture's attempt to collapse them all under the heading of the aberrant, the perverse, the Other—I advert to these parallels only briefly and attempt throughout to preserve a sense of the different difference, as Alain Finkielkraut puts it, that constitutes Jewish difference. Indeed, my goal here is not so much to provide a history of this difference as to explore some of the things we can do with it. I want to show how taking Jewishness into account can help us tell richer, more complicated, more serendipitous stories about our culture; by the same token, I want to show how thinking about the close inter-twining of assimilating Jews with the rise of new ideologies of culture can sharpen the narratives we tell about the social and cultural work these Jews did in the course of this process.

Thus in my first chapter, I try to assess the precise valences of my two con-tested terms "culture" and "Jewishness," preparatory to the task of trying to figure out how they might work in tandem with each other. In the case of each, I consider myself an agnostic or, perhaps it would be better to say, a nominalist, with respect to the virtues and salience of the term. If, as we have gotten used to saying after Raymond Williams, the very idea of "culture" has a history, if that notion as we understand it was a product of the German Enlightenment and its Victorian exponent, Matthew Arnold, and spread throughout Anglo-American culture in the later years of the nineteenth century,[4] then it comes with a full load of ideological baggage that makes it difficult to apply in a world increasingly understood to be divided by competing interests of class, race, gender, and so on. Yet the very fact that this ideal has a history—has exerted a social power over the passage of time—makes its social efficacy a powerful subject of inquiry even after two generations of demystification. That its history is powerfully con-nected to the experience of assimilating Western Jews, both as its object (Matthew Arnold's Hebrews) and as its subject (those Jews who sought to assimilate by bearing the torch of a high culture that marginalized them), makes it even more resonant—from a social point of view, to be sure, but also from an affective or psychological one.

If the ideal of high culture exerted a powerful social force, after all, it did so because it appealed to something in the emotional as well as the intellectual makeup of those who enrolled in its service. This is even more powerfully the case when it comes to those cultivated Jews who sought to wager their social legitimacy on the powers of "high culture" in a country—America—where respect for "culture" and its exponents has been contested, to say the least.[5] The payoff for Trilling or the writers of the *Partisan Review* or even the first generations of Jewish English professors would seem to be as much the assertion of a certain kind of refined superiority to the hurly-burly of a commercial society and its mass culture as the achievement of social power. Certainly economic success has never been the prime goal of people like professors, and until recently anything more than a life of shabby gentility has seemed something of an embarrassment to them.[6]

A similar complicating process confronted me when it came to thinking about Jews. Like many of my generation, I incline toward an anti-essentialist view of Jewishness, on account of both my historical position and my intellectual orientation. As far as the former is concerned, for example, it is impossible in 1999 to view the condition of Jews in the world as a single unitary phenomenon; if one needs proof of this, one simply has to look to the current debates in the State of Israel about the viability of Conservative and Reform Judaism to see just how fully the notion of Jewishness has been split—and not only by doctrinal differences but by considerations of nation, class, ethnicity, even race. And with respect to the latter, it is difficult to believe that everything has a history—has varied over time and will presumably continue to mutate over the course of the future—without extending that belief to the power of that mysterious amalgam of religious, racial, cultural, and social continuities that compose whatever sense one has of being Jewish. Paul Lauter puts the anti-essentialist position provocatively and well: "Jewishness, or even Judaism, is what it has always been: what people acting in history have chosen to make of it."[7]

But two problems with Lauter's formulation trouble me, hence this project. If one defines either Judaism or Jewishness as the ability of people to say what Judaism or Jewishness is, then what is the force of defining oneself, one's beliefs, one's acts, in tandem with these things at all? Like Lauter, I quickly add, I believe that Jewishness may be best defined not so much as a reified entity or even as a Rortyan conversation but as a loud, pot-banging quarrel; and my midrash-steeped friends tell me that Judaism qua religious practice is not unsusceptible to this definition, either. But unlike Lauter, I don't know how even to begin to assess these quarrels without acknowledging that, at least for its participants, something larger than their own interests is involved in it, whether that thing be a deeply felt religious faith, a sense of communal identity, a national or regional project, a simple matter of survival. I have tried to keep this fact in mind in what follows, even when (especially when) I find myself in disagreement with the politics that flow from these impulses. But—and this is my second problem—Jews have not always been able to exercise their own historical agency freely; indeed, such a self-defining liberty would seem to be often more the exception than the rule, and more the product of conditions of isolation (ghettoization, for example) that one might not wish to valorize. For despite the best efforts of Jews and gentiles to keep apart from one another, at least in Western cultures, the exact lineaments of Jewishness, if not Judaism,[8] have frequently been negotiated in response to the dominant cultures in which Jews found themselves, whether in the *shtetl*, the sweatshops, or the faculty lounges. Just to complicate the matter further, the same has been true for what T. S. Eliot once called Christian culture. The gentile tradition, as I would call it, has a long and complicated relation with Jews and Jewishness, indeed, a nearly foundational one—without Jews, where would Christianity be?—and the subsequent unfolding of the cultures of Europe and America occurred with continuing reference to the figure of the Jew, sometimes as ideal, sometimes as abject Other, frequently as both. Jews participating in the cultures of the West thus entered into an equally fraught relation with a cultural system that relied, for its own sense of identity, on its edgy and conflicted construction of *them*.

To do full justice to the complexity of these interconnections would be impossible. What I have sought to do in this book instead is to look at this cultural interchange in one admittedly large situation—the cultural dispensations of England and America between 1860 and the present day—in the hope that I have avoided the pitfalls of either a knee-jerk essentialism or an equally reflexive anti-essentialism. Whether I succeed in this task I leave for the reader to judge. What I am aiming to do is not only to provide a history of the reciprocal relation between the figure of the Jew and the career of high culture in Anglo-America but to contextualize my own efforts and those of my fellow travelers on the assimilation-by-culture trail. For to see that such gentile constructions as the Jew as alien had a powerful effect on the shaping of such archetypal figures as the alienated intellectual, and that assimilating Jews donned this garb as a part of their own entry into culture industries of the twentieth century, is to trace the path by which Lauter, or for that matter my family and hence myself, negotiated a position for themselves in Anglo-American high culture. Whether people can or should continue to follow this route, whether it even exists at all, are the questions with which I conclude this book.

Thus after my exercise in definition, I turn to some of the specific ways in which the new ideologies and institutions of high culture were shaped in relation to the Jew in the late years of the nineteenth century. My choice of this social moment is not adventitious. For notions that we have come to see as central facets of twentieth-century life first rose to prominence in the later decades of the nineteenth century. This was not only the era when the ideology of culture passed, via Matthew Arnold, from the starry realms of German philosophy into common, middle-class parlance; it was the era in which levels of culture that had long been forming in relation to each other crystallized into sharply distinct arenas of experience. Thus "high" culture gets shaped at this moment, under the Arnoldian banner of "the best that has been thought and said"; so too does a fully articulated, well-defined mass culture, propelled into prominence by new technologies of production, distribution, and reception like mass market magazines, penny and dime novels, and so on. And so, to complete the picture, does a well-defined and self-promulgated middlebrow culture. In the late 1880s and 1890s in particular, such phenomena as reading groups and Browning and Ruskin clubs, mass-produced vade mecums to high culture, tours of art museums at home or abroad, and the beginning of a boom in higher education testified to a vast middle-class hunger for instruction in the lineaments of "proper" cultural response. To be sure, one can note these developments at many moments in literary and cultural history: what is the Gothic novel but a mass market phenomenon, what is Wordsworth's critique of the Gothic in the *Preface* to *Lyrical Ballads* but a highbrow response to lowbrow competition? What marks this era, however, is the coordinated and co-implicated rise of these three very different cultural phenomena and their closely related social and affective experiences. And it turns out that each of these powerful collocations of social experience and cultural response has much to do with Jews.

Consider, as I try to do in chapter 2, one of the most socially powerful forms of the nineteenth century—and one that faced, as an integral part of its self-definition, precisely the problem of cultural hierarchy I have been treating here: the Victorian novel. For even as this form developed in imaginative power and artistic ambition, even as it sought to slough off its mass cultural origins and define itself as high art, the novel was increasingly frequented by Jewish characters and concerns—and not just at the margins of the narrative action but at its very center. Where would *Oliver Twist* be without the malignant Fagin, or *Daniel Deronda* without the character who gives the novel its name and half of its plot? My suggestion here is that this increasing concern with Jews was the product of a crisis of self-definition posed for writers engaging with the increasing mass market for fiction in the mid– to late nineteenth century. For writers like George Eliot or Anthony Trollope this situation created powerful affective consequences. To be a successful writer involves (as Catherine Gallagher powerfully argued a few years ago) feelings of shame, particularly among intellectuals who define themselves against the marketplace in which they have found such spectacular success. Gallagher began to suggest that the resulting conflicts were embodied and to a certain extent evaded by George Eliot's representation of three figures for the female artist in *Daniel Deronda*: the usurer, the prostitute, and the Jew. I extend Gallagher's argument in two ways. First, I want to suggest, pleasure as well as pain, pride as well as shame, governed the Victorian writer's response to the marketplace—and this welter of feelings was as constitutive of the male writer's experience as the female's, although it was obviously differently inflected. Moreover, the figure of the Jew serves as the embodiment of this nest of new affective possibilities in the brave new world of the marketplace—and has done so from at least the early modern period forward. The new feelings of pride, shame, joy, pleasure, and even a self-disciplining pain that arise in the capitalist economies of the West get most fully embodied by the figure of the lascivious, passionate, gold-greedy Jew, whether Marlowe's Barabas, Shakespeare's Shylock, or Dickens's Fagin. And, I suggest, that figure enters into the fiction of the Victorian era as a way for its authors to figure their own experience in a mature capitalist economy. My example is Anthony Trollope, whose novels of the mid-1870s and early 1880s register the seismic shocks set off by the simultaneous arrival of parvenu Jews and excesses of finance capital in the seemingly stable world of Victorian London. Trollope represents and to a certain extent resolves the dilemma of living in a materially successful world by his representations of the Jew as a scapegoat-like speculator who embodies the author's own imaginative burdens in their most malign guise. But Trollope being Trollope—deceptively self-conscious and infinitely cunning—he also critiques his very position, and he tries to force his readers to do the same. Trollope's seemingly anti-Semitic texts thus serve as both an exemplar of the structures of feeling that are circulating within and around him and a test of their imaginative and ideological consequences.

A similar knot seems to be tied in my second test case of the relation between Jews and the making of culture in the late nineteenth century: the massive popular excitement occasioned by George du Maurier's novel *Trilby*. *Trilby*-mania, as it was known in the later years of the nineteenth century, was perhaps the most powerful of the many waves of popular enthusiasm for European high culture that swept through England and especially America in the latter years of the nineteenth century; not only was this novel a spectacular bestseller but it accompanied a frenzied wave of commercial activity the likes of which simply hadn't been seen before. Two crucial issues that obsess my project were brought together in this popular enthusiasm, and more specifically in the figure of Svengali who stood at its center: the figure of the artist as powerful but perverse magician and the figure of the artist as Jew. The bipolarity of the middlebrow—the enthusiasm for "culture" *and* the resentment that such enthusiasm brings with it—get negotiated if not reconciled through this doubly represented figure, the figure of the potent but pestiferous Jewish artist. This figure, I suggest, becomes a staple of the middlebrow's imagination of high-cultural response and with it, a persistent expression of the simultaneous idealization and abjection of "culture" that is, I think, the defining mark of the middlebrow.

Throughout these chapters, somewhat to my surprise, I found myself grounding my analysis in the category of affect—the rich set of contradictory feelings that constitute cultural response, whether in the context of life in marketplace society or in that of middlebrows' responses to their cultural positioning. This interest carried over, I discovered, to the case study that follows, the responses to Jews of that most crucial figure in the late nineteenth and early twentieth century, Henry James. I found myself writing on James in part because he constituted my own area of expertise, but I was also interested in him for less parochial reasons. First, far more than any other figure, James has always seemed to me fascinating because he is at once liminal and foundational. He is liminal because he existed on the borders between the nineteenth and the twentieth centuries, between the concept of fiction as entertainment (as he viewed it early in his career) and fiction as high art; between England and America; between Anglo-America and Europe. James is foundational because, as I have tried to suggest elsewhere, he established the very terms by which the twentieth century came to understand the art of fiction and the identity of the artist; indeed, as I have tried elsewhere to argue, high canonical modernism is not only indebted to James but is often a pale imitation of the audacious experiments and deeply contradictory investments of its magisterial predecessor. Second, and more relevant to this project, James's responses to the massive emigration of eastern European Jews to Anglo-America was both representative of his fellow members of the gentry elite and deeply idiosyncratic. James evinced much of the same patrician dismay at the arrival of Jews in Europe and America as did contemporaries like James Russell Lowell or Henry Adams or successors like T. S. Eliot and Ezra Pound, but his response was richer, more conflicted, at once more generous and more anxiety-ridden than their more notorious ones. His responses to Jews—verging from outright disdain to idealizing fascination and touching just about every place in between—not only trace out the full range of possibilities expressed by his contemporaries and successors; they also suggest some of the motivation for their reactions. For James's complexity of reaction is grounded in his sense of himself as an artist and a sexually nonnormative man at a moment when both figures were being put under pressure by the claims for their deep participation in the process of social degeneration. James's defensive response to the Jew represents a way of changing the subject—of clearing himself of the charge of degeneracy by nominating another figure for that role. The figure of the Jew thus becomes, as it is for an Adams or an Eliot, an odd double for the artist or the intellectual even as it represents the decline of cultural value and social cohesion.

But what about those figures I have called "real live Jews"? In chapter 5, I sketch the process of assimilation in America between 1880 (with the entry of millions of eastern and southern European Jews along with numerous other immigrants to these shores) and roughly 1980. My focus here is both broad and specific. I try to sketch some of the lineaments of the process I call assimilation-by-culture from the earlier years of the century and to suggest some of the affective complexities—the admixture of reverence and rage, accommodation and aggression—that governed this process. And I try to trace the consequences of this modality of response with respect to two of the most important culture industries of the twentieth century: publishing and the literary academy. In each, Jews entered previously WASP-dominated institutions with a powerful force in the 1920s and 1950s, respectively; in both, they changed the ways in which that arena conceived of itself as irrevocably as they themselves were changed by it. The notion of "literature," the relation of writing to the augmenting and reticulating reading public, the ways in which "culture" might be packaged, promoted, and distributed, the political work that culture might be seen as doing—all these were changed by such houses as Alfred A. Knopf (the first Jew to be employed in an editorial capacity in New York publishing), Simon and Schuster, and Boni and Liveright, and by the spectacularly anomalous figure of Emmanuel Haldeman-Julius, perhaps the most successful publisher of his era, who has faded into utter obscurity today. Similarly, the study of literature, the understanding of what writing can be and can do, got irrevocably transformed when, under the aegis of the GI Bill and the postwar education boom, Jews flooded into a literary academy that had been, at least in its most elite outposts, less than welcoming to their presence.

From these broad considerations, I turn to another case study: the reception, in the literary field broadly conceived, of the works of Henry James. For it is a remarkable fact, one little noted, that the so-called James revival of the 1940s and 1950s was the first effort in American canon formation in which Jews participated on an equal footing with gentiles. Figures like Philip Rahv, Lionel Trilling, and Leon Edel were as important as arch-WASP F. O. Matthiessen in this process; the house organ of the Jewish-dominated "New York Intellectuals," the *Partisan Review*, was as crucial to the James revival as any academic department or publishing house. And the encounter of Jews with the example of James has continued to ramify both within the academy and without for the next two generations. Indeed, as I conclude the chapter, the very differently positioned figures of Cynthia Ozick and Philip Roth have this one thing in common—they are both imaginatively attuned to and significantly involved with the writing of that most unlikely of literary fathers, Henry James.

The Henry James that Philip Roth invokes, however, is a prophet of perversion as well as art, an inciter to masturbation as well as mastery, and this James is a fundamentally different character from the one apotheosized by Rahv, Trilling, et al. I conclude this project with the hopes that Roth's construction of James can be accompanied by a new understanding of the vocation of the Jewish writer, critic, intellectual in a diasporic world—the understanding that, as I suggested earlier, I see breaking out all around me. The idealization of high culture that follows from the assimilation-by-culture project can be replaced by attitudes more open to different possibilities of behavior, identity, and cultural self-understanding—both with respect to a Jewishness that has to be neither disavowed nor affirmed in any simple way and with respect to an increasingly diverse culture that continues to transform itself in ways sometimes analogous to the transformation of Jews, sometimes subversive of them. At any event, I suggest in a brief coda, the critique of multiculturalism, the defense of the canon, and the privileging of the most high-minded notion of European "culture" that was undertaken by the Jewish intellectuals—frequently invoking the familiar rhetoric of cultural decline and social anarchy that has haunted their experience from the 1880s forward—can be understood as the last gasp of a generation that built a space for themselves via their poignant, heartfelt cathexis to the traditional high culture of the West. But when we look at the unfolding history of this cathexis, as I do in the latter pages of this book, we can see other possibilities built into the Jewish encounter with "culture"—aggressions against traditional high culture as well as appropriations of it, negotiations of a new American identity as well as confrontations with old traditions of prejudice, marginality, and exclusion. And, tellingly, these models seem quite relevant to the experience and imaginative production of other racial and ethnic groups struggling to find a place in an American society where they are understood to be aliens, foreigners, or just plain different. With the passage of time (and one can only hope, increasingly so) traditional animosities and antitheses increasingly come to seem less important; new angles of similarity between the experience of racial and ethnic others and Jews in Western cultures—the relevance of the concept of diaspora, the problems of "model minorities," the problematic of aggressing against and assimilating to a culture that both depends on and marginalizes you—are beginning to emerge, and with them new forms of cultural production or expression.

Whether or not these new admixtures of materials hitherto kept separate by older animosities and hierarchies can continue to emerge, the more capacious understanding of the Jewish experience of high culture I offer hereafter would go a long way, I think, toward dispelling the baleful effects of the culture wars undertaken by many Jewish intellectuals, and pursued sometimes with a reductive vigor by their antagonists on the cultural left, and move us closer to a more nuanced appreciation of the actual situation we face at our own fin-de-siècle moment. The old temple of culture, built on the floorplan of Hegel and Arnold by Jews and gentiles alike for the last hundred years, is indeed in rickety shape, but it is still standing, and much beautiful and important work is being done there. Services are still regularly performed in the academic chapel even as new frescoes (and even neon light sculptures) are being installed in the antechambers and hallways. Meanwhile, new sites of cultural experience and exchange are being erected around and about it, designed on entirely different principles; and equally important and interesting and beautiful work is getting created in these spaces.

The first may fall apart entirely or, more likely, be patched and restored and remade—I have no doubt that a hundred years hence, people will still be reading Dante and Shakespeare and even Henry James, although I doubt very much that we would recognize the terms by which they do so any more than Victorian readers would or should understand ours. Whatever the ultimate fate of the temple of culture, those of us who, by inclination or habit or will or desire or profession, attend its services (however irregularly) can still do so without losing our interest in new forms of building—and *bildung*—taking place every day, all around us.

1

The Jew in the Museum

THE ART INSTITUTE OF CHICAGO; 1994: a collection of recent acquisitions to the photography collection. The crowd swarms, though not quite as thickly as upstairs, where it encounters masterpieces dismally familiar yet unexpectedly moving in their full auratic presence. The avidity of these spectators is hardly deterred—it may, in fact, be enhanced—by signs posted throughout the photography exhibition informing us, in purest officialese, that "material in this exposition may prove offensive to some patrons." Nothing conspicuously shocking, overtly prurient, initially presents itself; luckily, a cluster of signs soon appears demarcating one room containing "potentially objectionable material." Here the crowd quickens with particular intensity; and here indeed is much to catch the eye: a Mapplethorpe (part of the Lisa Lyon series); Josh Wytkin's transsexuals; Richard Avedon's portrait of a bee keeper, nude, covered with swarming insects. On one wall stands a familiar-looking image, discreetly clothed amid this abundance of flesh: Leonardo's Christ, from the very center of the *Last Supper*. On closer inspection, negative marks band the image; to its side entirely stands a plaque announcing the title, *Delay*, and the name of the artist, William Anastasi. On the image itself, slightly to the left of center, superimposed over the body of Christ, appears a single word: "Jew."

A *Talk of the Town* column in the *New Yorker*, 1996: an account of a leisurely lunch in Oxford, whose participants are discussing a new book by Anthony Julius, Princess Diana's attorney and a recovering academic. The thesis of Julius's book is that anti-Semitism was not an isolated blot on T. S. Eliot's otherwise unsullied reputation but rather an essential component of his aesthetics and politics. The lunch that occasions the *New Yorker*'s interest follows a public lecture on Julius's critique delivered by James Fenton, the Regius Professor of Poetry at Oxford (a lecture given in the same series in which Matthew Arnold delivered *The Function of Criticism at the Present Time*). There, the Regius Professor has acknowledged the salience of anti-Semitism not only to Eliot's poetry but to the cultural project in which he and Eliot are both engaged. Anti-Semitism, Julius argues, Fenton agrees, and the *New Yorker* breathlessly reports, "is the price to pay for admission into the club of Modernism" and the cultural authority that comes along with membership.[1]

These two episodes suggest how forcefully the matter of Jewishness has recently come rushing into critical awareness, particularly into that zone where traditional high culture meets a mass audience. They suggest as well how loaded are the concerns it brings in its wake. In the case of the former, after all, the truly remarkable fact is not the recognition enforced in the Anastasi image—that Christ was a Jew—but that such a recognition should still in 1994 be thought scandalous, even in Chicago, City of Churches. In the latter case what is remarkable is that the anti-Semitism of modern poetry should be found noteworthy not only in Oxford wine bars but in the pages of a magazine whose enterprise is increasingly nothing if not middlebrow. For at a moment when the value of the traditional high culture that Eliot and Pound incarnated for a previous generation has receded in the face of postmodern culture and postmodern critique, the interrogation of Eliot's anti-Semitism has the odd effect of resurrecting a previous cultural dispensation in the very act of disenchanting it.

It is my argument here that the interconnection of these two concerns—with the matter of the Jew, with the nature and powers of traditional high culture—is neither adventitious nor insignificant, even if its critical articulation has been, as Anastasi's title suggests, embarrassingly belated. Rather, the question of Jewish difference has long been central to the delineation of the nature, scope, and power of the entity referred to as culture. Indeed, this intertwining dates to the very onset of that discursive regime: the German philosophers of the late eighteenth and early nineteenth century who first enunciated the ideal of "culture" did so in direct relation to what came to be known as "the Jewish question"—the question of what to do with a large, non-native-speaking, non-Christian, ethnic minority in the new nation-state. And this interweaving of the matter of the Jew and the idiom of culture reached a further complexity, at least for our purposes, in England and America. For it is a remarkable fact, one little noticed until recently, that those nineteenth-century Anglo-American intellectuals who theorized the lineaments when they were exemplifying the practice of high culture, figures like Matthew Arnold, Anthony Trollope, George Eliot—and, a little later, George du Maurier, Henry James, Edith Wharton, Willa Cather, F. Scott Fitzgerald, T. S. Eliot, Ezra Pound, James Joyce, Ernest Hemingway—were also powerfully engaged by the problematic of Jewishness.[2] Or to be more precise, for all these writers, and many more besides them, the nature and possibilities of culture, civilization, literary value, social cohesion, intellectual life—the possibilities of artistic vocation, that network of concerns and values that got originated with the eighteenth-century German philosophers, bundled into a social program by Matthew Arnold, and then played out by his successors—were frequently measured, their positive and negative valences assessed, by comparison and contrast with the figure of the Jew.

Moreover, this process was not limited to literary texts or even texts about literary texts. To this era, and to critics who read and responded to the figures I have just named, we owe the origins of "English" as a distinct conceptual field, and along with it a neoracial genealogy that rooted the origins of English literary genius in the spirit of the Anglo-Saxons.[3] It is to this era, moreover, that we owe the origins of the so-called New Criticism, that method of studying literature that sought through the organic unity of the self-contained literary text a purchase on a concrete universal explicitly understood by many of its adherents to be Christian in nature.[4] For both a model of culture built on the ideal of a racialized national unity and a model of literature built on an ideal either Anglo-Saxon or Christian, the figure of the Jew represented a distinct problem, calling into question as it did the very possibility of the cultural ideal placed at its center. Needless to say, such tensions were further heightened by the increasing presence of actual Jews in college English departments and the literary sphere in postwar England and America.

The figure of the Jew and the matter of Jewishness are so constructed, I am suggesting, as to compose fault lines lying beneath both the ideal of culture grounded on the high Arnoldian model and that of literary study built on the New Critical or philological plan. At the moment when the adequacy of both those models has been called into question and when Jewish intellectuals previously conflicted about or even ashamed of their Jewishness rediscover and renegotiate its terms, long-buried stresses are rising to the surface with increasing frequency and force.[5] As a Jew, an intellectual, a Jewish intellectual, I can only find refreshing these tremors and the critical rumblings they have engendered. Bryan Cheyette has suggested that they are analogous, and perhaps indebted to, those early stages of the feminist movement where a recognition of the historical oppression of women served as a powerful goad to the redefinition of the possibilities of female agency and power.[6] In my view, they are most fully comparable those stages in postcolonial discourse when Western-trained intellectuals recognized and eloquently responded to the complicity of Western high culture in the racializing ideologies that oppressed them. Yet I wonder if, as has been the case in both those spheres, this early shock of recognition—of the presence of the Jew in the cultural traditions of the West à la Anastasi or of the presence of anti-Semitism in those same traditions à la Julius—might be ready to give way to a more nuanced analysis. We might at the present moment be ready to tell the story of the mutually modifying, reciprocal engagement of dominant culture with its long-neglected Other—that other Other, as Jonathan Boyarin puts it, whose otherness has been oft acknowledged but then ignored—in such a way as to ignore neither the subtlety of their interconnections nor the effects of that process on both parties to it.[7]

Or such is my hope here. In what follows, I want to treat some important episodes in the mutual construction of "the Jew," of Jewishness, of real, factual Jews, and the delineation (and deconstruction) of an idiom and ideal of "culture" in such a way as to do full justice to all the various social, historical, cultural, and textual ramifications involved in this process. I turn soon to some of the theoretical and historical problems involved in my various categories: "the Jew," "culture," the Jew *in* culture. But first, I want more fully to describe how complicated and intricate, how rife with cathexes and countercathexes, unexpected affinities and unanticipatable disavowals, this process of mutual identification and cross-referencing turns out to be.

Consider, for example, the gentile side of the cultural coin: in the Anglo-American sphere that is my chief focus here, the figure of the Jew embodied a weirdly persistent paradox, in which the Jew was not only linked to something deeply problematic about culture, but also seen as integrally connected to its very operation. Although frequently installed as "culture" 's debased other, the Jew is oddly, perhaps even scandalously, perceived as being its hidden truth. Thus to Arnold, "the Hebrew" figured a single-minded Puritanism that must find correction by a Greek-inspired suppleness, yet the Hellenic is finally figured in terms and tropes drawn from the experience of Jews, and the figure of the Jew provides a shadowy but powerful type for the Arnoldian intellectual. Similarly, for du Maurier, the Jew embodied a primal, corrupting sexual power that is nevertheless connected to a basic principle of essential dramatic or musical genius. For Trollope, particularly the Trollope of *The Way We Live Now*, the Jew figured the corruption of art, culture, and indeed all principles of stable value by the forces of modernity and the market yet at the same time, powerfully, represented the attractions and deficiencies of marketplace culture. For James, at least the James of *The Golden Bowl*, the Jew figured as the ultimate expression of cultural degeneration and decay but was at the same time an emblem of the transience of civilization and empire. This tendency reaches something of a climax in the poetry of Eliot, for whom the Jew is "under the lot," the most debased of all the heterogeneous figures composing a racially promiscuous modern culture, yet oddly, problematically, foundational to the culture: "under the lot" in the sense of part of the ground, something foundational, something ineradicably, inexpungibly *there*.

Whatever one wants to say about the matter of culture, then, it's clear that the Jew remains a resolute exception to the rule, or, to put it another way, it's clear just why throughout the nineteenth century the Jewish question remained for so long exactly that: a question. To put the matter this way, however, is to suggest that the Jewish question was one posed by gentiles to each other or, occasionally, Jews (who were, of course, quite literally put to the question at one spectacular moment in the deployment of Western power/knowledge). But on the other side of the coin, it's important to see that Jews themselves had a role in articulating, revising, contesting, and (ultimately) remaking the very terms under which they were articulated within the idiom of culture. One spectacular instance of this, as I show in more detail hereafter, is the challenge posed by Moses Mendelssohn to Enlightenment philosophers like Hegel and Kant, especially by his assertion that the essential Jewish contribution to the very possibility of Christianity and hence to a Christian-centered cultural dispensation demanded a political emancipation about which these philosophers remained profoundly ambivalent. And as assimilated German and Austrian Jews sought inclusion in the central organs of high culture that worked increasingly to exclude them— especially the high mandarinate, as one of its most influential scholars has called it, of the German university—a number of Jews sought to exert a certain counterpressure over both their own representation and that of their culture.[8] Indeed, such counterpressure is virtually synonymous with our understanding of modernity: figures like Proust, Freud, Benjamin, and Theodor Adorno have arguably had more influence over the ways that modernity has understood the nature and possibilities of "culture" than have any other such critics since Kant, Herder, and Hegel.

Nor was this counterpressure applied merely by ascribed male Jewish intellectuals, although in both Germany and England they found it easier to find a place in the public sphere than did their female counterparts, who were doubly constrained by traditional Jewish family structure and the relative absence of vocational possibility for intellectual women in early-nineteenth-century culture. Nevertheless, Jewish women functioned at the same time to exert an influence over dominant culture that shaped the views of Jews and Jewishness held in that culture.[9] One thinks here of the salon Jews of late-eighteenth-century Germany, who first modeled the possibilities of being an intellectual woman and about one of whom, Rahel Varnhagen, a twentieth-century intellectual woman, Hannah Arendt, wrote with such power early in her career.[10] My main focus here, England and America, initially provided less spectacular venues for such Jewish women, but their salons and cenacles did afford a certain kind of agency. In nineteenth-century England, Elizabeth Davis famously upbraided Dickens for his portrayal of Fagin and helped him reformulate his portrayal of Riah in *Our Mutual Friend*. Louisa Rothschild, the wife of the second son of the British clan, conducted an elaborate and complicated flirtation with Thackeray (who remained, nevertheless, a confirmed anti-Semite) and was a close, and perhaps also flirtatious, companion of Arnold. Indeed, like Elizabeth Davis, Louisa Rothschild served as a combination native informant and editor to her gentile friend. She not only corresponded with Arnold about matters Jewish but also fed him essays on the Talmud while he was composing *Culture and Anarchy* and *Literature and the Bible*. As Jews assimilated and secularized in England and America, moreover, a number of Jewish women broke fully into the world of literary culture-making: Amy Levy, Emma Lazarus, Anzia Yezirska, and Mary Antin, to cite four crucial examples.

But these entrances were made, by and large, late in the nineteenth and early in the twentieth centuries. For the most part, throughout the nineteenth century, Jewish women entered the realm of high culture in a more mediated way: under the sign of performance, especially theatrical performance. For many reasons, Jewish women were among the most famous actresses of the time, exerting palpable effects on the litterateurs who flocked to the theater. The French actress Rachel, for example, lived a prodigious afterlife in the poetry of Arnold; indeed, in a completely unexpected way she came to serve as an exemplar of imaginative expansiveness and cultural liminality that provided the model of the Arnoldian intellectual. Rachel served something of the same function for Henry James, for whom she came to symbolize the very possibility of a life devoted to art. So, to cite another example, did Sarah Bernhardt for Proust.

In all these different ways, in other words, those prominent Jews who moved in high-cultural circles were able to exert a certain force over their own cultural representation, even in the most prominent representations and most powerful theories of culture in the mid– to late nineteenth century. But at the same time, socially ambitious but less well-placed Jews had to come to terms with the ways they were represented in the new professions constructed and authorized by these discourses and idioms. As Jewish writers, intellectuals, critics, and teachers started to make their way into the cultural arena (largely, though not exclusively, because so many other arenas remained closed or limited), they had to come to terms with the patterns of thought that constructed them in such double terms at the very center of this arena. In Anglo-America, this meant having to deal with the complex legacy of Arnold, George Eliot, and Trollope, with the ways in which their thinking about culture and the practice of culture dealt with Jews in the work of successors like James, Wharton, Cather, T. S. Eliot, and Pound. And this was true throughout the twentieth century: even as late as the 1950s and 1960s, Jewish literary academics had perforce to deal with an Eliotic modernism that took its idealizing rhetoric from Arnold but added to it a particularly nasty brew of Anglicanism, imperialism, and anti-Semitism. To be a Jew in the Anglo-American literary academy in the 1950s, for example, usually meant being a New Critic, and to be a New Critic meant coming to terms with (T. S.) Eliotic Anglicanism, an enterprise that meant both coming to terms with oneself as a Jew and coming to terms with Western anti-Semitism, or at least choosing whether or not to do so.

The resultant confusions, complexities, and reshapings are the story that this book has to tell. Its narrative is a double one. To begin with, I want to trace the ways in which the figure of the fictional Jew enters intimately but problematically into the Anglo-American idioms of high and mass culture in the later nineteenth century; in the chapters that follow, I want to look at some of the consequences of this process for real, live Jews seeking to make their way in the cultural terrain of England and America for the last fifty years. That terrain, I have been implicitly arguing, was carved out in the late Victorian cultural sphere, which was a period marked by the rise of a mass-culture industry and a consequent crisis of self-representation for high-cultural writers and poets; a period that saw the construction of "culture" as a secularized religious faith that might, its adherents hoped, forestall class conflict; an era that witnessed the creation of new professional identities and career paths: the modern author, whether of bestsellers, or of audience-challenging high-art hermeneutic puzzles; the intellectual, whether alienated or hegemonic or even both; the literary academic. The construction of that arena, or, more precisely, that temple—that place where culture was sacralized, its powers preached to a social collectivity that was alternately awed, impressed, and scornful—and the activity that took place within it, I shall be suggesting, were intimately connected with the nature and fate of secularizing, assimilating, Westernizing Jews. Indeed, this connection has been so intimate that, at the moment when this arena begins to fall apart, those Jews who took their place in it are engaged simultaneously in the demolition *and* in the defense of that temple, the temple of culture.

THEORIZING "THE REAL JEW"
AND OTHER IMPOSSIBILITIES

No reader of this book will find it easy to put himself in the emotional position of an author who is ignorant of the language of holy writ, who is completely estranged from the religion of his fathers—as well as from every other religion—and who cannot take a share in nationalist ideals, but who has never repudiated his people, who feels that he is in his essential nature a Jew and who has no desire to alter that nature. If the question were put to him: "Since you have abandoned all these common characteristics of your countrymen, what is there left to you that is Jewish?" he would reply "A very great deal, and probably its very essence." He could not now express that essence clearly in words; but some day, no doubt, it will become accessible to the scientific mind.

> —*Sigmund Freud, preface to the Hebrew translation of* Totem and Taboo (1930)

You're what Grammy Hall would call a real Jew.

> —*Annie Hall to Alvy Singer in* Annie Hall

Before I continue, I need to establish some definitional clarity, and to do that I need to make some theoretical noises. I first need to clarify the notion of the Jew that I am deploying here, then turn briefly to the idiom of culture, before I show in more detail the intercourse of the two in the later nineteenth century and the consequences thereof in the twentieth. For in the case of each, I am writing at a specific historical moment of deep revisionism, if not utter skepticism—a moment, in other words, when both the idea of the Jew and that of culture have been complicated to the point where they no longer seem practicable as conceptual entities, at least not without a large degree of clarification and revision. But this complication or revision is grounded in utterly different situations: in the case of the idea of "culture," it results from a severe skepticism, at least among the ephebes of high culture, about the nature and possibilities of that idealized term. In the case of the Jew, however, it results from precisely the opposite: an efflorescence of scholarly, religious, and ethnic interest, perhaps so much so that one feels justified in using the somewhat inappropriate term "renaissance." In the Anglo-American academy, for example, a recent cornucopia of criticism has emerged out of a dialogue within Judaic studies and in its relations to other fields and programs: I am thinking of the splendid work of Daniel Boyarin and David Biale in constructing a powerful dialogue between Jewish theology and gender theory; of Jonathan Boyarin in creating an interplay between Jewish studies and anthropological theory; of Sander Gilman in moving within and without psychoanalytical theory and the question of Jewishness; of Michael Rogin's spirited critiques of the racial politics of assimilating Hollywood Jews; of Geoffrey Hartman, Robert Alter, Shira Wolosky, Susan Handelman, and a host of others in mediating between Jewish studies and midrash and postmodern literary theory; of Ragussis, Bryan Cheyette, and a host of others in tracing the responses of nineteenth- and twentieth-century novelists to the Jew.[11]

This efflorescence of Jewish-centered discourse, however, is not an academic phenomenon: outside the academy, in America alone, stands the powerful revival of Jewish musical and popular traditions that complicate the standard narratives of assimilation and identity-formation. I am thinking here of the recent revival of Yiddish (until the 1960s the embarrassing language of grandparents, now a subject of study in synagogues) and the related revival of klezmer music—the latter being brought more fully into contact with vibrant African-American jazz and blues traditions by the Klezmatics and jazz clarinetists David Krakauer and Don Byron. And outside America altogether stands an even more powerful revival of Jewish art, religion, philosophy; setting aside the question of cultural production in Israel—for reasons I'll explain hereafter—we can turn to the remarkable (if highly various) rethinking of Jewish identity offered in the Diaspora-affirming art of R. B. Kitaj, in the cultural criticism of Alain Finkielkraut, in, most powerfully of all, the philosophical theology (or is it theological philosophy?) of Emmanuel Levinas.

In this welter of cultural production, philosophy, critique, and theorization, a notion of *the* Jew—of a single unitary model for Jewish identity and cultural practice—seems a quaint anachronism at best. Replacing it in practice is a model of Jewishness as decentered, hybrid, de-essentialized; of "Jewish identity" as mobile, complex, "disarticulated."[12] This vision of Jewishness exults in the possibilities contained within the Jewish experience; it celebrates the very heterogeneity, the multiplicity, the variousness of practices, traditions, and cultural achievements that have marked the Jewish experience from the Diaspora to the present day. Like other forms of contemporary racial and ethnic identity-formation, the recent recrudescence of interest in Jewishness has led both to revival (e.g., the new school of Talmud studies centered in France, sparked by Levinas but by no means limited to him) and to revision (e.g., the Klezmatics' attempt to play the klezmer tradition off against the African-American rhythm and blues tradition) and, like other forms of ethnic and racial self-scrutiny, reaches out—at times tentatively, at times critically—to other arenas of ethnic identity-formation. And despite the notorious tensions between Jewish and other minority discourses, particularly in America, there are some recent signs that many in those arenas are beginning to reach back: I am thinking here, for example, of Paul Gilroy's remarkable account, in *The Black Atlantic*, of the adoption of the trope of the Diaspora by African-American criticism and his remarkably nuanced treatment of the interplay between Jewish and African-American narratives of the experience of exile.[13]

This new understanding of Jewishness, it must be said, reflects the actual conditions of Jewish life itself in 1999: the continuing and accelerating deep divisions of culture, religion, and practice between Ashkenazic and Sephardic Jews (not to mention the numerous splits within these two main branches of Jewish identity and practice); between orthodox and assimilating Western Jews (not to mention the divisions within each of these branches); between Jewishness as a cultural and Jewishness as a religious identity; and among those who accept, those who deny, and those who critique the legitimacy of the State of Israel. But as increasingly ramified as the always-already-ramified nature of Jewish identity may have become, the theorization of its complexity remains incomplete, tentative, problematic. Although postmodernist languages of antifoundationalism, hybridity, and performed identity might seem to lend themselves to a retheorization of Jewish identity, they have been less than effective in doing so, at least to date, perhaps because that identity has always been so internally contested and quarreled over, at least since the time of the Jewish Emancipation in eighteenth-century Europe.

We can see some of those problems—and understand how theorizing the de-essentialized nature of Jewish identity can put into perspective the problematics of theorizing an essentialized, foundationalist Jewishness as well—by looking at the introduction to a recent important volume edited by David Theo Goldberg and Michael Krausz, *Jewish Identity*.[14] The volume is devoted, its editors tell us, "to the reconcilement of personal and cultural identity from postmodernist or postfoundationalist perspectives"; the essays therein are subtle and wide-ranging, and help to push the formulation of Jewish identity toward a more theoretically sophisticated awareness. (Krausz's own essay is particularly exemplary in this regard.) It is thus all the more startling to come upon the following paragraph on the last page of the introduction, where Goldberg and Krausz assert that the establishment of Jewish identity

> in filial identification with the state of Israel is an identity to be resisted only by unapologetically recalling the central place of wandering in the Jewish imagination. It is, perhaps paradoxically, only from this space of "in-betweenness," of "going and resting" and going again that the moral burden of the Jew as witness to oppression can be satisfactorily borne. And this diasporic condition of Jewishness, split between reflection of past belonging and future commitments, may serve in turn as symbolic of the increasingly cosmopolitan and nomadic condition of postmodernity's personal-as-cultural identity. (12)

Politically one may find this appetizing or problematic (my own view inclines toward the latter); intellectually, it is somewhat vague. But its mushiness is of a particularly nutritional sort—it gives food, at the very least, for thought. For in the guise of de-essentializing Judaism, Goldberg and Krausz re-essentialize it: defining Jewishness as an exclusively "diasporic condition" is as thoroughly foundational a move as I can imagine, since it excludes the possibility that Jewishness can have any positive meaning in and of itself—that it can have any value or purpose other than that of bearing witness to oppression and affirming the value of exile. Moreover, the authors thereby perform a highly exclusionary maneuver, eliminating from full Jewish identity all Jews who do not wish to identify themselves as secularized, diasporic nomads-cum-cosmopolites—not an inconsiderable number, and not just one that includes Israelis (many of whom, to add to the problem, consider themselves just as cosmopolitan as do Goldberg and Krausz). More problematic but yet more symptomatic is the language Goldberg and Krausz use to establish this de-essentialized essentialism: the language of "symbolism." In doing so, they not only reveal themselves to be bad postmodernists—isn't the aim of a postmodern turn precisely to question the legitimacy of the symbol itself?—but heavily infatuated with Christian-centered discourse. As Paul de Man has argued, the concept of the "symbol" is loaded with the move to the metaphysical, the ontologizing, literally the logocentric: Christ, the alpha and omega, stands in Coleridge, in Hegel, in generations of German metaphysical thought, as the very symbol of symbols, the guarantee of the order and coherence of the "translucence of the eternal into the temporal" (Coleridge) that the symbolic accomplishes.[15] And, as one commentator suggests, in this discursive tradition, Judaism "with its *deus absconditus*, its radical alienation, its stark dualisms, and its rigid inflexible obedience to the letter of the law, is identified with lifeless mechanism, repression, and death.... Judaism represents the dead world of allegory in contrast to the living world of symbol."[16]

Precisely to undo this Hegelian hierarchy Benjamin turns, in the *Origins of the German Tragic Drama*, from the symbol to allegory as a means of thinking about language—and it is not the least of the ironies generated thereby that he had his greatest influence over a closeted Nazi collaborator who, working together with an assimilated Algerian Jew, reoriented critical discourse in the academy away from logocentric New Criticism to one more suspicious of the Christian-inflected move to the metaphysical that had been one of its staples.

Just how infatuated with a Christian metaphysic Goldberg and Krausz remain, in contrast with a Benjamin or a Derrida, is further revealed in their adoption of the trope of "wandering" as a master-image of Jewish identity. If "wandering" indeed "has a central place in the Jewish imagination," it is not exactly a happy or a healthy spot—or an exclusively Jewish one. It is a trope that has also functioned throughout *Western* accounts of Jewish identity to describe the eternally and unhappily homeless condition of Jews: Jews, of course, are routinely described as being condemned to wander the earth because of their participation in the murder of Christ in the sacred and secular literature of the West from the Middle Ages through the end of the nineteenth century. Jews may wish to identify themselves with the idiom of exile and with the tradition that comes along with it of sympathy for the oppressed and the homeless: and this may lead them, as it leads me, to sympathy with the Palestinians and hope that two historically unhappy people might at last be able to pursue their desires in peace. But to adopt a trope used to construct Jews as aliens antithetical to the spirit and practices of civilized peoples and to claim that that trope stands at the center of the Jewish imagination strikes me as taking hybridity a bit too far—right into the adoption of the worst, the most banal and limiting, stereotypes that have been mobilized to marginalize Jews and Jewishness.

It might seem that I am accusing Goldberg and Krausz of a species of self-hatred, the internalization of anti-Semitic stereotypes as a way of dealing with the shame of being Jewish in a hostile world. Such is not, however, my intent. To the contrary, what seems most remarkable to me about Goldberg and Krausz's quest for a postmodern, postfoundationalist Jewishness is how quickly it falls prey to—hence dramatizes the power of—the desire to reify Jewish identity as a way of coping with its always-already-de-essentialized reality.

For just about every Jew writing about Jewish identity claims, no less than do Goldberg and Krausz, that their position, no matter how de-essentialized or contingent it might seem, touches on the very essence of Jewishness: consider the quotation from Freud that begins this section. There are good reasons for this definitional habit, of course, going back to the time of the Babylonian exile, during which the rabbis shifted the locus of Jewishness from a land-centered to a matrilineal matrix of identity. Without any connection to a territory or terrain, some way of ascertaining an essential Jewish identity that transcended nation or region had to be affirmed as a way of eliminating the perpetually lurking threat of extinction via cultural assimilation. The importance of the idea (or ideology) of an essential but mysterious essence of Jewishness only grew further in the West after the time of the Enlightenment, when the quest for a scientific, rational accounting of Jewish identity, climaxing in the *Wissenschaft der Judenthums*—the systematic scientific inquiry into Jewishness undertaken by Jewish scholars as a conscious part of the Enlightenment process—was countered by the rise of the Hasidic movement, with its emphasis on a mystical, emotional, inclusive Jewishness. Enlightened, Westernizing Jewry's quest to "separate the 'kernel' from the 'husk' of Judaism" by the exercise of reason, rationality, and science was countered by an impulse, largely felt in eastern European Jewry, to define the *really real* Jew in terms of feeling, faith, and mysticism, and the two impulses have battled it out ever since.[17] And the battle over *real* Jewishness has not been ended, has in fact been enhanced, by the establishment of the State of Israel, which, instead of resolving the question, has only added new possibilities to the stew (e.g., the anti-Zionist leftist Jew, the anti-Israeli Crown Heights Hasid, the Brooklyn-born fanatic). While internally split, and representing a split or hybrid set of possibilities for Jewish identity, each position is argued for with a passion and a sense of mission that thoroughly undermines the Jew-as-hybrid position—a position that, I have been arguing, qualifies in form what it argues for in substance.

My own position in this discussion is one of limited acceptance of its irretrievably inconclusive nature. Rather than seeking to deny or negate the multiplicity of identities that governs the establishment of Jewishness at our moment, I seek to embrace it—and to embrace the dissonances that come with such a project. My best understanding of Jewishness is that it is an endless dispute—a quarrel—that has been going on since at least the destruction of the Second Temple and that doubtless preceded it. This is not to say, however, that Jewishness is or can be re-essentialized under the sign of its de-essentialized, contingent nature. What makes the category so interesting, and so tricky, is that the notion of the "real" or "authentic" Jew is one of the more important weapons or turns in this dispute, one, in fact, that is indispensable to it.

My position is one that seeks support in a number of recent critics, named earlier, who have sought to place the mysterious facts of Jewishness in the context of gender theory, critical race theory, and the cultural anthropology of religion. But it is one that has been best articulated, I think, not by a critic but by a literary character, Smilesburger, in Philip Roth's *Operation Shylock*. According to Smilesburger,

[i]nside every Jew there is a *mob* of Jews. The new Jew, the old Jew. The lover of Jews, the hater of Jews. The friend of the goy, the enemy of the goy. The arrogant Jew, the wounded Jew. The pious Jew, the rascal Jew. The coarse Jew, the gentle Jew. The defiant Jew, the appeasing Jew. The de-Jewed Jew. Shall I go on? Do I have to expound upon the Jew as a three-thousand-year amassment of mirrored fragments . . . ? Is it any wonder that the Jew is always disputing? He *is* a dispute, incarnate![18]

And in *this* incarnation—an incarnation that, as opposed to the orthodox version of the Christian one, brings with it only the fragments of a resolved identity, the shards of a unified visage—only "dispute" can provide a field on which a collective identity can be forged, then broken and remade.

This book understands that it, too, takes part in this quarrel, both internal and external; it is in part, that is to say, written by an American Jew, the product of an assimilated German-Jewish identified family that managed, by various means, to escape the Holocaust at something like the last minute and make careers in the American high-culture industry: his father and mother and wife are or have been college professors; his uncle, naturally, is a psychoanalyst. I identify with many of the sentiments expressed heretofore; I freely admit that I am trying to figure out exactly what position in the quarrel I wish to affirm, and how. In terms of the larger "dispute" or debate, I am resolutely agnostic, that is to say, I treat the nature and existence of Jewishness as a set of possibilities to be interpreted, explored, and understood rather than as a given; but I understand that the very possibility of this position is itself a contingency, the result of a century of assimilation, semitolerant immigration laws, and a few historical circumstances (the Hitler-Stalin pact, for example, which gave my grandmother the chance to escape Germany via the Trans-Siberian Railway and hence to lecture me, thirty years later, on the glories of the German language and the evil of the barbarians who had corrupted it). In short, my position in the quarrel is to try to stay out of it, but I am not so naive as to believe that this is not a position.

Indeed, my goal in what follows is not to resolve this quarrel but to historicize it: to understand the particular circumstances under which this dispute was produced, the multiple and dialogical quality of the discursive interplay that influenced it, and the social and cultural work it did. This is the only productive response or position left that has not been fully and polemically performed or explored, and it may, perhaps, move the quarrel of Jewishness and its uncomfortable place in the cultures of the West to a somewhat higher plane. And here my second point is relevant: the work of constructing Jewish identity is one that must take into full account the reciprocal relations between Jewish and gentile culture in constructing the very concepts of Jewishness—and, as I argue hereafter, of gentile culture as well. Goldberg and Krausz's slippery slide from the idiom of the exile to the trope of the wandering Jew represents what happens when this process is merely assumed, is not articulated in its full historical and social specificity; and their response is in turn best read historically, contextually, as telling us much about their own position as Jewish intellectuals in the 1980s academy.

It is precisely at moments like this one, in other words, that the task of historicizing the matter of Jewish identity is most urgently needed. Doing so helps us recognize two somewhat contradictory things: that there is no such thing as a pure, unmediated Jewish identity because this identity has been shaped by non-Jewish discourses on cultural identity that worked to construct their categories, in no small measure, by representing the figure of the Jew; but, complicating the matter, that that identity has itself been shaped, in great ways and small, by the imaginative and creative efforts of assimilating (and nonassimilating) Jews, who have helped make the very notion and the very practices that are deployed to construct Jews. Goldberg and Krausz cannot help but turn to the Christian-centered discourse of the symbol because they are philosophically sophisticated academics trained in Hegel, Kant, Marx; we cannot help but critique them because Walter Benjamin wrote a dissertation about German tragic drama that critiqued, hence changed, the ways that the culture of the West came to think about language, cultural production, identity. Putting both these moments together, reading them alongside and against each other, is what I mean by historicizing; and it is my aim in what follows to do so as fully as I can.

Let me make this point clearer by returning to *Annie Hall*. When Annie Hall tells Alvy Singer that he is what Grammy Hall calls a *real* Jew (or a real *Jew*), she does so in a hall of fragmented mirrors very much like Smilesburger's: her reflection of Grammy's reflection of Alvy as Jew is clearly marked as a Jew's reflection of a WASP's reflection of Jewishness—its attractions (to Annie), its pitfalls (to Grammy). Like Moses Mendelssohn, Disraeli, Rebecca Davis, Louisa Rothschild, Freud—like the whole host of assimilated or assimilating Jewish intellectuals—Woody Allen thereby seeks to intervene in the discourses by which Jewishness is made, maintained, staged, theatricalized. But as he does, he also seeks to enter into a non-Jewish discourse on the nature and possibilities of American culture and civilization itself, whether represented by New York (that "dying city") or Los Angeles (whose greatest contribution to American civilization, we are told, is the right turn on red) or the decline of public entertainment, represented in the film by Alvy's movement from Coney Island to stand-up comedy to the canned-laughter factory of the television industry. And this intervention as cultural critic is enabled by Allen's own Jewishness as represented by the satiric portrayal of Chippewa Falls, Minnesota, where people do not understand a world without swap meets and Sunday ham and where Alvy Singer sees Grammy Hall seeing him dressed as an Orthodox rabbi. Precisely the condition of outsider to which he is relegated by Chippewa Falls offers Allen the comic distance to satirize all aspects of American life, including, in one spectacular instance, his own liberal Democratic Jewish family.

Such a complex admixture of assimilation to and aggression against non-Jewish forms of cultural understanding and organization can be taken as this book's emblem for Jewish identity formation in non-Jewish culture, and vice versa. *Here*, we might say, is the really real Jew, which is also at one and the same time a version of what Alain Finkielkraut calls the imaginary Jew: a Jew whose understanding of him- or herself is always connected to a non-Jewish imaginary that itself was partially imagined by Jews. And here is the moment when the Jew as Jew inserts himself into a culture—and an idiom about culture—that treats him with the dutiful acceptance of the Hall family but still doesn't quite know where to seat him at the table, or whether or not to serve ham.

"Everything was Culture, Culture, Culture"

My second problematic term, "culture," demands further clarification and re-examination, particularly at the moment of the rise of something called, variously, cultural materialism or cultural studies. What's interesting about both these terms, I should begin by saying, is that each of them complicates (to say the least) the noun that is put to adjectival, and perhaps subordinate, use in the term: the notion of "culture" that cultural materialism/cultural studies deploys or advances has an ironic relation at best to the idioms of "culture" that shaped the practice of literary study, cultural criticism, anthropology, and sociology from the mid–nineteenth century to the present moment. The traditions of Matthew Arnold or Edward Tylor are not faring well these days—much less those of Theodor Adorno or Clifford Geertz.[19] Instead, within each tradition, we can witness the turn toward something that we might want to call postmodern culture-critique: a distrust of if not outright hostility to traditional high culture, the privileging of the mass-cultural as a site of resistance, and the deconstruction of the distance and authority of the cultural or social critic. The result has been a crisis in those traditional disciplines without the full emergence of new ones—a proliferation of inter- and intradisciplinary rearrangements without a concomitant methodological or institutional structure-building to replace them. "Cultural studies" may mean many things, but one thing that it does *not* mean is the systematic study of culture, much less "culture."

Or at least this has been the case in the academy. In the public sphere, however, precisely the opposite impulse has been felt. The academy may have rejected the notion of traditional high culture arranged as a body of coherent knowledge that, when studied, yields insights into, or deeper knowledge of, social, moral, or psychological truths; but such notions have found a rich and rewarding ground in middlebrow culture, where they have sprouted with remarkable rapidity. Witness first the extraordinary success of Allan Bloom's venture into Straussian culture-critique, *The Closing of the American Mind*, followed by a spate of similar efforts, reaching a crescendo with Harold Bloom's recent attempt to reinvigorate the entire corpus of Western literature, *The Western Canon*. We live in strange and interesting times indeed, when books arguing that Nietzsche has corrupted a generation of college students (to which one can only reply, in the words of Alicia Silverstone, "as *if*!!") or that knowledge of one hundred books will maintain Western civilization (a conceit last glimpsed in Ray Bradbury's *Fahrenheit 451*) can garner million-dollar advances and extraordinary sales. We live in stranger times, when those people who might once have been counted on to argue the primacy of ideas and art in the world at large, college professors, are the very last people in that world to accept them. But this is the world we have made; and it is the argument of what follows that it has been made as such in large measure both in a reciprocal struggle between Western discourses on "culture" heavily engaged in defining themselves with reference to Jewishness and by Jewish intellectuals seeking to use those discourses to win a place for themselves within the social dominant.

My goal here, in other words, is to step back a little from the battle of the books, from those who over- and those who under-cathect to high culture, and to think about the ways in which the idiom of "culture" has also been a language in which the Jewish presence in Western society has been formulated—and vice versa. For, as I argue more fully hereafter, from the Enlightenment forward, the concepts of Jewishness and of culture were irrevocably linked with each other by gentile intellectuals through Jews' resolute failure to fit into any of the categories for organizing social experience.

The key to this process can be found in the later years of the eighteenth and the early years of the nineteenth centuries. For, as Raymond Williams has reminded us, history of the idea of "culture" in the high Arnoldian sense (and, complicating the matter, the descriptive anthropological sense as well) begins with German Romantic philosophy, with Fichte and Hegel and Herder and Humboldt.[20]

But, it is important to remember, these philosophers were also socially committed intellectuals dedicated to the creation of a German nation-state by asserting the linguistic and imaginative—in short, *cultural*—homogeneity of the German people. And both the epistemic and the geographic coherence of this project were called into question by one overwhelming social fact: the presence within the territories of the German-speaking people of a large number of foreign-looking, foreign-acting Jews.

In other words, the population of Jews existing within the territory, both geographic and epistemic, of the German nation challenged the very grounds on which its philosophers and aestheticians were thinking about the overlapping categories of culture and its relation to the emergent idioms of nation, race, and language. If "Jews" are members of a nation, for example, and if the nation is defined by linguistic identity, why did they speak so many languages? If Jews are members of a religiously defined community, then how do we think about them in a new, secular nation-state? If they are a race, why do they look so different from each other? As Alain Finkielkraut writes, in words that are drawn from contemporary France but apply to the cultural situation of Napoleonic France, imperial Germany, or nineteenth-century England as well,

> the foreignness of Jews is a kind of difference *unlike others*. They are "those people" whom no label fits, whether assigned by the Gaze, the Concept or the State. . . . [F]or Jewishness, the type is the exception and its absence the rule; in fact you can rarely pick out a Jew at first glance. It's an insubstantial difference that resists definition as much as it frustrates the eye: are they a people? a religion? a nation? All these categories apply, but none is adequate in itself.[21]

And it is the essence of my argument hereafter that because all these crucial categories apply in such inadequate ways, the Jew became one of the prime means by which nineteenth- and twentieth-century cultural critics, anthropologists, philosophers, and philologists sought to define the nature and limits of their own discourse of culture and its relation to the emergent categories of race, language, and nation.

The contemporary social theorist Zygmunt Bauman has given us a more precise language for understanding these dynamics. He reminds us that it is precisely this indefinable quality of Jewishness, its resistance to easy compartmentalization in the boxes that the Enlightenment constructed, that created both the fascination and the fear that nineteenth- and twentieth-century culture exhibited toward the Jew. Bauman suggests that this undefinable quality of Jewish identity became the ground not only of Enlightenment attempts to use the Jew to define the world but of the most unenlightened surfacing of a distinctive species of anti-Semitism at the moment of modernity. He usefully distinguishes between thinking of anti-Semitism as an exemplary instance of heterophobia, or fear and resentment of others, and as proteophobia, or fear of that which stands outside of, and subverts, the cognitive categories by which the world is organized and hence by which even the category of otherness itself is established. Bauman writes:

> The great fear of modern life is that of under-determination, unclarity, uncertainty—in other words, ambivalence . . . the Jews had entered modern times as ambivalence incarnate. . . . In the mobile world, the Jews were the most mobile of all; in the world of boundary-breaking, they broke the most boundaries; in the world of melting solids, they made everything, including themselves, into a formless plasma in which any form could be born only to dissolve again. As the eponymical ghetto dwellers, the Jews were walking reminders of the still fresh and vivid memories of stable, transparent caste society; among the first to be released from special laws and statutes, they were walking alarms alerting one to the arrival of the

strange new world of free-for-all.... They embodied incongruence, artificiality, sham and the frailty of the social order and the most earnestly
drawn boundaries.[22]

And the response to ambivalence, Bauman reminds us, is often a violent one:
"the temptation is to 'de-ambivalentize' the ambivalence by condensing or focusing into one obvious and tangible object—and then burn ambivalence down
in this effigy" (215).

What's most useful in Bauman, it seems to me, is the ways he gives us a more
precise language for figuring the different kind of difference the Jew makes in
the discourses of the West—and for the ways that that different difference produces a different kind of prejudice against Jewish otherness after the period of
the Enlightenment, that period when the world was mapped with such special
fervor. His work has been enormously productive in the criticism I mentioned
earlier—it has been particularly influential on Cheyette's formulation of the construction of the Jew as a "semitic discourse" in which the attempt to map Jewish
identity charts shifting relations of *gentile* culture, particularly British national
identity. But Bauman also reminds us, perhaps inadvertently, of the inadequacy
of telling the story only this one way—as a narrative of gentile culture's construction of the Jew in the image of its own ambivalence. For what makes the situation
even more complicated than Bauman recognizes is that the moment of modernity
for "Europe" was also the moment of modernity for European Jews: the time of
Emancipation, the era in which Jews were incorporated—sometimes with reluc-
tance, sometimes with enthusiasm—into the lineaments of the new nation-state.
And that process brought with it as many challenges to Jews as it did to the
nation-state itself. It meant the breakup of traditional social arrangements, and
it meant new possibilities for moving out of traditional communities into an
uncertain and problematic modern world governed by a greater seeming tolerance
of Jews on the one hand and gusts of anti-Semitic sentiment on the other.

Assimilating (and traditionalist) Western Jews adopted many differing stances
and responses to this dismayingly complex, bracingly open brave new world. And
for many of those Jews who sought purchase and a place in such a world, "culture," in the highest and most exclusive sense of the word, played a crucial role.
The ideal of culture, not to mention its practices—the practice or knowledge or
both of art, music, writing, journalism—promised the rapid conferral of social
acceptance through the acquisition of cultural legitimacy. This was particularly
true in the very center of the hypostatization of "culture," the emerging nation-
states of Austria and Germany; and, while I can't tell this tragicomic tale in these
pages, it hangs so heavily over the experiences I seek to narrate that I must briefly
glance at it, if only to provide texture to the Anglo-American terrain I seek to
travel.[23] George Mosse, who has spent a long and distinguished career both living

and reflecting on the story of culture-loving German Jews, describes this process with the greatest precision.

> The liberal *Bildungsburger* as defined by Wilhelm von Humboldt provided the model of German citizenship for the newly emancipated Jew.... Through fostering the growth of reason and aesthetic taste, each man would cultivate his own personality until he became an autonomous, harmonious individual. This was a process of education and character-building in which everyone could join; only the individual mattered.[24]

These terms, it is important to stress, were constructed *for* German-speaking Jews as much as they were constructed *by* them. Throughout the later eighteenth and early nineteenth centuries, gentile authorities who were sympathetic to the cause of Jewish emancipation stressed the importance of educational instruction for their Jewish peers in order to overcome their putative limitations, their "Oriental" or "Asiatic" origins, their non-Western identities. Education, it was reasoned (in terms soon to be brought to the colonial endeavor as well as that of integrating lower classes into political culture), was necessary to prepare Jews for the mantle of citizenship. Thus Christian Döhm wrote, in the first German Enlightenment argument for the full citizenship of Jews, *Über die burgerliche Verbesserung der Juden (On the Civil Betterment of the Jews)* that, precisely because centuries of ghettoization and discrimination led to the degradation of the Jewish people (not to mention their indulgence in shadier business practices), the state needed to reeducate the Jew in the language, the culture, and, most important, the *feelings* appropriate to citizenship as it emancipated Jews from the ghetto. "Let the government allow each of [its] special groupings to indulge in its pride," Döhm writes (and the Jew here, naturally, symbolizes the problem of diversity of all sorts in the face of "the great harmony of the state"), "but let it also strive to instil yet more love in each of its members, and it will have achieved its great task when the nobleman, the peasant and the scholar, the Christian and the Jew [become,] beyond and above all that, a *citizen*."[25] Political projects of emancipation often followed precisely this path. Thus Emperor Franz Joseph II of Austria-Hungary agreed to facilitate Jewish marriages, which required the emperor's permission; but he demanded in return a promise that married Jews send their children to secular schools for proper instruction in German culture, language, and civilization.[26] And, later in the century, Wilhelm Humboldt's educational reforms—later to be so influential on Matthew Arnold's programs of educational reform to socialize the working class—were explicitly directed at this very end.

To be assimilated into such a culture, that is to say, meant not only to move into a new political form of citizenship; it meant to be reoriented into a new form of subjectivity appropriate to life in a "civilized" or cultured world: one in which feeling, sensibility, and responsiveness to the finer emotions and the finer cultural productions was the guarantee of belonging to the larger collective identity, the larger collective project, of the German people. It meant, in a term that, again, was to be deployed in colonialist discourse, being "civilized"; but "civilization" here is not a matter of knowledge or even behavior. It is a matter of affect, of sentiment—of being responsive in the proper way to the feelings encoded in art, literature, and music.

The results of assimilation under these terms, as part of the project of Culture, were dramatic indeed. Under the sign of cultivation, *bildung*, and reason, Jewish men (particularly those of families who had already entered the middle class via business) flocked into universities and the professions, and, as Hannah Arendt memorably put it, "what the nation state once feared so much, the birth of a Jewish intelligentsia, proceeded at a fantastic pace."[27] Historian Marsha Rozenblit notes that when Jews composed 8 percent of the population of Vienna, they made up close to 30 percent of the students who attended the Gymnasium.[28] These young men (and to a lesser extent women) moved rapidly through the educational system with an eye toward the professions: according to Peter Pulzer, 33 percent of the students in universities in Vienna: 39 percent of medical students, 23 percent of the law students.[29] Jews were overwhelmingly present in the Viennese and German social and cultural worlds; it might be argued, in fact, that their entry resulted (at the very least) in psychoanalysis, Marxism (and critical theory), the law of relativity, twelve-tone music, analytic philosophy, free market economics, and expressionist theater, art, and film. "In the invigorating air of this remarkable cosmopolis" (Vienna but, it might also be added, Berlin as well), wrote a contemporary, "Jewish talent blossomed as vigorously as it did in Granada under Moslem rule."[30] So too, it might be added, did the host culture.

This matrix has been frequently anatomized, theorized, and historicized, so much so that I don't want to do more than gesture at it here; but I would like to draw attention to the resonances of the process of assimilation-by-culture among middle-class Jews, even those who retained their sense of Jewishness.[31] The contemporary philosopher (and concentration camp survivor) Emil Fackenheim remembers, to cite but one example, a particularly rich moment in this process:

What we had was like Conservative Judaism—but with an organ. That may sound funny, but in a Liberal synagogue in Berlin, an organ made sense, in part because of German-Jewish composers, notably Lewandowski. Did you know that even Franz Rosenzweig once wanted to bring the music of Bach into the synagogue? And nobody ever accused *him* of being an assimilationist. It's just that we believed in the symbiosis of German and Jewish culture. Nobody has ever done justice to the ordinary German Jews who believed in all sincerity that it was possible to be an upright Jew and a German at the same time.[32]

This book, too, can't do justice to these "ordinary German Jews"—or even the extraordinary ones; what it can do, however, is to note how even for Fackenheim, being "an upright Jew and a German at the same time" was coterminous with believing in the symbiosis of "German and Jewish culture": that the cultural sphere was not only the means of assimilation but its validation. And herein lies the source of the tragedy that was the experience of assimilating German Jewry. German Jewry was undone because of its belief that cultural symbiosis and social integration would lead to political protection from the resurgent forces of anti-Semitism and class envy; to enhance the irony, these sentiments were put into social play, given cultural validation, precisely in the very universities and professions through which Jews sought assimilation. As George Mosse puts it, "*bildung* and *sittlichkeit*, which had stood at the beginning of Jewish emancipation, accompanied German Jews to the end, blinding them, as so many other Germans, to the menace of national socialism" (*German Jews*, 144).

Precisely because of this lack of justice, then, I offer just one of the countless stories of problems of assimilation via high culture, one that encapsulates all the thematics that Mosse, Fackenheim, Pulzer, and countless other commentators have noted, with a kind of an ironic twist that gives them individual, if tragic, heft. In his memoirs, Gershom Scholem records with searing understatement the story of his aunt Käthe,

> whom I have already mentioned as one of the first female doctors admitted to practice in Berlin, [and who] at the age of thirty-eight married a colleague who was ten years her junior. . . . They lived in an ivory tower in Friedenau, practically around the corner from my uncle, and yet there never was any contact between them. The little house they rented was full of Far Eastern art; Buddhas and Kwanyins were everywhere. Everything was culture, culture, culture, and high-class journals . . . seemed to be their daily fare. They associated with each other, and a small circle of friends consisting entirely of Jews, but only those who tried to make little or no use of their Jewishness. . . . The big test came in 1933. After a while my uncle discovered, following a marriage of more than twenty years, that he was an "Aryan" and asked my aunt Käthe to release him so that he could marry a German. Thus my aunt was later taken to the ghetto of Theresienstadt, where she died.

This story is just one of countless such narratives, and Käthe's betrayal by her husband is emblematic of the betrayal by a cultural sphere into which so many Jews had poured their social hopes, dreams, and aspirations—frequently, as Fackenheim reminds us, retaining their identities as practicing Jews while doing so. This sense of betrayal may explain the investment of so much of the post-Holocaust criticism of German-born Jewish intellectuals in the matter of "culture"—witness the enormous power of Adorno's famous dictum that there is no poetry possible after Auschwitz or, in a positive vein, Marcuse's attempt to reinvoke the Kantian/Schillerian idiom of the aesthetic as the space of freedom in an administered world.[33] But it may also serve to remind us of the different but analogous paths that assimilating Jews in England and, yet more powerfully, America, pursued more successfully in the pre- and postwar periods. The fate of "culture" in Germany, Austria, France, and central Europe serves as both a kind of a brooding countertype and a powerful antonym to the similar kinds of processes in Anglo-America. Here too the idiom of "culture" proved enormously useful to the project of assimilation; here, too the professions of cultural creation and anatomy—writing, reviewing, journalism, and increasingly the literary academy—served as powerful routes to social status or, at least, legitimacy. Although catastrophe was averted or was perhaps never at real issue, the powers of anti-Semitism in both national cultures were nevertheless palpable and pernicious, needing, at the very least, to be negotiated with, if not overcome entirely. The consequent relation of Jewish writers, critics, and intellectuals to the social dominant is a complex tale, one as fully involved in acts of aggression or transgression against the dominant WASP high-cultural orthodoxy as in acts of accommodation to it, frequently at one and the same time. And in this process, the idiom as well as the instantiation of "culture" were profoundly at stake, defined and redefined in the flux and contest that so many of these Jewish intellectuals undertook as part of their own struggle both with their own tradition and with that of the high-cultural sphere.

The results of this process can only be gestured at briefly here before I go into them in greater depth; they are, in sum, the subject of this book. But as a brief prelude, let me point to the two most powerful culture-affirmers currently operative in the public sphere (about whom I have more to say in the coda): Allan and Harold Bloom. Both were or are Jews, and the latter, at least, writes about that Jewishness in interesting and powerful ways. Even though they have entered into the public sphere, they have done so as either students of or a synecdoche for an entire generation of critics and public intellectuals who made a place as promulgators of traditional high culture, sometimes explicitly in relation to their Jewishness, sometimes less so: Leo Strauss and Lionel Trilling, for example, or Saul Bellow and Irving Howe. These figures admittedly have little in common, but they do have two similarities: a powerful cathexis to Western culture and civilization and a habit of negotiating the terms of their own Jewishness through that cathexis.

At the very same moment, another phenomenon is perceptible, particularly in Jewish academics of a slightly younger generation. Michael Rogin, Judith Butler,

Walter Michaels, Eve Sedgwick, Amy Kaplan, Eric Cheyfitz—these figures may have little or nothing in common, too, except for two things: a powerful skepticism about traditional notions of Western culture and civilization and a problematic relation to their own Jewishness in that culture, a relation that only some of them have written about, despite its clear salience to their own counterhegemonic concerns.[34] This is the other side of the story this book narrates, one in which Jewish intellectuals mediate both their Jewishness and their responses to other cultural players through their critical, revisionary intervention in the construction of Western culture—English and American literature, stable canons of taste and aesthetic value—a culture that, to repeat one more time, is a fraught and unstable ideological construction jury-rigged in large measure through its responses to the Jew.

The task I set myself in the next few pages, accordingly, is to understand this interplay in its full historical complexity from the Enlightenment forward and to seek through that understanding a kind of analytic purchase on it. For, as I will show, both the positive and the negative cathexis to "culture," and specifically the culture of the West, mimic the highly ambivalent relation of that culture itself to Jews—one in which philo- and anti-Semitic understandings play off each other in the quest to establish a positive relation between the culture of the West, understood as a unitary phenomenon, and the figure of the Jew, a figure whose very presence both confirms and disrupts that unitary identity. And to see *that*, we need to return to the moment of the first full entry of the Jew and of the idiom of culture onto the Western stage: the German Enlightenment.

THE JEW AND/IN "CULTURE"

For just as the eighteenth century witnessed Europe's discovery of the non-Western world and the birth of an anthropological taxonomy of otherness in response, so too was it marked by the discovery of the "Jew" as the limit case of the categories the Enlightenment sought to valorize: the state, reason, and the innate rights of man; and both philosophically and politically, the question of establishing the nature of Jewish difference and its proper place in the culture of "the West" became one crucial way for those categories to be shaped, articulated, defined, and sharpened. To be sure, this period witnessed a remarkable interplay between those Jews who were escaping the internal and external lineaments of the ghetto and the gentile intellectuals who were attempting to promulgate an ethic of universal human rights and reason: I am thinking especially of the remarkable interchange among Moses Mendelssohn, Kant, and Schiller that eventuated in both some of the most enlightened writing about Jews and some of the best Enlightenment philosophy and literature. Nevertheless, precisely this increasing presence of Jews in both the social and the public spheres posed a powerful challenge to the Enlightenment programs of delineating new concepts of state, nation, language, culture, and (ultimately) race.

This problem was inflected differently in different national arenas, but particularly salient for my purposes are the difficulties faced by German theorists and philosophers we might group under the name nationalist-idealists—those who theorized linguistic and cultural identity as a way of forging a national identity out of the diverse welter of duchies and states composing greater "Germany." For the very presence of the Jew within the boundaries of the nation-state posed severe challenges to such a project. Were Jews, segregated in distinct communities within Europe, practicing a distinct religion, speaking a distinct language, already an alien nation living parasitically within the body of the new national dispensation? Fichte, for one, thought they were; he defined Jews as members of "a mighty state stretch[ing] across almost all the countries of Europe, hostile in intent and engaged in constant strife with everyone else": while willing to grant Jews human rights, the right, that is, to exist as resident aliens, he would deny them citizenship in a German state unified by a common linguistic identity. (And at his worst, in his *Addresses to the German Nation* [1807], Fichte mingled appeals to national identity with anti-Semitic rants in the service of opposing Napoleonic rule—hardly the first, but perhaps one of the most doleful, examples of the uses of anti-Semitism in the service of nation-building.)[35]

Herder was somewhat less overtly prejudiced, but his insistence on a fundamental national character and the linkages he suggested for that of the Jews proved even more problematic. Herder's work is of course the origin of what we would call cultural relativism or even multiculturalism; and much of Herder's sense of the validity of cultures other than his own grew out of his admiration for the Hebrew Bible as a representation of the national genius of the Jews and found expression in his advocacy of civil rights for Jews in the new German state. But this vision is also a problematic one: precisely in his understanding of the Jews as a distinct nation he defined them as inextricably foreign, un-European, Asiatic. Even his most benign comments on the Jew occur in a chapter entitled "Foreign Peoples in Europe"; and while Herder looks forward to the day "when in Europe one will no longer ask who be Jew and who Christian" he sees the Jew's ability to contribute to the "good of the state" as limited: a "barbarian constitution may impede him from doing that [good] or render his ability dangerous." And even Herder's more benign claims had unfortunate aftereffects. Not only did his delineation of the Jew as Oriental (a staple of the race-thinking of his moment) become a staple of the anti-Semitic popular movements of the later nineteenth century, whether conducted under the banner of "Young Germany" or extending into the mass anti-Semitic movements in the 1880s and 1890s; but also his emphasis on the linguistic basis of national identity legitimated critiques of the Jews as debased by virtue of their mysterious yet corrupt language—critiques that, as Sander Gilman has recently argued, shaped anti-Semitic discourses for the next century.[36]

In both Fichte and Herder, not to mention the countless polemicists and theorists who surrounded them in the booming German public sphere, the Jew served as one of the chief means by which crucial notions like state, race, nation, and culture could be defined. More accurately, the ontological slipperiness of the category "Jew"—its intimate relation to but ultimate transcendence of all of these categories—positioned the Jew in a particularly fraught, hence a particularly productive, relation to these very classifications. Precisely because that figure fit, but fit only partially, into the most contested categories of nineteenth-century Europe, the Jew both incited frenzies of definitional activity and frustrated such endeavors. As a result of this interplay, the nature of the Jew and that of a putative German national culture were defined by each other, to the chagrin both of those actual Jews who were struggling for legitimation within a new cultural order and of the gentile ideologists of their moment. The former resulted in figures like Heine, who introjected an idealized version of Western Enlightenment culture and, in turn, gave birth to the dialectical vision of that culture as a battle between Hellenism and Hebraism that was profoundly to affect that culture's imagination of itself. For the latter, Jewish difference remained a problem to which no small amount of intellectual effort and ingeniousness was devoted to overcoming.

A fine case in point is Hegel, and all the more so because, as the prominent Jewish philosopher and theologian Emil Fackenheim has powerfully argued, "Hegel does greater justice to Judaism, than any other modern philosopher of the first rank."[37] In his early theological writings, echoed in his mature view of Judaism as a primitive stage in human consciousness that persisted as a kind of living atavism into the contemporary world, Hegel pointedly figures Jews in terms that define their resolute otherness to the career of Europe. The Jew's unchanging identity is that of Abraham, the nomad,

> a stranger on earth, a stranger to the soil and to men alike. Among men he always was and remained a foreigner, yet not so far removed that he needed to know nothing of them whatever. . . . He steadily persisted in cutting himself off from others, and he made this conspicuous by a physical peculiarity imposed on himself and his posterity.[38]

At once circumcised and circumscribed—proudly self-defining as Other yet at the same time forced to live in proximity and at times even close contact with non-Jews—the Jew's fate for Hegel is

> no Greek tragedy; it can rouse neither pity nor terror, for both of these arise out of the fate which follows from the inevitable slip of a beautiful character: it can arouse horror alone. The fate of the Jewish people is the

fate of Macbeth who stepped out of nature itself, clung to alien Beings and so in their service had to trample and deny everything whole in human nature, had at last to be forsaken by his gods (since these were objects and he their slave) and be dashed to pieces on his faith itself. (204–5)

These lines in *The Spirit of Christianity* deserve some further glossing, not only because they anticipate so much of what is to come later but also because they figure in such interesting ways the uses to which the Jew's alterity could be put. Writing with his customary combination of power and obscurity, the early Hegel conflates those familiar fantasmatic tropes of the wandering and the Oriental Jew with Christian claims that the Jew embodies an adherence to narrow legal forms rather than spiritual truths. Elsewhere, the ethnographic imaginary—the invention of entire new categories of otherness under the impact of European expansion—provides Hegel with an entirely new language for thinking about the Jew's otherness, for literally casting the Jew out of Europe in figure, if not in fact.

Truth is beauty intellectually represented; the negative character of truth is freedom. But how could they have an inkling of beauty who saw in everything only matter? How could they exercise reason and freedom who were only mastered or masters? How could they have hoped even for the poor immortality which the consciousness of the individual is reserved ... who never enjoyed any life or consciousness above eating and drinking? How in such circumstances should it be a merit not to have sullied by restriction something which was not present, to have left free something which no one knew (i.e., the Jewish God)? Eskimos might as well pride themselves on their superiority over any European because in their country no excise is paid on wine, and agriculture is not made harder by oppressive taxes. (196–7)

It is remarkable to see both the depth with which Hegel works out his marginalizing logic and how completely it is embedded in the dialectics of German philosophy in the early years of the nineteenth century. Hegel is writing here in counter to Moses Mendelssohn's arguments for full emancipation and religious tolerance—not necessarily, it must be stressed, the same thing—based on the indispensability of Judaism to Christian belief. Mendelssohn argued that Christians need to allow emancipated Jews to be religious Jews, rather than demand their conversion, in order to maintain the coherence of *Christian* identity, an identity that rests upon Judaism itself. And as Kant—contemporary, rival, and friend of Mendelssohn—recognized, acceptance of Mendelssohn's argument would lead to the utter undoing of the typological house of cards in which the Jew is deemed essential but made subordinate to a Christian dispensation, since the Jewish faith itself is, according to the avowal of Christians, the substructure upon which the superstructure of Christianity rests, the demand that it be abandoned is equivalent to expecting someone to demolish the ground floor of a house in order to take up his abode in the second story. [Mendelssohn's] real intention is fairly clear. He means to say: first wholly remove Judaism itself out of your *religion* (it can always remain, as an antiquity, in the historical account of your faith); we can then take your proposal under advisement.[39]

But this is precisely what Hegel tries to do, at least figuratively: he denies the salience of the Jew's monotheism to the Christian project by comparing Jews to a species of Eskimo, a people not only living outside the bounds of both European religion and geography but failing to possess the civilizing relation to nature that Europe claimed for itself. In countering Mendelssohn's cleverly dialectical argument against the hegemony of a Christian-centered European culture, Hegel constructs the Jew in the image of the primitive, the aboriginal, the "savage"—or, in Boyarin's terms, reconstructs the "other within" as quite literally an Other without.

The Jew, then, is culturally expelled from the precincts of European identity by the very terms within which Hegel struggles ontologically to *include* that figure; and this exclusion has the double effect of tracing the lineaments of a Western cultural identity even as it works to repress the ontological priority of the Jew. This double movement is also present in Hegel's invocation of Shakespeare's Macbeth, in which the Jew implicitly stands to Christian Europe as does the heathen Scot Macbeth to Christian England, a barbarian outside the gates. The vehicle of the metaphor does as much work here as the tenor; the invocation of Macbeth alludes metonymically not only to the putative barbarism of the Jew but also to the genius of Shakespeare—to the power of what stands within the gates as well as what stands without. In the next section, Hegel takes this process one step further: he uses the same tactics both to distance the Jew from European identity and to define his own philosophical position vis-à-vis his most problematic precursor, Kant. As he builds his dialectical argument for Christ by arguing that the latter embodies the Jew's "precise opposite, a human urge and so a human need," he finds himself linking a putative blind Jewish obedience toward law with the Kantian emphasis on duty as a prerogative of moral life. For what is true of the Jew is also true of Kant: "woe to human relations which are not unquestionably found in the concept of duty . . . for this concept excludes or dominates all other relation" (212). Tellingly, the minute he makes this argument, he turns, again metonymically, to invoking the opposition of Western identity and otherness. Responding to Kant's claim in *Religion within the Limits of Reason Alone* that, while there is no difference between the Siberian shaman of the Tungus and the pope and the Siberian tribe of the Voguls and the Puritans, since all rely on "positive authority" or external compulsion for moral sanctions, the man of reason is free, obligated only to a moral law grounded in his own reason. By contrast, Hegel claims that the precise contrary is true.

> By [Kant's] line of argument, however, positivity is only partially removed, and between the Shaman of the Tungus, the European prelate who rules church and state, the Voguls, and the Puritans on the one hand, and the man who listens to his own command of duty, on the other, the difference is not that the former make themselves slaves, while the latter is free, but that the former have their lord inside themselves, while the latter carries his lord inside himself, yet is his own slave. (211)

Hegel's argumentative slide from the Jew to Kant to the non-Western Other works by implication to suggest a chain of identification that places those three in a pool of common alterity, ready to find their dialectical completion in the hands of Christ and the Christian principles of freedom and love, of a freedom achieved precisely through love. The resulting effect is complex, to be sure. It is *not* to posit the political or civil ejection of the Jews from the bounds of a Christian Europe nor even to suggest a religious expulsion; Fackenheim is right to see Hegel working here, and later in his work, to find a place for the Jew as Jew in his dialectical system, and right to find this a relatively "enlightened" response. (Hegel was, to put it another way, no Fichte.) But here again the thrust of the argument—the basis of its problems—is a *cultural* one, one that works by placing the Jew on the margins of Europe through implication and metaphor and that traces as it enacts a common thread of Western identity stretching from Greek tragedy through Shakespeare through Hegel himself—an identity that is constructed by, and dependent on, the contrast with that figure of troubling contiguity to this cultural project, that figure who, as Mendelssohn might also have suggested, is indispensable to it: the Jew.

As German philosophy continued to elaborate a theory of culture and its relation to the state and to language and to enact that philosophy in practice—in Humboldt's educational reforms, for example—the problematic conjuncture between the Jew and the idea of a common Western culture retained this problematic force and continued to do this complex Hegelian work of marginalizing while incorporating the Jew. Shaped by and shaping the traditional hostility toward Jews in Germany, a hostility that was particularly accelerated among the elites in the later years of the nineteenth century and that was impelled by the role of the Hellenic—that is, ostentatiously non-"Hebraic"—ideal throughout post-Enlightenment German culture as a midwife of German nationalism (as Ludwig Marcuse put it, established German intellectuals could be best described as worshipping "Prussian army barracks adorned with Doric columns and Corinthian capitals"), the Jew remained a problematic presence in the construction of models of Western culture—precisely the problematic presence that I have noted as recently as the Anastasi exhibit at the Chicago Art Institute.

THE JEW AND THE CAREER OF "CULTURE" IN ANGLO-AMERICA, 1860–1920

As that example suggests, it would be a mistake to limit this problematic to Germany or to the nineteenth century alone. Hegel's move to acknowledge Jewish difference but to marginalize Jews from the bounds of European cultural identity is central to later thought about European or Western cultural identity. For that notion of "culture," like Hegel's, acknowledges the Jew as such and even acknowledges the Jew's right to practice her or his religion, but wishes to distance "the Jew" from a legacy to which Jews have made impressive contributions of their own and to which they have a good argument for having begun in the first place. But Hegel's argument also suggests, by the same logic, why such a marginalization can never be complete or effective: both as the other within the geographical confines of the nation and as the other within the self-conceptualization of Western culture, the Jew serves as an ongoing reminder of the limits of such self-conceptualizations and an incitement to making new ones.

The clearest example of this process and its ramifications in the theorization of "culture" is of course the work of Matthew Arnold, perhaps the most influential literary and cultural critic of nineteenth-century England, one who powerfully reshaped the study of literature, the practice of education, and the ideology of "culture" throughout the nineteenth and twentieth centuries in both England and America. At least in the context of our subject, the importance of Arnold ought never be underestimated, for what he so successfully did was to take the idiom of culture out of the starry realms of German philosophy and into the life-practices and institutions of the middle classes. Arnold is no less important, at least for our purposes, for the way he seamlessly sutures the Jewish question into the German idealist idiom while he makes the latter part of the idiom of a new Anglo-American dogma of "culture." Bridging gaps between German and English thought, ethnology and literary history, and—most important for my purposes— eighteenth- and nineteenth-century philo- and anti-Semitic inscriptions of Jewishness, Arnold reorganized the discursive links between the Jew and these various terms and understandings. In so doing, he shaped the ways the next generations were to conceive the relation between these terms—and suggests a deeply problematic, because fundamentally covert, relation between the very process of affirming cultural value and the endlessly vexing figure of the Jew.

To understand the specificities of Arnold's contribution to it, we need first to think through the place of the Jew in the discourse of English identity-formation and, more saliently, the possibility of a coherent English national culture. A good deal of recent work has been done on this very question, pointing to an English version of the problematic appropriation of Jews in the service of establishing a German national identity: that anti- and philo-Semitic currents played off against each other in the British national frame, too, creating in their eddies powerfully conflicting genealogies for English cultural identity. For despite (or perhaps because of?) the relatively small number of Jews who lived in England after the great expulsion of 1190, Jews occupied a powerful place in the English national imaginary, and not entirely a negative one. The meticulous historical work of David Katz has demonstrated that Jews in Renaissance England existed in greater number and were received with greater tolerance than has previously been acknowledged; that many Protestant divines in the seventeenth century turned to Jews as bearers of the Adamic, pre-Babel language; that many seventeenth- and eighteenth-century theorists thought of Jews as precursors of the English nation— sometimes under the argument that since the descendants of Gomer, the son of Noah, emigrated to ancient England, Jews were really the aboriginal Englishmen; sometimes in religious and national narratives told in quarters frequently though not exclusively Puritan, where Jews (persecuted, it was argued, largely by Catholics) were seen as the origins of a distinctly Protestant dispensation.[40] Howard Weinbrot has extended the argument further into the eighteenth century, arguing that the increasing toleration of Jews was part of a larger process by which a "national self-esteem" was transformed into market-based multiculturalism via the "acceptance of Dutch and German kings, Dutch and French Protestant artisans and merchants, Scottish frauds, intellectuals and prime ministers, and Jewish merchants and stock brokers, one of whose sons would be baptized in the Church of England, become Prime Minister in 1867, and the first Earl of Beaconsfield in 1876 while . . . remaining suspiciously alien."[41]

Writing about exactly the same cultural moment, dealing with much of the same material, Frank Felsenstein has observed precisely the opposite phenomenon.[42] He shows the persistence of anti-Semitic stereotypes throughout eighteenth-century culture, from Hogarth through the pamphleteers, from the Restoration theater through the debates in the Houses of Parliament. Specifically, Felsenstein reminds us that blatantly anti-Semitic versions of Shylock proliferated on the eighteenth-century stage; that the proposal of the "Jew Bill" (the Jewish Naturalization Act) in 1753 was met with an outpouring of anti-Semitic pamphlets, caricatures, and polemical denunciations, and that its defeat was greeted with a recrudescence of nationalist sentiment throughout England, complete with celebratory bonfires and church sermons. Disputing Katz's Whiggish narrative of the increasing toleration leading ineluctably to the Second Jew Bill of 1867, Felsenstein argues that Jews won grudging acceptance only at the price of denying their difference, their distinctiveness, their Jewishness.

The truth of the matter would seem to lie somewhere between Katz and Weinbrot's optimistic narratives and the more pessimistic story told by Felsenstein.

Or rather it would, I think, incorporate both—would see the dramas of expulsion and reintegration, and those of anti- and philo-Semitism, as essentially co-implicated with each other and hence isomorphic with (at the very least) the larger ideological pattern we have been looking at in Western culture: the attempt simultaneously to incorporate and expel Jews from the boundaries of a presumably monolithic West. And in England in particular, the figure of the Jew was a shifting signifier that could be used to establish cultural, social, and religious continuity or to define historical, cultural, and religious rupture. Thus the Jew both authenticates the historical reality of Adamic language and enacts the process of that language's transformation into mere babble. The Jew provides a distinguished historical pedigree for the motley racial admixture that composes the English nation—and embodies the problematic racial and national mixing from which English national identity must be rescued. The Jew provides historical grounding for Protestantism (either Nonconformist or C. of E., depending on whom one is reading), hence grounds English identity contra its Catholic antagonists, or the Jew is understood as the heathen Other to the Christian entirely: a position that Cromwell's opponents quickly took when he proposed repatriation, the point the Tories raised as part of a project of enlisting nationalist sentiments against their Whig antagonists around the occasion of the first "Jew Bill," the point that Disraeli's antagonists constantly raised against him. (It was not coincidental that Disraeli's pious, Nonconformist antagonist Gladstone asserted that whatever the possible linkages between British and Hebrews might be, "the Hebrews were Semitic; Christendom is Aryan.")

The point is not only that the sentiments toward the Jew were irretrievably mixed or even that unstable narratives of British nationality, and the relation of that nationality to a larger Christian-centered narrative, were told with reference to the Jew. It is that those narratives could only be told through the complex drama of incorporation and expulsion, of admission and expelling, that it was the Jew's office both to define and to instantiate. For the Jew is not only "ambivalence incarnate," as Bauman puts it; the Jew is also that border or boundary figure that calls into question the viability of any model of racial, national, or cultural identity (including, as I have shown earlier, the Jew's own). Hence the Jew may be not only invoked for the purposes of a "violent de-ambivalentization," as Bauman puts it, but identified *with* as a kind of figure of bounded boundlessness, one who can image the very possibility of existing within a social or a national or an ethnic identity without being completely subsumed by it.

Here Arnold's famous invocation of the term "Hebrew" as one part of the dialectical argument that composes the most prominent chapter in *Culture and Anarchy* assumes its greatest significance. For one thing, placing Arnold's argument in the context of European responses to "the Jew" helps us understand why (other than its origins in his culture-hero Heine) Arnold seizes upon the

"Hebrew" as the antonym to the Hellene—why, to put it a bit more complexly, he feels he must posit a dialectical alternative to the Hellene at all. As far as the first is concerned, Arnold's famous association of the middle-class, Protestant spirit with the Hebraic—with a rigid and unbending adherence to the Law and a Puritan zealousness—resonates with full meaning when understood against the identification of an anti-Catholic, anti-European, pro-Puritan program with the Jew in eighteenth-century philo-Semitism. And placing Arnold's argument in its larger cultural frame accounts for the odd tipping of the scales toward the Hellenic. For the very form with which Arnold argues for the balancing of the Hebrew and the Hellene—the dialectic—privileges the latter even as (indeed precisely because) it argues against its priority. The act of balancing the two positions Arnold's own text on the side of that form of apprehension that enacts as it valorizes balance, suppleness, dialectic. And insofar as that text performs as it advocates "culture"—the equilibrium of Hebrew and Hellene, sweetness and light, sentiment and "right reason"—it redefines "culture" as a species of Hellenic suppleness, one whose suppleness is performed, in fact, by the very act of incorporating into its purview the figure of the Hebrew.

In other words, exactly like Hegel, Arnold invokes the Hebrew as a figure in his drama of culture in such a way as to subordinate that figure to the larger dilemma of European culture itself. That this effort involves more than mere rhetoric becomes clear when Arnold brings his terms in line with the new racial theorizing, theorizing that gives him a more authoritative language with which to accomplish this dual project:

> Science has now made visible to everybody the great and pregnant elements of difference which lie in race, and in how signal a manner they make the genius and history of an Indo-European people vary from those of a Semitic people. Hellenism is of Indo-European growth, Hebraism is of a Semitic growth; and we English, a nation of Indo-European stock, seem to belong naturally to the movement of Hellenism. Eminently Indo-European by its *humour*, by the power it shows, through this gift, of imaginatively acknowledging the multiform aspects of the problem of life, and of thus getting itself unfixed from its own over-certainty, of smiling at its own over-tenacity, our race has yet (as a great part of its strength lies here) in matters of practical life and moral conduct, a strong share of the assuredness, the tenacity, the immensity of the Hebrews.[43]

For Ragussis, this moment in Arnold's thought represents the incorporation or absorption of the Jew into the drama of a national culture, "like the absorption of Judaism in Christianity, or Hebrew Scripture in the Christian Bible, authorizing himself to limit and even eradicate the elements of difference by which Hebraism undermines his . . . racially pure definition of the English nation."[44] Like Ragussis, I see this moment, which occurs very near the end of *Culture and*

Anarchy, as the final sign of the incorporation of the Jew under the sign of the Hellene, although I think that it is, oddly enough, the careful balancing of Hellenic and Hebraic identities with which the passage performs its maneuver that does this amalgamative work. But unlike Ragussis, I see Arnold here as performing a fundamentally defensive maneuver, one that predicates a "share" in one side of Hebraic identity in order to distract our attention from deeper, more dangerous connections between Arnold and the Jew, particularly as both are grouped (or group themselves) under the sign of a common otherness.

For in a distinctly odd turn, one that was to have unexpected consequences in later critical thinking and writing, the language, if not the actual figure, of the Hebrew returns under the sign of ambivalence to haunt Arnold's self-imagining. When Arnold shifts from the language of the Hebrew and the Hellene to that of class—whose divisions he describes as those between Philistines, Barbarians, and populace—he also discerns the lineaments of a new class, a classless class, a class wholly devoted to the idea of culture rather than their own personal or partisan interests: those "persons who are mainly led, not by their class spirit, but by a general *humane* spirit, by the love of human perfection" (196). And to this class— a class in which, though a "child of the Philistines," he eloquently includes himself—Arnold gives a particularly resonant name: "Therefore when we speak of ourselves as divided into the Barbarians, Philistine, and Populace, we must be understood always to imply that within each of these classes there are a certain number of *aliens*, if we may so call them" (196).

This description has been frequently (and correctly) cited as the origin of the ideal of the critical, alienated intellectual in Anglo-American culture; and it is particularly crucial that in describing that figure Arnold deploys terms that Enlightenment culture and his own country both associated with the Jew, that paradigmatic outsider in Europe's new cultural dispensation. Moreover, the notion of the alien explored herein defines that figure in the culturally fraught idiom of the alien *within*—the alien whose place in the social ensemble is one of profound and self-reifying otherness yet for whom some kind of place must be negotiated in the social ensemble. And, as Bryan Cheyette notes, many of Arnold's descriptions of the cynosures or embodiments of culture identify that figure with actual Jews. For example, an entire essay in *Essays in Criticism* is devoted to Heine— from whom, of course, the Hebrew/Hellene distinction itself springs; there Heine serves as a militant anti-Philistine whose enthusiasm in the battle for culture leads to fanaticism and poetic failure. Spinoza is similarly recognized; indeed, he underwrites Arnold's own attempt to reimagine biblical hermeneutics in the wake of the Higher Criticism. Indeed, these Jews work typologically in order to establish a genealogy for Arnold himself: his description of Heine as failed poet chimes with Arnold's vision of his own poetic failures, and his delineation of Spinoza's expulsion from his own community eloquently glosses Arnold's own cultural position vis-à-vis insular, "Hebraic" England of the nineteenth century: those who condemned him "remained children of Israel, and he became a child of modern Europe."[45] Finally, of course, Arnold identifies himself explicitly with these figures in his most sustained exploration of the possibilities and difficulties of the scope of intellectual life, *The Function of Criticism at the Present Time*. There, he not only defines himself in the language of alienness familiar from anti-Jewish propaganda—as the member of a small circle dedicatedly pursuing an arcane but vital study in which true cultural value inheres—but identifies himself as a second Moses poised in the wilderness, espying from afar the Promised Land.

The point here is not only that Arnold's praise of the critical intellectual seeks to affirm a certain alienness whose cultural embodiment is the Jew, although there is a good deal of truth to that assertion. It is that the figure of the Jew represents the very possibility of representing this alienness: that the career of the Jew is not only that of the alien within, indistinguishably subversive of the cultural dominant, but that of the alien who stands in opposition to all forms of cultural inhibition and social power, the alien who affirms his alienness as the very ground of his being (even, in the case of Spinoza or Heine, to the extent of alienating himself from his own community). Arnold's relation to the Jew, then, partakes of the kind of ambivalent fascination Eric Lott has discerned in the relation of American working-class audiences to African-American others via the figure of the blackface minstrel,[46] and it is no coincidence that here, too, the connection is fraught with both liberationary and libidinal potential, and turns on the matter of performance. For perhaps the most revealing moment in Arnold's treatment of the Jew is his composition, in 1863, of his sonnets on the death of the French actress Rachel. These three sonnets are redolent with the dynamics of identification and projection; they are in fact structured as a series of boundary confusions, in which Arnold mourns the passing not only of Rachel but also of the young Matthew Arnold who had traveled to Paris to see her:

> She follows the gay world, whose swarms have fled
> To Switzerland, to Baden, to the Rhine,
> Why stops she by this empty play-house drear?
>
> Ah, where the spirit its highest life hath led,
> All spots, matched with that spot, are less divine;
> And Rachel's Switzerland, her Rhine, is here![47]

The "playhouse" figures a place—call it (as Arnold did in his youth) Switzerland or the Rhine; call it poetry, call it, as increasingly Arnold does, "culture"— where a kind of imaginative amplitude and an expansion of spirit can find its local habitation and name: this is a "spot," like Wordsworth's "spot of time," which spatializes and reifies the aspirations of the imagination and allows for a full renovation of the self. But the only way for Arnold himself to gain access to this "spot" is through an imaginative identification with the Jewish actress who actually inhabits that space: only by seeing her seeing it is he able to grant himself the right to participate in that experience.

Rachel literally embodies the ability to enter into contact with the imaginative amplitude and the suppleness that Arnold associates with culture. To a certain extent, of course, she does so because she is an actress—that figure in the nineteenth-century imaginary who conjoined sexual appeal with the power to represent falsely, to impersonate a multitude of personalities and inhabit an abundance of beings. But to a certain extent (and Arnold is not of course the first to make the connection) she does so because she is so spectacularly a public Jew, a Jew on the stage at precisely the moment when Jews were entering the public sphere, the sphere of "culture." This point is made clearly in the final sonnet, where Rachel's Jewishness becomes the ground not only of Arnold's boundary confusion vis-à-vis Rachel but of Rachel's vis-à-vis the culture of "the West":

> Sprung from the blood of Israel's scattered race
> At a mean inn in German Arrau born,
> To forms from antique Greece and Rome uptorn,
> Tricked out with a Parisian speech and face
>
> Imparting with renewed, old classic grace
> Then, soothing with thy Christian strain forlorn,
> A-Kempis! her departing soul outword
> While by her bedside Hebrew rites have place—
>
> Ah, not the radiant spirit of Greece alone
> She had—one power, which made her breast its home!
> In her, like us, there clashed contending powers,
>
> Germany, France, Christ, Moses, Athens, Rome,
> The strife, the mixture, in her soul are ours,
> Her genius and her glory are her own.

Here, Rachel's polynational origins and her attempt to negotiate "the strife, the mixture, in her soul" place her in the familiar Arnoldian position of internal warfare; within her very being, as on Dover Beach, "ignorant armies clash by night." But she is most Arnoldian in her project of cultural assimilation—of assimilation by culture, for it is through quite literally performing the masterpieces of Western culture that Rachel is "uptorn" from her humble Jewish origins. Rachel as Jew figures, that is, not only Arnold's characteristic ambivalence but also his response to it; she enacts it, represents it, and in so doing holds in a kind of taut suspension all the possibilities contained within the seemingly unified notion of "the West." And Rachel's performative heterogeneity becomes the very ground of her "genius" and her "glory": she is like all of us, Arnold writes in one last boundary confusion, except that she can represent her mixed cultural identity in the public arena, on the public stage.

In all these moments, then, Arnold subverts his own sublation of the Hellene by covertly identifying the Hellenic, the pursuit of sweetness and light, with the drama of the assimilating but not fully assimilated Jew—and by identifying, as well, that figure who pursues Hellenism, the alienated intellectual, with the same figure. In doing so, he neatly reverses the pattern of simultaneous incorporation and expulsion of the Jew that I have explored in the drama of European culture-building. Instead of deploying the Jew, as does Hegel, as the means of defining the bounds of European "culture," Arnold seizes upon and makes his own the Jew's marginalization to distance himself from his own provincial, "Philistinish" national culture and to identify himself with a larger, European cultural project and ideal. Like Heine, like Spinoza, like Rachel, Arnold stages himself as an alien struggling not only to comprehend but to correct the vicissitudes of a national culture with which he identifies himself but by which he finds himself wholly rejected. And, most saliently like Rachel, he is bound endlessly to perform his own marginalization, his own multiplicity, as he struggles to figure out the fit object of his own address; indeed, in its positive guise, his stance becomes the very embodiment of the alienated suppleness that constructs the Arnoldian intellectual. The intellectual, like Rachel, is defined as that person who publicly performs ambivalence, or to put it positively, who refuses to be captured by any one party or program and hence displays the virtues of that refusal to be confined by narrow boundaries.

The very metamorphic, boundary-challenging qualities that Bauman ascribes to the Jew in post-Enlightenment culture thus become the ground of Arnold's covert, almost libidinal, engagement with that figure; instead of demanding its repression, as Ragussis and Cheyette suggest, Arnold's identification with the Jew under the sign of the alienated intellectual crucially depends upon, and returns repeatedly to, precisely the qualities of Jewishness that cause the Jew to pose such large-scale cultural problems. This deployment of the Jew in the construction of ideas (and ideologies) of "culture" had important consequences for later generations of writers and artists, gentile and Jewish alike. For writers, artists, and critics, who conceived of themselves in the Arnoldian tradition as devotees of high culture in an irrevocably Philistine world, it established a powerfully problematic set of conflicting equations. Insofar as they so located themselves, they found themselves occupying a position homologous with, and at times identical to, that figure most fully identified by their culture as the prime Other, the Jew; and it is the drama of that figure that most neatly encapsulates the cultural trajectory of the would-be alienated intellectual and the polyglot, polycultural "West" with which such critics sought to identify. Much of Eliot's early anti-Semitic poetry, for example, can be read as a reaction-formation to precisely this situation—one in which the Jew represents an alienated cosmopolitanism that is covertly connected, almost beyond the poet's knowledge or desire, to surpassing qualities that define the culture of the West. As I show in the next chapter, Trollope's representation of Melmotte in *The Way We Live Now* as a species of monster is grounded in a covert identification of Trollope's own fictional act, the writing of fiction for an unstable and troubled marketplace, with the figure of the Jew, the writer of empty IOUs. Or, as I show in subsequent chapters, George du Maurier and Henry James both face a cultural identification with the Jew as artist under the sign of degeneration and both attempt, variously, to clear themselves from this powerful identification.

The result of the identification with the Jew by partisans of Arnoldian high culture is, then, a complicated series of cathexes and countercathexes, coalitions and hesitations, which would have a lasting effect on the Anglo-American cultural imaginary from their time to our own. The weird, contradictory, at times disgraceful, at times unexpectedly sympathetic response to Jews—and the use of "the Jew" as a figurative and/or characterological resource—that runs through the works of writers as diverse and as crucial as George Eliot, Trollope, James, du Maurier, Wharton, Cather, T. S. Eliot, Virginia Woolf, and Pound flows directly from the social and cultural position these figures found themselves occupying. For in and through their response to the figure of the Jew as emblem of the artist and the intellectual—of the possibilities of transnational culture itself—these writers work to assert and to define the authorial stance and to test the limits of their own cultural power.

This, then, is one side of the story I have to tell in the pages that follow: a variant of the familiar one in which Western writers work to construct narratives of cultural identity in ambivalent relation to problematical others, it suggests that much of what we have come to know in the last hundred years as the idea or ideal of "culture" in both its positive and negatives guises was shaped in identification with and struggle against the Jew. But it is crucial to remember, as I noted earlier, that this was a moment in which Jewish identity, too, was at powerful and problematic stake, and in precisely the same social field.[48] Playing out their own variously cathected dramas of assimilation, identification, and resistance in a cultural milieu marked on the one hand by an unprecedented openness to Jews and by all-too-familiar frenzies of anti-Semitism on the other, Jews of all varieties—ranging from the assimilated to the observant and passing at various points in between—remade as they responded to the cultural milieu they faced. To add to the complexity of the situation, they were in turn remade by their role in the interchange—given new social powers and scope, at times, or made better able to negotiate their way through the charged and complicated cultural field of turn of the century Europe and America alike. To cite but three examples, consider the roles played by Sigmund Freud, Cesare Lombroso, and Max Nordau in the construction of idioms of cultural identity and decline (and consider as well how thoroughly Nordau and Freud were shaped by the various forms of anti-

Semitic frenzy whipping through the Austro-German polity in the later portions of the nineteenth century). Or consider the quite different examples of Disraeli in England, Marx in Germany, and Proust in France—three wildly different products of Jewish parentage each of whose responses to his Jewishness had, to say the least, a powerful impact on the respective spheres he entered.

The causes and consequences of this discursive tendency are complex, so much so that much of this book is devoted to tracing just one small aspect of them. A few brief observations may be ventured here. One is to note just how crucial was the cultural arena as a space of social struggle for would-be assimilating Jews and how various were their dialectical wrestlings with normative ideals of "culture" that only partially acknowledged or included them (at the very best). The established and newer professions, the universities, the press—in all these arenas Jews found both opportunity and opposition; and in their fight for recognition and full participation they had to master the reigning discursive idioms that constricted as they constructed them. John Efron has recently stressed how ethnographers of Jewish descent like Joseph Jacobs had to deal with racist deployments of anthropological discourse in the course of their work, and as they did so, they attempted (with varying degrees of success) to turn or transform the slurring representations of the Jew encoded in that discourse to ends less prejudiced, more inclusive.[49] Or one thinks of Freud's wrestlings with German Romantic poetry and philosophy and the writings of Nietzsche and Schopenhauer—a body of thought that served at one and the same time as an imaginative burden to be overcome, a resource to be appropriated, and a species of legitimation, one that he sought to remake, to turn against its more exclusive or exclusionary aspects.

Or, to turn to the Anglo-American literary sphere that is my prime focus here, one thinks of the special salience of the Arnoldian ideal of culture and the cathexis to culture, in the high Arnoldian sense of the word, to Jewish intellectuals in Anglo-America in the latter years of the nineteenth and the early years of the twentieth centuries. One sign of the intensity of their cathexis, and of its ramifications, is the degree to which they wrestled with the legacy of Arnold himself. One of the most prominent Jewish literary critics of the 1920s, for example, Ludwig Lewisohn, identified his reading of Arnold as the crucial event in the formation of his identity as an alienated Jewish intellectual: "My father discovered the volume containing Culture and Anarchy and Friendship's Garland and urged me to read it. I felt the impact of a kindred mind and the book became one of my deepest experiences, although its full import was revealed to me only years later."[50] That "full import," Lewisohn later wrote in the progressivist pages of the *Nation*, was as a guide to people exactly like himself, alienated intellectuals adrift in George Babbitt's America.

> [W]e all talk Arnold, think Arnold, preach and propagate Arnold. In the dead and almost fabled sixties of the nineteenth century, he discovered

Main Street with its "imperturbable self-satisfaction," its devastating "provinciality," its dangerous hostility to the "free play of mind," to any flexibility of intellect." He discovered the eternal Philistine of an industrialized and standardized civilization, who boasts of the output of his factories and the speed of his trains and never stops to consider that these "trains only carry him from an illiberal, dismal life at Islington to an illiberal, dismal life at Camberwell." It was Arnold who diagnosed the central Philistine heresy of substituting means for ends.[51]

Adopting and internalizing Arnold's own words, making them his own, Lewisohn discovers a genealogy for his own position exactly as Arnold discovered in the figure of the Jew a genealogy for his own identity as an alienated intellectual.

Lewisohn's reverent response was not the only way Jewish intellectuals responded to Arnold. When Horace Kallen, to cite another example from the period, began to construct the current of thought that was to eventuate in the ideology of cultural pluralism, he found himself taking on Arnold quite directly, adopting the term "Hebraism" to designate Jewishness at large and attempting, contra Arnold, to resuscitate the philosophic virtues of a "Hebraic" attitude toward life: one that emphasizes "flux, mutation, immanence, disorder" as opposed to the Hellenic ideal of "structure, harmony, order immutable, eternal."[52] And Kallen makes a second, more aggressive, move as well: to identify this position with Augustine and Hegel as well as Philo and Mendelssohn; with Darwin and James as well as Bergson; with the coming dispensation rather than with preceding ones. Kallen's vision totters on the edge of grandiosity when it proclaims this second coming of Hebraism, this universal triumph of the doctrine of the flux over reason and chaos over order.

> It is easily demonstrable that this relation holds not only in philosophy but in innumerable other intents of life—that all which Hebraism supplied that was potent, in the history of nordic Christian civilization, was merely a new language for an unabandoned vision, that the gigantic reconciliation which Christian institution and thought attempted between Hellenism and Hebraism never took place, that Hebraism has never dominated European life to the degree in which Hellenism dominated it, that the "supremacy" of Hebraism is, if one reads the signs of the times aright, yet to come.

But precisely this grandiosity has the effect of reorienting Arnoldian discourse, of pitting Arnold (and Carlyle, who gets quoted explicitly here) against themselves as avatars of an over-Hellenized past that is due for a bracing cultural renovation at the hands of a Hebraic-identified modernity. Thus Arnold's implicit typology, the Hebraic as a fallible predecessor of a Hellenistic consummation, and his implicit tropology—the Hellenic as mobile and fluid, metamorphic and modern, the Hebraic as stubborn and fixed—are turned inside out and directed against

Arnold's own argument, which is seen (in pointedly anti-Arnoldian thrusts) as "true only in the schoolmaster's sense of true. It represents a conventional, traditional attitude and the effect of tradition is invariably to harden living fact into dead literature and so to falsify its essence" (8).

This kind of dialectical wrestling with Arnold's dialectical vision of culture was to have powerful aftereffects in the writings of Anglo-American Jewish intellectuals. But I leave this particular turn of the Arnoldian screw for a later chapter: for the time being, it's perhaps more important to note that similar accommodations to—or departures from—the Arnoldian problematic challenge the work of subsequent Jewish writers, critics, and intellectuals as fully as the identification of the artist and cultural producer with the Jew challenges their gentile counterparts. The result is an interlocking series of affinities, contradictions, reversals, and ironic accommodations, all of which involve a shifting, ramifying relation between at least three terms: assimilating Jews who seek to enter the terrain of high culture; ideas and ideals of culture and art that significantly trope or were themselves constructed in relation to Jewishness (or, as Kallen would put it, "Hebraism"); and a prevalent but shifting anti-Semitic cultural dispensation, particularly but not exclusively among the elites who formed the center of literary and intellectual culture. If I were to put this interrelation in narrative terms, it would go something like this: through their responses to that oddest of figures, "the Jew," the fin-de-siècle Anglo-American literati created new notions of high culture and shaped such enduring figures as the marginalized artist and the alienated intellectual. And in coming to terms with Anglo-American literary culture, assimilating Jewish intellectuals attempted to delineate a new, nonethnic identity for themselves. But the result of these interchanges was a powerful set of reversals, transpositions that shape our own cultural imagination (and our imagination *of* culture). The intellectual and the artist got constructed on the model of the stereotypical Jew—estranged, corrupt, yet mysteriously potent. And many Jews came to define themselves as conservers of Western culture—self-appointed bearers of literary tradition in that era of ceaseless change we call postmodern. To this process I now turn.

2

The Temple of Culture and the Market for Letters

The Jew and the Way We Write Now

In CHAPTER 1 I argued that Jews were much on the minds of nineteenth-century intellectuals in England and America, and in a completely new way, as they began to think of themselves *as* intellectuals, using the conceptual equipment bequeathed them by their German and other Continental counterparts. But it needs to be added that some of the most important deployments of the figure of the Jew can be found in the genre that, at precisely this moment, was simultaneously experiencing huge popular success and struggling to affirm its artistic prestige: the novel. In this chapter, I want to parse this particular deployment of the figure of the Jew by asking the most vexing (and unanswerable) question of literary analysis: *why*? Or, more specifically, why *here*, why in the sphere of high-cultural literary production?

After all, in the category-mad nineteenth century, it is unsurprising to find that race theorists, sexologists, and ethnographers all grappled with the question of Jewish difference. At a time when the mass literary market was booming and evangelical culture predominating, it is also unastonishing to discover solemn, didactic romances of Hebrew history circulating in the low- and middlebrow arenas of popular fiction. General Lew Wallace's *Ben Hur* (1880) climbed the first bestseller lists in America; Marie Corelli's *Barabbas* (1892) did the same in England. Nor, when we turn from the philo-Semitic 1880s to the anti-Semitic, anti-alien 1900s, is it odd to find Edgar Wallace's paranoid fantasies of world domination by Jewish aliens, anarchists, and Bolsheviks—books like *The Four Just Men* (1904) or *The Council of Justice* (1908)—supplanting their more benign biblical precedents in a march into bestsellerdom. What *is* startling is that Jews should figure with such prominence in a literary culture that was beginning to think of itself as just that, as a distinct zone of imaginative endeavor possessing a distinct and powerful, even redemptive, social mission. And it is equally startling that the matter of Jewry should have been so prominent in the project of self-validation undertaken by writers entering into that zone.

To be sure, changing social conditions are part of the story. By 1880, the Jewish population in England had doubled, as it had done in America; legal barriers against Jewish citizenship and voting rights in both countries had tumbled; Jews began to move in the highest social circles not as exotic exceptions but as common facts of social life; the son of a Jew had been elected prime minister. But the Jews so entering were interestingly, and increasingly, heterogeneous. In England, the dominance of a longstanding, socially prominent Sephardim-dominated community was challenged by the augmentation of Ashkenazim from western Europe. In America, the dominance of German Jews ("Our Crowd") was similarly challenged by the arrival of eastern Europeans. In both cases, the arriving Jews were poorer, spoke a variety of languages, and seemed to assimilate less easily than had their predecessors. These newly arriving Jews thus troubled the prospect of establishing a national culture in both locales—a project increasingly central to the concerns of an intellectual caste eager, as intellectuals always are, to negotiate a space for themselves in the burgeoning nation-state. When an anxious Henry James looked out on New York's Lower East Side and saw in the influx of Jews a threat to the cultural and linguistic identity of the recently riven American nation, he spoke not only for his own fears but for those of his high-culture contemporaries in both England and America.

Yet even the capacity of these newly arriving immigrants to jangle the nerves and push the buttons of anxious high-culture intellectuals explains only one side of the response of novelists, cultural critics, and intellectuals in the high Victorian era. In this chapter I want to suggest another dimension to their response, one that cuts, indeed, to the very core of the social experience of the writer in the high Victorian moment. It will be my argument in what follows that Victorian writers were fascinated with the figure of the Jew, and in an entirely new way, because that figure allowed them to negotiate their relation to the dominant fact of their existence: the burgeoning, but segmenting, market for letters.[1]

In making this claim, I extend a line of inquiry begun by Catherine Gallagher about a decade ago. Countering celebratory narratives like those offered by Sandra Gilbert and Susan Gubar in the classic *Madwoman in the Attic*, Gallagher emphasized that for women (and for men, too) entering the booming sphere of letters was a profoundly transgressive act. Although vast fortunes could be made in the arena George Gissing dubbed New Grub Street, success in this marketplace exacted severe psychic costs (although, as Gissing's endless and gloomy novel reminds us, nearly starvation wages and all-too-frequent failure were a far more common danger). For to prosper in this marketplace was psychically tantamount to selling one's self on the open market or opening oneself up to the endlessly proliferating play of language—a play that generates economic value out of nothing in the same way a usurer generates value from money, not labor. In either case, material success is streaked with shameful similarities to prostitution or usury, and such shame is inevitably touched with consequences on the plane of race as well as gender. In "Victorian economic thought," Gallagher argues,

> a marketplace not directly bound to production, the value of a commodity wildly incommensurate with the value of the labor embodied in the commodity, is almost universally regarded as a bad thing. And as this economic discourse finds more popular expressions in either the liberal or the socialist traditions, one detects a growing hostility towards groups that seem to represent a realm of exchange divorced from production: for example, traders in general but especially costermongers in Mayhew . . . prostitutes in the works of Mayhew, Acton, W. R. Greg, and Jews in the works of almost everybody.[2]

Gallagher's jaunty joke and her quick swerve to other concerns—the essay is almost wholly taken up with the question of the image of the woman writer as prostitute—are both very much of the moment in which she was writing, when consideration of Jews qua Jews was not fully on the critical map. Nor has she, nor any other critic I know, taken her line of argument much further. But this hardly vitiates the power of her insight into the relation between the profusion of Jews in Victorian fiction and the swelling of the literary marketplace. Nor do its implications stop here. Gallagher's argument points beyond its own materialist horizons to an even more profound and perhaps more destabilizing insight: that rather than or in addition to being a matter of shame or confusion, a fact to be avoided or evaded, participation in the market economy via the literary career could provide the writer with material abundance, sensual delight, imaginative zing. If the figure of the Jew was particularly powerful to these writers and intellectuals, we might suggest, it may well be because representing and responding to Jews allowed them to experience the guilty pleasures as well as the grinding pains of living in a capitalist world.

For such a world brought with it a whole new range of sensations, entirely new species of feeling, both positive and negative. A maturing capitalist culture brought for the middle classes in general new possibilities of material sustenance and bodily enjoyment as well as an increased sense of vulnerability. For intellectuals in particular it brought an experiential calculus difficult to quantify but perhaps just as important. They juggled the new imaginative possibilities afforded by the very decomposition of stable certainties that capitalism wrought, the chance to vend or sell their own wares as intellectual property on the open market, the exhilarating task of self-fashioning in a culture where individual identities were very much up for grabs, the debilitating fear of the failure of that task of self-remaking. And what better way to resolve the resulting contradictions, to master the conflicting emotions of life in a fully developed market culture, than to project them onto the culturally available figure and repository of ambivalence itself, the Jew?

In this chapter, then, I want to focus on this process with particular reference to two novels by Anthony Trollope that generate a rich profit off this authorial investment: *The Prime Minister* (the penultimate and by far the best novel in the Palliser sequence) and his concurrent endeavor at cultural diagnosis, *The Way We Live Now*. I do so for two linked reasons. Although Jews appear quite frequently in fiction of the high Victorian period—even setting aside the inevitable and inimitable Daniel Deronda or the Dickensian Jews I mentioned in chapter 1, one thinks of Mrs. Swartz in *Vanity Fair* (1848) at one end of the era and the evil Jewish stage manager of Oscar Wilde's *Picture of Dorian Gray* (1890) at the other—Trollope is the novelist of the period who turned most frequently to the figure of the Jew as a sign of social debasement, and he did so frequently in his most ambitious fictions. A brief inventory of characters identified as Jews (as I will suggest, matters are more complicated when one actually encounters them) includes a swindling forger (Melmotte in *The Way We Live Now*), a rapacious speculator (Lopez in *The Prime Minister*), a thief and quite probably a murderer (Emilius in *The Eustace Diamonds* and *Phineas Finn*), as well as a number of more sympathetically rendered characters who are nevertheless linked to the world of finance capital: Breghert in *The Way We Live Now*, for example. Whether sympathetic or rapacious, moreover, the presence of these Jews in contemporary London is explicitly glossed as a matter linked to changes in the tenor of national life. As Mr. Wharton puts it in *The Prime Minister*, thinking of his beloved daughter's prospective marriage to the man he calls a "swarthy son of Judah," "the world was changing round him every day. Royalty was marrying out of its degree. Peers' sons were looking only for money. And, more than that, peers' daughters were bestowing themselves on Jews and shopkeepers."[3] This crisis in social value occasioned by the ubiquity of Jews and the possibilities of intermarriage was articulated not only by Trollope's character but throughout the culture. In " 'the smart set,' " wrote T. H. S. Escott, editor of the *Fortnightly Review*, in 1885, "the Israelites are the Lords paramount. . . . English society once ruled by an aristocracy is now ruled by a plutocracy. And this plutocracy is to a large extent Hebraic in its composition. There is no phenomenon more noticeable in society than the ascendancy of the Jews."[4] Similar sentiments could be found in *Punch* cartoons and *Times* editorials, in the broadsides circulating in the aftermath of Disraeli's attempt to extend citizenship to Jews in 1868, or indeed in the many political attacks on and critiques of Disraeli to be found in the opposition press—and in the halls of Parliament.[5]

Second, and notoriously, Trollope's is one of the first, most successful, and certainly least self-mystified examples of the fully professionalized career in the new literary marketplace of the later nineteenth century. Although many of his contemporaries were equal or greater commercial successes, few presented themselves in such thoroughly disenchanted terms as does Trollope, both through the demystifying, balloon-pricking narrative voice he adopts in his fiction and in the canny, completely unsentimental accounts of his enterprise he offers in his *Autobiography*. Indeed, I want to suggest, his response to Jews and his authorial self-imagining are quite closely related. It is my suggestion in what follows that Trollope's avid participation in the literary marketplace—and his relation to market culture itself—led to a series of complex and quite contradictory responses that in turn were negotiated through as they were represented by his Jewish characters. His work thus becomes the exemplary site of the Victorian interplay between racial representation (in Bryan Cheyette's term) and economic affect: a place where we can see just how much was at stake in the Victorian writer's conflicted self-conception in the market culture of high Victorian England and how fully the Jew came to externalize and hence partially resolve those contradictory impulses and feelings.

Before I turn to Trollope, it is important to remember that his deployment of the Jew as a way of figuring marketplace pleasures and anxieties is historically overdetermined. The figuration of the Jew has been related to cultural responses to the market over many centuries—and ambivalence about the social, cultural, and affective consequences of capitalism has long been channeled into, and managed by, the long and not-so-glorious tradition of economic anti-Semitism. To be sure, this tradition of thought has been shunted aside in recent years: the foremost historian of anti-Semitism, Leon Poliakov, impressively argues that even nineteenth-century

> economic anti-Semitism remains rooted in theology and only continues to exist by virtue of it, since without the theology, propertied Jews would only have been money-grubbers, like any other money-grubber. . . . The Jew's theological function preceded and determined his economic specialization, and it is the composite image resulting from these two functions which continued to single him out as Jew within the new bourgeois society.[6]

Similarly, most students of the rise of anti-Jewish sentiments of the past decades have turned their attention from economics to other factors in the making first of anti-Judaism and then of anti-Semitism. For Zygmunt Bauman, as I have suggested, it is the categorilessness of Jews that is at stake; precisely because modernity works in such a way as to call all stable identities into question, those figures that challenge stable identities are recategorized as (in Bauman's terms) viscous, fluid, grotesque; and for Bauman, this match has to do with the rise of modernity of which the marketplace is a subset rather than the other way around. So too for the most influential reader of anti-Semitism of a previous generation, Hannah Arendt, for whom the rise of anti-Judaism and thence of anti-Semitism is intimately tied to transformations in the power of, and attitudes toward, the state, from the rise of the court Jews in the sixteenth and seventeenth centuries through the process of assimilation (and the challenges posed to it by Jews) in the nineteenth century to the extermination of Jews wrought by the totalitarian extension of the state in the twentieth century. As the last example suggests, one can see, in both these cases, why economic anti-Semitism should play so small an explanatory role. Not only the disciplinary imperatives that govern their fields—sociology, cultural criticism, political philosophy—but also the example of the Holocaust loom over their explanatory paradigms. Something about genocide makes even economic anti-Semitism seem trivial, insubstantial: one must seek for explanations on the level of Modernity with a capital M or on that of Theology with a capital T to account for an evil that seems so all-embracing.

To return to economic anti-Semitism, in some sense, is to turn back to the pre-Holocaust world, a world where many cruelties could be and were imaginable and accomplished but where mass extermination of Jews was not (yet?) understood as an option: where the evil of the Jew could be experienced and negotiated as such precisely because the reactions it elicited were "only" prejudice, fear, hatred—and the occasional pogrom. To return to that world, the wildly shifting, eddying, perpetually self-reinventing world of nineteenth-century capitalism, is to see that the figure of the Jew was so constructed as to become bonded to the affective and experiential structures of the market economy. It is not merely that Jews played a crucial role in the construction of this economy through their capacity as moneylenders or traders or through their role in the creation (and crashes) of international capital, as in the case of the Rothschilds—and then got scapegoated for their efforts. Rather, or perhaps in addition to this dynamic, Jews have long been defined as figures of false appetencies, as beings linked to unnatural (hence perversely pleasurable) emotions of all sorts. It is my suggestion here that, particularly in the new capitalist economies of the early modern and modern eras, the Jew increasingly stands as a malign embodiment of the possibility of gentile pleasure at their own success in a capitalist economy—a twisted alibi for the tabooed pleasures that such an economy brings along with it; or, to be a bit more precise and less Manichean, a way to negotiate the tangle of new affects that the transition to a mature market economy brings with it and which the ceaselessly metamorphosing social facts of capitalism are constantly eliciting in turn.

As Slavoj Zizek puts it, in a language I find overdrenched in Lacan but nevertheless, I hope, comprehensible:

> What we gain by transposing the perception of inherent social antagonisms into fascination with the other (Jew, Japanese . . .) is the fantasy organization of desire. The Lacanian thesis that enjoyment is always enjoyment of the Other, i.e. enjoyment supposed, imputed to the Other, and that

conversely the hatred of the Other's enjoyment is always the hatred of one's own enjoyment. . . . What are fantasies about the Other's special, excessive enjoyment—about the black's superior sexual potency and appetite, about the Jew's or the Japanese's special relationship towards money and work—if not precisely *so many ways for us to organize our own enjoyment?* . . . And . . . is the anti-Semitic capitalist's hatred of the Jew not hatred of the excess that pertains to capitalism itself, i.e. of the excess produced by its inherent antagonistic nature?[7]

Zizek here does more, however, than give us an analysis of this phenomenon; he also puts its imaginative habits and their consequences on display. He follows but extends Lacan in arguing that desire—diffuse, proliferating, multiple, decentered, decentering—gets brought under control for the self-stabilizing subject by means of a relation to an absent Other, that figure that crystallizes pleasure, enjoyment, *jouissance* that the subject must deny itself in order to attain a stable sense of social identity. And, as it must, Zizek's text symptomatically performs as it depicts this process. Its proliferation of Others reveals the diffusion or proliferation of desire itself, as figures of abjected or denied pleasure slip and slide into different and contradictory guises—black, Japanese, capitalist. But, tellingly, there remains one constant in this parade of alterity. The black's supposed superior enjoyment of sexual pleasure, the Japanese's "special" relation to money and work, the capitalist's relation to his profits—all these contradictory nodes of enjoyment are associated with that figure who is everywhere in this text and yet who constantly dissolves or disappears back into the various avatars of otherness: the Jew. It is, in other words, the Jew who stabilizes the discourse on the Other in Zizek's account itself; it is the Jew who provides the master trope for otherness that allows one to see the family resemblance between these heterogeneous and proliferating others. It is, in fact, the stereotypical Jew who allows us to see these others as Others at all.

And this is what is so fascinating in the tradition of anti-Jewish sentiment from the early modern period to the current moment: the ways that responses to the Jew have served to organize in a thoroughly Zizekian manner the wildly complex set of affects, conscious and unconscious, aroused by the rise of a fullfledged market economy in Europe and, thereafter, those called into being by its ceaseless metamorphoses in the modern era (that referred to for the past eighty years, for example, as late capitalism or that labeled, in more recent years, disorganized or postmodern capitalism).[8] The affective life of capitalism (Zizek's real subject, it seems to me, rather than, or perhaps it would be better to say in addition to, nationalism and nation-formation) is of course too large a subject for me to do more than glance at here, but I do want to note briefly two things: first, that social and cultural historians are beginning to pay more attention to the ways in which capitalism depended not only upon coldhearted rationality but on a wide range of affects and responses and, second, that transformations in the construction of the Jew are intimately tied to this process.

Thus, to turn briefly to the first point, the classic and not entirely incorrect take on the historical development of capitalism has been the line of analysis so famously initiated by Max Weber, a line of analysis that squarely poses capitalism against anything that might resemble emotional or affective life, much less a pleasure principle. In *The Spirit of Protestantism and the Rise of Capitalism* the rise of capitalism is tied to denial of the body, to ascesis, and hence (looking backward) to monasticism and Puritanism and (looking forward) to the imprisonment of the mind in ever more rational manacles of its own devising. But increasingly, critics have seen that the cultural dynamics of capitalism or, to put it more broadly, capitalism as a cultural system with wide-spreading ramifications in the life of its subjects, is (to paraphrase Raymond Williams) a way of feeling as well as a way of being. Moreover, and more important, the feelings it relies on are not only those Freud anatomized as being at the center of the subject's relation to money—anality, domination, control—but also a wide variety of affects, including pleasure, ease, grandiosity, expansiveness, and joy: "animal spirits," as Joseph Schumpeter, thinking of the early entrepreneurial stages of capitalist development puts it; "irrational exuberance," as an economist of greater worldly power and somewhat less insight, Alan Greenspan, has recently called it.[9]

It is true that major theorists of capitalism cast this development in the neo-Weberian narrative of rationalization, not feeling. One of the greatest theorists of capitalist culture, Georg Simmel, claimed that it was precisely the effect of a money economy to produce a predomination of the intellectual over the emotional throughout the social sphere. Although Simmel also shows with dialectical finesse the wide range of emotions created and nourished by a society in which money mediates human interactions—emotions running the gamut from the intensities of greed to the detachment of "the blasé attitude"—the construction of value by money finally leads to an effort to render calculable, commensurable, all differences and hence to render reason hegemonic in spheres of society and subjectivity alike.[10] Marxist critic Georg Lukacs took Simmel one step further; for Lukacs reification—the understanding of living human processes as calculable, objective, and "thinglike," governed by iron laws of necessity—becomes the fundamental mindset of a capitalist world, and the individual subject is rendered powerless and passionless, given over to a "contemplative attitude" of seeming detachment from the phenomenal world. Critics of the so-called Frankfurt School like Adorno followed in Lukacs's wake: indeed, the results of reification and objectification can be said to form the very basis of Adorno and Max Horkheimer's critique of the means/ends thinking of the Enlightenment that is productive of capitalism, not the other way around.

But this perception of the death of feeling in the epistemic regime of capitalism is not only a product of the Left, particularly that element of Marxist thought that Michael Löwy has called—following the subject of his study, Georg Lukacs— romantic anticapitalism.[11] It is also offered, albeit with a different spin, by the more benign theorists of capitalism who emerged in Vienna at precisely the same moment that Marxist thought was flourishing in Berlin and Paris. For Schumpeter, the inevitable decline and fall of capitalist economies is based on the defeat of entrepreneurial high-spiritedness by the progress of rationalization as well as by the disenchantment of intellectuals. For Friedrich Hayek, what his contemporaries on the Left would decry under the heading of reification is precisely what is to be celebrated. The mechanism by which the marketplace sets prices is a form of thought; the price of things is a means by which millions of people communicate information to each other with super-rational speed and efficiency.

> Assume that somewhere in the world a new opportunity for the use of some raw material, say tin, has arisen, or that one of the sources of the supply of tin has been eliminated. It does not matter for our purpose— and it is significant that it does not matter—which of the two causes has made tin more scarce. All that the users of tin need to know is that some of the tin they used to consume is now more profitably employed elsewhere and that, in consequence, they must employ less tin. . . . The whole acts as one market, not because any of its members survey the whole field, but because their limited individual fields of vision sufficiently overlap so that through many intermediaries the relevant information is communicated to all. The fact that there is one price for any commodity . . . brings about a solution which (it is just conceptually possible) might have been arrived at by one single mind possessing all the information which in fact is dispersed among all the people involved in the process.[12]

Following but extending Hayek, the neoclassical tradition of economic thought has taken, in Wai Chee Dimock's paraphrase, "human reason itself [to be] fundamentally economic in nature" and vice versa; and following the work of Nobel Prize–winner Gary Becker, this tradition of thought has taken the goal of optimizing outcomes to be the mainspring of human behavior in any number of arenas generally thought to be affective or emotional in nature: racial discrimination, marriage, drug addiction, art purchasing.[13] In other words, exactly as in Simmel or Adorno, for the neoclassical school the rational logic of economic calculation infiltrates or leaches into all precincts of human life, even or most powerfully into those that seem most removed from its means/ends calculus, except that here, that form of thinking is taken to be a force even more determinative—and ultimately far more benign—than those unleashed by the human sentiments.

From the critique of rationalization to the celebration of rational self-maximization, there seems to be little room for the emotional, the intuitive, and the affective in the discourses of either Left or Right vis-à-vis a market economy. But these lines of analysis defy common sense. Merely to observe a mature capitalist economy in action—to witness the interplay of impulses and desires that motivate individual transactions, the ups and downs that govern markets in goods, commodities, stocks, the pleasures of avid consumers, the grinding despair of poverty—is to sense something more complicated: that powerful bursts of feeling are as much a motivating force for the capitalist system as cold-headed rationality, and maybe even more so. To put the matter facetiously but not inaccurately, they don't call them manias or depressions for nothing, a fact that even the fiercest advocates of reason- or information-based theories of market behavior are beginning to concede.[14]

This debate cannot be settled here. But one thing can: whatever one's feeling about capitalism and feeling, it is clear that a *discourse* on feeling has long entered into and complements the discourse on rationalization and impersonality that governs the major critical theories of capitalism. Three directions in particular can be foregrounded here—and each bears a complex relation to the figure of the Jew. One is that so elegantly outlined by Albert Hirschman, whose excavation of the imperatives organized by and around the early phase of capitalism shows how powerfully early thinkers about the market economy were engaged in a discourse of subduing human ardors, of rationalizing or controlling the passions as they are reshaped by the invisible hand of the marketplace into the impersonal force of the interests.[15] The paradox of capitalism in this formulation is that it relies on the most problematic forms of human sentiment—greed, avarice, the desire for power—in order to work, but that in so doing it subordinates them to the force of the larger good. Selfishness and avarice get gently corrected by the invisible hand of the marketplace as they enter into the play of interests that defines a larger moral economy and that makes the amoral-seeming marketplace itself moral. Yet precisely how fully subdued these passions may be soon seemed problematic. As Hirschman puts it, for its early defenders "capitalism was supposed to accomplish exactly what was soon to be denounced as its worst feature" (132); to put it another way, capitalism was soon seen to enhance the unfettered exercise of human appetencies and aggressions that its early defenders claimed it would correct. Thus, to cite a salient example, antimarket middle-class reformers in England and America alike located the degrading effects of the market economy in precisely the ways that the economy enhanced the very passions their predecessors thought it would sublimate into the interests they celebrated. The unbridled lusts of the working classes, the rapacious desires of malevolent capitalists, the corruption of good-hearted middle-class citizens: all these manifestations of the excess of animal spirits in the body politic are seen as grounded in the loss of self-control and orderliness that is elicited by the free market and the industrial system, producing (in the words of one social reformer) "a population that is young, inexperienced, ignorant, credulous, irritable, passionate."[16]

One more such set of affects deserves to be mentioned before I move on to the effects of these new ways of feeling upon the racialization of identity—one for which there is surprisingly little language in the available literature: the affects produced by (and indeed in many cases constitutive of) the deal, the ups and downs of transaction itself: the joy of the bargain, the delight at the sharp trade, the uncertainty or even terror that produces less fulfilling ones, the interplay of greed and fear that makes buyers buy and sellers sell. Observable in the smallest flea market and massively on display in stock exchanges, these affects are perhaps the most powerful of all, operating on the level of the mass or collective identity and shaping the destiny of nations. Like Smith's invisible hand, this sequence of ups and downs is, in the view of many observers, ultimately rational, or at least rationalizable—as I have shown, contemporary economic theory stresses the market as the most effective conveyor of information. Yet at the same time, the history of economic experience in a postcapitalist world is virtually coterminous with the chronicle of these tides of sentiment, ranging from tulip mania in the seventeenth-century Netherlands through the booms and crashes that accompanied the extensions of Europe into the non-Western world, from the aptly named Great Depression through the California real estate boom of the 1980s (not to mention the American stock market of the 1990s). An entirely new academic field has recently been born to study "patterns of irrational behavior that might explain market anomalies": behavioral finance—the addition of which to the curriculum sparked a major controversy at the bastion of rational-choice economics, the University of Chicago.[17]

My point in inventorying the rich affective possibilities opened up by the rise of a capitalist market and sensibility in the Western world (and there are many such possibilities besides them) is to suggest two things: first, how complex, eddying, co-implicated and ultimately unruly those affects are on the level of both the individual subject and the collective culture and, second, how thoroughly salient each and every one has been to the figure of the Jew. The stereotypical Jew is notoriously selfish in the Hirschmanian sense: rapacious, desirous of profits, greedy for gold, the Jew reaches out his quite visible hand to grasp the fruits of the earth and clutch them to his body, withholding or even stealing them from worthy gentiles. This stereotype has been repeatedly glossed by anti-Jewish thinkers from (at least) the early modern period to our own, for whom the Jew's special qualities image the central moral problematic of capitalism itself: greed. Marx puts the matter with his usual asperity in his infamous essay *On the Jewish Question*: "What is the profane basis of Judaism? *Practical* need, self-interest. What is the wordly cult of the Jew? *Huckstering*. What is his worldly god? *Money*."[18] Or, to cite but one example of literally countless instances, an anti-

Semitic contemporary of Marx wrote with less dialectical finesse (at least for Marx the egoism is grounded in material deprivation, in "practical need"): "[It] is not by work or the exercise of any particular virtue that the Jews have arrived at the top of the ladder. It is exclusively intrigue, brazenness, the ability to exploit one's neighbor, insatiable rapacity. . . . What fruitful work has he accomplished? All that he has done, he has done for himself."[19]

Here (and these two instances are hardly unique) the figure of the Jew embodies all those passions that were problematic in the earliest formulations of capitalism and remained so in its later instantiations and, perhaps more important, does so by virtue of the very essence of his Jewish being, which is inscribed in the language of feeling. And more: the unrestrained nature of the passions unleashed in the figure of the Jew is not turned to the larger good by means of a putatively invisible hand but rather is directed at theft from more honorable, and deserving, gentiles. "He has become rich, infinitely richer than the Christians, and at the expense of the Christians. All they have gained by their work, enlarged by their thrift, and saved with the most minute care, he has robbed them of," wrote one nineteenth-century anti-Semite (*The Jews*, p. 86). A German contemporary writes in strikingly similar language that brings the idiom of the passions directly back to the discourse on the interests by means of the Jew: "It is not the creation of riches, nor even their exploitation, which feeds the Golden Calf [which Jews worship]; it is above all the mobilization of wealth, the soul of speculation, which feeds it." He goes on to "quote" the (fictional) confession of a (fictive) Jewish power broker:

> We are the brokers who receive commissions on all exchanges, or, if you prefer the expression, we are the toll gatherers who control the crossways of the world and collect a tax on all movements of that wealth which is "anonymous and vagabond," whether such movements are from country to country or are the oscillations of market prices. To the calm and monotonous song of prosperity we are the passionate voices, raised in turn, of a rise and fall in market values. (105)

It is not only sheer greed or selfishness, in other words, that the Jew exemplifies and instills but the very frenzy of the speculative spirit, the very desire that moves markets large and small. The Jew as Jew embodies the very passions that govern capitalism itself.

If the Jew is associated with the passions that rule in the marketplace, so too that figure is associated with the pleasures, and vices, of consumption. Hence the common insistence on the Jew as a voluptuary even amidst an understanding of the Jew as a practitioner of a species of miserly self-abasement, which of course turns out to be an inverted form of voluptuousness, since miserliness is the adoration of gold or money as a thing in itself: the worship, as the anti-Semite just quoted has his Jews put it, of the Golden Calf. Most frequently, it is the former that gets stressed, usually in sexualized terms. Here is Marx: "That which is contained in an abstract form in the Jewish religion—contempt for theory, for art, for history, and for man as an end in himself—is the *real, conscious standpoint* of the man of money. Even the species-relation itself, the relation between man and woman, becomes an object of commerce. Woman is bartered away" (49). Note the metonymic slide here: the stretch from the spirit of the Jewish religion to that of the capitalist to that of the whoremonger links all three into a complex chain of pseudologic in which the putative Jewish principle of superiority corrupts what is for Marx (as it is for Freud) the very ground of human pleasure, sexuality. The image of the pimp that Marx plays with looks deep into the affective heart of capitalism itself—we remember that, for Marx, money is the "pimp" who brings pleasures to the subject in capitalist culture; but that image also effectively links capitalism's affective possibilities to both a perversity and a commercialism that is given an explicitly racial embodiment in the figure of the Jew.

This may help explain why over the long development of capitalism from the early modern period to our own, the medieval image of the monstrous Jew is supplemented by the image of the Jew as pander—almost invariably with overtones of sexual perversity, frequently aimed at children or young women. The Jew-as-perverted-pimp topos recurs with amazing frequency throughout these two centuries, at all levels of discourse and in all the societies of Europe. One can find it in the anti-Semitic writings of Luther, the etchings of Hogarth, the ravings of Drumont. But the topos reaches a new height of frequency (as should not surprise us) in the late nineteenth and early twentieth centuries when both the emancipation of Jews and the rise of finance capital brought this metonymy to a new pitch of cultural saliency. "Next to his lust for money," wrote the anonymous author of *The New York Jew* in 1888, "the strongest passion in the Jew is his licentiousness. This like every other vicious trait of which the Jew is possessed, takes a peculiarly prominent and objectionable form," which the author anatomizes in gory detail, including incest, voyeurism, "mashing," molesting women under sedation, industrial exploitation, and the following conflation of many of these habits, offered via a rewriting of Shylock's confusion between his affectional and his economic interests.

Upon one occasion, a young lady, while passing the corner of Park and Kearney Streets, was addressed by one of these Jew Lotharios of the street. Gazing upon the Jew dude with a pitying look, she drew a fifty-cent piece from her pocket and threw it at his feet, exclaiming, "You miserable thing! you don't look as if you were half fed. Go buy yourself something to eat with that."

The Jew masher gazed for a moment at the coin as it lay on the sidewalk, and then the instinct of his race conquered him. He stooped, picked up the money, and pocketed it.[20]

"A quick and efficacious way to get rid of the Jew masher," the text concludes, "is to throw him a little money. It will engross his attention, and secure a release from his importunities" (51). But, according to the author, even a financially secure Jew is a sleazy Jew. For, given a little financial success, the Jew launches into a frenzy that extends itself into every facet of his being.

> The spirit of gain and the desire for domination chase every other idea from their mentality, together with every affection, which is, as we know, the characteristic sign of obsession. The secondary troubles which engage them, like their obscene passion for young Christian girls, cruelty towards the poor, and the spirit of revenge, are episodic systems of this unhealthy state. . . . The millionaire Jews, those speculators on the Stock Exchange, seek out the purest, most innocent girls. Then, when the Jewish aristocracy has abused these unfortunates at their leisure, the Christian victims are simply abandoned to their misery and fall into the abyss of prostitution. As for the poor Jews, those of the lower classes, they excel in fulfilling the role of procurors. They know where to find young girls for the houses of ill-fame the world over. (52)

And so on and so on and so on, ad infinitum and ad nauseam, not only in this tome but in the writings of Drumont that the author of *The New York Jew* virtually transcribes, and in masses of anonymous anti-Semitic pamphlets and volumes circulating in France, Germany, England and America, the *Protocols of the Elders of Zion*, the tomes of Madison Grant, the writings of Rosenberg, the ravings of Hitler.

What interests me in this parade of anti-Semitic slurs are two things: the passionate and reiterated emphasis on the passionate nature of the Jews, their uncontrolled and uncontrollable bursts of feeling, particularly the thoroughly co-implicated sentiments of greed, passion, and sexual desire; and the relation between those bursts of emotion and the new sets of feeling emerging within an advancing, developing, maturing capitalist culture. As far as the former is concerned, we should note how different this image of the Jew is from the ones that became normative in the high philosophical tradition of Kant and Hegel and were passed down into the discourses of Arnold and high culture. In such a cultural scheme, the Jew embodies legalism, rationality, calculation in the place of true feeling: this creature of covenants and contracts has no understanding of grace and love, no deeper feelings, no sublime sentiment. But in the anti-Semitic writings of the later nineteenth century, by contrast, the Jew is a veritable embodiment of sentiment, albeit of the wrong sort: of the predominance of passion, greed, avarice, lasciviousness, desire for pleasure. To be sure, this emphasis on the Jew's Jewishness as a matter of excessive passion (and insufficient self-control) is common in descriptions of many demonized or marginalized social groups. If, as one anti-Semite puts it, "the Jew represents the lower side of nature . . . [i]n reality the Hebrew is the mental cripple among mankind, the type of intellectual deformity" (*The Jews*, p. 96), one could easily find similar language in descriptions of peasants, members of the working classes, Asians, Africans, and on and on.[21] What makes the passionate Jew different from these other abjected others, however, is that the Jew has been since the Middle Ages discursively positioned so as to be close to the *economic* experience of gentiles—positioned by historical circumstance and gentile hypocrisy, that is to say, at the center of the two institutions that did the most to generate the explosion of the capitalist system in the early modern period, moneylending and international trade.[22]

The passions ascribed to the Jew in the culture of capitalism, then, may serve as a powerful way of distancing the affects unleashed by this system from the normative life of Christian culture and gentile commerce. Indeed, the affect-drenched, passionate, lascivious Jew becomes a literal embodiment of all the irrationalities, the perversities, the greeds and lusts, that are arguably the motor, and undoubtedly the consequences, of an economic system that presents itself as a self-correcting and rational mechanism for the maximally efficient delivery of goods and services.

Before turning to Trollope's attempt to bring these wildly colliding sets of affects about marketplace feeling fully under control, I want to give an example of their complex functioning in the literary traditions Trollope studies and inherits. It's important to note that there are so many for me to choose from: that the great moments of representation of Jews are precisely coterminous with the structures of feeling about feeling in market economies that I am trying to anatomize here and that each of these representations contains moments when the Jew's affect crosses, glosses, and bears the burden of conflicting Christian affect vis-à-vis money, wealth, economy. I am thinking here of such moments as that scene in *Oliver Twist* where Oliver, in his first night *chez* Fagin, awakes from a dream to see Fagin greedily gazing at his stolen gold glittering in its opened hiding-place. Oliver's own dozy desire (and that of the normative Christian culture into which he escapes) crosses over into Fagin's, who seems here less the unadulterated Jew and more the dream-vision of a gentile culture that simultaneously enjoys and disavows its own eroticization of money. Or one thinks of Shylock, who is purposefully and fully juxtaposed to that other Merchant of Venice—the one who actually gives his name to the play, Antonio—to ends that are often mutually destabilizing, as in the famous moment in the trial scene when Portia, disguised as the lawyer Bellario, cries out, "Which is the merchant here? and which the Jew?"[23]

The text I wish briefly to draw our attention to here, however, is one that provides an ur-example of this sort of conflating (one, incidentally, that Trollope, a student of Renaissance drama, would have known well): Christopher Marlowe's *Jew of Malta*. For the eponymous Jew in that text, Barabas, is spectacularly defined from the first in precisely the affective terms I have just described. Neatly reversing Poliakov's analysis, Emily Bartels has sagely observed that while Marlowe's Barabas "does place himself within an international community of famous Jews . . . what secures his place (and theirs) on the roster is wealth, not religion."²⁴ One can extend this insight further by suggesting that what truly distinguishes Barabas from his fellow merchants is the affective afflatus that his wealth brings. Machievel, speaking the prologue, defines it as "the tragedy of a Jew / Who *smiles* to see how full his bags are cramm'd"²⁵; and Barabas is depicted as a representative of untrammeled emotionality amidst the new mercantile order. He is proud: when his fellow Jews attempt to comfort him for the confiscation of his fortune, Barabas turns on them, angrily crying: "You that / were ne'er possessed of wealth, are pleased with want" (1.2.200–1). As he rants, his fellow Jews perform the sixteenth-century equivalent of a shoulder shrug and define him as an irrevocably passionate character: "Come, let us leave him in his ireful mood: Our words will but increase his ecstasy" (210–11). (But of course Barabas is feigning outrage here, as he has secreted the best portion of his fortune.) His pride is mixed with greed; even when faced with a choice of keeping half his fortune by acquiescing to the duke's decree (or by becoming a Christian) he spiritedly refuses, leading to the confiscation of the entire amount. Like Barabas's fellow Jews, the duke Firenze diagnoses his condition as that of an emotional disorder when consoling him for his loss by urging on him—postconfiscation—a different psychic configuration: "Be patient and thy riches will increase; / Excess of wealth is the cause of covetousness, / And covetousness, O, 'tis a monstrous sin" (122–4). (But of course the duke is being equally disingenuous, since he has also told Barabas that he is confiscating the Jews' wealth not for their moral improvement but simply because war has exhausted the Maltese treasury, and "amongst you't must be had" [56].)

Barabas's frenzied emotionality, then, reflects upon even as it is played against cooler, more rational ways of experiencing and deploying wealth. And this habit of response is linked, as the duke suggests, to cupidity incarnate. In an ur-scene of economic anti-Semitism—a scene that Shakespeare, Dickens, and Trollope all rewrote—Barabas takes gold bags from his daughter (whom he has forced to pretend to be a nun) and proclaims:

> Oh my girl
> My gold, my fortune, my felicity;
> Strength to my soul, death to mine enemy;
> Welcome, the first beginner of my bliss!
> O, Abigail, that I had thee here too,
> Then my desires were fully satisfied.
> But I will practice thy enlargement thence.
> O girl, O gold, O beauty, O my bliss!
> [Hugs the money bags] (2.1.47–54)

What's striking here is the emotional lability of Barabas's response; his gold-induced greed spilling over into the assertion of a masculine "strength" (earlier on he has been taunted for being a merchant, not a soldier) and of pleasure, affects that then slide together into a truly weird response to his daughter. The double-entendres of Barabas's discourse on Abigail—"that I *had* thee here," "I will practice thy *enlargement* hence"—speak not only to Abigail's confinement but also of Barabas's desire, a desire at once sexual and economic in nature. "Enlargement" can refer not only to the freeing of Abigail (the meaning the Craig edition assigns to these lines) or to her swelling as with child, as I have been implying; it also might refer to the equally perverse practice of usury, of making money from money, of augmenting gold with yet more gold as if by magic (or alchemy) rather than by toil or (as the duke advises) patience. And in the final apostrophes, all these things—gold as girl, girl as gold, both as the very cynosure of beauty—cross into each other and are rendered as "bliss": as the full crystallization of that pleasure into a definitive affective enunciation.

But this "bliss," this pleasure at economic gain so intense that it is sexual in charge and perverse in instantiation, is demonstrated by the play to be virtually pandemic in the world of Malta—and by extension, the brave new world of mercantile capitalism that Malta represents. The duke would seem to represent an alternative to this structure of feeling; indeed, in a striking anticipation of the arguments about capitalism that Hirschman anatomizes, he urges Barabas to tame his greed for the sake of the community as a whole. But the duke's son's desires resemble Barabas's and in ways that suggest the ubiquity of Barabas's sentiments—and the ways that they get stapled onto or sutured to the Jew. Barabas's object is revenge, son Lodowick's object is Abigail, but when they meet their intentions are expressed via the language of the deal:

> LODOWICK: Well, Barabas, canst help me to a diamond?
> BARABAS: Oh sir, your father had my diamonds,
>   Yet I have one left that will serve your turn:
>   [aside] I mean my daughter, but ere he shall have her
>   I'll sacrifice her on a pile of wood. (2.3.48–53)

Here, gentile and Jew perform the same chiastic dance with each other, a dance, to be sure, that Barabas is better at than the clunky Lodowick: Lodowick approaches Barabas on what he thinks is Barabas's turf, that of diamonds, of trade; Barabas turns this discourse back on Lodowick and replaces that object with the object Lodowick is troping with the mention of diamonds, his daughter. But as his frequent asides let us know he knows, and as Lodowick's discourse lets us know as well, that substitution has in some sense already been made in Lodowick's mind before he meets Barabas; just before the encounter, he says: "I hear the wealthy Jew walked this way / I'll seek him out and so insinuate / That

I might have a sight of fair Abigail" (2.2.32–3). And in this scene, the mordantly performative Jew Barabas stages a gruesome commentary on the arrangement he has just reached with Lodowick (whose father, after all, has just confiscated Barabas's wealth): he strolls into the marketplace and purchases a slave, a bargain in which Lodowick nonchalantly participates. That is to say, he signals his own economic subjugation yet performs his continuing power within that system by buying another human being. To continue the proliferating ironies, the slave they purchase, the Turk Ithamore, becomes a yet-more-displaced version of the Jew Barabas's displaced enactment of gentile desires, scheming both to get Barabas's gold and Barabas's daughter, for whom he conceives a kind of insane but powerful lust that tropes yet transcends both Lodowick's chivalric kind (Lodowick has been disposed of in a duel with Abigail's *true* beloved, who is also slain, much to Abigail's chagrin) and Barabas's own economically implicated, sexually perverse sort of desire.

The Lodowick/Barabas and Barabas/Ithamore relations, then, suggest one model for the Jew-as-affect in the marketplace culture, a model in which that figure both reflects gentile lusts and appetencies and mediates between them and their more horrific "pagan" or "barbarous" alternatives: the Jew would seem to represent the "barbarous" within the polis, always already inside the confines of the gentile, mercantile state and indeed crucial to its continued financial flourishing. Marlowe's point, though, here and throughout, is to return to the affective center of capitalist culture, the complex stew of desires, appetencies, greeds, and energies that drive the engine of capitalist development and to see these affects as radiating out from the demonized, othered figure of the Jew. The Jew serves as an embodiment or a crystallization of the drives and desires that actually drive the mercantilist culture for which he speaks, and to which Marlowe speaks, and becomes Marlowe's way of diagnosing that culture to itself through the hyperemotional medium of theatrical spectacle. "What wind drives you thus into Malta road?" asks one traveler of another in Marlowe's play; the answer is: "The wind that bloweth all the world beside / Desire of gold" (3.5.3–4). The appetencies that Barabas incarnates, in other words, are integrally tied into the very project of mercantile imperialist expansion his spectators themselves profit from and are so tied by the language of desire, of impulse, of feeling via their affective response to the play. Marlowe's play thus offers its spectators a mirror in which they can witness the depth to which economic desire has become normalized, woven into the expectations and appetencies of everyday life: this form of desire is part of the air that audience breathes, part of the winds that blow them to and fro. As they watch its Grand Guignol effects with mingled attitudes of pity and terror and laughter—the responses that Marlowe's play inevitably elicits—they are asked to respond with a heightened set of feelings to their own experience, and to the pitfalls and pleasures of living in a world defined by economic appetency.

As I have suggested, Marlowe is of particular importance to a study of literary anti-Semitism—or, more properly, literary versions of economic anti-Semitism—because he establishes crucial tropes that get worked out in subsequent texts: the line from Barabas's primal scene with Abigail to Shylock's choice between his daughter and his ducats to Marie Melmotte's attempt to steal her own fortune from her father—and Melmotte's violent response—is direct. Marlowe is important, too, because he establishes certain patterns of thought from the very first that persist in later versions of writing and thinking about experience in a capitalist world by means of the figure of the Jew. Indeed, the last may be his greatest and most important contribution to later writers: both the emphasis on the Jew's emotionality and the reflexive turn toward the audience's own response are present throughout the entire subsequent tradition of writing and thinking about Jews. And as I show in greater detail in the rest of the chapter, nowhere are they put to greater, and more subversive, use than in the seemingly anti-Semitic writing of Anthony Trollope.

About midway through *The Prime Minister*, the swarthy, foreign-born, Jewish speculator Ferdinand Lopez is complaining to his business associate, Mr. Sextus Parker, about the tightfistedness of his father-in-law, Mr. Wharton. Lopez, of course, has been complaining from the first weeks of his marriage about Wharton's lack of generosity; knowing full well that Wharton disapproves of what he takes to be Lopez's Jewish origins,[26] his seeming effeminacy, and his greed, Lopez nevertheless keeps hoping against hope that his father-in-law will relax his iron grip on his money and allow Lopez to live in the style to which he wishes to become accustomed—and to speculate, grandly, in guano futures. But more seems to be involved here than Lopez's greed. The very means by which the father has come by his fortune is an affront to the son-in-law.

> "I suppose he's worth a quarter of a million."
>
> "By Jove! Where did he get it?"
>
> "Perseverance, sir. Put by a shilling a day, and let it have its natural increase and see where it will come to at the end of fifty years. I suppose old Wharton has been putting by two or three thousand a year out of his professional income, at any rate for the last thirty years, and never for a moment forgetting its natural increase. That's one way to make a fortune."
>
> "It ain't rapid enough for you and me, Lopez."
>
> "No. That was the old-fashioned way, and the most sure. But, as you say, it's not rapid enough, and it robs a man of the power of enjoying his money when he has made it. But it's a very good thing to be closely connected with a man who has already done that kind of thing. There's no doubt about the money when it is there. It does not take to its wings and fly away." (255–6)

As in Zizek, in other words, the crux of the relation between the figure of the Jew and that of the gentile culture to which he speaks seems to be the question of enjoyment, of pleasure. According to Lopez, Wharton is like one of Max Weber's Protestants: austere, penurious, pious (although, to be sure, he enjoys a good glass of claret). According to himself, Lopez is a particularly fun-loving capitalist: he asks not what he can do for his money but rather what his money can do for him. And the results of this approach, the novel insists, are disastrous. Lopez takes on greater and greater risk, flitting from get-rich scheme to get-rich scheme, taking up increasingly manic projects, ultimately draining the capital of his credulous investor, Sexty. Finally, in order to cover his debts and make a new start, he even propositions Lizzie Eustace, a woman who is known to favor shady Jews but still, doubtless, the least likely recipient of a proposition that she entrust all her money to a man and run off with him to Guatemala.

Pleasure and enjoyment, then, are not the only issues at contention here; an entire range of feelings is implicated in and expressed by this "half-foreigner, half-Jew, all pauper," as Lady Glencora Palliser so delicately puts it after Lopez's death (166). "Though this man had lived nearly all his life in England, he had not quite acquired that knowledge of the way in which things are done which is so general among men of a certain class," the narrator sniffily writes (23); and one of the prime ways that Lopez shows his lack of breeding (his father, a peddler, had struck it rich and sent him away to school) is by acting out. Not only does he lust visibly, if not passionately, after wealth, he swears at and speaks bitterly to his father-in-law, gambles giddily with other people's money, and explodes with rage when crossed or confuted. To add to this affective confusion, he is something of a sincerely sentimental lover—he shows, in fact, an unsettling conflation of high sensibility and low avarice. He woos Emily (for whom, the text insists, his feelings are initially quite genuine) with ardent caresses and billets-doux. And when he propositions Lizzie, he quotes Byron:

"Lizzie Eustace, will you go with me to the land of the sun

> Where the rage of the vulture, the love of the turtle
> Now melt into sorrow, now madden to crime?

Will you dare to escape with me from the cold conventionalism, from the miserable thraldom of this country bound in swaddling clothes? Lizzie Eustace, if you will but say the word I will take you to that land of glorious happiness." (472)

Lopez's "Guatemala" is a nirvana as impalpable as the one that arch-aesthete Walter Pater celebrated a decade later; but it is one bound via the Byronic tag to a world of affect, a realm of authentic feeling that is thoroughly opposed to the "cold conventionalism" of middle-class England. And Lopez's yearning after this spot reminds us that his covetousness is indissolubly linked to his imagination, his rapacious grasping after wealth to his passion. In this sense, it is quite appropriate that none of his ventures ever involves the real purchase of actual goods: Trollope reminds us of the deepest sense of the idea of speculation, one that involves as much the projection of imaginative desires as the making of profit from those desires.

Lopez's Jewishness is a crucial part of this conflation and adds further depth to its portrayal. Not only, as some critics have suggested, do the slurs against Lopez emanate from Wharton or from other members of Emily's family—the grandmother, for example, who thinks of Lopez as "a man without a father, a foreigner, a black Portuguese nameless Jew" (36). In addition, the plot underscores the point by enacting these slurs. The Jew's putatively parasitical relation to the Christian's hard-earned capital we saw adverted to in the anti-Semitic writing I surveyed earlier, for example, is put into sharp focus from our first encounter with Lopez—when he is scheming to use Sexty Parker's capital, funds he drains with ruthless efficiency—and in his obsessive desire to access Wharton's capital. Indeed, the terms in which he puts that project—his desire to "get close to" Mr. Wharton's money—suggest to us not only the ways in which, like Shylock or Fagin, he has conflated the affective and the economic but also the Barabas-like power of his desire to get intimate with money itself. Implicated in Lopez's character, too, are a host of familiar discourses on usury. At the center of those discourses is the Aristotelian notion that money may be made to increase either naturally or unnaturally—and that indulgence in the latter is linked to unnatural forms of reproduction and hence perverse forms of sexuality. Wharton's reliance on the "natural increase" of money—socking it away in a bank and relying on compound interest to build a fortune for fifty years—plays off against the Jew's interest in more rapid and by implication unnatural forms of growth. Such growth is implicitly related to Lopez's perverse but palpable sexuality, one that seems to exert (in Mr. Wharton's phrase) an "incubus-like" effect on young women like his daughter (130). (In this Lopez prepares the way for Svengali.) The link is made explicit to Emily by her lower-class acquaintance Mrs. Sexty Parker. "Them men," she tells Mrs. Lopez, "when they get onto money-making,—or money-losing, which makes 'em worse—are like tigers clawing one another. . . . There ain't no fear of God in it, nor yet no mercy, nor ere a morsel of heart. It ain't what I call manly, not that longing after other folk's money" (404). At once a figure of economic desire and sexual passion, Lopez is the very archetype of the depraved, perverse Jew that circulated in anti-Semitic circles as Trollope was writing the novel.

No wonder, then, that according to one of the most important critical studies of the figure of the Jew in Victorian fiction, Michael Ragussis's *Figures of Conversion*, the work of this text is to banish Lopez from the normative sphere of Christian culture. "The Christian fantasy of *The Prime Minister*," Ragussis writes, is to keep "the Jew outside the social order in both the public and the private domain: he is ejected from the domestic plot by failing as a husband, and he is ejected from the national plot by failing as a candidate for Parliament" (258). Yet interestingly, in a third realm, neither fully public nor fully private yet determinative of both in capitalist culture—the realm of the economic—things are more complicated. For here, it is important to note, Mr. Wharton and the economic principles he embodies fare no better. His purpose in keeping his money whole is to leave it to his children; hence his financial plans are connected to the normative, Aristotelian principles of capital accumulation and sexuality alike: his money makes money in a way that is tied to proper reproduction. But Wharton's progeny fare disastrously, and in a way that indicts his economic master plan. Emily marries the very antithesis of her father—a swarthy, poetry-quoting hunk—in large part to escape his control over her, only to find a far more domineering and money-mad man in that figure. More problematic still, son Everett (who actually introduces Emily to Lopez) becomes a gambler who saddles his father with his debts, that is, indulges in the very form of behavior of which Lopez as speculator and son-in-law is consistently accused. (The height of hypocrisy comes, perhaps, when the wastrel Everett reviles the recently deceased Lopez as "a foolish gambler" [271].) In both cases, it is strongly hinted, the father's penny-pinching leads to acts of filial rebellion that undo the very raison d'être of his savings. At the very least, Wharton is clearly guilty of the sin for which he indicts Lopez, using money as a form of emotional leverage: "If the man were to his liking," he thinks, just before Emily's marriage, "there would be money enough" (138). In the mobile, ever-changing world of the novel, making money the old-fashioned way, the "natural" way, the un-Jewish way, proves to be no more successful than its newfangled, and Semitic, alternatives.

The economic world that the text depicts, in other words, is one that is deeply scored by fault lines that run back and forth between money and love, wealth and desire, economics and sexuality—and this is as true on the normative, gentile, Christian side as on the aberrational, demonized, Jewish one. There is no hard and fast rule for living in this new economic world—an enterprise best emblematized, perhaps, by the campaign of Plantagenet Palliser, the novel's eponymous prime minister, to decimalize the British currency, that is, to make rational, regularized sense of a traditional, and famously irrational, monetary system. (Needless to say, Palliser fails.) If Lopez, like Barabas, stands at the center of that world, he does so as a literal embodiment of the repressed but omnipresent affective spirits of capitalism, a world where stable criteria of value vary and new feelings—greed, arrogance, desire, bodily pleasure, speculative zing—proliferate. To adopt Zizek's trope, he "organizes" this aspect of experience; he gives it shape and form, allows us to perceive it as such at all. Or Lopez brings into temporary shape all its seemingly complex and contradictory elements until his highly resonant end. For, as his life enters a downward spiral, Lopez walks to the very center of the new capitalist order—Tenway Junction, a place where all the rails coming into London converge—steps in front of a train, and is "knocked into bloody atoms" (520). He is, that is to say, decomposed into the very proliferation of diverse, dispersing elements that he once brought together and thus becomes the truest embodiment of the entropic world of high capitalism even as his body is knocked into smithereens by it.

Lopez's suicide is, predictably, glossed by his fictional contemporaries as a form of madness: the dementia of the marketplace, as it were. Yet, clearly, it is also a sign of his creator's inability to resolve the conflicts that structure the novel. And, it might be added, his own career as well. The same tussle between speculation and reason, desire and restraint, that is written into *The Prime Minister* structures Trollope's own representation of himself as a writer and is inscribed into his account of his career in the literary marketplace of which he was such a thoroughly demystified master. Throughout that account, too, a Lopez-like investment in the double act of "speculation"—in making one's fortune in the new marketplace through the unfettered exercise of the imagination—is at perpetual war with the other side, the sober side, the side associated in the novel with the tragic figure of Mr. Wharton. Certainly to read Trollope's *Autobiography* is to encounter a tale told more or less by Mr. Wharton; this work, written in 1876 but published after Trollope's death, famously ends with a list of exactly how much the author has received from the sale of each and every one of his novels and contains along the way many hymns to the work ethic. Here is one, culled from the very last pages of this work: "What remains to me of life I trust for my happiness still chiefly to my work; hoping that when the power of work be over with me God may be pleased to take me from a world in which, according to my view, there can be no joy."[27] Elsewhere in the *Autobiography*, this side of Trollope—the side that notoriously wrote exactly the same number of words per day; the side that caused Trollope to lash himself to his writing desk while making rough passage through the Cape of Good Hope—is put into service in the articulation of a self-controlled, self-controlling producerly ethic applied to the rationalization of the act of writing itself:

> All those I think who have lived as literary men—working daily as literary laborers, will agree with me that three hours a day will produce as much as a man ought to write. But then, he should have trained himself that he shall be able to work continuously during those three hours—so have tutored his mind so that it shall not be necessary for him to sit nibbling his pen, and gazing at the wall, till he shall have found the words with which to express his ideas. (336)

Max Weber couldn't have done a better job of tracing the line from the doctrine of salvation by work to the refinement of the productive process, or of tracing the thoroughgoing asceticism, the almost religious chastening of the body, that such a movement involves and profits from.

But even or especially at the apogee of this style of response, we encounter another. Here is an equally well-known passage from the *Autobiography*'s penultimate page, just before the quotation just cited:

> If the rustle of a woman's petticoat has ever stirred my blood; if a cup of wine has been a joy to me; if I have ever thought tobacco at midnight in pleasant company to be one of the elements of an earthly paradise; if now and again I have somewhat recklessly fluttered a £5 note over a card-table; —of what matter is that to any reader? I have betrayed no woman. Wine has brought me no sorrow. It has been the companionship of smoking I have loved, rather than the habit. I have never desired to win money, and I have lost none. To enjoy the excitement of pleasure, but to be free from its vices and ill effects—to have the sweet and leave the bitter untasted— that has been my study. The preachers tell us that this is impossible. It seems to me that hitherto I have succeeded fairly well. I will not say I have never scorched a finger—but I carry no ugly wounds. (335–6)

Christopher Herbert has reminded us that the Shakespearean vision of comic pleasure is never far from Trollope's value system, but Herbert goes on to suggest that it is a pleasure that is accommodated to a larger moral system by restraint, modesty, and chasteness.[28] Here, by contrast, we encounter a Trollope articulating the most immodest aspirations of the modern consumer society: a world where all wants indeed are satisfied and where the cycle of desire and unfulfillment that governs the dialectic of consumerism is permanently stilled through a permanent satisfaction. It is an earthly paradise indeed, where one can smoke and drink and gamble and ogle without suffering any of the consequences. It is also, one senses, the dream of Lopez: of a something-for-nothing sensibility that achieves a state of boundless pleasure through "speculation," albeit in this case a purely imaginative one. This is Trollope's own private Guatemala, as it were. And not only does he apotheosize this place of consumerist bliss, he evinces a kind of Lopez-like hubris in the terms by which he hymns it. Trollope here claims to have achieved a feat that "moralists" deem impossible, and furthermore claims so on the authority of his own person, however modestly he expresses this claim.

Henry James beautifully captured both sides of Trollope with his reminiscence of encountering his English counterpart on the latter's return from his 1874 trip to Australia, New Zealand, and America: "We also had Anthony Trollope," James wrote his brother William, "who wrote novels in his state room all morning (he does it literally every morning of his life, no matter where he may be), and played cards with Mrs. Bronson all the evening."[29] James's Trollope—or even Trollope's Trollope—represents the split at the very center of capitalist self-imaging: between production and consumption, the amassing of capital and the expenditure of funds, reason and emotion, calculation and pleasure. As the *Autobiography* suggests, this split moves directly into the experience of the professionalized writer, that figure who cultivates his own pleasure-making faculty and his own capacity for imaginative "speculation," subjects them to an austere discipline, and then profits from them to produce yet more pleasure *and* pride in its subjugation or control. It is a delicate balance, to be sure, but it is one that is deeply constitutive not only of the identity of the professionalized writer but of the subject itself in the epistemic regime of capitalism.

It is this split, finally, that is expressed by Trollope's representation of the Jew: the figure, that is to say, who most fully embodies the emotional, pleasure-centered, consumerist, imaginative side of his authorial being, and pushes that impulse toward its logical, if suicidal, extreme. This set of equations, and its close relation to the work of writing, is most fully enacted in Trollope's 1875 novel *The Way We Live Now*, and is brought there as close to the crisis point as he is capable of bringing it. Written just after Trollope's trip to Australia, New Zealand, and the United States and just before *The Prime Minister*, the novel is, as its title suggests, a despairing piece of auto-ethnography—the investigation, from the inside, of a culture gone spectacularly wrong. It is also, technically, something of a Juvenalian jeremiad (to mix classical and Hebraic): a stunning anatomy of just about every form of social degeneration possible, all flowing from the wholesale substitution of economic for human values and of the credit nexus for that of genuine human relations. Given the preceding discussion, it will hardly surprise the reader to learn that what has gone most spectacularly wrong in this culture are three things: the rise of high capitalism, particularly finance capitalism; the proliferation of writers; and the ubiquity of Jews. It will also come as no surprise to learn that these three are thoroughly intertwined, related in a brilliant series of metonymic substitutions in which causal links are hard to determine but in which effects are manifest and malign. Indeed, all three of these things soon collapse into one figure who combines all these formations and the complexities of affect associated with them: that of the splendiferously evil (or so he seems) Jew (or so he seems) Melmotte (or so he is called).

But fully to understand Melmotte's role in the novel, we need to turn first and foremost to the equations that structure it. In many ways, this novel illustrates the side of Gallagher's argument that she herself neglects—the one that links the usurious Jew to the work of writing—with a kind of precision that is almost uncanny; but it does so, as Gallagher would also predict, through the paralleling of the speculating Jew Melmotte with an actual novelist: Lady Carbury. Lady Carbury is, of course, a nightmare version of Trollope's own maniacally prolific novelist mother, but she is also and most powerfully a reflection of himself as pleasure-loving professional in the literary marketplace. "Commenced partly from a sense of pleasure in the work, partly as a passport into society," her "dabbling in literature" had "been converted into hard work by which money if possible might be earned."[30] "[A] career in literature," this novel makes clear, is not one of imaginative creation; "to puff and get oneself puffed," she writes Mr. Alf, editor of the *Evening Pulpit*, "have become different branches of a new profession" (14). There are sexual implications to Lady Carbury's language here, and throughout the novel she is represented as the very type of radiant female physicality. But despite—or perhaps in tandem with—this embodiment, she also represents literary activity as a process of hardheaded rationalization that has the ironic effect of negating the value of the product itself. She does not so much produce a product for a market as offer it up as an object of exchange, of reciprocal "puffery"—one item in the exchange of favors that constitutes the literary career. The effect on the level of language is (as Simmel or Marx would suggest on the model of economics) to empty writing of any intrinsic value whatsoever. This is best summarized by Trollope's description of Lady Carbury's *Criminal Queens*, a nonfiction tract through which she hopes to cement her reputation. Founded on an absolute ignorance of the historical events upon which it is based, cobbled together from other suspect sources inadequately understood, the book betokens her own regal "criminality"—her own participation in a system that the novelist calls "absolutely and indominably foul" (15). But it also signifies the emptiness of that cultural system itself: the reviewer who decries Lady Carbury's ignorance of the facts upon which her book is based is himself working in such haste that he, too, gets the facts with which he corrects her completely wrong. When words become markers in the game of puffery, language is voided of any connection to the real—and the project of the novelist becomes (by implication) both thoroughly self-referential and utterly debased.

I have dwelt on Lady Carbury because she offers such a compelling model for the conflation of economics and semiotics, and because she brings a crisis in value posed by a participation in a capitalist economy firmly into the sphere of literary production. But I have also done so in order to note that precisely because she is a woman, the threat that she embodies is easily stilled. Lady Carbury ultimately marries one of her "puffers" (Mr. Broune), on the condition that she retire from the field of literature, and the novel disposes of her by turning her back into the society matron she once had been: her "house in Wellbeck Street was kept, and Mrs. Broune's Tuesday evenings were much more regarded by the literary world than had been those of Lady Carbury" (760). In significant contrast to threats posed on the level of gender, however, the threat represented by Gallagher's other model for the degradation of writing in the culture of capitalism— the usurious Jew—is not so easily dispelled. The central and most compelling irony in the novel is that it is the Jewish financier Melmotte who is the novel's most successful writer. Melmotte is spectacularly a writer in the sense of being a fiction-maker: we learn on his first appearance in the book that his name may or may not be his own; that the Esquire he sticks on the end of it may or may not be appropriate; that his reputation as market-mover may or may not be earned; all is a matter of rumor, of hint, of fiction. Indeed, his financial power crucially depends on the narratives that circulate around him. "It was said that he had made a railway across Russia, that he provisioned the Southern army in the American civil war, that he supplied Austria with arms, and had at one time bought up all the iron in England. He could make or mar any company by buying or selling stock, and could make money dear or cheap as he pleased" (31). "All this was said in his praise," the narrator adds, but the novel demonstrates that even more than inducing praise, these fictions are what cause the credulous and penurious British aristocracy to invest in his company—itself, of course, merely a fiction, since Melmotte's firm makes nothing, buys nothing, and for that matter sells nothing—and to marry their bankrupt sons to his daughter, attend his grand fete for the emperor of China, make him a member of their political party (both vie for his services; appropriately, the Disraeli-led Conservatives win), elect him to Parliament. "The tradesmen had learned enough to be quite free of doubt," at any rate, "and in the City Mr. Melmotte's name was worth any money—though his character was perhaps worth but little" (33).

Made by fictions, Melmotte is also the cause of fiction-making in others. In this, of course, he is like many of Trollope's morally flawed but imaginatively endowed characters—like Lopez or, perhaps more accurately, Lizzie Eustace.[31] But far more than that of these two, Melmotte's narrative infectiousness—his ability to make others share in his own imaginative schemes—makes the people around him rich, at least, for the time being, in their perfervid imaginations. Appropriately enough, it is Lady Carbury who understands this aspect of speculation and who issues a powerful defense of it and the risks associated with such acts of economic (and imaginative) adventurism:

> "If a thing can be made great and beneficent, a boon to humanity, simply by creating a belief in it, does not a man become a benefactor to his race by creating that belief? . . . You cannot send a ship to sea without endangering lives. . . . You tell me this man may perhaps ruin hundreds, but then again he may create a new world in which millions will be rich and happy." (231)

Significantly, her skeptical interlocutor, Mr. Booker, does not quarrel with Melmotte's financial chicanery or malevolent effects on people's lives: it is Melmotte's lack of "veracity" that offends Booker. His crimes, finally, are, like Lady Carbury's, those of the aesthetic or the imaginative itself: like Lady Carbury, he is "false from head to foot" (31). But, as Lady Carbury reminds us, falsity—the creation of factitious expectations—is built into the nature of speculation itself, and such speculation fuels the very capitalist enterprise from which all the characters in the novel seek to profit, and from which the novelist, too, profits, whether that novelist be Lady Carbury, or Frances Trollope, or the more successful version of both, her son Anthony.

But Melmotte's reputation is an example not only of the power of fiction or "speculation," in all the senses that word takes on for Trollope, but of the arbitrariness of the sign; it is linked (as is Lopez's) to the decoupling of signifier and signified, the free-floating quality of language in a culture where name guarantees character, not the other way around. It is no surprise, then, that like Lady Carbury, but even more effectively than she, Melmotte generates economic value quite directly through writing: that his grand character turns out to be nothing but characters, marks on the page. For Melmotte may be a practitioner of the kinds of Ponzi schemes that proliferate in capitalist economies, but his frauds all depend crucially upon the act of writing for their consummation. In his many dealings—most spectacularly, with an impecunious aristocrat mockingly named Longstaffe and his wastrel son, appropriately named Dolly—he pays debts with IOUs based on his rich expectations, which he grandly signs, and then, when he is called upon for payment, he offers stock in a valueless company, a great railroad to Veracruz, a railroad the narrator explicitly describes as a fiction. Then, in an utterly gratuitous gesture, he forges Mr. Longstaffe's signature on a document that corroborates a transaction that has been verbally agreed to by all parties to it—an act that causes his discovery and demise. Melmotte is both made and unmade by acts of writing; and the novel links explicitly the acts of semiotic and economic making and unmaking to the culture of capitalism:

> It was part of the charm of all dealings with this great man that no ready money seemed ever to be ready for anything. Great purchases were made and great transactions completed without the signing even of a check. . . . As for many years past we have exchanged paper instead of actual money for our commodities, so now it seemed that, under the new Melmotte regime, an exchange of words was to suffice. (345–6)

And what is true of Melmotte is spectacularly the case with every other sphere of experience in the text: the exchange of written words or scraps of paper is the governing principle within each of the novel's separate plots and the spheres of experience they emblematize. Lady Carbury not only offers reciprocal puffery through writing novels; she also spends much of her time writing letters through which she guides both her professional and amatory life. When Melmotte stands for Parliament, his opponent is none other than Mr. Alf, a (German, perhaps Jewish) magazine writer and editor, who uses journalism as well as oratory to undo his opponent. When the novel's upstanding Jew, Breghert, seeks to marry Georgina Longstaffe, their courtship is ratified by a contract and revoked by an exchange of letters. Even in the Beargarden, the gambling den frequented by the novel's young men, written chits are exchanged in place of cash. Here all goes well until an American, Fisker, joins the game:

> When IOUs have for some time passed freely in such a company as that now assembled the sudden introduction of a stranger is very disagreeable,

particularly when that stranger intends to start for San Francisco in the morning. If it could be arranged that the stranger should certainly lose, no doubt then he would be regarded as a godsend. . . . When these dealings in unsecured paper have been going on for a considerable time real bank notes come to have a loveliness which they never possessed before. . . . [But] from the very commencement Fisker won, and quite a budget of little papers fell into his possession—bearing . . . a "G" intended to stand for Grasslough, or an "N" for Nidderdale, or a wonderful hieroglyphic which was known at the Beargarden to mean D—L—, or Dolly Longstaffe, the fabricator of which was not present at the occasion. (78–9)

The intricate making-good of these IOUs, which takes several pages and much further chicanery to unravel (the basic problem is that they are all that Felix, who has also lost heavily, has in his bank account), is perhaps less important than their Melmottean overtones. The shell game of exchanging writing for writing, paper for paper, stock for IOUs and further paper for stock, not only unites the diverse worlds that structure the novel in exactly the way that a mature market economy brings together diverse social spheres via the act of exchange. It also makes all the players in its economic sphere mini-Melmottes: social actors who perform acts of inscribed fiction-making that nevertheless seem to have real economic backing and consequently to exert a genuine worldly power.

This, then, is the way we live now: a way of life based not so much on credit as on a play of inscribed signifiers, backed up only by our faith in language and the power of fictions themselves. And it is a way of life that is best encapsulated by, and whose consequences are most fully negotiated through, a Jew: all identities aspire to the condition of Melmotte, the self-naming, self-making, fiction-creating fraud who generates false value by means of fraudulent writing. (Significantly, in Trollope's notes for the novel, Melmotte was intended to be arrested—that is, put on public display—for his act of forgery, then die in prison.)[32] And Melmotte is not just *a* Jew but rather *the* Jew: a veritable walking assortment of Jewish stereotypes. Melmotte's forging invokes the image of the Jew as usurer—as maker of money by false, perverse means, in both its original sense and the sense it acquired in the nineteenth century of the Jew as maker and unmaker of false value on the stock exchanges—"the passionate voices, raised in turn, of a rise and fall in market values," as the anti-Semitic text I quoted earlier, would have it, deeply opposed to "the calm and monotonous song of" true "prosperity" (*The Jews*, p. 74). His forging also conjures, with an age-old topos I have not fully dealt with here, the image of the Jew as representative of false, degraded language, of proliferating words, not backed up by the true Word of God. A third is elsewhere brought to bear on the text by Melmotte's attempt to sell Marie Melmotte on what the text quite nakedly refers to as "the matrimonial market" (92): this is the Jew as pander, the dealer in young virgins who is quite often incestuously connected with them. Trollope does not merely suggest the salience of these stereotypes; just about every calumny circulating throughout European culture with respect to the Jew lands on Melmotte's quite substantial shoulders:

> People said that Mr. Melmotte had the reputation throughout Europe as a gigantic swindler—as one who in the dishonest and successful pursuit of wealth stopped at nothing. People said of him that he had framed and carried out long and premeditated and deeply laid schemes for those who trusted him, that he had swallowed up the property of all who had come into contact with him, that he was fed with the blood of widows and orphans. (61)

We remember these ascriptions and aspersions from the topoi of economic anti-Semitism I inventoried earlier, so it will come as no surprise that to this set of circulating and self-implicating associations Trollope adds another. Melmotte is both a spectacularly embodied and a deeply passionate character and as such resembles the image of the licentious, lascivious, overemotional Jew I have shown coursing through nineteenth-century thought. Unlike Lopez, Melmotte is not a passionate, Byronic lover—far from it. But he is like Lopez in being indecorous, rude—and violent: indeed, in one of the most shocking moments of the book, he beats his daughter Marie when her attempt to run off with Felix Carbury is frustrated. More salient still is the series of associations that follow from popular suspicions of Melmotte, the public belief that he swallows up property, that he is engorged with the blood of women and children. These hints look back to the anti-Semitic emphasis on the Jew as participant in ritual murder (one that eventuated in frequent images in nineteenth-century anti-Semitic propaganda of the Jew as blood-sucking monster), but they also look forward to the understanding of consumption, in its most literal sense, as the introjection of pleasures on the model of the human's first experiences of consumption—ingestion—and the protuberant swelling of the body that follows. They remind us that throughout the novel Melmotte is not merely a successful capitalist but also a spectacularly *embodied* character, one whose physical appearance is conjoined with strong oral cravings. From the moment we first meet him, his implacable bulk, broad shoulders, and thick waist are emphasized—and the other characters in the scene find themselves rather timidly moving themselves around these. Melmotte does not hesitate to use his physical power to his own advantage, especially when first intimidating and thereafter striking his daughter Marie. There are constant references to his embodiment or to body parts, either metaphorical or literal, usually conjoining them to the capacity of speculation. Melmotte is, according to a furious Sir Felix Carbury, "a bloated swindler . . . a surfeited sponge of speculation, a crammed commercial cormorant" (184). "Melmotte was not only the head, but the body also, and the feet of [his grand enterprise]," Mr. Fisker observes (268).

Trollope goes one step further in the inventorying of the Melmottean body and in linking this embodiment to the process of generating money from money:

> The magnificence of Mr. Melmotte affected even the Longstaffe lawyers. Were I to buy a little property, some humble cottage with a garden—or you, O reader, unless you be magnificent—the money to the last farthing would be wanted. . . . But money was the very breath of Melmotte's nostrils, and therefore his breath was taken for money. (268)

The transvaluations that Marx describes, the personification of money as pleasure-making pimp and the hollowing-out of the genuine appetencies of the human body in the culture of capitalism, would seem to be themselves personified by Trollope's bloated Jewish money-man. So too is the culturally powerful association between the Jew and the act of consumption. Melmotte not only spends much of the novel planning that cynosure of conspicuous consumption, a grand party, but also is affiliated with consumption in its most literal sense. When we see him he is frequently eating, drinking, or partaking of less nutritious oral delights: "It may be supposed [that on Sunday afternoon] he was meditating on millions, and arranging the prices of money and funds for the New York, Paris, and London exchanges. But on this occasion he was waked from slumber, which he seemed to have been enjoying with a cigar in his mouth" (181). Later in the novel, as his reputation suffers its inevitable decline, he responds to his woes by calling first for endless rounds of whiskey and sodas (he is thoroughly drunk in the Parliament scene), then ends his life by adding prussic acid to that drink and downing it.

Melmotte, then, conjoins the anti- or un-Weberian qualities or characteristics in his bulky Jewish body as thoroughly as Lopez does in the more graceful mein of a "swarthy son of Judah." In that body, the novel metonymically symbolizes speculation—the swelling of money by illegitimate means, means other than work (which no one in this novel seems to do, save Lady Carbury) or land (which nobody in this novel is able to hold on to, save the thoroughly attenuated Roger Carbury); it also figures consumption, the swelling of the body through the assiduous pursuit of pleasure: all are deemed to be the essential lineaments of life in the new capitalist London. The novel continues to extend its self-referential logic by using Melmotte to include writing in general, and its own imaginative act in particular, in this process. For Melmotte as embodied consumer is conjoined at a crucial moment with Melmotte as self-deconstructing literary producer: one step ahead of his creditors, he burns most of his papers, then picks up the document on which he has forged a signature and eats it.

This gesture, it seems to me, brings together the novel's concerns with appetency, writing, and consumption into a complex whole that poses questions not only to our analysis of it but to our reading of Trollope's culture. It reminds us at the very least that Trollope is setting out to question both the production and the consumption of writing, of fiction, of the culture of capitalism itself by creating in Melmotte a figure who figures all these and who brings them to the point of ontological vertigo and moral collapse. The implications of this gesture do not end here; they point not only out to the character Melmotte but even further, toward the audience, which has been swallowing, wholesale, the images the novelist has been producing for its enjoyment. Trollope accomplishes this most brilliantly at the end of the novel when, in the aftermath of his suicide, we learn along with his daughter Marie that Melmotte may not in fact be a Jew of mysterious European origins:

> [Marie] was alone in the world . . . not even knowing her father's true name, as in the various biographies of the great man which were, as a matter of course, published within a fortnight of his death, various accounts were given as to his birth, parentage, and early history. The general opinion seemed to be that his father had been a noted coiner in New York—an Irishman by the name of Melmody—and in one memoir, the probability of his descent was argued from Melmotte's skill at forgery. (747)

To be sure, this moment enhances yet again both the ubiquity and the undecidability of writing itself: the medium through which Melmotte creates and destroys his own identity (and the fortunes of countless others) here performs its work with merciless efficiency after his death. But this moment of deauthentication is itself authenticated by the novel that has preceded it. It implicitly asks us to return to all the descriptions of Melmotte in the text and to see that, while his wife and her relatives are all explicitly Jewish, there is no positive indication whatsoever that Melmotte himself is, well, anything at all. Indeed, given his facility at forging, the genealogy provided for Melmotte at the end of the novel is considerably more convincing than the ones that were provided by the impersonal wisdom of the crowd. But to say this is not to suggest (as some critics have done) that we can *not* read him as a Jew. Not only do the people who surround him do so in all the ways I have discussed, but Trollope's text persistently does so as well. In its invocation of anti-Semitic topoi in describing Melmotte, in its conscious rescripting of the Shylock/Jessica scenario from the *Merchant*, most fully of all in the culturally contumacious habit of linking a Jew to the structures of affect that circulate in the marketplace: in all of these ways, Trollope has fully mobilized the powerful cultural metonymies that circulate in and around the figure of the Jew. It would be naive (at the very least) to pretend that these are unmotivated by the author, and have no effect on the reader.

If we cannot read Melmotte as a Jew but cannot *not* read him as a Jew, at the end of the novel we are caught in the trap of our own readerly expectations. And this would seem to be Trollope's point. As thoroughly as he includes himself and his own authorial endeavors via Lady Carbury in the parade of corruption that is the way we live now, he wishes to include the reader in that very process. And more: he wants to include the very yen for anti-Semitic fictions that the novel itself profits from in this process. Trollope here asks the reader to question why he or she should have understood Melmotte as a Jew, and by so doing he wants us to question the ways in which those anti-Semitic associations circulate in a culture of capitalist appetencies where fictions and facts are inseparable from each other and where both are devalorized as they are made into objects of consumption and exchange. Trollope explicitly as well as implicitly asks his readership, in other words, to consider what consuming desires of their own are served by the metonymies that circulate in and through the fictions of the Jew; he does so by making fictions stick in our craw. Given the financial failure of the novel, the ultimate effect of this maneuver is, to say the least, equivocal. From a position that privileges anti-anti-Semitic responses, it is difficult to say whether the failure of the novel to win the plaudits of the Victorian readership is heartening or distressing: whether the fictions of the Jew that circulate in and through Victorian culture were unpopular or whether the deconstruction of those fictions for the audience was itself the problem. Certainly Trollope's more anti-Semitic contemporaries—Thackeray, for example, or the *Punch* cartoonists—never experienced this slide in popularity.

Whatever we can say about its Victorian success, the lessons of *The Way We Live Now* for our endeavor are clear. Like *The Prime Minister*, it suggests how culturally contumacious the association is between the Jew and the new species of affect available, and necessary, in the world of high capitalism: how easily and how fully the figure of the Jew comes to fulfill the imaginative and social needs of the bourgeois novel struggling to find a language to express these new desires, sensations, and emotions—not only for the writer, as I have been arguing, but also for the reader to whom, as Trollope so intensely knew, his work must appeal. For both, the figure of the Jew becomes both the embodiment of and a scapegoat for the new kinds of attitudes, understandings, and experiences that a capitalist culture creates, a way of giving body to those experiences and attitudes while distancing the writerly and the readerly self from them. The novel's reception ironically suggests as well how that vehicle of the experiencing of the new capitalist world itself assumes a powerful force in it: that economic anti-Semitism became a part of the life of the culture not only because of the needs it managed but also because its fictions would *sell*. As indeed they did, in the later years of the nineteenth century and the early years of the twentieth.

As we turn to those fictions and to the various pieces of cultural work that they did, we might pause over the honesty and prescience of Trollope and note that the associations he brings together—not only between the Jew and capital, but more powerfully between the capitalist Jew and the act of *imaginative* speculation—get more fully developed in the fin de siècle and the early years of the twentieth century. As they do so, as I will suggest in the next chapter, the ambivalent interest of the reader, as well as that of the writer, in the figure of the Jew continues to compound. For the failure of Trollope's novel was followed in the very next decade by the wild popular success in England and, especially, America of *Trilby*, a novel with a character—the pestiferous Svengali—who contains within his filthy Jewish body the qualities Trollope tries to keep separate: artistic genius and perversion, imaginative success and bodily appetencies. Ironically, then, Trollope's diagnosis of the cultural appetite for the figure of the Jew was confirmed not by his own novel's fate but by that of du Maurier's, for the success of that novel was in no small measure due to its use of the very stereotypes Trollope had so brilliantly deployed and so thoroughly critiqued.

Svengali conducts, Trilby sings.

A Svengali for our times: Leonard Bernstein conducts, Frederica von Stade sings.
Courtesy of the New York Public Library for the Performing Arts,
Astor, Lenox and Tilden Foundation.

"The New Jerusalem, Formerly New York." From *Judge*, July 22, 1882.
Courtesy of the American Jewish Historical Society.

E. Haldeman-Julius (right) meets with Sir Allan Lane, founder of Penguin Books, at his Girard, Kansas farm. Courtesy of Leonard Axe Library, Pittsburgh State University.

"'Who Owns Henry James?' Biographer Edel and Subject." Time Magazine,
November 20, 1962. Courtesy of Time Magazine, Time-Warner Communications.

3

The Mania of the Middlebrow

Trilby, the Jew, and the Middlebrow Imaginary

IN THE PRECEDING CHAPTER, I attempted to suggest that writers of the high Victorian period inflected the figure of the Jew so as to articulate their own tangled structure of affects about marketplace culture and to negotiate a new place for themselves in that culture—ironically enough, as a version of precisely that problematic figure, "the Jew." But this argument raises in its wake another question: what about the audience—those readers Trollope confutes and confuses so vigorously at the end of *The Way We Live Now* and who responded to their own indictment with such startling indifference? There is no hard and fast way of answering the question. Despite the very fine efforts of critics like Norman Holland and Janice Radway, the empirical phenomenology of reader response—of what actually happens when people read and how their reading practices enter into their daily lives—remains conjectural and murky. Despite the excellent work of Richard Altick, Martha Vicinius, and Regenia Gagnier on the constitution of working- and middle-class readerships, the question of how readers of the past actually responded to texts on a quotidian basis remains murkier still.[1]

Luckily, there is one phenomenon through which we can more fully probe these dynamics: the literary mania. The nineteenth century was a time of vast waves of popular enthusiasm for literature, high, middle, and low, which, although registered on many social levels, was particularly intense among the booming middle classes in England and especially America. Frequently, this response took on forms anticipatory of the celebrity culture the emergence of which we date to a later century: mobs rushing the Brooklyn docks anticipating the next installment of Dickens's *The Old Curiosity Shop*, tumult during the tours of Oscar Wilde (con) and Jenny Lind (pro), and of course the famous Astor Place riots of 1849, when a production of *Macbeth* stirred class fervor exploding in violence that left ten dead.[2] At other times, this enthusiasm took the more sedate guise of organized clubs or reading groups. As one commentator put it, middle-class Browning reading groups proliferated in "[n]ot only more than one University quadrangle, but every mercantile town, from London where the poet dwells to the farthest outpost of the western continent . . . from which dependents radiate like little spiders that spin their tiny strands near the maternal web."[3] And largely but not exclusively through the efforts of the enthusiastic Frederick Furnivall were founded the Chaucer Society, the Shakspeare Society, the New Shakspeare Society, the Sunday Shakspeare Society, the Wordsworth Society, the Shelley Society, the Brontë Society, the Morris Society, the Ruskin Society—not to mention the Wycliff Society, the Dunbar Society, the Malone Society and the Omar Khayyam Society;[4] as with Browning societies, these clubs soon spread to America, where, joining with the already powerful women's club movement, they helped make avid study of literature an integral part of middle-class culture.[5]

In one other spectacular instance, that wave of public interest in the literary conjoined both these responses and turned not toward an author but a book: the novel *Trilby*, by George du Maurier. More to the point, this response assumed a thoroughly imitative guise; readers took to re-enacting scenes from the novel, singing the songs contained in it, modeling ice sculptures on its characters, and buying clothes and other accouterments based on its artist-author's designs. It is no coincidence that this mimetic enthusiasm was associated with two topics that it is my task to anatomize: on the one hand, the fate of high culture in a world governed by the vicissitudes of an increasingly powerful and self-conscious mass readership; and, on the other, the Jew. Indeed, I argue in what follows, *Trilby*-mania and its complement, Svengali-phobia, worked to delineate a new kind of audience response in which insecure readers avidly turned to high culture as a way of affirming their social status; along the way, it bound their concerns with the nature and powers of art to the figure of the Jew in a form that continued to resonate throughout the next century.

In this chapter, then, I want to look at *Trilby* the text and *Trilby*-mania the phenomenon for what they can tell us about the texture of responses evidenced by the new mass audience for fiction; for what the spectacularly labile response of that audience to *Trilby* tells us about its charged investment in the mythos and the practices of high culture; and, finally, for how that doubled response made its way with such spectacular force into representations of that culturally powerful image of doubleness, the Jew. In *Trilby*-mania and its complement, Svengali-phobia, we witness the consummation of a nineteenth-century cultural suturing that is going to have powerful aftereffects in the twentieth: the linkage of the Jew to the image of the high-cultural artist in such a way as to affiliate the ascriptions made about one to the other and back again in a chiastic crisscross of cultural ambivalence. Looking back to George Eliot's Klesmer or Disraeli's hymns to the power of Jewish music in *Coningsby* and forward to the complicated associations between art, power, and perversity that run through anti-Semitic discourses of the twentieth century, the mania that focused on *Trilby* is a benign reminder of the kinds of sometimes not-so-benign work that get done through the figure of the Jew. This work, as I will argue, is constitutive not only of racial identifications that crawled to the surface in the later years of the nineteenth century but of the role those ascriptions played in the making of ideologies of culture in the early years of the twentieth.

TRILBY AND TRILBY-MANIA

On March 25, 1889, Henry James wrote in his notebook:

> [L]ast evening, before dinner, I took a walk with G. du Maurier, in the mild March twilight on Hampstead Heath . . . and he told me over an idea of his which he thought very good—and I do too—for a short story. . . . Last night it struck me as curious, picturesque and distinctly usable; though the want of musical knowledge would hinder *me* somewhat in handling it.[6]

James toyed briefly with the idea of writing this story of a "servant girl with a wonderful rich full voice but no musical genius who is mesmerized and made to sing by a little foreign Jew who has mesmeric power, infinite feeling, and no organ [*sic*] . . . of his own" (97). Soon thereafter, however, he thought better of the project and remitted it to du Maurier. Five years later, just as James was beginning to despair over his attempted conquest of the London theatrical audience and hence over his ability to survive at all in the brave new world of the fin-de-siècle marketplace, du Maurier's version of his own tale began to appear in *Harper's*, under the title *Trilby*.

To James's chagrin and du Maurier's delighted embarrassment, *Trilby* rapidly generated precisely the enthusiasm that James had been hoping in vain to kindle, partially in England, more largely in America. It was not without reason that *Trilby* headed the first bestseller list, published in the *Bookman* shortly after the novel's publication: over one hundred thousand copies were sold within the first two months of publication; over two million in two years. If anything, these figures understate the novel's popularity. One hundred copies circulated at the Mercantile Library in New York but still proved inadequate to reader requests; public libraries in Boston and Chicago also reported unprecedented demand. A librarian from the latter reported, with the hyperbole that characterized all aspects of *Trilby*-mania: "every one of our 54,000 cardholders seems determined to read the book" (*Trilbyana*, p. 105).

The public excitement occasioned by *Trilby* was not confined to literary manifestations. Sir Beerbohm Tree adapted the play for the London stage, giving it, significantly enough, the name *Svengali*; it ran for three years. Due to ill health, du Maurier was not able to follow the likes of Dickens, Wilde, and Matthew Arnold onto the lecture circuit—particularly lucrative, of course, in America, where *Trilby* was already such a sensation; nevertheless, the public appetite for *Trilby* led to numerous tours by traveling companies of the theatrical version of the novel—twenty-four separate troupes were simultaneously touring at one point in 1896. *Trilby*-mania did not end at the theater. Other forms of entertainment centered on the novel. A New York society matron, Mrs. Charles Ditson, organized an evening at Sherry's restaurant, for the benefit of the New York Kindergarten Association, devoted to "Scenes and Songs from *Trilby*"; *tableaux-vivants* reproducing du Maurier's illustrations with painstaking fidelity alternated with the performance of songs from the novel. (Twenty-five hundred dollars was raised.) Meanwhile, at a burlesque house, the Eden Musée, a certain Miss Ganthony impersonated Trilby, as did Miss Marie Meers in Barnum's Greatest Show on Earth, "riding bareback . . . around the tan bark to the snapping of ringmaster Svengali's whip." Literary and charitable societies devoted meetings to the novel; the Daughters of the American Revolution sponsored a *Trilby* evening to benefit the St. Luke's Home for Indigent Christian Females, "a literary criticism of the book was read . . . and the songs oftenest alluded to sung"; as far afield as Omaha, "An Evening with Trilby" was held during which seven papers (e.g., "Could *Trilby* Be Successfully Dramatized?" and "The French of *Trilby*") were read and music associated with the novel was performed. Finally, but not least significantly, a host of what we would call commercial tie-ins proliferated: to this cultural moment we owe the origins of Trilby hats and overcoats, of course, but it also witnessed a proliferation of Trilby shoes, Trilby hearth-brushes, Trilby hams, and, particularly in England, the Trilby sausage, which, its advertisers claimed in language perhaps not entirely unfamiliar to the current reader, "is something new, and fills a long-felt want; they melt in your mouth."[7]

The passing of "the germ" of *Trilby* from du Maurier to James and back again, then, might appropriately symbolize the cultural situation of the novel itself at the end of the nineteenth century; and the explosion of this germ into a full-blown "mania" in both England and America might suggest some of the ramifications of that condition. If James was increasingly to learn the lesson of *Trilby*-mania—that writers like himself were now thoroughly alienated from the genteel but not unremunerative readership whose affections he had seemed to win with the publication of *Daisy Miller* (1878) and which he had last successfully addressed with *Portrait of a Lady* (1881)—du Maurier discovered the converse: that a new audience had risen from this earlier one, an audience similar in social aspiration but different in its size, its lack of firm social variegation, and, perhaps most significant, its enthusiasm for a version of high or elite culture now being made available through the organs of a booming and reorganizing mass culture. Or, to translate into a different kind of language, both men were forced to recognize and to reckon with the birth of a style of audience response that critics were later to dub the middlebrow.

To be sure, it's difficult to get a take on exactly what one means by this vexed and contested term, especially since its critics tend to be implicated so powerfully in the very effort to critique it: the middlebrow, whatever else it is, is what the academic or intellectual critic is *not*, and is not in large measure by virtue of the critical analysis of this contested category. And it's even more difficult to get a sense of precisely *when* the middlebrow rises to full articulation in Anglo-American culture. Virginia Woolf firmly set the rise of the middlebrow in England in the 1920s (she did *not* approve) and associated it with the fiction of H. G. Wells.[8] Henry Nash Smith located the rise of the middlebrow in mid-nineteenth-century America and identified it with the popularity of sentimental fiction by women. Joan Shelley Rubin focuses her attention on the period between the world wars and identifies it with the rise of institutions like the *Encyclopedia Britannica*, the quiz show, and the Book-of-the-Month Club. Janice Radway concentrates on the Book-of-the-Month Club from the 1920s to the present day and focuses on the complex interplay of class and taste in the process by which the club's selections are made.[9] My own view, which synthesizes the views of the critics I have named here, is that the middlebrow as such emerges in the 1880s and early 1890s with the rise of new professional/managerial classes in both England and America and with the concomitant rise of a culture increasingly attuned to the ethos of consumption. For in the consumer-oriented world of this period, members of these new elites sought increasingly to legitimize themselves by invoking the authority of taste, aesthetics, and "culture"—all of which were made available to them by the newly status-conscious mass market magazines as well as by the reading clubs and literary societies I mentioned earlier and by the burgeoning social institutions devoted to the promulgation of "culture."[10]

Whatever spin one wants to give it, the rise of "middlebrow" tastes had profound cultural effects, leading to a wholesale transvaluation of the work of high culture, particularly in the literary sphere. In and around the sites of culture-making—in the new art museums that opened in this period in Chicago, New York, Toledo, San Francisco, Omaha; in periodicals, like *Poet-Lore*, that were devoted to spreading the gospel of literature and art to a large reading public; in the reading groups I have described; in the new courses that began to proliferate throughout colleges and universities, literature, music, art—"culture"—were seen as possessing sacred meaning and value, if only one could pierce the veil, understand the mysteries; and cultural entrepreneurs became increasingly interested in both supplying this need and in augmenting it by using the technologies of advertisement and direct sales via subscription. The 1890s are officially known as the Gilded Age, but they may also be thought of as the great era of the cultural how-to kit: the moment when new encyclopedias and dictionaries were prepared by companies like Funk and Wagnalls or the Century; when guidebooks to cultural knowledge were published by houses like Scribner's or Henry Holt;

when fine, de luxe editions of Shakespeare and the classics were sold by houses like Dodd and Mead and cheap paperback editions of the classics were vended at railway stations via Tauchnitz—when a new style of appropriating or appreciating cultural artifacts became evident. It is crucial to remember that this activity shaped what we know as the high culture of the era. To cite but one example, William James's *Principles of Psychology* (1890) was commissioned by Henry Holt for its New Science series, and it rapidly became a bestseller, which James augmented by writing *A Briefer Course in Psychology* and, later, *Talks to Teachers on Psychology*, which, to continue the process, was adopted by a number of reading groups eager to gain access to this most exciting new arena of knowledge.

To a certain degree, this is the response that Lawrence Levine has anatomized under the heading of "highbrow" sacralizing of culture. Levine argues that this process had the purpose and the effect of enhancing social control—disciplining audiences, restraining the more pervervid responses to cultural phenomena, and ultimately anticipating the rise of a more reified, detached spectatorial response to come later in the century. Levine's populist argument (highbrow bad, lowbrow good) has been quite influential, although critics have recently shifted the focus from efforts at social control undertaken by cultural authorities to the reactions of their audiences, and from the image of social hierarchy to (to use Anne Gere's wonderful trope) that of a recalibration of social position through the experience of culture. For me, the greatest drawback of Levine's analysis of the "sacralization of culture" is its misreading of the complex affective dynamics that governed this process. As *Trilby*-mania's conflation of the reverential and the undignified (if not out-and-out wacky), of sedate reading groups and bareback riders, may remind us, tomato-tossing and polite applause were not the only sorts of emotions evidenced by audiences of the period. Not only did a whole range of affective responses occur to culture in between these polar opposites, but cultural reverence and cultural rage coalesced and played off of each other in unexpected and complicated ways in the very same audience at the very same moment. There is real mania in *Trilby*-mania, and its existence reminds us of just how complicated the cathexis to "culture" that that phenomenon instantiated really was.

Indeed, I want to claim in what follows, that what made the fin-de-siècle "middlebrow" a middlebrow, what distinguishes these new sorts of consumers from their predecessors (avid nineteenth-century novel readers, for example) and prepares the way for their twentieth-century avatars is a powerful collocation of emotions: an uneasy combination of reverence for and insecurity in the face of the high cultural, a mingling of overestimation of the virtues of traditional high culture and a self-deprecation of the reader's own abilities to encompass it, and odd refluxes of resentment that follow upon this set of feelings and give further resonance to them. Or such at least is the analysis I extrapolate from the brilliant and prolific French sociologist Pierre Bourdieu. Bourdieu's work does have its problems, particularly when applied to the American scene (which I inventory in note 11). But what attracts me to Bourdieu is that unlike Virginia Woolf—in fact unlike any of the critics I cited earlier, with the possible exception of Radway, and even she writes about the middlebrow under the sign of shame—Bourdieu attempts to read the middlebrow immanently, sympathetically. For Bourdieu, the middlebrow is a figure of perpetual, but perpetually frustrated, cultural aspiration, one expressed "inter alia, by a particularly frequent choice of the most uncon-ditioned testimonies of cultural docility (a choice of 'well-bred' friends, a taste for 'educational' or 'instructive' entertainments), often combined with a sense of unworthiness ('paintings are nice but difficult')."[11] Bourdieu's middlebrow is de-fined by the quest for status through the attainment of high-cultural competence. But, denied by birth, education, and social circumstance easy access to the fund of cultural data and, more important, ready assurance in making aesthetic judg-ments, the middlebrow is perpetually conscious of "the fact that legitimate culture is not made for him (and is often made against him) so that he is not made for it; and that it ceases to be what it is as soon as he appropriates it—as would happen tomorrow to the melodies of Fauré or Duparc if sung, well or badly, in petit-bourgeois living-rooms" (337).

To Bourdieu, the middlebrow is more than just a docile numskull; he is some-thing of a comic hero impaled on the horns of a cultural dilemma. (Tellingly, Bourdieu compares the middlebrow to Leopold Bloom, that perpetual outsider who brandishes his shards of erroneous cultural knowledge as a ticket to the social acceptance his origins deny him.) For the very cultural *reverence* of the middlebrow places that figure in the midst of a self-defeating paradox. Although the middlebrow always gets it *wrong*, he also gets what no other social player possesses—a genuine involvement in the cultural that is as emotionally intense as it is perpetually frustrated. In the middlebrow's "symbolic class struggle with the certified holders of cultural competence" (330) "avidity combines with anx-iety" (328), and the middlebrow grasps as hard as he or she can at cultural artifacts as if they were objects of sacred value. Neither the dominant classes, who treat taste as their birthright, nor the working ones, who make a virtue of their exclusion from the culturally canonical, need or are able to establish so vibrant, complex, and *cathected* a relation to high culture. Yet it is precisely this cathexis that frustrates the social ambitions of the middlebrow. For the middle-brow yearns to achieve the very antithesis of his or her own response: the ease, effortlessness, and self-confidence that mark the "sense"—and the reality—of *true* high-cultural "distinction":

> The petit bourgeois do not know how to play the game of culture as a
> game. They take culture too seriously to go in for bluff or imposture or
> even for the distance and casualness which show true familiarity; too se-
> riously even to escape permanent fear of ignorance or blunders, or to

sidestep tests by responding with the indifference of those who are not competing. (330)

There are two possible outcomes to the ensuing dilemma. The first, which Bourdieu tellingly fails to consider, is to reject high culture altogether: to demonize it or subject it to the symbolic violence of parody or satire. Rage *at* high culture, in other words, is as likely an outcome of the middlebrow's social drama as is rage *for* high culture. A second, less extreme solution is for middlebrows to generate a cultural system of their own or, more accurately, to turn to a cultural system created for that purpose. The middlebrow turns for aid and comfort— for the legitimation that legitimate culture withholds—to those authorities who mediate between high culture and the mass audience, who provide

> accessible versions of avant-garde experiments, film "adaptations" of classic drama and literature, "popular arrangements" of classical music or "orchestral versions" of popular tunes, vocal interpretations of classics in a style evocative of scout choruses or angelic choirs, in short, everything that goes to make up "quality weeklies" and "quality shows" which are entirely organized to give the impression of bringing legitimate culture within the reach of all, by combining two normally exclusive characteristics, immediate accessibility and the outward signs of cultural legitimacy. (323)

But—and this is a point Bourdieu sketches but does not sufficiently emphasize—the organs of middlebrow culture do not necessarily adopt a passive relation to their clientele. Considering themselves part of legitimate or high culture, the makers of middlebrow culture frequently enhance and exploit as they pretend to allay the cultural insecurity of the middlebrow audience. Claiming to be neutral or "objective" translators of culture, they select, block, or critique elements of that culture even as they transmit it. College teachers or museum guides or bestselling vade mecums to culture impart a powerful spin all their own to the culture that is positioned as such, that is understood as legitimate or powerful by the middlebrow audience that turns to them for instruction in the lineaments of "taste."

Americanists like Levine, Joan Shelley Rubin, and again, in a more nuanced way, Radway have noted this phenomenon and used it to mount a neopopulist critique of middlebrow taste-makers. Sympathetic as they are to the project of middlebrow culture-making, they frequently see these gatekeepers as seeking to claim an illegitimate cultural authority for themselves. In so doing, these critics supplement the ahistoricism that Bourdieu succumbs to but they miss the affective dynamics that make his analysis work. If the rise of the middlebrow is two-pronged, calling into being middlebrow consumers and cultural authorities who increasingly make middle-class careers of instructing those consumers in the lineaments of proper cultural response, then what locks these two in relation is a dance of ambivalence. The very terms of their interrelation guarantee resentment on the part of the large middlebrow public on the one hand and condescension and disaffection on the part of the exponents of middlebrow culture on the other. The former feel patronized, the latter disaffected, each pricked into irritation by their dependence on the other—the need of the middlebrow public for cultural instruction, the dependence of the adherents of middlebrow culture on their middlebrow clientele for food, shelter, and security. And in American culture in particular, rife as it is with a bias for practical knowledge and against abstract thinking and impractical art, the result is the coalescence of cultural esteem and cultural disdain, civic pride and anti-intellectualism, that courses so complexly through the body politic, surfacing in such differing controversies as the conservative Republican critiques of the Writer's Workers' Project in the thirties, the repeated attacks on the National Endowment for the Arts in the 1980s and 1990s, the critique first of high theory and then of soi-disant political correctness in the academy. In all these we see contradictory investments and counterinvestments in the cultural sphere: on the part of middlebrow consumers looking to art for social esteem and finding instead—well, what they find; and on the part of cultural authorities seeking to instruct them in the proper responses to culture and finding instead resentment, if not *ressentiment*, then responding with a flat dismissal of their audience as rubes, boors, and philistines.

The result of the interplay of middlebrow consumers and the mediators of middlebrow culture, in other words, is a complicated and highly labile set of cathexes and countercathexes in which knowledge of art or culture as such is at one and the same time made crucial to the larger reading public and rendered suspect, foolish, or even fraudulent. The ensuing stew of mutual affect, it seems to me, is worked out for the first time in *Trilby* and given an explicitly racially charged exposition there. For in that text that was crucial to the construction of the middlebrow qua middlebrow and in the thoroughly middlebrow response to it, we see middlebrow audiences and exponents of middlebrow culture negotiating and renegotiating their shifting and ambivalent relation to each other through their responses and counterresponses to a highly charged third party, Svengali, the pestiferous, sexually threatening musician who is also a spectacularly gifted artist—and a Jew.

TRILBY AND THE MANIA OF THE MIDDLEBROW

To turn, first, to the text: *Trilby* may not be as familiar to a contemporary audience as it was to the fin-de-siècle one, so I briefly summarize its plot here. My aim in doing so is not merely to familiarize the reader with this text, but more powerfully to inquire what it is about the novel that might have caused the middlebrow mania that greeted its publication. As the novel opens, we encounter three young British artists who have sought to make their fortunes in Paris: a muscular Yorkshireman nicknamed Taffy; a Scottish laird, Sandy; and, the only one among them truly gifted with artistic genius, a delicate-framed and deeply feeling artist named Little Billee. (Readers of James will instantly note an homage to du Maurier's novel in the equally delicate, although finally happier, "little artist-man" of *The Ambassadors*, Little Bilham.) The milieu in which these three move is a version of the world portrayed by Henri Murger earlier in the century in *Scènes de la Vie Bohème* and by Puccini in *La Bohème*; a world of would-be artists, writers, grisettes, and grifters, facing poverty with bohemian gaiety, wild parties, and passionate affairs. But du Maurier's Paris is thoroughly benign: while poverty, prostitution, and drunkenness are hinted at, his characters remain untainted by its worst aspects. Thus when the Englishmen meet up with a beautiful young model, Trilby, she remains as innocent as she is beautiful; she may model in the nude, smoke cigarettes, and give herself carnally in her love affairs, but it is true love that she offers. And when she and Little Billee fall in love, she may offer to be his mistress; but when he proposes marriage, she refuses his proposal and disappears from Paris, breaking Little Billee's heart but preserving his name and honor.

The one exception to this rule of uniform benignity is the musician Svengali: spectacularly gifted, unequivocally villainous, and—not coincidentally—unmistakably Jewish. Outside his musical genius, Svengali is marked by a lack of interest in hygiene and an overabundance of interest in Trilby, the latter being manifested in the desire to hypnotize her in order to cure her of migraine headaches. Shortly after her disappearance, he too, decamps; five years later, both suddenly reappear on the public stage. Now Svengali is married to Trilby, and she has mysteriously become an international sensation as a diva, all the more mysterious because the only flaw that could previously be discerned in her was absolute tone-deafness. The three Englishmen hear Trilby (now *la Svengali*) sing and find themselves entranced by her performance—and horrified by Svengali's seeming mastery of her. After plot contrivances too dreary to summarize, Svengali withdraws from conducting and observes one of Trilby's performances from a seat. She is now unable to sing—indeed, she croaks out a tune in her previously tone-deaf manner, causing the audience to riot. After the crowd clears, Svengali is discovered stone dead in the box facing her, victim of a heart attack. Trilby sickens and dies, with Svengali's name on her lips. The still-lovesick Little Billee soon follows, heartbroken that she had died speaking his rival's name. The novel ends with Taffy and the Laird learning the secret of Trilby's vocal success from Svengali's villainous assistant, aptly named Gecko: Svengali had hypnotized Trilby into artistry and into loving him; only under his mesmeric spell could she perform.

This summary can only begin to suggest the sources of the novel's popularity. It fits generically into a number of narrative structures extremely popular at the time: fin-de-siècle occultism, for example, and sheer sentimental melodrama. Its treatment of bohemian Paris, too, was doubtless a powerful incentive to popular esteem. Much of that world was indirectly known to the Anglo-American reading public—Murger was not translated into English until 1895, but articles in the British periodical press communicated the essence of his Parisian sketches in the 1870s and 1880s. Du Maurier's novel made *la vie bohème* widely available, but with a sense of safety: his racy Paris, with its spicy intimations of free love and nude modeling, is nevertheless depicted with large doses of bourgeois nostalgia for youthful indiscretions pleasantly remembered but safely past.

But neither of these facts explains the link between the novel and the spectacular cultural enthusiasm of its audience—its ability to generate the frenzy that greeted its arrival. The best explanation I can supply here is that this text was perfectly suited to meeting the multiple cultural needs of the middlebrow class fragment—hence the lack of equivalent rages for other contemporary texts that appealed to other audiences: although there were sales aplenty, there were no *Barabas* or *Quo Vadis?* manias, for example. The novel provided a painless thumbnail sketch, almost a taxonomy, of the European artistic and musical world, ranging from an idealized portrait of the Parisian *vie bohème* to a thoroughly satirical representation of "the most bourgeois of bourgeois living rooms" and stopping just about everywhere in between.[12] The novel offered itself, that is to say, as a cultural how-to kit; it provided a handbook to the facts and figures of the high-cultural experience, painless instruction in the minutiae of high culture. Indeed, with its grammatical lapses, its colloquial zest, its racy narrative, its violation of generic norms ("freedom of mind, freedom from artificiality, absolute freedom from conventionality," wrote Charles Dudley Warner in *Harper's*, conflating du Maurier's authorial skill and his heroine's unconventional morals),[13] even its abundant illustrations, the novel addressed its readers with an unpretentious immediacy enacted on all levels: language, grammar, plot, and the physical appearance of the book. More important, the text also offered the middlebrow reader a vivid account of the experience of being *truly* cultured, a reproduction of the inner processes of high-cultural response—an account that makes those processes not only available to this particular audience but, more important, their property.

The novel performs the latter task with particular force in the vivid and prolonged passages that are devoted to Trilby's musical performances—"the chapters, the wonderful chapters," Warner wrote, "in which the author gives a hint to all singers of the power there may be in the simplest song" (636). Here du Maurier's treatment of his musical culture is particularly significant: he thereby offers the reader entry into the most privileged precincts of distinction. For, as Bourdieu acutely if somewhat sardonically observes,

> nothing more clearly affirms one's class, nothing more infallibly classifies, than tastes in music. This is of course because . . . there is no more "classificatory" practice than concert-going or playing a "noble" instrument (activities which, other things being equal, are less widespread than theatre-going, museum-going, or even visits to modern-art galleries). But it is also because the flaunting of "musical culture" is not a cultural display like any other: as regards its social definition, "musical culture" is something other than a quantity of knowledge and experiences combined with the capacity to talk about them. Music is the most "spiritual" of the arts of the spirit and a love of music is a guarantee of "spirituality." (18–9)

Music, in other words, is a site of particularly intense struggle on the battlefield of taste. Since responses to music are defined by custom, convention, and the dominant discourse of Western aesthetics as expressions of an inner nobility of spirit that—ideally—depends on neither class nor circumstance and is, at least in theory, free from the determinations of cultural capital, it is by affirming the power of their intuitive response to music that listeners claim most immediately a social éclat and value. *Trilby*'s vivid depictions of the music, the lyrics, the effects of "even the simplest song upon all singers"; its use of the second person throughout these sections; its narrative depiction of an ordinary, tone-deaf woman transformed magically into a singer of genius: all these endow its audience with a powerful sense of its own capacities of aesthetic response and hence arm it for battle on the terrain of taste.

In these chapters the novel offered its audience another gift as well: an uncannily precise guidebook to *Trilby*-mania. For in its musical sections, *Trilby* is nothing if not a novel about the public reception of art, and specifically a spectacular, a frenzied, public reception of art. An audience, any audience, has only to hear Trilby sing to fall into a Bacchic delirium:

> When the song was over, the applause did not come immediately, and she waited with her kind wide smile, as if she were well accustomed to wait like this; and then the storm began, and grew and spread and rattled and echoed—voices, hands, feet, sticks, umbrellas!—and down came the bouquets, which the little page-boys picked up; and Trilby bowed to the front and right and left in her simple *débonnaire* fashion. It was her usual triumph. It had never failed, whatever the audience, whatever the country, whatever the song. (251)

Nor does the Trilby craze stop with her audience. The press is similarly infected—Trilby's performance is met with "a chorus of journalistic acclamation gone mad, a frenzied eulogy in every key" (269). And in a striking anticipation of the mass marketing of Trilby (or is it *Trilby*?) shoes and boots, the novel tells us that "casts of her alabaster feet could be had at Brucciani's, in the Rue de la Sourcière St. Denis. (He made a fortune.)" (280).

I want to designate this quality of the text as the most telling, and most problematic, aspect of its middlebrow status: the fact that the audience responding to *Trilby* could learn the lineaments of its own behavior from the novel—learn from that text itself, that is, how to respond to the cultural experience it depicts in such vivid detail. In so doing, the novel provided that audience with a critical perspective on its own conduct: the novel reflects on the nature and implications of *Trilby*-mania through an analysis of the causes and consequences of "Trilby-mania." In a literalizing echo of fin-de-siècle cultural commonplaces and a remarkable adumbration of twentieth-century mass culture theory, those performances are portrayed as a kind of a mass mesmerism, a hypnotic spellbinding of the crowd that induces both fascination with and a slavelike dependence upon the figure of Trilby herself. In their experience of the novel, in other words, *Trilby*'s readers were both learning to act as *Trilby*-maniacs and invited to see themselves as *Trilby-maniacs*: learning simultaneously to act out their cultural enthusiasm and to see that enthusiasm as something lower or lesser.

Consider, for example, the positive and negative charges that accrete to the analogy between Trilby as hypnotic subject and the audience that Trilby both cultivates and enthralls. When hypnotized, Trilby is told that she "shall *see nothing, hear nothing, think of nothing but Svengali, Svengali, Svengali*" (57, emphasis du Maurier's); similarly, after they encounter Trilby, her audience can see, hear, and think of nothing but Trilby, Trilby, Trilby. Indeed, we are shown that what we might want to call (in allusion but contradiction to Brecht's "A-effect") Trilby's "T-effect" lasts not only for the duration of her performance but leaches into the very subsoil of her audience's psyche; following their exposure to Trilby's song, Taffy, the Laird, and Little Billee can quite literally dream of nothing else—when they can sleep at all. (In this they are like Trilby herself, who dreams incessantly of Svengali after he hypnotizes her.) The same is the case with the audience, which has not had the pleasure of knowing and loving Trilby since youth; the songs of Trilby affect it, too, on the most basic, the most elemental, of psychic levels. We are told, in a lengthy description of Trilby's performance in Paris, that just as Svengali's voice does to Trilby so Trilby's voice "forces itself on you" until you feel as though "all your life is changed for you":

> Waves of sweet and tender laughter, the very heart and essence of innocent, high-spirited girlhood, alive to all that is simple and joyous in nature
> ... all the sights and scents and sounds that are the birthright of happy
> children, happy savages in favoured climes—things within the remembrance and reach of most of us! All this, the memory and the feel of it
> are in Trilby's voice ... and those who hear feel it all, and remember it
> with her. It is irresistible; it forces itself on you, no words, no pictures,

could ever do the like! So that the tears that are shed out of these many French eyes are tears of pure, unmixed delight in happy reminiscence! (257)

But, as the conflation of the language of possession and domination with that of regressive soothing suggests, Trilby's hypnotic voice has a dual effect on the audience. On the one hand, the effect of Trilby's voice is therapeutic, cathartic, curative. Just as Svengali's hypnotic voice heals Trilby of her migraine head-aches, so Trilby's mellifluous voice cures her audience of its heart-ailments: it brings even the jaded, misanthropic French public in touch with buried feelings and repressed memories, with, in short, "happy reminiscence." On the other, less benign hand, her voice induces what can only be called a species of collec-tive insanity. Even "an audience made up of the most cynically critical people in the world" "burst into madness" on hearing Trilby; indeed, it regresses all the way to a state of prehuman monstrosity: "the many-headed rises as one and waves its sticks and handkerchiefs and shouts" in acclamation (252, 257, 258).

This lability of the T-effect—its power to induce both intense anxiety and soothing, healing peace—is the prime example of the novel's own intense am-bivalence on the question of the audience and the source of its extraordinary effect on an equally divided middlebrow public. The novel evinces a fundamental conflict in attitudes toward spectatorship itself, suggesting that a spellbinding artistic representation is to be understood both from a perspective that valorizes the vision of the highbrow and from one that reinforces the vision of the low-brow—to be viewed both *in bono* as a therapeutic dip into the daemonic, or *in malo* as a pernicious and terrifying species of mass madness.

This multidimensional ambivalence is expressed—and sexualized—by the re-lation between Trilby's efforts and those of her ostentatiously Jewish "master," teacher, and husband, Svengali. It is one thing, that is to say, to image intense audience response in terms of a beautiful young woman whose native purity of spirit, whose pristine and innocent spontaneity, speak directly if enthrallingly to the emotions of her listeners; it is quite another to think of that young woman as being merely an extension of the will of an evil genius. And the questions raised by Trilby's submissive relation to Svengali—a relation whose sexual di-mensions a shocked and titillated nineteenth-century audience did not fail to note—point increasingly and problematically beyond her to the audience itself: to that audience that, to follow this chain of argument through, is asked to experience through Trilby's manifestly beautiful voice neither an intensified ver-sion of its own repressed emotions nor a purified version of Trilby's ennobled ones but rather an odd and troubling reproduction of Svengali's least benign sentiments and impulses. The more they imitated Trilby, the more they imagined themselves falling under the spell of Svengali.

This ambivalence—this increasing negativity—about the effect of public performance on the audience is, I think, the key to *Trilby*'s function at its historical moment. For if, as I have been arguing, the moment of *Trilby* is also the hour at which forms of cultural response were crystallized, then the precise ideological work in which the novel and its own readership collaborate is both robust and overdetermined. Through its representation of that audience, the novel simultaneously endorses and problematizes the idea of cultural enthusiasm itself; it sketches for its middlebrow audience a highbrow vision of a lowbrow audience response, but it does so in such a way as to render high and low indistinguishable from one another. In so doing, it both sketches and creates a space for a new form of cultural experience, that form I have been calling middlebrow.

Thus on the one hand, the enthralled and hypnotized but wildly enthusiastic audience in this novel resembles nothing so much as the highbrow's dream of the once boisterous, now thoroughly tamed mass audience, a dream that, as historians have shown, late-nineteenth-century conductors and concert impresarios struggled mightily to achieve and in the construction of which the genteel audience seemed increasingly willing to collaborate.[14] Indeed, the treatment of this crowd by Svengali and his instrument Trilby is of a piece with the behavior of those new cultural authorities who presented themselves as experts in the gentle arts of high-cultural crowd control in both England and America. "Nothing seems to have troubled the new arbiters of culture more than the nineteenth-century practice of spontaneous expressions of pleasure and disapproval in the forms of cheers, yells, gesticulations, hisses, boos, stamping of feet, whistling, crying for encores, and applause," writes Lawrence Levine of these conductors, and to tame the savage audience Theodore Thomas, Frederick Stock, and a group of martinet-cum-conductors following in their footsteps (usually European in origin and Germanic in demeanor) all deployed tactics ranging from the posting of regulations ("No spitting," "no hats") to sarcastic gestures from the podium, to the public humiliation of offenders. It was, for example, reported of Thomas that "when his audience relapses into barbarism on the subject of encores, he quietly but firmly controls them. I have seen him . . . leave the stand and quietly take a seat in a corner of the orchestra, remaining there until he had carried his point."[15]

Similarly, while Svengali and Trilby excite their audience into frenzies of emotion and paroxysms of enthusiasm, they also chasten, order, and discipline their crowd—and they do so without resorting to the heavy-handed tactics their contemporaries deployed. Contrary to custom and convention, Svengali makes the audience stand enthralled for exactly one hour until he releases them into frenzies of approbation and, exactly like Theodore Thomas, sends them out into the night without benefit of the expected encore. But unlike Thomas, his efforts require no exceptional gestures, no extraordinary efforts; all he needs to perform this task is the melodious, mellifluous, and thoroughly enthralling voice of Trilby.

If its representation of the crowd comports itself to the most extravagant high-brow dreams of social order–making, other elements in the novel enact a powerful subversion of the highbrow imaginary—just as, as I will argue soon, the novel's labile popular reception undermines the picture Levine draws of disciplining authorities and self-punishing audiences. The crowd this novel depicts is, surprisingly, not one composed exclusively of the lower orders. To the contrary, it is the elite that is most visibly infected by Trilby-mania—at least within the space of *Trilby*—a mania they conspicuously refuse to display under other circumstances. Du Maurier is quite unsparing in his representation of the boredom of the haute bourgeois salon or the snobbery of an aristocratic English cenacle. *Even* the most socially exalted, this text tells us, are susceptible to the effects of Trilby and Svengali, and when they are so affected, they adopt the mannerisms and the behavior of the lower classes; they become at once maddened and obsequious, frenzied and subservient. When a "famous composer" named Herr Kreutzer describes Trilby's acclaim in Vienna, he makes clear that the spectators are of high—of the highest—social standing and that their behavior works to strip them of the lineaments of aristocratic reserve even as they strip themselves of the signs of their status: "Ze women all vent mad, and pulled off zeir bearls and tiamonts and kave them to her—vent town on zeir knees and gried and gissed her hands. . . . Ze men schniffelled in ze gorners, and looked at ze bictures, and tissempled—efen I, Johann Kreutzer! efen ze Emperor?" (202). Not only does the diegetic Trilby-mania know no social bounds, it works actively to undo social difference, to level social hierarchies, to reduce all classes and orders to the same frenzied common denominator.

The result is, however, overdetermined, if not confusing. The novel portrays the establishment of cultural hierarchy without endorsing the reification of social hierarchy; it speaks a classed discourse about taste without sanctioning, while in fact contesting, the class assumptions that underlie that discourse. It thus simultaneously moves in two directions, toward what we might call elitist and anti-elitist assertions about the effect of art on its audience. In what might be best described as a populist move, the elite audience for culture is shown to act exactly like its lower-brow counterparts; but in an antidemocratizing, indeed highly elitist move, the novel images both in the terms of hypnotic mind control, recapitulating both the imagery and the logic of class difference in the very means it uses to deny it.

The novel's message to its culturally insecure audience is equally dual. While its readership is theoretically empowered by the novel, the means of that empowerment are ultimately constraining. The novel's audience is endowed with a conceptual apparatus for thinking of its own response that leads to a sharply bifurcated vision of itself as an audience. Readers are asked simultaneously to identify with the enthusiasm of the listeners and to critique their very enthusiasm—to participate vicariously in the response of the audience and to see that response from a critical position exterior to it. This knot of intensely contradictory subject-positions is fully tied at the end of the novel in the last representation of audience response it has to offer us, in which Trilby fails to sing. None of the seductive intimacy of the earlier scenes is evident here; the audience, Taffy, Little Billee, and the reader all stand in uncomprehending alienation from Trilby, as Trilby herself does to (the now dead) Svengali. At this moment of utter estrangement, the crowd is fully personified and is represented in terms that bring to a dizzying climax the novel's play between highbrow and lowbrow: "Then came a voice from the gods in answer [to Trilby's incomprehension, voiced not in French but in English]: 'Oh, ye're Henglish, har ye? Why don't yer sing as yer *hought* to sing—yer've got *voice* enough, any'ow! why don't yer sing in *tune?*'" (295).

At the moment when hypnotic control is withheld, in other words, du Maurier's audience significantly speaks with one voice, and that voice possesses a distinctly lowbrow intonation. But the class position of that crowd contrasts utterly with its own words; the crowd's focus on Trilby's linguistic identity (a matter of mystery throughout the book) and its emphasis on vocal propriety ("sing as yer *hought* to sing") both stand in ironic contradistinction to its own demotic diction. At this moment, the pattern of taste and class allegiances we have seen throughout the novel is significantly reversed. Instead of a highbrow audience acting with lowbrow frenzies, here a lowbrow audience acts with a highbrow concern for dictional and musical proprieties. But this reversal only indicates the true nature of the control to which the audience is now subjected; it reveals that that control is now thoroughly internalized. Released from the gentle discipline of Trilby and the domineering mastery of Svengali, the audience demonstrates how well it has learned its lesson from them. At precisely the moment of freedom, the audience turns its own inner anxieties about cultural response outward and disciplines the figures who hitherto have disciplined it.

I would like to locate at this moment within the text the full unfolding of what I am calling mania of the middlebrow—and a full unfolding of its labile dynamics. The switch from valorization to demonization is shown by the text itself to be not an outbreak of carnivalesque populist critique but a thoroughly middlebrow response, a response that conjoins cultural squeamishness with cultural excess; this is a moment in which the critique of the embodiments of high culture like Svengali and even Trilby is shown to be predicated upon an impossibly idealized vision of high-cultural propriety, and in which the response swings from adulation into revulsion at the sight of any deviation from a hyperbolized and overinvested norm.

This moment bears further significance for my current project. In the actual historical as well as the textual Trilby-mania, too, we witness what we might appropriately label a mania in the sense not only of "enthusiasm" but also of "rage": a "rage" expressed simultaneously for and at the products and possibilities of high culture, a rage predicated upon the idealization of high culture that the negative moment of that response contests. The lability of this rage is perhaps best represented in the shifting centers of popular response to the text within *Trilby*-mania itself. Just as the fictional audience switches from the idealization of Trilby to her denigration at the moment her voice disappears, so too the readers switched from idealizing Trilby to denigrating Svengali. We can already see the figure of Svengali lurking behind the early stages of *Trilby*-mania—as the evil ringmaster, for example, snapping his whip in the Greatest Show on Earth. As I suggested earlier, the enormously popular stage version of the novel, starring the illustrious Sir Beerbohm Tree, was entitled *Svengali* and focused its attention on that malevolent figure. As *Trilby*-mania faded into the mists of cultural memory, the figure of Svengali exerted an increasing force. The tale was made into two movies: a silent film of the twenties entitled *Trilby* was followed by a marvelous 1937 British film called *Svengali* and starring John Barrymore, a vehicle more or less carried by his remarkable performance (and far more faithful to the illustrations and plot of the novel than its predecessor). And when the novel is mentioned at all today it is usually remembered not for the culturally apotheosized and oft-imitated Trilby but for the figure of Svengali, whose name has even entered, I was delighted recently to learn, the *Dictionary of American Slang*.

This increasing focus on Svengali, however, is merely an instance of the more general cultural ambivalence I see lurking within *Trilby*. For Svengali, too, expresses in acute form the ambivalence that governs the text's response to high culture itself:

> Svengali playing Chopin on the pianoforte, even (or especially) Svengali playing "Ben Bolt" on that penny whistle of his, was as one of the heavenly host.
>
> Svengali walking up and down the earth seeking whom he might cheat, betray, exploit, borrow money from, make brutal fun of, bully if he dared, cringe to if he must—man, woman, child, or dog—was about as bad as they make'm. (45)

Within the very character of Svengali, in other words, ambivalence about "culture" becomes structural, definitional; he is at once, and by the very same logic, a representative of the cultural ideal and the cultural abject, the purest of the pure, the filthiest of the filthy. And it is no coincidence that Svengali is so spectacularly a Jew. Indeed, in some sense he could not have been anything else; to put the matter differently, the ambivalence of cultural affiliation that the novel both enacts and constructs could only find its full expression in the culturally dual figure of the eastern European Jewish artistic genius. This move, I think, marks *Trilby*'s greatest contribution to the very field of culture it defines; and by far the most interesting aspect of this development is the way that the racialized, anti-Semitic discourse used to delineate the artist participates in the same cultural bends and folds, the same large-scale ambivalences, that make *Trilby*-mania such a powerful and important model of middlebrow taste-formation.

MIDDLEBROW MANIA AND RACIAL HYSTERIA

In making this argument, I take issue with some of the most insightful studies of the late-nineteenth-century representation of the Jew, all of which suggest the centrality of *Trilby* to the construction of the literary image of the Jew in the fin de siècle but which end up seeing in the novel only a negative stereotype, a stereotyping that prepares the text for (at the very best) complicity in the nascent world of Nazism. Thus Edgar Rosenberg has argued in his sprightly and humane study of representations of the Jew in English literature, *From Shylock to Svengali*, that Svengali is a veritable compendium of the various stereotypes that get loaded onto the figure of the Jew: the wandering Jew, the demonic Jew, the bestial Jew, the occult Jew, and so on. But more important for Rosenberg, Svengali translates age-old stereotypes into modern form, preparing them for yet more sinister twentieth-century deployments.

> Svengali survives: Svengali leering, Svengali screaming anathemas, Svengali rumbling "dors, ma mignonne," Svengali having his face bashed in, Svengali baring his yellow fangs in a rictus of hate—the smutty genius, the sticky spider-cat, the Devil bedeviled, the Errant Jew solemnizing his glory and his death behind the taffeta curtain of a London music hall.[16]

For Rosenberg, little or no credit is to be given to the other side of Svengali's character—to his undeniable expression of a kind of musical genius; instead, "we get in Du Maurier a fairly clear double-intention, a case of wanting one's cake and eating it . . . and since Svengali's sordidness is really, as Shaw says, a good deal more impressive in the long run than Svengali's genius, one is apt to remember the smuttiness after one has forgotten the power and the glory" (251).

It is as difficult utterly to reject Rosenberg's position as to quarrel with Shaw's epigram. But I think Svengali's double nature needs to be taken more seriously than Rosenberg takes it, and for several reasons. The first is my distrust of what we might call the Shylock effect: the well-known tendency of abjected figures to hijack critical response to the works that represent them. As with Shylock and *Merchant* criticism, Svengali obsesses Rosenberg so much that his prose comes to take on the very cadences of du Maurier's slangy depiction of Svengali in denouncing him. In doing so, he ignores what seems to me the most important feature of Svengali, a feature that suggests the salience, I would argue, of Jewishness to the issue of the middlebrow itself. Through Svengali, the book conflates Jewishness and artistry *tout court* in ways that have powerful implications for the avid middlebrow audience that confronts both. Indeed, as I will now more fully argue, the most important cultural work that this text performs is accomplished in and through that conflation.

To be sure, it's important to acknowledge not just Svengali's villainy but its larger implications. Indeed, this representation of the Jew as sexual corrupter of innocent gentile women ascended to a virulent power at this moment in racial and cultural history. "Du Maurier belonged to the era when anti-Semitism acquired its scientific pedigree," notes Olivier Cohen-Steiner. "The diffusion of racist theories that argued for the superiority of the German race [in this period] was to give aid and comfort to visceral anti-Semites." More than "aid and comfort" was involved here for anti-Semites: at this cultural moment in particular, too, European culture responded to the increasing presence of eastern European Jews in western Europe with a burst of racist collocations centering on sexual hysteria, stressing the "prepotency" of the Jewish blood surging forth, like Svengali, from the mysterious East. Like Freud, Svengali was born in a small Austro-Hungarian village; unlike Freud, he carries with him unmistakable traces of the Jew as understood and interpreted by nineteenth-century ethnographic thought: he is filthy, both morally and physically; he is dark; he is hook-nosed; he is endowed with mysterious sexual power yet suffused with a sense of deep powerlessess; his extended family, which moves about with him, lend to him vague suggestions of promiscuity and incest. Mesmerism has been habitually associated with the figure of the Jew in contemporary anti-Semitic discourses as well. His hypnotic power combines with his sexual appetencies, as I have already discussed, to suggest that we read the novel quite directly as a parable of the power of the miscegenating Jew to overcome the purity of the Western European stock. As Cohen-Steiner puts it, "if Svengali were successfully to consummate his union with Trilby, it would no longer be the crime of sorcery of which he would be guilty, but rather that of *Rassenschande* [the Nazi term for shameful race-mixing]."[17]

But there are more specific cultural associations to be brought to bear on Svengali at the same time. For the connection of the Jew to musical genius (or the lack thereof) was a particularly hot topic in the nineteenth century, both in England and on the Continent, and one that places Svengali in the middle of a full-scale cultural debate about Jewishness and artistry negotiated in terms of music. From an English point of view, this battle was joined by no less a figure than Benjamin Disraeli. In *Coningsby*, the sexually ambiguous Jewish financier Sidonia rhapsodizes to his young charge Coningsby about the innate superiority of the Jewish race's "passionate and creative genius" in ways that quickly turn to the musical as a prime instance of that genius:

> The ear, the voice, the fancy teeming with combinations, the imagination fervent with picture and emotion, that came from Caucasus, and which

we have preserved unpolluted, have endowed us with the almost exclusive privilege of MUSIC; that science of harmonious sounds, which the ancients recognized as most divine, and deified in the person of their most beautiful creation. I speak not of the past; though, were I to enter into the history of the lords of melody, you would find it in the annals of Hebrew genius. But at this moment even, musical Europe is ours. There is not a company of singers, not an orchestra in a single capital, that is not crowded with our children under the feigned names which they adopt to conciliate the dark aversion which your posterity will some day disclaim with shame and disgust. Almost every great composer, skilled musician, almost every voice that ravishes you with its transporting strains, springs from our tribes. . . . [T]he three creative minds to whose exquisite inventions all nations at this moment yield, Rossini, Meyerbeer, Mendelssohn, are of the Hebrew race; and little do your men of fashion, your muscadins of Paris, and your dandies of London, as they thrill into raptures at the notes of a Pasta or Grisi, little do they suspect that they are offering their homage to "the sweet singers of Israel."[18]

Sidonia's wisdom rapidly became a commonplace of philo-Semitic thought, particularly in the era of racializing discourse, as for example in the studies of Hebrew hymns that filled the pages of the *Jewish Chronicle* in 1887, where the power of those sorrow-songs was linked to a native Jewish propensity for musical genius; as in the portrayal in George Eliot's *Daniel Deronda* (1876) of Herr Klesmer (his name means "music" in Yiddish but also chimes with that of Mesmer), who may embody the sexual attractiveness of a Liszt (or a Svengali) but speaks in the sternest voice of high culture when he dissuades Gwendolwen Harleth from a career as a singer; as, most impressively, perhaps, in the ethnographic writing of Joseph Jacobs, the foremost Anglo-Jewish student of Jewish racial identity. Writing as late as 1905, sixty years after Disraeli and ten after *Trilby*, Jacobs speculated that "the custom of separation between the sexes in Jewish religion following Leviticus" might have some "connection with Jewish proficiency in music, which in its origin seems to be also regulated sexual emotion."[19] The association between Jew and musical genius that was so tendentious for Disraeli had become commonplace for Jacobs, and the tinge of sexual feeling associated with the musical Jew for Disraeli and du Maurier alike had passed entirely into the matter of Jewish identity *tout court*.

But the anti-Semitic side of the coin was also present throughout this period. *Coningsby* was widely reviled by a number of Victorian periodicals, none more so than *Punch*, which offered a parody by one of its foremost contributors, William Makepeace Thackeray, entitled *Codlingsby*. At the center of that parody (which offers a farrago of standard anti-Semitic insults of the time, ranging from an emphasis on the Jew's nose to suggested connections between the Jew and sexual perversity, especially incest) the author offers a precise counter to the scene in which Disraeli rhapsodizes the special Jewish genius for music:

> When Miriam ... at a signal from her brother, touched the silver and enameled keys of the ivory piano, Lord Codlingsby felt as if he were listening at the gates of Paradise, or were hearing Jenny Lind.
>
> "Lind is the name of the Hebrew race; so is Mendelssohn, the son of Almonds; so is Rosenthal, the Valley of the Roses: so is Lowe or Lyons or Lion ..." Rafael observed to his friend; and drawing the instrument from his pocket, he accompanied his sister, in the most ravishing manner, on a little gold and jewelled harp, of the kind peculiar to his nation.[20]

Whatever else one can say about it, the deflationary turn from the aggressive claim of special Jewish musical powers by Disraeli to the insistence on the Jew's harp—the most debased of instruments, indeed, an instrument that requires no special talent to play whatsoever—suggests that a negative reaction accompanied claims for Jewish artistic genius in England. This reaction, at least in the British Isles, was only exacerbated by the popularity of operas written by Jews on the Continent; for that very form was suspect, and brought to the lips of British high-culture observers denunciations of the mass public that strongly resemble the passages I have quoted from *Trilby*. According to the *Contemporary Review* of 1868, to cite but one example, "opera's popularity can be explained by one fact: the public in all ages are children, and react like children. Let one person clap and others are sure to follow."[21] Even if Disraeli claimed for "the sweet singers of Israel" a special power and ubiquity, the increasing popularity of Jewish composers on the Continent was also ascribed by these reviewers to the decadence of musical tastes of the times—Meyerbeer and Halévy come in for particular disdain in the same review. And when, ten years later, the *Saturday Review* noted that the last great composer who had written in England was Mendelssohn, it was not meant as a positive indicator of musical health.[22] Indeed, these denunciations enter into *Daniel Deronda*, ironically enough, in no small measure through the voice of Herr Klesmer, whose denunciations of Meyerbeer echo the more overtly anti-Semitic ones circulating on the Continent that firmly bound the Jewish influence in music, especially opera, to a full-scale cultural degradation.

But, as this last example suggests, the fullest expression of this anti-Semitic tendency can be found not in England, which was, after all, a musical backwater at this time—hence the presence of the Herr Klesmers—but rather in the Continental discourse on music itself, particularly that offered quite contemporaneously with Disraeli's by Richard Wagner. Indeed, there is little better evidence of the strange similarities of the anti- and philo-Semitic imaginaries than the continuity between Disraeli's claims for Jewish superiority in music and Wagner's for Jewish inferiority. The power of Mendelssohn, Halévy, or Meyerbeer designated for Wagner a crisis of cultural value that led him to a perception strikingly similar to Disraeli's: "utterly incapable of announcing himself to us artistically through either his outward appearance or his speech, and least of all through his singing, [the Jew] has nevertheless been able in the widest-spread of modern art varieties, to wit in Music, to reach the rulership of public taste."[23] But for Wagner the triumph of the Jew designates the degeneration of musical value itself, particularly of the inner spiritual essence that once powerfully obtained in Europe and that the essentially inert, dead, deadening, uncreative Jew was so massively destroying.

> The Jews never could take possession of this art, until *that* was to be exposed in which they now have demonstrably brought to light—its inner incapacity for life. So long as the separate art of music had a real organic life-need in it, down to the epochs of Mozart and Beethoven, there was nowhere to be found a Jew composer: it was impossible for an element entirely foreign to that living organism to take part in the formative stages of that life. Only when a body's inner death is manifest, do outside elements win the power of lodgement in it—yet merely to destroy it. Then indeed that body's flesh dissolves into a swarming colony of insect-life; but who, in looking on that body's self, would hold it still for living? (99)

Only an entirely new form of musical drama, indeed of art itself, would be capable of replacing this dead body—and of repelling any further Jewish degeneracy or rot.

This double representation of the Jew as master or maggot, as inspired plucker of the sacred harp or "a wretched take in—a miserable lyre" (*Punch*'s description of the Jew's harp in yet another denunciation of Disraeli),[24] fits exactly with the labile dynamics of the middlebrow taste-fragment. In the discursive context surrounding the figure of the Jewish musician-genius stands, on the one hand, the language of cultural value, on the other, that of cultural degeneracy; the figure of the Jew embodies each at one and the same time yet is positioned to do so in thoroughly antithetical ways. And if the question of the nature and powers of art, imagination, and artistry thus becomes here inevitably and irretrievably part of the racial politics of the late-nineteenth and twentieth centuries, it is also the case that the politics of Jewish identity become a part of the battles that occur within and around the rise of middlebrow culture. The devotées of high culture, the mediators or masters of middlebrow culture, find in the Jewish composer (and hence Svengali) an instigator of the social corruption that goes along with the rise of a mass audience for art, for music, for literature; middlebrows act out their own cultural aggression vis-à-vis these authorities by embodying their own worries over the proper nature of high culture in bourgeois society—its links to the bohemian or avant-garde, its intimate relation to the body and to the experience of pleasure—in the very same figure. The lability of the figure of the Jew, its ability simultaneously to exemplify or symbolize utterly antithetical positions in a cultural debate, is the key to its deployment. Neither the Wagnerian position (which has so many weird echoes in the language of Adorno, for whom Mozart and Beethoven represented the last moment of cultural power) nor the Disraelian position (which has its afterimage, as I discuss hereafter, in philo-Semitic theorizing about the special connection of the Jew to genius, artistic and otherwise) achieved hegemony either in the mid–nineteenth century or thereafter. Instead, they have played off against each other in ways that bring the conflicted, conflictual discourse on culture and the Jew from the starry flights of German philosophy or the ironic meditations of Matthew Arnold directly into the experience of would-be cultural enthusiasts.

Here too du Maurier's text shows the way, although in a highly complex and fraught manner. The Disraelian and Wagnerian impulses make their way into the representation of one more character besides Svengali (or his assistant Gecko); in addition to the hypersexualized Jew carrying on his merry miscegenating way, there is another character who contains what the novel refers to as "Jewish blood"—none other than the novel's other truly talented artist, Little Billee. In a remarkable passage early on, the narrator describes this sensitive artist, a genius in painting as fully as Svengali is in music, as follows:

> [I]n his winning and handsome face there was just a faint suggestion of some possible very remote Jewish ancestor—just a tinge of that strong, sturdy, irrepressible, indelible blood which is of such priceless value in diluted homeopathic doses, like the dry white Spanish wine called montijo, which is not meant to be taken pure; but without a judicious admixture of which no sherry can go round the world and keep its flavor intact; or like the famous bulldog strain, which is not beautiful in itself, and yet just for lacking a little of the same no greyhound can ever hope to be a champion. So at least I have been told by the wine-merchants and dog-fanciers—the most veracious persons that can be. Fortunately for the world, and especially for ourselves, most of us have in our veins at least a minim of that precious fluid, whether we know it or show it or not. *Tant pis pour les autres.* (5)

The passage is a fascinating one, and briefly to unpack its obscurities can help guide us through not only the racial politics of this text but those of the middlebrow taste-fragment in the years that follow. The balance between anti- and philo-Semitic inscriptions of the artistic genius of the Jew is precisely articulated, for example, in the notion that Jewishness in small doses and small doses alone connects to artistic genius—indeed, in "homeopathic" ones, which is to say that somehow the presence of a little bit of Jewishness in the "blood" counteracts the possibility that too large a dose would lead to Svengalism, ugliness, and moral evil. Thus, to suggest how complicated this nexus of affects proves to be, the very *Rassenschande* that Cohen-Steiner tells us lurks as the ultimate nightmare of the embrace of Trilby and Svengali itself begins to be the salvation *from* Jewishness: the quite literal hybridity of the Jew, the intermingling of the Jew with "native" gentile stocks that has been undertaken from time immemorial, is both the guarantee of a certain quickening in those stocks and the best defense against a rampant Jewishness. Most powerfully and most importantly, we are told that this is the essential condition of the novel's middlebrow audience as well; it is the condition that defines "us" as readers and places "us" in exactly the same condition of hybridity as that which constructs Billee: "most of us have in our veins at least a minim of that precious fluid, whether we know it or show it or not." Insofar as we are readers interested in culture, excited by music, thrilled by art— insofar as we are middlebrows—we are Jews. And more: du Maurier tells us not only to feel this guiltily but to exult in it, to adopt the Disraelian idiom of distinction, of specialness, as the very sign of our own artistic distinction, of the powerful assertion of our own taste: *"tant pis pour les autres."*

The knot of subject positions I have been tracing in both *Trilby* and *Trilby*-mania, then, has this larger salience: it suggests that the interplay of philo- and anti-Semitic understandings of the Jew and culture we have been seeing at the center of the Arnoldian project lives a prodigiously double afterlife in the projects of middlebrow culture. In the middlebrow imaginary, to be cultured is to be dangerously (or pleasurably) touched with the alien force and sexual energy socially ascribed to the Jew; it is also to be, however temporarily and within reason, touched with the aura of specialness, distinction, and superiority that is also culturally ascribed to that figure. Yet, at one and the same time, to be middlebrow (rather than highbrow) is to be saved from the fate of being *too* Jewish, too outré, too extreme, too powerfully connected to this model of identity and response that is so visibly connected with the powers of otherness. The brilliance of this formulation is that it allows both the middlebrow and the maker of middlebrow culture like du Maurier to express a certain rage at or contempt for each other— as high-cultural perverts, as a massified audience of inept lemmings—even as they keep their mutually constitutive relation going unaffected. The former gets to have its philistinism and its valorizaton of art; the latter gets to proclaim his or her access to the transcendent powers of culture yet express superiority to that version of it proffered to the middle-class readership. And as I have been suggesting throughout this chapter, it is the Jewishness of the Jew that allows both to do so. The double construction of that figure by du Maurier and the ambivalent response to that figure by the mass audience of *Trilby*-maniacs allow what Bourdieu calls "the game of culture"—the process of social positioning by means of cultural knowledge or competence—to go forward without undue friction or conflict.

The concern of the rest of this book is to trace the way that game continued to get played in the rest of the twentieth century by means of the figure of the Jew. As I will show in more detail in the next chapter, the associations worked out in middlebrow culture between the Jew, artistic genius, and sexual perversity only augment in the first decades of the twentieth century; indeed, we shall see them affecting a nervous fin-de-siècle novelist by the name of Henry James. Middlebrow relations to "culture" evince this set of conflations in England and America for the rest of the century (although, to be sure, it goes underground or is expressed in less dire ways after the Nazi exploitation of it in their campaign against "decadent" Jewish art), creating unexpected and odd associations and affiliations in the years to come. I want to conclude by looking at one powerful example from a century after *Trilby*-mania; one has merely to look at the career of the greatest exponent of classical music to the popular market, Leonard Bernstein. Definitively Jewish, he refused the suggestion of his mentor, Serge Koussevitsky, that he change his name to Leonard Burns, offended Catholics by including Jewish material in his Mass, and persistently brought Jewish material to his secular music—e.g., the *Jeremiah* symphony. Fluent in popular musical modes, and powerfully able to use the new media like television to reach the mass audience with his famous *Young People's Concerts*, Bernstein was persistently thought of by his audiences and the press as a kind of modern-day creator of the Trilby-effect, one who could translate his own complex emotional states to orchestra and audience alike with absolute immediacy. As his career progressed, he found exactly the kind of celebrity that Svengali and Trilby discover on their European tour. Far more than any of the other great conductor figures of the 1940s and 1950s—Stokowski or Toscanini in particular, both of whom powerfully prefigured his appeal to the media—Bernstein became a celebrity ratified as such in language that echoes du Maurier's with uncanny accuracy: "This Bernstein of the vanities was mobbed by adulators wherever he went. Groupies thronged his green room and kings and presidents asked him to dinner. To the man in the street, he was the most famous living musician. In New York and Jerusalem, he was a living god."[25]

The overtones of sexual perversity that du Maurier brought to his character were not missing from Bernstein's popular reception, either. His homosexuality was more or less an open secret in the musical world, and that secret rapidly spread over into the public sphere as well. He was more or less "outed" shortly after his death; the full extent of his voracious promiscuity (with members of both sexes but more with men than women) and its effects on the politics of preference was retailed to the public by Joan Peyser in 1987 and has been explicated by any number of other biographers and critics since then. These revelations, as one might expect, have had no discernable effect on his public reputation. Bernstein's recordings with both Columbia and Deutsche Grammophon have all been reissued, often in that surest sign of middlebrow appeal, special "collectors'" editions, and have sold splendidly; more important perhaps, much of his own music has recently been revived with great success. Indeed, it is precisely his most "middlebrow" music that has been received most spectacularly; as I write, Bernstein's failed musical *1600 Pennsylvania Avenue* is running quite successfully on Broadway, and his other failed musical, *Trouble in Tahiti*, has been equally successful in the West End of London.

As should not surprise us: for one lesson of the cultural reception of *Trilby* is that for the augmenting middlebrow audience of the twentieth century—one even further built, as I will discuss in more detail hereafter, by the paperback revolution, the rise of mass media like radio and television, the spread of art and music education in secondary schools, the growth of populations attending colleges and universities—the artist as artist is always already a charismatic genius, sexually potent and perverse, and irrevocably Jewish. In some sense, Bernstein's performance of that role was increasingly just that; and later in life he took to playing the very part of Svengali—by not only seducing promising young protégés but also affecting a melodramatic cape and dressing in such a way as to emphasize his exotic, Levantine appearance. As such he became the very embodiment of a figure that had, from the nineteenth century forward, delighted the vast new audience for traditional high culture, the artist as the charismatic Jewish pervert— who terrified James.

But before I move on to Henry James, it's important to mention a matter that preoccupies me later in this book. The career of this modern-day Svengali teaches us another lesson: that in the field of cultural production opened up by the middlebrow, spaces get created for racial and ethnic others who were previously denied entry there—and that the first group to make its way onto this field was Jews. For in the early twentieth century, Jewish writers, artists, and intellectuals negotiate a space for themselves in a progressively less anti-Semitic culture in precisely this guise: as authorities dispensing cultural guidance to the awed and insecure middlebrow audience that was prepared by texts like *Trilby* to identify cultural authority with Jewishness in both its benign and malign aspects. All the cultural mechanisms I have cited as being crucial in the making of both the middlebrow qua middlebrow and middlebrow culture, especially the changes in the publishing industry that wrought the paperback revolution and the rise of college and university attendance as a normal part of middle-class life, created significant if contested vectors of Jewish entry into the cultural mainstream in the period beginning in the 1920s and continuing to the present day. There, as I will suggest, Jews had to wrest authority from genteel, largely Protestant cultural mediators by deploying a series of tactics ranging from transgression to appropriation and stopping just about every place in between. (It is not insignificant, to cite Bernstein again, that he spent much of his later years as the conductor of the most notoriously anti-Semitic orchestra in the world, the Vienna Philharmonic—and that he made his late reputation by reconverting it to the music of Mahler, himself, to complete the chain of ironies, a Jew who had converted to

Catholicism in order to conduct that very orchestra in the 1910s.) It is not the least of the attending ironies that the end of this process for many of these figures was precisely the unmaking of their own Jewishness, their assimilation to a cultural and social sphere that has had little space for the kind of maniacal energy and cultural lability so spectacularly epitomized by Svengali, so spectacularly enacted in the fin-de-siècle mania of the middlebrow.

4

Henry James and the
Discourses of Anti-Semitism

POWERFUL LINKAGES BETWEEN THE IDEA, and the ideal, of culture and the figure, and fact, of the Jew circulate, I have suggested, throughout Anglo-American high culture in the nineteenth and twentieth centuries. Such conjunctions were particularly prominent in the 1910s and 1920s, the period when anti-Semitic and anti-immigrant sentiment boomed in England and America, climaxing politically in the Immigration Restriction Act of 1924 but resonating throughout the next decades before receding in the aftermath of World War II. In the works of many writers of this era, the Jew is invoked as a corrupt agent debasing culture with a thoroughgoing commercialism, insistent sexuality, and resolute neuroticism. Such a representation notoriously animates the poetry of Pound and Eliot; the topos filters into Fitzgerald's *Gatsby* and (ironically) Hemingway's *Sun Also Rises*; it is present, in a somewhat more subtle form, in Willa Cather's *Professor's House*.

Over the past decades an abundance of critical attention has been paid to these works and to the questions they pose; so much so, as I suggested in chapter 1, that even the *New Yorker* treats the anti-Semitism of high modernism as an emblem of High Culture gone hideously wrong. The anti-Semitism of an Eliot or a Pound or their confreres is by now a scandal so often reiterated that it has become less than scandalous, the thrusts of accusation and the counterthrusts of defense so familiar that one has difficulty remembering just how much ought to be at stake in the combat.[1]

In this chapter, I want to probe more deeply into this association between the Jew and the corruption of a putative cultural ideal—trace the work it does, note the problems it poses, parse the solutions it offers—in the work of a somewhat earlier figure, who has arguably stood the test of time more successfully than the figures I just named: Henry James. Specifically, I want in what follows to inquire into the relation between Henry James and the genteel, high-culture anti-Semitism of the 1890s and the early years of the twentieth century. I do not propose to do so by staging an inquisition of Henry James the historical subject. If *I* were put to the question on this matter, I would state for the record three things: that, like many in his class and caste (although with the significant exception of his brother William), James subscribed reflexively to a number of bigoted beliefs; that among these were beliefs we could and should label anti-Semitic; but that James's *explicit* anti-Semitism is of a garden variety at best. It is not as wildly pestiferous as that of his contemporary Henry Adams (whose anti-Semitic expressions are closest to those of a writer like L. F. Céline in his association of Jews, vermin, and filth); it is not as interestingly weird as that of his predecessor and friend James Russell Lowell (who was both a partisan of the superiority of the ancient Hebrews and an exponent of the view that contemporary Jews were a debased lot who should be done away with); he was not even as cunningly snobbish vis-à-vis Jews as his great friend Edith Wharton (whose heroine Lily Bart faces the choice of dying of consumption or marrying a rich Jew—and chooses the former).[2] But James's textual responses to the figure of the Jew, particularly in the last three decades of his career, were neither unnuanced nor insignificant. These responses originated in the matrix of associations we saw in *Trilby*-mania, one that was evident throughout the fin de siècle and the early years of the twentieth century: the set of discourses that conflated Jews, art, and social degeneration. James's reaction to this discursive intertwining was not anti-Semitic in any simple sense of the term. Indeed, precisely because that figure embodied so many of the qualities he valued, the Jew became the vehicle through which James staged an encounter with his deepest anxieties about himself, his art, and the relation of both to his culture. But the result of this response was also problematic. The Jew got placed by James in a position as culturally resonant—particularly in the works of the moderns who were to follow him—as it is ethically untenable: that of the scapegoat who bears the burden of social degeneracy so that the writer or artist or intellectual can be absolved of it. How James's response came to be, how it is related to those of his contemporaries, and how it points beyond that of his successors even as it anticipates their own patterns of anti-Semitic sentiment, is my subject here.

I focus in particular on James's final and greatest novel, *The Golden Bowl*, for it is here, I think, that the connection between the Jew qua Jew and the very principles of Jamesian art is put at its most problematic, and it is here, too, that James's responses to the figure of the Jew ramify most fully. But first I turn to some of the problems involved in thinking of James under the sign of Jewishness by spending some time with a crucial text, *The American Scene*. And with good reason: this record of James's travels in the United States in 1903 and 1904—the height of Jewish immigration to American shores—presents his most extensive and most explicit commentary on the presence of Jews in American life, climaxing in an encounter with what he calls "a Jewry that had burst all bounds" on the Lower East Side of New York. One's first reading of these pages inclines one to the view of James as a card-carrying anti-Semite. There is here, to give a taste of the Jamesian anti-Semitism I just termed trivial, a bit of physiognomical tomfoolery whose ugliness is not so much concealed by the circumlocutions of simile as revealed by the very casualness with which it is drawn into James's textual net: "It was as if we had been thus," James writes, "at the bottom of some vast sallow aquarium in which innumerable fish, of over-developed proboscis, were to bump together, for ever, amidst heaped spoils of the sea."[3] Such efforts at ethnic comedy recur frequently in James's writing—there are jokes about Jewish noses in *Roderick Hudson* (1874), in the short story "Glasses" (1898), in James's critical dialogue on *Daniel Deronda* (1881)—and its appearance here may remind us why, of all the many studies of James that have proliferated over recent years, the one entitled "The Homespun Humor of Henry James" has yet to appear. But these expressions have a more problematic side as well. In nineteenth-century race theory, the concept of the Jewish nose was installed in scientific discourses as well as popular ones as a prime marker of Jewish racial identity.[4] And the explanations for its alleged protuberance pointed to just how slurring those discourses could be. American physical anthropologist Robert Bean hypothesized that the so-called Jewish nose was a classic example of a Lamarckian acquired trait—a piece of adaptive behavior that rapidly becomes genetically encoded; the Jew's nose elongated and upturned, Bean thought, because it was "the hereditary product of a habitual expression of indignation."[5]

When we put *The American Scene*'s Jewish nose joke in this context, we begin to see the problems of thinking about James under the sign of anti-Semitism. If James's little piece of ethnic stereotyping represents nothing more than a failed piece of ethnic humor, then it deserves to be little noticed and quickly forgotten. But if it indicates his deployment of contemporary racial categorizations that render him complicit in the dominant course of late-nineteenth-century race thinking, then we need to regard his responses to the Jew with a high degree of suspicion. The latter tendency is heightened later in the same passage at the moment when James discusses "the intensity of Jewish aspect," which, according to James, "makes the individual Jew more of a concentrated person . . . than any other human, noted at random." "Or is it simply rather," James continues, "that the unsurpassed strength of the race permits of the chopping into myriads of fine fragments without loss of race-quality?" (132).

This last note, the note of racial essentialism, is ominous indeed; and it may incline us to move more in the direction of a negative opinion of James. Language like this reminds one of Sartre's eloquent unveiling of the irrational "primitive conviction" that lies behind the tissue of "intellectual principles" held by the anti-Semite: "For the anti-Semite what makes the Jew is the presence in him of 'Jewishness,' a Jewish principle analogous to phlogiston or the soporific virtue of opium. . . . Without the presence of this metaphysical essence, the activities ascribed to the Jew [by the anti-Semite] would be utterly incomprehensible." More to the point, language like this reminds one of a similar expression of sentiment among Anglo-American intellectuals at James's moment: eugenic theory.[6]

Both the gentry anti-immigration activists of the fin de siècle and their successors in the full-blown eugenics movement of the early years of the twentieth century claimed that Jews composed a homogenous racial body whose identity was signified by their distinctive appearance and whose entry into American society, if not forestalled, would lead to a corruption of the native Anglo-Saxon stock.

> The foal of a Percheron dam by a Percheron sire is, of course, a Percheron. . . . The children of Jews have their parents' prominent nose and other physical attributes. Like breeds like, and when the unlike mate together the progeny have some of the characteristics of both parents. It is beyond question that the vast infusion of southern European blood which is each year passing into American veins is certain to work marked changes in the physical appearance of Americans. It is reasonable to conclude that the future American will be shorter in stature, swarthier of skin, that his skull will be shorter and broader, that probably his nose will be more prominent than is the case today.[7]

If one continues to pursue the analogy, disturbing parallels between James and his eugenicist contemporaries continue to present themselves. For, as this quotation suggests, it is not a far step from positing Jewish race qualities to fantasizing Jewish race conquest. Two vectors of such Jewish racial triumph persist in the eugenics literature. The first and most common is the concept of "overbreeding"—promiscuous overproduction that has been held against virtually every social out-group (the lower classes, Irish, African Americans, Italians, Asians) from the time of Malthus to the present day. The second, more specific to this moment, is the hypothesis that Jews were intrinsically better able to negotiate the demands of the urban environment, precisely because of their physical deficiencies and over-developed intellectualism. Unfit for a healthy life of rural toil, the Jew will triumph precisely because such a life is being replaced by that of the dreadful, sprawling city. Here, too, James's response to what he calls the "Jewish conquest of New York" is troublingly similar to that of his more explicitly racist contemporaries (131). Their language of immeasurable reproduction, moreover, suffuses James's description too. His dominant tropes are those of a thoroughly urban population "swarming," "bursting all bounds" and, most tellingly, "multiplying." "Multiplication, multiplication of everything, was the dominant note," James writes, and then continues: "[the] children swarmed above all—here was multiplication with a vengeance" (131). To play with James's terms, the vengeance that these proliferating progeny quite literally embody is one that will soon be wrought on the civic life of the American nation. For while it is the sheer plentitude of humanity crowded into the Lower East Side that James the social observer notes, it is the "agency of future ravage" that James the "incurable man of letters" fears. This rapidly reproducing minority, James argues, will transform utterly the English language and hence frustrate the already tenuous possibilities of a national culture (138).

James's response to the Jew in *The American Scene*, then, possesses disturbing analogies to the most offensive slurs that circulated through elite gentry circles—slurs that, it is important to remember, widely circulated in the popular press of his time.[8] Given these kinds of continuities of thought and language, it is no wonder that many critics from Maxwell Geismar forth have treated James as a raving anti-Semite of the worst sort. "Quite logically," Geismar wrote,

> for this frightened, insecure, snobbish temperament, that is, he substituted the later [Jewish] immigrants as a new scapegoat, demon, and villain on his own "native scene." . . . Reaching backwards, as for refuge, into the Victorian myths of his history, James called upon the resources of Anglo-Saxon romance to combat this tumultuous and threatening menace to the American tradition. . . . But no modern St. George emerged in answer to Henry James's appeal, unless it was the Germanic Hitler who used a more barbarous mythology, combined with all the skills of scientific-industrial technology, to quell the same alien presence.[9]

Given the hyperbolic move at the end here, few Jamesians followed quite so far into denouncing the Master's anti-Semitism.[10] And, as I suggest in the next chapter, Jewish Jamesians of the 1950s and 1960s frequently ignored James on Jews in the process of remaking him in their own image. But historians of American anti-Semitism—John Higham, Michael Dobkowski, Robert Singerman—treat James as the literary embodiment of the eugenics-minded anti-Semitism of his moment, and when they do so, they point to the passages from *The American Scene* I have noted here.[11]

But merely noting the similarities between James's language and perceptions and those of his anti-Semitic contemporaries is not, in my view, sufficient. Indeed, it errs in precisely the same way that anti-Semitism does, by mistaking metonymies for identities, confusing similarity and same. For when one places these passages from *The American Scene* in the context of elite eugenic theorizing and anti-immigrant activism, one's prevailing impression is one of James's mildness. For all his worrying about the threat posed by Jews to the English language, there is a countervailing and envious sense of the vitality of Yiddish culture. Indeed, James's real worry here seems to be the deadening effect of American mass culture on intellectual and cultural activity on the Lower East Side; he even goes so far in his culture-critique as to valorize the Jew as a potential bearer of enlightenment to a stultifying American cultural scene. And despite his horror at the sheer numbers of bustling aliens, he goes to some lengths to distinguish between the Lower East Side and the "dark, soul-stifling Ghettos of other remembered cities"; the former represents, he argues, in a trope that tellingly resembles the most resonant figurations of an earlier New England elite, a shimmering city on a hill. "For what had it really come to but that one had seen with one's eyes the New Jerusalem on earth? What less could it have been, in its far-spreading light and its celestial serenity of multiplication?" (133). In this "city of redemption" the very signifiers of the eugenics movement are transformed. "Multiplication" figures here as a trope of enlightenment and redemption, not one of cultural despair.

Moments like this tempt us to see James as a kind of a philo-Semite, performing the opposite maneuver of his friend James Russell Lowell. If Lowell moved from a philo-Semitic appreciation of the ancient Hebrews to an anti-Semitic denunciation of contemporary ones, James shuttles from a sense of horror at the Jew's degeneracy to an appreciation of that figure as the very emblem of a redeeming modernity. This movement has been noted by contemporary critic Ross Posnock, who cunningly argues that James's labile representation of the Jew enacts his most profound response to the problem of modernity itself. Posnock suggests that James generates from his encounter with the Jew a new model of subjectivity that prizes otherness without incorporating the Other and a politics of nonidentity that valorizes the alien without plotting the alien's extinction through assimilation into the American mold.[12]

Both the philo-Semitic and the anti-Semitic readings of James have their merits, although my own sense of the matter inclines me closer to Posnock's pole than Geismar's. But each misses, I think, the main thrust of James's engagement with the figure of the Jew. That engagement, I suggest, is one that we have seen expressed in *Trilby*-mania and that gets further worked out in the poetry of the modernists; it is the one that connects here James's response to the Jew with the role he names for himself in the passage cited earlier as "the incurable man of letters" (138). I take that self-description quite literally, and am struck not only by its compulsive naming of the author or artist as bearer of disease but by its presence in the middle of a description of Jews. For one of the topoi of the anti-Semitic discourses I have just described is precisely the incurably diseased quality of Jews: these figures are frequently defined as unhealthy bearers of germs, as harbingers and agents of social and cultural sickness. James's self-representation as an "incurable" man of letters signifies his participation in larger discursive currents that identified variously high culture, Jews, and the artist as irrevocably diseased—as, in fact, the bearers of a quite literal social disease, that of degeneration. Indeed, in late-nineteenth- and early-twentieth-century discourses on degeneration, all the terms I have been discussing in James's response to the Lower East Side are present in shuffled but similar combinations. Jews, writers, overcrowded urban environments, anxieties over sexuality, fears about cultural identity: all these circulate through the fin-de-siècle debates about a putative cultural "degeneration"—and all, except one, point the finger of degeneracy directly at

James himself. That one—and it is one that James, somewhat against his better instincts, seizes upon as his own candidate for locus of cultural corruption—is none other than the Jew.

JAMES, THE JEW, AND THE DISCOURSES OF DEGENERATION

The nineteenth-century degeneration debate, like its more recent incarnation, the late-1980s American controversy over "national decline," constituted an extraordinarily powerful controversy over a resonant pseudoquestion, one that involved medical authorities, cultural critics, and imaginative writers in protracted struggle over the causes and consequences of the alleged deliquescence of that highly problematic entity, "western civilization."[13] And one major strain in European discourse identified the agent and embodiment of a putative cultural degeneration as the Jew. One associates this current of thought most powerfully with that supreme dialectician of decadence, Nietzsche, for whom Jews are both more degenerate and more vital than their Christian successors:

> Considered psychologically, the Jewish nation is a nation of the toughest vital energy which, placed in impossible circumstances, voluntarily, from the profoundest shrewdness in self-preservation, took the side of all the *decadence* instincts—*not* as being dominated by them but because it divined in them power by means of which it can prevail against "the world."[14]

But Nietzsche's meditations were not composed in a vacuum; rather, he was responding to and writing against the most powerful currents of his own social moment. As Sander Gilman has observed, the Jew was located throughout nineteenth-century medical and evolutionary discourses as a pernicious atavism, a remnant of a past stage in history's Hegelian march toward the consummation of a Christianized Spirit.[15] But the Jew was more than just an evolutionary relic. In that coupling of ontosenetic and phylogenetic logic that provided so much of the buttressing for nineteenth-century scientific racism, Jews—along with Africans, Asians, and the lower classes—were seen as the incarnation of instincts that individuals and societies alike needed to outgrow. Childish, primitive, and thoroughly inbred, the Jew embodied a "stage of sexual development which was understood as primitive and perverse and therefore degenerate" (214–5).

The Jew embodied another form of "degeneration" as well—mental enfeeblement or madness. Such propensities, it was claimed, resulted from Jewish endogamous marital practices—precisely the quality, of course, that constituted Jews as a distinct and identifiable "race" at all. "Nervous diseases of all sorts," according to the authoritative voice of Charcot, "are innumerably more frequent among Jews than among other groups," and he identified the prime cause of such illness as Jewish inbreeding (quoted in Gilman, 115).[16] Charcot's diagnosis was confirmed in a number of discursive arenas and professions. In the established professions of law and medicine and the newer ones of psychiatry, physical anthropology, and criminal anthropology, the image of the fatally inbred, sexually aberrant, and congenitally neurasthenic Jew rapidly became canonical.

The link between this strain of medicalizing discourse and the topos of cultural degeneracy was both powerful and problematic. On the one hand, inbreeding was seen to result in weaker nervous systems, lesser degrees of self-control, and a decline in physical well-being. On the other, cultural degeneration was seen as the result of *inter*breeding, assimilation, a mingling that, in the terminology of the time, resulted in the mongrelization of the races and thence a corruption of Western culture.[17]

The force of this paradox, it might be noted, was activated with particular power among the Anglo-American social elite, and the burden of its double imperatives was largely borne by that increasingly demonized figure, the eastern European immigrant. As in Nietzsche, the eastern European Jew was paradoxically defined by Anglo-American race theorists as being more degenerate *and* more vital than his gentile counterparts. "In the community of rascals," wrote Paul Popenoe, editor of the house journal of the American Genetic Association, the greatest rascal might do best. "In the slime of the modern city the Jewish type, stringently selected through centuries of ghetto life, is particularly fit to survive, although it may not be the physical ideal of the anthropologist."[18] Indeed, in a paradox repeated throughout the eugenics movement, the Jew was constructed as a figure whose very sexual degradation—his lack of sexual self-control, the size of his families, his omnipresent lechery—betokened his extraordinary vitality, all the more so for a WASP elite obsessed at the turn of the century with its own falling birth rate and the multiplication of Ostjuden and other European immigrants. We shall see, not to anticipate the argument too fully, precisely this fear at work in the reproductive anxieties of James's *Golden Bowl*, where the sterility of the ironically named Adam Verver (and the limited family constructed by his daughter, who bears only one child) is contrasted with the unchecked proliferation of the Jewish antique dealer, the ominously named Gutermann-Seuss.

Following directly from this paradox, linked to it by the bemusing metonymies of racism, was another double bind. As a result of the Jew's insistence on maintaining his "race and religious purity," it was claimed, the ameliorative influences of intermarriage and cultural assimilation could not curb the potent force of his race energy; yet the assimilation of the Jew by means of marriage was not, to say the least, a consummation devoutly to be wished. For the eugenicists, Jews' refusal to intermarry or intermingle only heightened the decline of the native stock when they did. The Jew "stubbornly resists absorption and assimilation by the peoples among whom he casts his lot," complains Henry Suksdorf on one page of his

1911 racist-eugenicist tract *Our Race Problems*, but then on another he turns around and worries about precisely that possibility:

> the strong current of inferior quality has set in from the unprogressive east and north-east of Europe.... This bodes no good for the American nation. If this rising flood will continue to pour into this country, and if this undesirable human element will continue to be absorbed and assimilated, American manhood and womanhood, and American civilization, will certainly deteriorate.[19]

The only acceptable solution is to limit immigration—or worse; and it bears repetition at a moment when similar anxieties pervade our culture that the most extravagant fantasies of nineteenth-century eugenicists anticipated the most nightmarish realities of twentieth-century history.[20]

In fin-de-siècle Europe, by contrast, the brunt of this discursive current was borne not by lower-class immigrants but rather by those figures then entering the mainstream of high-cultural life: assimilating Jewish intellectuals. For, as I observed in chapter 1, those intellectuals sought to enter precisely the professions that occupied themselves with denouncing Jews for promoting social degeneration—and at precisely the moment in which these denunciations began to crescendo. This situation put assimilating Jewish intellectuals in a position that could only be described as problematic. If they accepted the dominant terms of their own professions, they would reinforce the anti-Semitic tendencies of their own social moment. But if they failed to accept those terms, they would consign themselves to the very social margins they were entering those professions to escape. The response of these intellectuals and professions was appropriately complex. While they tended to accept the terms of the degeneration debate and even, frequently, identification of the Jew as a prime source of degeneracy, many sought to shift the burden of degeneracy to other forms of causation and consequence. Gilman has influentially argued that Galician-born Freud constructs the neurotic in precisely the image of the eastern European identity he was sloughing off at this moment, and for these very reasons. Equally telling were the efforts of Caesare Lombroso, the Italian-born criminologist and Zionist. On the one hand, Lombroso argued that the Jewish struggle against persecution was responsible for the high levels of mental illness detected among Jews. On the other, he sought to shift the burden of degeneracy by focusing his efforts on such groups as Africans, prostitutes, and that entirely new social type, homosexuals.[21]

This discursive task was central to the most influential writer on the topic of degeneration, the one who bundled together medical and anthropological treatises on degeneracy and packaged them for broad public consumption: Max Nordau. Nordau's activities were wide-ranging; originally trained as a doctor, he settled into a career as a journalist, freelance cultural critic, and Zionist activist. In this last role, I believe, his antidegeneration polemics are most accurately to be read. His writings on degeneracy and those on the conditions of the Jews share a common anti-anti-Semitic agenda. Like Lombroso, to whom *Degeneration* is dedicated, Nordau's Zionist writings adopt much of the accepted linkage between Jews and forms of degeneracy: if ghetto-dwelling eastern European Jews and city dwellers are shown to be afflicted with the physical and mental signs of degeneracy, then the salvation of both is to be found in the physical vigor and self-assertion embodied by a new, affirmative concept of Jewish identity that Nordau labeled "the muscle Jew." Nordau's massively influential tome also continued the Lombrosian shift away from the identification of the Jew as prime degenerate to a broader definition of degeneracy, one that scapegoated other marginalized figures and groups as instances of degeneracy.

Indeed, Nordau expanded the notion of degeneration to include just about any deviation from just about any norm, norms that were often antithetically related to one another. Excitation and exhaustion, sexual indulgence and asceticism, criminality and aspirations to sainthood: all these incompatible qualities are to be read as signs of degeneration. And its causes are equally global; they consist for Nordau in nothing less than modernity itself. When the pressures of modern urban life impacted the weakened nerves of the "cultured classes"—those removed from the bracing life of manual labor and relentlessly exposed to cultural expressions of pessimism and gloom—the result was nothing less than a mass "derangement of the nervous system" leading to fatigue, exhaustion, and boredom.[22] This derangement, perceptible in the very nerves and brain cells of the modern urbanite, may have been caused by environmental factors but, Nordau continues, soon came to be encoded on the very level of the genotype, passing from one generation to the next in that parade of cultural declension Nordau calls degeneration.

The efficacy of such a move, from an anti-anti-Semitic point of view, is obvious. Nordau redefined the degeneration debate by identifying the effeteness of the elite and modernity itself, not the hypercontagious Jews, as the source of cultural decline and social corruption. Indeed, it is a sign of both his intent and his effectiveness that Nordau was ultimately able to turn the discourse of degeneration against those who would use it to demonize Jews—against the anti-Semites themselves. "German hysteria manifests itself in anti-Semitism, that most dangerous form of the persecution mania, in which the person believing himself persecuted is capable of all crimes (the *persecuté persecuteur* of French mental therapeutics)" (209). But Nordau did more. He nominated a figure to replace the Jew as arch-degenerate: the avant-garde artist. Contemporary literature's preoccupation with morbid subject matter like crime, sexuality, slum conditions; its defiantly antibourgeois attitude; its evocation of decadence, gloom, pessimism, malaise; the well-publicized nonnormative sexualities of so many fin-de-siècle artists: all these provided Nordau with evidence of the fundamental degeneracy.

And in a move tellingly similar to that of those who read the degraded conditions in which Jews were forced to live as evidence of their racial inferiority, Nordau defined the artist as not merely the witness of degeneration but also its source. Focusing first on the sex lives and nervous breakdowns of actual fin-de-siècle artists and then sliding to their efforts at formal experimentation, Nordau argued that the works of contemporary artists and writers functioned as the vector of "mental contagion" through which these "graphomaniacal fools and their imbecile or unscrupulous bodyguard of servants" were able to spread the "Black Death" of "degeneration and hysteria" throughout the social body. "The feeble, the degenerate will perish," Nordau prophesies. "The aberrations of art have no future. They will disappear when civilized humanity will have triumphed over its exhausted condition" (233).

It would be tempting but misleading to treat the degeneration debate as a conflict between anti-Semites and Zionists proposing Jews and artists as competing candidates for the role of prime agent of cultural decline. (For one thing, the two positions were far from incompatible, as the Nazi conflation of "degenerate" and Jewish art suggests.)[23] But what one can conclude about this debate is that the particular spin that Nordau wished to give to the issue, the shifting of the burden of degeneration from the Jew to the socially and sexually marginalized artist, fell on receptive ears in Anglo-American middle-class culture, already prepared to think the worst about that last figure from *Trilby*-mania. *Degeneration* was translated into English in 1895 and instantly became an object of popular enthusiasm and dinner party discussion; a rough analogue would be the vogue surrounding Allan Bloom's *Closing of the American Mind* in the late 1980s. William Dean Howells recorded in *Harper's* with characteristic sanity both the extensiveness of Nordau's popularity and some of the reasons for it.

> The most interesting fact in regard to this book is that it has made any stir in the world [at all], and Dr. Nordau's success here, where a great many people are now reading his book, is another proof of the advantages of living in Europe. . . . If some ill-conditioned American had written his senseless and worthless book, we should scarcely have troubled ourselves to say it was senseless and worthless, far less tried to prove it. But it comes to us with authority, coming across seas, and because it comes from Germany, where the critical thinking is somewhat slow, it is believed to be deep and thorough.[24]

For all his nationalist scorn, Howells reminds us that Nordau achieved a considerable degree of cultural authority, at least to those for whom the discourses he invoked were novel and unfamiliar. Howells also reminds us that Nordau achieved this authority because he used his patter of pseudoknowledge to give a name (many names, in fact) to the anxieties that the middle-class audience faced throughout their social experience. What some middle-class folk called Svengali,

Nordau named "Degeneracy," and in so doing (without intending to do so; he was a man of the utmost tolerance and sophistication) he lent a patina of respectability to the strains of anti-intellectualism, homophobia, and philistinism that coursed through the middle classes in fin-de-siècle England and America. The moment of Nordau, it is important to remember, was also that of the Oscar Wilde trial, and the public outrage directed at Wilde fed and was fed by Nordau's reflections on the artist as agent of degeneration.

That current in the discourse of degeneration that Nordau emblematized had an energizing effect on many artists and writers, some of whom took to proclaiming themselves degenerates with an enthusiasm bordering on zeal. But this discursive tendency posed a serious threat to an eminent, if deeply depressed, fin-de-siècle writer named Henry James. To this (probably closeted) gay man and (undeniably) audaciously experimental writer, the cultural linkage between degeneration, stylistic hypertrophy, nonreproductive sexuality and madness carried a powerful charge. The responses of his critics, many of whom were at that very moment lamenting the obscurity of his style and decrying his participation in "decadent" journals like the *Yellow Book*, only served to heighten the association between what James felt were the very grounds of his psychic health—his art— and corruption, madness, and disease. James's despairing response is partially registered in his private communications of the period, particularly those letters following the public brutalization of his play *Guy Domville*, in which he lashes out at the insensitivity of the brutish, philistine public and positions himself as a martyr to the cause of art. But it is in his stories and novellas of this period that James evinces his greatest defensiveness in the face of this cultural indictment, and to a certain extent, his internalization of its terms. Writers in his tales of this period are aging, diseased, dying, or dead; their writing is cryptic, crabbed, incomprehensible, ignored; those readers who do take them up rapidly become obsessed monomaniacs. Authorship is connected with an inability or disinclination to enter modes of reproductive sexual relation—sometimes charmingly ("The Lesson of the Master"), sometimes problematically ("The Figure in the Carpet"); tellingly, these tales are collected in volumes with titles like *Terminations* and *Embarrassments*. This tendency reaches something of a climax with *The Sacred Fount*, which provides a virtual textbook of the topoi of degeneration. The obsessive ravings of that novel's voyeuristic narrator, who decides that one member of each couple he spends a country weekend with is draining the life energy of the other and spends his time attempting to verify his hypothesis, firmly link the enterprise of fiction-making itself to madness, sexual eccentricity, and, ultimately, exhaustion and decrepitude. And at this very same moment, James begins to use the language of the degeneration debate itself to define his art. Many of James's most famous ascriptions and assertions demand to be read in light of the culturally resonant links between madness, nonnormative sexualities, and the vision of the artist as carrier of the disease of degeneracy. "The madness of art";

"that queer monster, the artist": expressions like these suggest a James who finds himself inscribed in a position of dementia and monstrosity even as—especially because—he turns those suspicious definitions of his office into a badge of authorial pride.

With this context in mind we can best understand James's responses to the Jew in the 1890s and the early years of the twentieth century. For even as James turns his authorial attention to the link between the artist and "the degenerate," references to Jews appear in his fiction with increasing frequency. Many of these, to be sure, are relatively innocuous, if still somewhat offensive. The narrator of the 1896 story "Glasses," which I mentioned earlier, notes the proliferation of Jews at French resorts at precisely the moment that Jews are being excluded from American hotels: "there were thousands of little chairs and almost as many little Jews, and there was music in the open rotunda, over which the little Jews wagged their big noses."[25] While the point of the story, as its title suggests, is to limn the perceptual apparatus of the somewhat unattractive speaker, there doesn't seem to be any implicit or explicit ironization of this slurring position. Jews make similar minor but still disturbing appearances in many of James's fictions of the 1890s. For example, a vulgar Jew named Tischbein romances Maisie's mother in *What Maisie Knew*, to the embarrassment of all concerned; and in a short story published in the same volume as *The Turn of the Screw*, "Covering End," James depicts a group of boorish Jewish visitors to the country house that gives the story its name, describing them as

> four persons so spectacled, satcheled, shawled and handbooked that they testified to a particular foreign origin and presented themselves indeed very much as tourists who, at a hotel, casting up the promise of comfort or the portent of cost, take possession, while they wait for their keys, with expert looks and free sounds. . . .
>
> They met Mrs. Gracedew with low salutations, a sweep of ugly shawls and a brush of queer German hats. . . . The only lady of the party—a matron of rich Jewish type with small nippers on a huge nose and a face out of proportion to her little Freischutz hat . . . [broke] the spell by an uneasy turn and a stray glance [at a portrait of the owner of the house]. "Who's *dat?*"[26]

To be sure, these moments all suture Jews to the decline of traditional institutions like marriage or resorts, or the commodification of culture; indeed, the last of these is the focus of the action of the rest of "Covering End," which turns on how much a country house and its portraits may or may not return if they are sold. Despite these ramifications, these finally are instances of the kind of anti-Semitism I find trivial—no better than that of many of James's contemporaries, to be sure, but also no worse. More important, in my view, are the responses to Jews and the deployments of Jewishness to be found in two important texts of James, his 1890 novel *The Tragic Muse* and his 1904 masterpiece *The Golden Bowl*. Here, the Jew enters James's fiction both as a character-type and as a figurative resource in a manner that can only be described as overdetermined. Characters, sustained metaphors, and offhand references all connect, in a manner one could label either compulsive or consistent, the Jew to the making of art and the transmission of cultural value.

I want to concentrate on the second of these texts in some detail, both because it is one of James's richest and most important fictions and because the roles played by Jews and Jewishness in it resonate most fully in the definition of James's artistic endeavor. But I need briefly to parse *The Tragic Muse* because it sets the stage so brilliantly for the kinds of complex work that get done through the Jew in the later text (and, indeed, in *The American Scene*). The eponymous heroine of that novel is a woman named Miriam Rooth, an actress modeled on the actresses Sarah Bernhardt and Rachel, whose preternatural dedication to her craft is played off against the other central character, Nick Dormer. Nick spends most of this interminably long fiction trying to decide between a career as a portrait painter and one as a Parliamentarian: urging him to the former is an aesthete by the name of Gabriel Nash; rewarding him for the latter is a beautiful and wealthy widow, Julia Dallow. Life in politics promises heteronormative as well as monetary fulfillment; a life dedicated to art is at least as potentially bereft of heterosexual intimacy as it is of financial security. It is this life that the monomaniacal Miriam chooses. Gifted with an exotic Levantine beauty and an ability to manipulate appearances but not, originally, a full acquaintance with the dramatic classics, Miriam dedicates herself to artistic success with a ferocity that other characters—Nick's sister Biddy, for example—find "monstrous."[27] The life of art, as in all of James's narratives of this moment, is associated with forms of human conduct that stand outside the norms of social and sexual conduct alike. And here, virtually alone in James's fiction, those qualities are associated with a Jew.

Or they are so associated for much of the novel, but—unlike a Rachel or a Sarah Bernhardt—the more successful she becomes, the less Jewish Miriam seems. At the end of the novel, much is made about the fact that she has married her non-Jewish manager, and this act is associated with the loss of her ethnicity. "A servant opened the door and was ushering in a lady.... 'Miss Rooth!' the man announced; but he was caught up by a gentleman who came next and who exclaimed with a gesture gracefully corrective: 'No, no—no longer Miss Rooth!' " (523). This "gracefully corrective" gesture is meant to signify Miriam's new identity as a married woman—to announce that she is no longer *Miss* Rooth. But it more fully announces her metamorphosis from a Jewess into another racial identity—that she is no longer Miss *Rooth*. It announces what the rest of the book confirms, that Miriam has transformed herself into "Miriam," the culturally apotheosized tragic—and comic—muse of the London stage. As such, she knows no ethnicity or race. She is merely—magnificently—herself, which is to say that her only race or ethnicity is that of the artist.

I want to designate this swerve as the key to James's deployment of the Jew in the moment of full-scale debates about art and degeneracy. Here James comes close to the conflation of Jewishness, artistry, and nonnormative sexuality that filtered through his culture; but he severs the first term from the second by showing Miriam sloughing off her Jewishness in her accession to full artistic genius. And, in a truly perverse and highly ingenious move, a non-Jewish character is invested with Jewishness precisely as Miriam divests herself of her own. Tellingly, considering the sense the novel gives us that Miriam remakes herself into an entirely new racial or ethnic entity, this figure is her gentile mother, a wealthy woman seduced by her Jewish music instructor, who then turned financier and died before providing for his family. While painting the transforming Miriam (who, it should be added, is spending no little time at this point in the novel attempting to seduce him), Nick Dormer looks at her mother with new eyes.

> Mrs. Rooth's vague, polite, disappointed bent back and head made a subject, the subject of a sketch, in an instant: they gave such a sudden glimpse of the pictorial element of race. He found himself seeing the immemorial Jewess in her, holding up a candle in a crammed back shop. There was no candle indeed, and his studio was crammed, and it had never occurred to him before that she was of Hebrew strain, except on the general theory, held with pertinacity by several clever people, that most of us are more or less so. The late Rudolf Roth had been, and his daughter was visibly his father's child; so that, flanked by such a pair, good Semitic reasons were surely not wanting to the mother. Receiving Miriam's little satiric shower without shaking her shoulders, she might at any rate have been the descendant of a tribe long persecuted. (444)

In this truly weird passage, James initially seems to reinforce the link between the two discourses we have seen brought together with such problematic intensity—the racial identity of the artist and the racial identity of the Jew. But on further examination, it turns out that he does so to dismantle that connection. The work the passage performs is to deconstruct the notion of race itself. Jewish characteristics may be passed on genetically, as Rudolf Roth does to his daughter Miriam; but they may also be passed on by prolonged contact, something like a bad habit, a cold, or a venereal disease. Because she has been seduced by a Jew, then has given birth to her daughter, the gentile is transformed directly into a Jew, even as her daughter transforms herself into a gentile. Indeed, at the end of this passage, it would seem that the two have fully changed places. It is as if there is a certain amount of Jewishness in the Roth/Rooth clan, and when one member of that family divests herself of it to become a punitive gentile, her Jewishness has to pass on to another who becomes the persecuted Hebrew.

Artists and Jews, then, are conflated with each other in this text only so as better to differentiate them; it is as if James is tracing out the terms of the degeneration debate in order to rearrange them in ways that will exculpate him and the artistic vocation he claims for himself and in so doing finds himself almost absent-mindedly inculpating the Jew. A similar dynamic is evident in *The Golden Bowl*, but taken to an even more culturally resonant pitch. Indeed, this work bridges the kinds of concern we have seen in the discourses of degeneracy and James's response to them in the 1890s and in the larger cultural crises centering on immigration and the transformation of host cultures evident in *The American Scene*. For *The Golden Bowl* plays out the drama of racial degeneration on a national, indeed an international scale, and in such a way as firmly to connect James's own artistic crisis to a crisis in cultural value that is negotiated through, as it is represented by, the figure of the Jew.

The Poetics of Cultural Decline: Degeneracy, Assimilation, and the Jew in *The Golden Bowl*

At the center of the knotty and problematic work that concluded James's career as a novelist stands a racial drama that has cultural ramifications. That racial drama centers on the radically ambiguous figure of Prince Amerigo—lover, husband, adulterer and, in the novel's final turn, husband again. Amerigo is represented throughout the text as a figure of racial and cultural degeneracy encoded in his free and easy Italianness; his return to his wife, as a successful assimiliation of the norms and even the identity of the dominant Anglo-American order. Given the concerns of this chapter, and given James's linkage of the remaking of Amerigo and Maggie's marriage to the making of a work of art, it will not surprise the reader to learn that the benchmarks of Amerigo's progress are those other Others who embody cultural degeneration, encode racial difference, and attempt to assimilate but who, in contrast to him, conspicuously fail to do so: the novel's Jews. And more: precisely because they refuse to be assimilated, they play a crucial role in the novel's most problematic narrative actions, the purchase of the Golden Bowl itself by Amerigo and his lover Charlotte as a wedding gift for Maggie Verver and the echoing purchase of Damascene tiles by Adam Verver for his wife-to-be, none other than Charlotte. Indeed, by their very status as stereotypical Jews, the mysterious *antiquari* and the Jewish antique dealer Gutermann-Seuss make themselves indispensable to the novel's narrative action: without them, and without their Jewish commercialism, the novel would not have a plot at all. In so doing, they bring to the novel the full force of their racial equivocality as Jews, allowing James to clarify further his attitudes toward race, art, and the making of cultural value itself. It is not the least, or the least Jamesian, turn of the screw that in so doing the novel's Jews also bring into focus the possibility, if not the necessity, of transcending the category of race itself.

Before I turn to these two crucial, if marginalized, Jews, I want to discuss the novel's thematics of racial and cultural degeneration, concerns that are both faced and finessed through its representations of the two. My claim that *The Golden Bowl* is related to the rhetoric of cultural decline ought not to prove surprising; as critics have frequently observed, that concern is announced on the novel's first page, with its invocation of the representative of the attenuated Italian aristocracy musing on the *translatio* from the Roman imperium to Victoria's thoroughly commercial empire. What is less frequently observed is the topicality of this concern—that the novel was written at a moment when the questions of the decline of the British Empire, the alleged degeneration of the Anglo-Saxon (or British) "race," and the putative deliquescence of Anglo-American high culture all rose to the fore of public discussion and debate. The death of Victoria, the passing of the nineteenth century, and the difficulties of the Boer War provided the immediate occasions for these musings, but they were more credibly motivated by the fact that economically, Britain *was* in a state of decline, at least in comparison with its booming rivals, Germany and America. Whatever the source of the decay—and historians are still debating its causes—its symptoms were noted throughout the English-speaking world; in the years during which *The Golden Bowl* was being written and read, a profusion of books and articles detailed every imaginable sign of the social, cultural, and economic deterioration of England. The decrease in productivity, literacy, health, and public-spiritedness shown by British workers (not to mention their unwillingness to indulge in healthy sports like boxing or football); the deficiencies of the educational system in comparison with those of the Continent and even America; the rise of cheap penny journalism and other forms of mass entertainment; the diminished quality of English literary life: all these were adduced by writers of the Left and Right alike as ominous signs of a more general national deterioration. If I cite the most programmatically stupid of these accounts—an essay in *Blackwood's Edinburgh Magazine* of 1904 on the subject of "[t]he degeneracy of the race"—it is not only to point out how frequently the diagnosis of enfeeblement unwittingly illustrates its own argument but also to give a flavor of the rhetoric that motivated even the less rabid meditations on the future of England in such respectable journals as the *Fortnightly Review* (which posed the question "Will England last the century?" in 1901) or the *Westminster Review* (which asked, "What should England do to be saved?" also in 1901).[28] Here, then, *Blackwood's*:

> The causes of the nation's decay are manifold. Yet in the first rank we must place the prevailing passion for life in town. . . . [T]he decline of agriculture and the sudden wealth of the factories drove the working man to the town and the gin-palace. . . . [The working man's] amusements, no

doubt, increased with his wages,—but he lost self-respect; he lost independence; he paid more for a single room than erstwhile for a cottage; and in spite of easy dissipation, he is to-day far less his own man than formerly. In brief, he who was strong became weak, and he cared not what he lost in strength if he gained in cunning.

And, then, some thirty years since, came education. ("Musings," 272–3)

For *Blackwood's*, "education" was an unmitigated disaster, since it drove students away from the simple pleasures of the body to the debilitating life of the mind. Only if "we could contrive a system of teaching...which did not give way to the snobbish impulse of reading about foreign countries to those from whom physical strength was more precious than the ability to find Timbuctoo upon the map, something might be done in the schools to check the race's degeneracy" ("Musings," 275).

I cite *Blackwood's* not only to point to the currency of the discourse of degeneration but also to direct attention to its racial agenda. Those last words— "the race's degeneracy"—resonated vigorously for an Anglo-American elite contemplating the decline of England, its loss of empire, and the implications of that loss for a booming, nationalist America; indeed, it would seem that fears of racial degeneration frequently and powerfully superintended those recognitions. If it was, as argued John Randolph Dos Passos (whose illegitimate son was the twentieth-century novelist), "an Anglo-Saxon century" and if—as *Harper's Weekly* paraphrased his argument—the "Anglo-Saxon will be the dominant race a century hence," then any possible imperial decline in that century raised the specter of racial degeneration itself. Such decline seemed to many observers inevitable, built into the very nature of things. According to Rear Admiral Lord Charles Beresford, in an essay tellingly entitled "The Future of the Anglo-Saxon Race" and equally tellingly published in the *North American Review*, the question of the moment was whether "the Anglo-Saxon will follow the path of Degeneracy, as other nationalities have done, or whether there is some vitality in the blood and in the heart of the dominant race of to-day which will keep it from decay and preserve it from the fate of its predecessors." Great dangers confront the race, largely from within: "The sea which threatens to overwhelm [the Anglo-Saxon] is not the angry waters of the Latin races...but the cankering worm in its own heart, the sloth, the indolence, the luxurious immorality, the loss of manliness, chivalry, moral courage and fearlessness which that worm breeds." For Beresford, the future of the Anglo-Saxon is guaranteed by two factors. One is that its greatest triumphs were commercial rather than military in nature, guaranteeing a continual circulation of new cultural productions into and out from the imperium and preventing the stagnation that threatens even the gaudiest military power. The second is that the Anglo-Saxon race, unlike others, is ceaselessly renewed by racial admixture. In this argument, Beresford goes a good deal beyond the commonly held belief that Anglo-Saxons were themselves a composite or amalgamated race and hence immune to the inbreeding that caused the deterioration of other genetic stocks.[29] For Beresford extended his logic from the historical past into the lived present and the imagined future.

> [T]he race has had the immense advantage of being constantly invigorated by new blood. . . . Her sons who sailed across in the Spanish wake to the shores of the New World carried this love of the stranger with them, and in the United States to-day we see the old principle of incorporation going on; the race ever enriching its blood with that of the best and most enterprising of other nations. (803–4)

It is true that Beresford's was only one voice in a chorus preaching Anglo-American unity in the face of British national decline; indeed, as *Blackwood's* may also remind us, his was a voice of relative but nevertheless undeniable progressiveness in that chorus. Whether representative or not, Beresford's was also a voice that found its truest echo in that of Henry James. For, I want to argue, Beresford's drama of the de- and regeneration of the Anglo-Saxon race chimes with James's portrayal of the translation of empire in *The Golden Bowl* and glosses James's representation of the Jew in that text. The imperative that Beresford endorses, the maintenance of an Anglo-American cultural and racial identity under the threat of a seemingly inevitable decline by means of the careful infusion of other racial "bloods" and cultural experiences, is the imperative affirmed by *The Golden Bowl* as well. The fear the novel explores, further, issues from Beresford's program: that these processes of transmission will corrupt rather than renew, will contribute to the process of degeneration, not of regeneration. It is first to express, then to contain, this threat that the Jew is deployed in James's novel.

Indeed, we are made aware of this danger on the very first pages of *The Golden Bowl*, as we are invited to witness a representative of a degenerate empire and a thoroughly diminished race, the Prince, ruefully contemplating his acquisition by that oddly inoffensive embodiment of the new Anglo-Saxon mercantile world order, Adam Verver. "No one before him," Amerigo thinks, "never—not even [his ancestor] the infamous Pope had ever sat up to his neck in such a bath [as that provided by the wealth of Adam Verver]. It showed for that matter how little one of his race could escape after all from history."[30] The Prince's racial identity, in other words, *is* his history; and although he is, the text assures us in its first sentence, "one of those Modern Romans who find by the Thames a more convincing image of the truth of the ancient state than any they have left by the Tiber," he is, nevertheless, so thoroughly a representative of his now thoroughly degenerate lineage that it might as well be burned into his racial identity (23:3). "There are two parts of me," the Prince tells Maggie before their marriage. "One is made up of the history, the doings, the marriages, the crimes, the follies, the boundless bêtises of other people." But, he continues, "there's another part, very much smaller doubtless, which, such as it is, represents my single self, the unknown, unimportant—unimportant save to *you*—personal quality" (23:9).

Maggie banteringly reassures the Prince that it is less his "unknown quality, [his] particular self" than "the generations behind . . . [him], the follies and crimes, the plunder and the waste" that had initially attracted her to him; but it is precisely her failure to reckon with those factors, and his failure to ameliorate the racially encoded vices they represent, that lead to the problems of the novel (9–10). For we learn repeatedly over the course of the narrative that Maggie and the Prince have both mistaken the power of his race as overruling the dictates of his "particular self." "Personally," the Prince thinks,

> he hadn't the vices [of arrogance and greed]. His race, on the other hand, had them handsomely enough, and he was somehow full of his race. Its presence in him was like the consciousness of some inexpungible scent in which his clothes, his whole person, his hands and the hair of his head, might have been steeped as in some chemical bath; the effect was nowhere in particular, yet he constantly felt himself at the mercy of the cause. (16)

Despite his desire to "*make* something different" of himself, the Prince succumbs to some of the less attractive elements that he, Fanny Assingham, and the narrative voice all ascribe to the "inexpungible scent" of his "race"; he is indeed, as Fanny calls him (and as he agrees to be described) "a Machiavelli," if Machiavel *malgré lui* (23:31). For the Prince is placed first by Maggie's and then by Adam's native American naiveté in a position so resolutely double that it can only be responded to by drawing, first reflexively, then systematically, on his rich racial reservoirs of duplicity.

The Prince thus represents an image of the unassimilated, unassimilable alien—a noble, indeed thoroughly distinguished, version of that figure, but one whose full integration into the Anglo-Saxon sphere is at least as questionable as that of the eastern European Jews who were entering London's East End or New York's Lower East Side in such extraordinary numbers at that very moment. But it is precisely this process that Maggie must perform in order to save her marriage. The Prince must, he thinks early in the book, be perpetually "unlearning, with people of English race, all the little superstitions that accompany friendship"; Maggie's task is to guide this process, to help him "unlearn" certain of his "superstitions" and relearn others, ones more compatible with the belief systems of the "English race" (23:35). And in this process the interplay of racial, national, and cultural experiences is as delicate as it is problematical. For, as Maggie herself thinks, her husband is constituted by the facts of race and history alike to be unassimilable, and she, by the same token, is equally constructed by her culture and (complex, perhaps already fatally mixed) race, to be nothing if not supple:

> [S]he recognized her having had . . . to "do all" . . . while he stood as fixed
> in his place as some statue of one of his forefathers. . . . It was strange, if

one had gone into it, but such a place as Amerigo's was like something made for him beforehand by innumerable facts, facts largely of the sort known as historical, made by ancestors, examples, traditions, habits; while Maggie's own had come to show simply as that improvised "post"—a post ... with which she was to have found herself connected in the fashion of a settler or a trader in a new country; in the likeness even of some Indian squaw with a papoose on her back and barbarous beadwork to sell. (24: 323–4)

Yet we learn in the last chapters of the novel that neither Maggie nor the Prince can remain where or what each was. The trajectory these chapters plot is one in which the identities of both wife and husband must be altered in order to produce a new order—a new marital, a new genetic, and thus ultimately a new racial order—of identity. If the Prince does finally make good on his early claims and affirms his bonds (in all senses of the word) in ways that, the novel insists, are alien to his national temper, historical circumstance, and racial constitution, it is also the case that Maggie must be analogously transformed. For in order to maneuver in the face of the Prince and Charlotte's intimacy, Maggie must acquire precisely those elements of the Prince's character that are most alien to her, and most race-specific to him. "He had noticed ... [that] it was the English, the American sign that duplicity, like 'love,' had to be joked about. It couldn't be gone into," the Prince thinks early in the novel (23:15). In order to save her marriage, Maggie must learn to "go into" precisely these things. In order to love, she must learn to become a Machiavel of equal—of greater—subtlety than her husband or his equally supersubtle lover. To drive home the connection between his propensities and her behavior, she acquires these capabilities precisely by modeling herself on Amerigo's own capacities for dissimulation and betrayal. The precise mechanism involved here is spelled out for us with the greatest of clarity as Maggie meets Charlotte's explicit challenge—Charlotte's challenge to Maggie to make Maggie's implied accusation *of* Charlotte explicit *to* Charlotte. For in response, Maggie pursues her strategy of disingenuous prevarication ("I accuse you of nothing") with wrenching inner reference to Amerigo's example:

Maggie, to go on, had to think with her own intensity of Amerigo—to think how he on his side had to go through with his lie to her, how it was for his wife he had done so, and how his doing so had given her the clue and set her the example. ... He had given her something to conform to, and she hadn't unintelligently turned on him, "gone back on" him, as he would have said, by not conforming. ... The right, the right—yes, it took this extraordinary form of humbugging, as she had called it, to the end. It was only a question of not by a hair's breadth deflecting into the truth. (24:250)

At moments like these, the racial agendas established by the book activate themselves with particular clarity—and demonstrate their implications with compelling force. As Maggie learns to lie like the Prince and the Prince learns to act (as he claims at the end of the novel) "in good faith" like Maggie, a mutually transformative alteration takes place between the two of them, leading both to modify their respective behaviors in order to refabricate their strained marriage—a process in its turn that will, the novel assures us, produce a new racial and cultural admixture, first in their marriage, then in their child (24:330).[31] The Prince fantasizes about this latter process early on, and in explicitly genetic terms. He imagines that his "blood" might mingle with that of the hyperinnocent Ververs to produce a more worldly and sophisticated offspring: "they were good children, bless their hearts, and children of good children; so that verily the Principino himself, as less consistently of that descent, might figure to the fancy as the ripest genius of the trio" (23:334). Maggie's development in the second half of the novel, somewhat to the contrary, shows that the identical result can be accomplished by social interaction and marital intimacy as well as by genetic interfusion. But both these means—genetic and social—end at the same point, the creation of a new order of identity, one that combines elements of both Maggie and the Prince's racial and national characteristics and qualities and makes of them a different, distinctive, and unprecedented amalgam.

A degenerate race regenerated; a regenerated race successfully kept from falling into decline—the kind of decline that surrounds them in the decidedly decadent precincts of what the Prince and the novel alike rather contemptuously describe as "English society" (a society composed of Mister Blints and Lady Castledeans who cheerfully cuckold their spouses in the precincts of the appropriately named Matcham)—this is the ultimate act of cultural, historical, and ultimately *racial* translation plotted in *The Golden Bowl* (24:328). As that formulation suggests, this process faces many threats, some external, more internal—most prominently, the very tendency toward laxity, luxury, deceit, and unending and unsatisfying conspicuous consumption that (as Lord Beresford argued) lies within the very heart and leads to the decline of "civilization." And, I would suggest, it is in order to express and control this threat that that culturally potent figure of unassimilability and racial degeneracy, the Jew, is brought on stage, and made to perform a crucial role in two acts of exchange that significantly structure the novel's two marriages: the vending of the Golden Bowl and the purchase of the Damascene tiles.

What I want to focus on here, accordingly, is the strange admixture of centrality and marginality accorded to the figure of the Jew, and the echoes between that combination and the novel's drama of racial decline and renewal. Renewal through boundless procreativity is suggested by the figure of Gutermann-Seuss, who embodies rather delicately, even sympathetically, the stereotype of the Jew deployed by those racial theorists and eugenicists who constructed the Jew as being at one and the same time prodigiously reproductive and fundamentally unassimilable. "To the casual eye" he is "a mere smart and shining youth of less than thirty summers, faultlessly appointed in every particular, he yet stood among his progeny—eleven in all, as he confessed without a sigh, eleven little brown clear faces, yet with such impersonal old eyes astride of such impersonal old noses" (213). It is doubtless distasteful to linger on James's characteristic insistence on the Jewish nose as marker of racial identity; accordingly, let me direct my attention to the other notable element of this description: the ways Gutermann-Seuss's marital productivity stands in contrast to that of the other characters in the novel. Indeed, of all the pairings we encounter in the novel— Maggie and Amerigo, Charlotte and Adam, Fanny and Colonel Bob—the Gutermann-Seusses alone produce more than one child. And if the "graduated offspring" of the Gutermann-Seuss clan contrast ironically with the diminished productivity of the other marriages in the novel, they also serve to remind us of the anxieties over the proliferative tendencies of the Jew and the lack thereof of the Anglo-Saxon "race" that circulated throughout the fin de siècle (213). To put the matter bluntly, Gutermann-Seuss not only is as sweet as the German of the second half of his name suggests, but also lives up to the German sense of its first half: measured in terms of mere productivity, at least, he is indeed a good goods-man, better than that sterile and asexual connoisseur so ironically named Adam Verver.

There is another way in which Gutermann-Seuss serves to bring the discourse of racial degeneration ironically to bear on the novel's plot, one that links him not merely with the Verver-Stant marriage he presides over but also to the Jewish antique dealer who performs an analogous function in the novel's other marriage. That is the way that he embodies not only the fear of proliferating progeny, but also the reality of cultural detritus. The "Damascene tiles" Adam buys as a wedding gift and test for Charlotte (her ability to appreciate them is the sign that she deserves to have them) are icons of a premodern, pre-Christian, non-Western past, brought within the purview of the new capitalist imperium by means of the eternally present but eternally alienated Jew. Those tiles, in other words, serve as a kind of marker of the translation of empire that it is this text's mission to celebrate; but they also serve as a marker of the very tendencies that cause that translation to go awry—if only, perhaps, by working too effectively. For the tiles represent the effluvia of empire, the detritus, however lovely, of long-dead rulers being passed on to the new potentate of the capitalist Anglo-American world; they represent as well the luxury and corruption that, according to Beresford, foretell the decline of even the most puissant imperial order. "The infinitely ancient, the immemorial amethystine blue of the glaze, scarcely more meant to be breathed upon, it would seem, than the cheek of royalty": these tiles bespeak not only the imperial power that first called them into being but also the transience of all imperial powers, including, one assumes, the power of that modern-day "Alexander furnished with the spoils of Darius," Adam (24:215).

That heavily loaded Jamesian word, "spoils," is the key to the novel's ambivalence not only toward these Damascene tiles but toward the status of cultures past in the capitalist imperium of the present—the question that it is not only Gutermann-Seuss's function but, as I will show, also that of the antique dealer to raise in the text as a whole. These Jewish characters are uniquely suited to raise that issue because, by virtue of their racial identity, they endure over the course of many civilizations yet also embody the ethos of the latest, the capitalist world order whose presiding figure in the novel is none other than Adam Verver. And the representation of Gutermann-Seuss expresses fully, even more fully than the portrayal of Adam, the text's ambivalence over this new imperial power, one that, as in Beresford, can either be read *in bono*, as representing a relatively bloodless translation of empire untainted by the elegant violence of the Prince's Roman ancestors or the "campaigns of cruelty and licence" in which the Hun-like Colonel Bob Assingham has participated; or *in malo*, as representing tendencies toward "sloth, indolence, luxurious immorality," and ultimately imperial decline (James, 67; Beresford, 807). The role Gutermann-Seuss plays in the plot seems to bear both these possible readings, just as the first half of his name hovers between the German meaning I have just alluded to and its English pronunciation. He is himself the sweetest embodiment of the commercial spirit, yet by that very fact he reminds us of the gutterlike taint of commerce that adheres even (especially) to the two transactions in which Adam Verver has engaged him, the buying of objets d'art for a museum in America (which seems unobjectionable enough) and the acquisition of a wife to protect Adam from gold-digging American widows (which seems to be of a different order entirely).

The point is not that Gutermann-Seuss explicitly links the Jew to a corruption of culture by forcing its entry into commerce or its confusion with the order of intimacy. Quite to the contrary: the novel maintains a studied silence on these vexed questions. What Gutermann-Suess does, however, is literally embody the processes of individual and social reproduction—and suggest ways in which those processes might lurch out of control. As hyperprolific father and as vendor of cultural artifacts of a bygone era to the highest bidder, he is intimately connected to, and works intimately to connect, the reproduction of families and the circulation of cultural artifacts, and suggests ways in which the process of the genetic circulation afforded by the former and the cultural revitalization enhanced by the latter might fail precisely because they work all too well. Unchecked sexual reproduction might produce a motley ensemble of "graduated offspring . . . fat earringed aunts and cocknified uncles, inimitable of accent and assumption"; cultural reproduction might, by the same logic of unchecked proliferation, produce an equally perpetual, and equally deracinating, circulation of cultural artifacts from nation to nation, empire to empire, subtended by and wrought through the relentless power of capitalist exchange that it is the Jew's role here (as it has dolefully been throughout history) to embody and that it is Adam's role here to harness and exploit (216).

Precisely because he is so fully connected to the things the novel seems to value most intensely—the creation of a family, the translation of empire, the "spoils" of high culture, the logic of capitalist accumulation—Gutermann-Seuss suggests the potential for degeneration and decay that lurks within even these seemingly benign sociocultural projects; further to complicate the matter, he does so precisely by embodying their fulfillment. In so doing, he pushes James's concerns to the point of crisis—and begins to suggest why the stereotypical terms in which he is portrayed are so pointed. These terms are, it would seem, useful, for only by being encased in the lineaments of the Jewish "race" is Gutermann-Seuss's taint kept from extending to the rest of the novel. Gutermann-Seuss can serve as a kind of suggestive analogy for the characters and enterprises of the rest of the novel, but, because he is so spectacularly a Jew, because he is invested so thoroughly with the capacities stereotypically associated with the Jewish "race," he remains a suggestive analogy alone.

In so doing, he anticipates the work performed by the novel's other, more important, Jewish character, the mysterious, unnamed antique dealer who tries to sell the Golden Bowl to Charlotte and the Prince and whose successful vending of it to Maggie precipitates her discovery of that pair's previous intimacy. Like Gutermann-Seuss, the antique dealer is only briefly onstage, but even more than Gutermann-Seuss, his role is (literally) central to the most important aspect of the plot; by vending the bowl, he causes the novel to have a plot, he enables its action to occur at all. Of equal importance, this figure functions as a crucial player in the novel's representation of national and imperial decline, a role in which he too pushes the novel nearly, but not quite, to the point of a crisis that it is the Jew's role, as well, to contain.

The linkage between the novel's thematics of cultural decline and the *antiquari* is implicit from our first meeting with him, an encounter that begins with Charlotte and Amerigo wandering together one last time just before the latter's marriage. For throughout that scene, it is as if the couple is not only moving away from their accustomed haunts in the West End but also moving onto the periphery of the West itself: when Charlotte and Amerigo pass out of Regent's Park through the Marble Arch, they make their way to such barbarous locales as the "Baker Street Bazaar" where Charlotte banteringly proposes to buy Maggie a "pin cushion"; or a Bloomsbury filled with low-class antique stores aspiring to the condition of junk shops—places filled with a "redundancy of 'rot'" (23:104). Such "rot" initially seems absent from the *antiquari*'s well-appointed store, the place where their peregrinations end; but as Charlotte and the Prince look closer, they see that it is filled with another kind of detritus, the detritus of empire. Among the list of goods in this shop, pawned by the "too-questionable great," are "a few commemorative medals of neat outline but dull reference; a classic monument or two, things of the first years of the century; things consular, Napoleonic, temples, obelisks, arches, tinily reembodied" (23:107).

In other words, in the *antiquari*'s store among the piles of bric-a-brac pawned by a penurious British aristocracy, whose economic supersession by American millionaires like Adam Verver is not the least of the echoes in this novel of the discourse on national decline, can be found mementos of the previous effort at imperial world domination: Napoleon's. These miniatures contain, in fact, a tidy history of Napoleon's imperial venture in (as it were) miniature. These mementos of Napoleon's Egyptian triumph and retreat simultaneously betoken the flood and ebb tides of empire—betoken as well the miniature appearance that even the gaudiest human achievements take on in retrospective view. To ring the final change on this passage, they prophesy directly the fate of the British imperial adventure as well. The "tiny reembodiment" of a triumphal arch found in a London junk shop reminds us of the life-size Marble Arch that Charlotte and the Prince have passed through to get there; and this diminutive echo of an imperial simulacrum—of a British imitation of a French copy of a ruined Roman triumphal arch—offers not a sign of the power of imperial mastery but rather a token of the vanity of imperial wishes.

It is thus appropriate that the owner of this antique store–cum–cultural symbol be a Jew, that perpetual witness of the vicissitudes of history and the fallibility of empire. It is particularly crucial that this figure be a Jew because of the role of the "spoils" he vends in the plot. Even more than the Damascene tiles, the Golden Bowl connects the novel's historical drama to its racial and familial one. In addition to what it signifies in the novel's marriage plot—which, as Laurence Holland has so magisterially shown, is something like the possibility of fulfilled but bounded desire, abundant but contained plenitude: in short, that impossibility of Jamesian impossibilities, a successful marriage—this resolutely overdetermined symbol itself takes on the by-now-familiar sense of racial degeneration or cultural decline and hence links these social thematics to Charlotte and Amerigo's disruption of the most intimate precincts of the domestic order itself. Found among but privileged beyond the geegaws of bankrupt lords and empires past, passing, or to come, the Golden Bowl implies the social conditions by which it was itself produced and which, its very presence in an antique store suggests, might no longer obtain. Made "by some very fine old worker and some beautiful old process," the bowl symbolizes first a "lost art" and then, according to the *antiquari*, "a lost time"—an art by which, a time at which, gilt surface and crystalline substance were fashioned to be at one (23:114). But, as has often been noted, the accent here is decidedly on the "lost"—a loss that is simultaneously wrought in both the public and the private spheres. So when Charlotte offers the cup to Amerigo, she is enacting the very process that the cup symbolizes: the passing of a time of felt or imagined social and personal unity; the sundering of social and individual bonds; the severing of gilt surface from cracked substance.

Here again, in other words, we see an unassimilated, ostentatiously foreign Jew standing in close proximity to those things that James's novel values most fully—standing, literally, as the figure who allows those possibilities to circulate throughout the degraded world of the novel, even if he mimics the essentially commercial nature of that world by seeking "coaxingly" to vend the cheaply acquired bowl at a near-bargain price to Charlotte. Or at least this is one of the perspectives we are allowed to hold on this figure, largely through the sympathetic eyes of Charlotte. But it would seem that the very connection of the Jew to the things that the novel wishes to valorize demands a countermovement as well, one that acts to distance that figure from these very possibilities. For, as if by clock-work, such a distancing is provided by Amerigo, who stands angrily outside the shop while Charlotte lingers inside with the *antiquari*, and then denounces the dealer as a fraud. Indeed, it is Amerigo who identifies both the Golden Bowl as cracked and the *antiquari* as Jew—who, in fact, links these two together at a particularly significant moment in the novel. When he decides to accept the "gift" of Charlotte's love—"risk[ing] the cracks," in Charlotte's glorious and ominous phrase—the Prince turns all his scorn on the antique dealer for vending an item that symbolizes so presciently the condition of his affectional life (23:359). " 'Do you remember,' " Charlotte asks him (winsomely, seductively), " 'the beautiful [bowl] that I offered you so long ago and that you wouldn't have?' " " 'Oh yes!'— but it took, with a slight surprise on the Prince's part, some small recollecting. 'The treacherous cracked thing you wanted to palm off on me, and the little swindling Jew who understood Italian and backed you up!' " (23:359).

It is doubtless a sign of just how far things have gone between Amerigo and Charlotte that she is willing to dally with him after this remark; but the Prince's remark is also a sign of the remarkably complicated uses to which the novel puts the matter of Jewishness. Here the reflex against the Jew is deployed by a figure for whom we are asked to have somewhat complicated feelings, and at a moment when they are at their most complicated. Yet the novel oddly endorses the Prince's vision. For the Prince turns out to be right—the bowl does indeed have a hidden flaw, and is practically worthless; and hence the Jew is, as the Prince suggests, something of a swindler. But the identification works both ways; the Italian-speaking Jew brings into sharp moral focus the double-dealing of the Italian prince who is so quick to note his duplicitousness. The cultural associations invoked by the racial identity of both—the common identification of Italians and Jews with the Levant, the exotic, and the fraudulent—reinforce each other at this moment in the text, and the Prince and antique dealer serve as figures for each other's chicanery.

But—and here the plot turns become vertiginous—the Jew turns out to be more than, or precisely the opposite of, a swindler at the second transaction, the transaction that reverses and in effect annuls the first one. Maggie's knowledge of the Prince and Charlotte's liaison is made possible by the agency of the "little man in the shop" who performs a racially uncharacteristic act: an act of economic sacrifice. Returning to tell Maggie that she had paid too much for the Golden Bowl that she, like Charlotte, had picked out of his antique shop as a present for the man in her life—in Maggie's case, problematically, her father—his act is portrayed by Maggie as a gesture of unqualified "friendship."

> "He liked me. I mean—very particularly. It's only so I can account for afterwards hearing from him—and in fact he gave me that today," she pursued, "he gave me that frankly as his reason . . . I inspired him with sympathy—there you are!"
>
> [Amerigo] saw her so keep her course that it was as if he could at the best stand aside to watch her and let her pass; he only made a vague demonstration that was like an ineffective gesture. "I'm sorry to speak so ill of your friends; and the thing was so long ago; besides which there was nothing to make me recur to it. But I remembered the man's striking me as a horrid little beast."
>
> She gave a slow headshake—as if, no, after consideration, *that* way were an issue. "I can only think of him as kind, for he had nothing to gain. He had in fact only to lose. It was what he came to tell me—that he had asked too high a price, more than the object was really worth. There was a particular reason which he hadn't mentioned and which had made him consider and repent"—

namely, the fact that four years ago, the Prince had "guessed the flaw" in the bowl and refused it as a gift from Charlotte. Maggie, however, does not want or ask for her money back—particularly after the shopman sees photographs of the Prince and Charlotte in the drawing room and tells Maggie of their ease with one another on the day of her wedding with Amerigo. She receives, she tells the Prince, "nothing but an apology for empty hands and empty pocket; which was made me—as if it mattered a mite!—ever so frankly, ever so beautifully and touchingly" (24:196).

This passage is crucial both to James's representation of the Jew and to the plot of the novel as a whole; indeed, it reminds us of the indissoluble if thoroughly subterranean connection between the two. The antique dealer's "repentance" both controverts and confirms common anti-Semitic stereotypes—confirms, that is to say, precisely what it seems to controvert. The odd conversion of this Jew to a form of behavior identified by the text as Christian, or at least not Jewish, in effect endorses the Prince's calumnies even as it redeems the *antiquari* from them. Most important, it is absolutely central to the novel's emplotment. Not only does this conversion of the Jew, that is to say, make that plot happen at all; it also anticipates the similar conversion of the Jew's greatest antagonist and most exact double: Amerigo. Just as the Jewish antique dealer undoes the slightly shady bargain he had made with Maggie by turning around and comporting himself to a higher—a non-Hebraic—standard of behavior, so too does Amerigo repent of a breach of faith and comport himself to a redeemed standard of behavior, one in which, far more than the antique dealer, he loses his own racial identity in order to take on that of Maggie. Indeed, the resemblance between the two goes further, if somewhat paradoxically, to a significant differentiation. For the Jew's "repentance" here is, the text suggests, a slightly disingenuous one; since he claims to have "empty hands and empty pocket," it would seem, he makes good on his slightly shady business transaction only verbally, without any of the financial remuneration that, the text seems to imply, is the real ground of his concern. And, as we have begun to see, the Prince must go even further, to a recasting of his very identity and behavior.

I am suggesting, then, that the ultimate function of the Jewish antique dealer is to serve not only as the agent by which the plot of the novel is wrought and turns but also as the benchmark against which the assimilation of Amerigo is measured. When so measured, Amerigo's project appears all the more successful and all the more terrifying. In its final stage, for example, Amerigo reaches a point analogous to that of the antique dealer—one in which he shows the final signs of his racial identity, only to foretell their departure. Just as the Jew here retains his Jewishness even in the final moment of his conversion, so too does Amerigo hold on to his Italianness, even though (unlike the Jew) he recognizes that it must be fully expunged. That moment of recognition occurs in the remarkable penultimate conversation between Maggie and Amerigo, in which, it would seem, the masks that each member of that couple wears are fully and formally doffed, with Maggie's resonant question: "Am I to take from you then that you accept and recognize my knowledge?" The Prince does not answer directly, speaking only in "ambiguous murmur[ings]" that descend through fragmentary bursts of speech into a single phoneme:

"Ah, my dear, my dear, my dear—!" It was all he could say.

She wasn't talking however at large. "You've kept up for so long a silence—!"

"Yes, yes I know what I've kept up. But will you do," he asked, "still one thing more for me?"

It was as if for an instant it had with her new exposure made her turn pale. "Is there even one thing left?"

"Ah, my dear, my dear, my dear!"—it had pressed again in him the fine spring of the unspeakable.

There was nothing however that the Princess herself couldn't say. "I'll do anything if you tell me what."

"Then wait." And his raised Italian hand, with its play of admonitory fingers, had never made gesture more expressive. His voice dropped to a tone. "Wait," he repeated. "Wait." (24:350–1)

At this moment, the Prince would seem to reach a point analogous to that attained by the antique dealer in his own dealings with Maggie; but it is a limit, the novel shows us, that he is willing to pass beyond. Prevarication, ambiguousness, an easy way with other people's emotions: these are, as we have seen, qualities genetically encoded in the Prince's Italianness as fully as are deceit and avarice in the Italian-speaking Jewish antique dealer; and the text reminds us of them with its last, and magnificent, mention of the Prince's Italianness. Appropriately, we learn with that very gesture that, while the Prince prepares to forgo these qualities once and for all, he is not ready *yet*, and asks for Maggie to give him until Charlotte and Adam have departed—"till we're really alone" (351)—before fully amending his behavior and, one assumes, resuming fully intimate marital relations.

The Prince here, in short, stands at a stage exactly analogous to that of the *antiquari*: ready to "consider and repent" for his flaws yet at the same time not yet fully prepared to amend his behavior. The gesture he makes here, like that of the *antiquari*, is generous, yet again like the *antiquari*'s, it is not generous *enough*. Not until the final pages of the novel, in fact, does the Prince fully accommodate himself to Maggie's expectations and understandings and turn to the new form of identity that I have been attempting to describe throughout this essay, one that is radically purified, altered, transformed, racially emended. It is appropriate, however, that I am having some trouble describing that new species of identity, for it is one that the novel quite literally has itself no language for. When what is identified at this moment as the Prince's "raised Italian hand" gathers itself, on the last page of the novel, to embrace Maggie, it is a hand that is no longer given a racial identification or appellation; and so too, we are to believe, the Prince is purged of racial characteristics in a way that the *antiquari*, for all his contrition, is not. But with the Prince established as an emblem of a race regenerated (and a token of the regeneration, too, of the Anglo-Saxon peoples whose embodiment is Maggie), the novel comes to its perfectly ambiguous end; it has nothing left to say about that character (or, for that matter, Maggie), preferring instead to close itself off in a silence that is as self-enclosing as the embrace it would depict. That ambiguous end seems to signify both that the novel understands the necessity of the new order of possibility represented by the newly established identity of the Prince and that it understands as well what this new order of possibility implies: a transcendence of the very notion of race that the novel has itself, until this moment, relied upon. Yet this moment also demonstrates the extent of James's imaginative failure; it shows that he has no means of imagining and picturing this new order of identity, no terms for encompassing the new form of identity that this triad, Maggie, the Prince, and the Principino, will create. All James can do, and it is not a small achievement, though also not an untroubling one, is to detail for us the ways that the Prince has moved beyond the *antiquari* into the ambiguity of his final embrace with Maggie. All he can do, in other words, is to show that the Prince has now fully transcended his own grand but corrupted race, and perhaps even race itself, but the only way James can do *that* is by showing how much further the Prince has progressed than his double, the member of an equally grand but far more degenerated "race": the Jew.

The drama of cultural degeneracy and racial assimilation that this novel plots, therefore, is a complex and overdetermined one, but its outlines are clear enough: Amerigo bears the burden but also achieves the possibility of a racially revitalizing assimilation that the novel takes as its ground of value. This process is glossed as an imperative, given the degeneracy both of Amerigo's own "race" and that of the Anglo-American world in which he lives; the novel suggests that by means of culture, will, or even the most intensely analyzed but finally mysterious species of love, a successful racial admixture will lead to a revitalization first of the family order, then of the West itself. Yet the presence of the Jew in the text as a counter-Amerigo—unassimilated, unassimilable, linked to the glories as well as to the decadence of the degenerated past—serves as a kind of an internal check on James's fantasies of this sociocultural-genetic *translatio imperii*. The process can go just so far, and no further; it can go no further because of the ineradicable realities of race; and those realities are represented in the novel by the figure of the Jew.

In doing so, his text takes on a social and cultural salience—for James's era, of course, but also, I fear, for our own. Both issues demand a good deal of attention, more than can be given here. But I want to gesture, in conclusion, to the outlines of each, if only to begin the task of unpacking their complexities. To link James's text to his cultural context is, of course, desirable but difficult, all the more because the figures of his own time were wrestling with the notion of racial, cultural, and national identity itself, and through precisely the means through which James performed this venture. But one does not want to move casually (much less causally) from James's texts to those of his milieu. There is a complex admixture of affiliations and differences between James and all his contemporaries. James resembles Beresford and other trans-Atlantic liberals, for example, in his desire to valorize a process of mutually modifying assimilation between Anglo-American and other "races" or nationalities. But, like contemporary racist ideologues, such as his American counterparts who founded the Anti-Immigration League or those who wrote for Tory journals in England, James fears the consequences of that process, and his fears are expressed in a language of terror at the prospect of sexual and cultural reproduction, racial and cultural degeneration. The residue of that fear—most fully expressed on the *formal* as well as the thematic level of the novel—is precipitated in the figure of the Jew: a figure of the unassimilable, the ineradicable alien, standing at the very center of the marital rearrangements the novel wishes to valorize, standing indeed at the very center of the aesthetic structure that this novel takes as the only possible means by which that valorization can be effected.

The novel thus takes on an even greater poignancy in the context of James's career-long endeavor to work out a position for himself in a culture obsessed with the dogmas of degeneration—a culture, moreover, that pointed the arrow of disapprobation straight at him. For in the twists and turns of the novel's vertiginous plot the very fear that James worked so hard to dispel—that the forces of cultural degeneration were intimately connected to his privileging of aesthetic values—gets reestablished through the very means by which he sought to banish it. Over the course of the novel, the process of cultural degeneration and the transmission of cultural value, the making of art and the moral corruption it claims to redeem us from, collapse into each other. They do so, in the last analysis, because the figure James invokes to keep them separate, the Jew, has intimate connections to both these possibilities. For all James's hard work to keep them separate, the artist and the Jew are finally so intimately tied to one another that they might well prove indistinguishable.

THE LESSON OF THE MASTER

The irony built into James's representations of the Jew points in two entirely different directions. It looks outward to his immediate successors, the modernists; it looks further still, toward us—toward contemporary critics who are attempting to come to terms with the problematic social affiliations of high culture in the post-Arnoldian era. To deal, first, with the former: the problems that bedevil James foreshadow those of his successors, especially those who admired him so intensely, Eliot and Pound. (Following James's death, these two, together with Ford Madox Ford, prepared a special memorial edition of the *Modern Review* and printed quite brilliant appreciative essays on James in that forum.) "The rats are underneath the piles / The Jew is underneath the lot," Eliot notoriously wrote some fifteen years after James published *The Golden Bowl*, imaging the cultures of the West as a wasteland like James's Bloomsbury, suffused with a "redundancy of rot" and locating a Jew as the source of that decomposition. But the same kinds of ironies that James's discourses face are evident in Eliot's. If Eliot's Jew is "under the lot" he is at once the most depraved character one can imagine and foundational, part of the ground on which the crumbling edifices of Western culture were built. And the work of these figures may be seen as more Jamesian still. In one of the best analyses of the anti-Semitism of the moderns I know, Maud Ellmann has recently written that Eliot and Pound "reviled in the Jew what they feared and cherished in themselves: their exile from their homeland and their diaspora among the texts that bear their name. [Their] antisemitism is founded on identification, and [their] writings represent a lifelong struggle to exorcize [the] unknown self."[32] This drama of identification and disavowal, of self-inquiry and self-negation, is precisely what I have been attempting to trace in novels written a generation before these figures, works that were enormously influential for them.

James's deployment of the Jew thus can help us contextualize the responses of his modernist successors. It can help us, for one thing, get beyond the clichéd question of whether the modernists were or were not anti-Semites; *pace* Julius, the point is not that they were obviously so but that their anti-Semitism was the consequence of an authorial stance and a historical moment that constructed them in such a position as to articulate anti-Semitic sentiments as an ineluctable consequence of their own self-imagining. As poets who had inherited the full set of fin-de-siècle suturings between the artist and the degenerate, and as subjects who faced the full complexities of this identification for their own desire for cultural and social power, their response to the Jew was an inevitable one, determined (if not overdetermined) by the accretion of associations I have been tracing in this chapter, as in the preceding chapters. To be an advocate of high culture at the moment of modernity, that is to say, is to be written into a complex relation to the figure of the Jew. And more: it is to encounter in that figure not only an inevitable expression of cultural nightmare but also an incarnation of possibilities and identities one wishes to access—at a safe distance. Precisely because the Jew was "the Jew" for these writers, they, like James, were able to explore a set of imaginative possibilities untouched by their more socially taboo aspects. But precisely because the figure of the Jew was connected to those possibilities by the very line of logic that distanced it from them, they, like James, could not help but discover in the Jew an uncannny, mocking double of themselves and their cultural projects.

As I implied at the beginning of this chapter, I find James far more complex and far more interesting in his response to the Jew than these later figures. Through him, rather than them, I believe, we should raise the question I have been circling throughout this chapter: how should the contemporary reader respond to this fin-de-siècle and early-twentieth-century discursive deployment of the Jew? I have been telling the narrative of that response in such a way as to stress both the Jew's marginality and the Jew's centrality to James's own literary and imaginative projects. The Jew functions most fully for James not as a concrete figure or even as a stereotyped one but as a receptacle: a figure onto which can be loaded all the sources of his inchoate anxieties and unacknowledged terrors. As such, my narrative is quite similar to the one Julia Kristeva has recently told of L. F. Céline: a narrative of expulsion, excorporation; of what she calls "abjection":

There looms, within abjection, one of those violent, dark revolts of being, directed against a threat that seems to emanate from an exorbitant outside or inside, ejected beyond the scope of the possible, the tolerable, the horrible. It lies there, quite close, but it cannot be assimilated. It beseeches, worries, and fascinates desire which, nevertheless, does not allow itself to be seduced. . . . Unflaggingly, like an inescapable boomerang, a vortex of summons and repulsion places the one haunted by it literally beside himself.[33]

I turn to Kristeva at this moment because the quality of her language is, to the Jamesian, uncannily familiar. I can think of no better words, for example, to describe James's habitual problematic in his more compelled writing of this period—in the ghost stories, for example, or the odd fables of artistic practice like *The Sacred Fount*. But there is more than linguistic affinity to note here. Like Kristeva's Céline, James seems more than usually "haunted" and "beside himself" when confronted with the figure of the Jew; and his own responses to the Jew do indeed at times seem to comport themselves to the pattern Kristeva traces: "the image of the Jew will concentrate negated love become hatred for Mastery on the one hand; and on the other and jointly, desire for what Mastery cuts out: weakness, the joying substance, sex tinged with femininity and death" (180).

Indeed, Kristeva's analysis suggests a possible juncture between the psychoanalytic and the cultural hermeneutic we have been looking at in James's treatment of the Jew. Briefly to sketch the narrative suggested by this juncture requires little effort: James's own, heavily culturally overdetermined aspirations to "mastery"—his projection of himself as consummate high-culture authority on the Art of the Novel—involved a process by which he was forced to repress with particular vigor all the messy, fluid formations of his own psyche; this self-limitation, we might further speculate, became all the more powerful when that material was brought to the surface by the degeneration debate. James, we might continue to argue, responded to this psychic roadblock with the classic defense of negation (of entertaining as the forbidden or the denied wishes or desires subject to the vicissitudes of repression). Inflating the power of the artist-Jew, James connects that figure to all the things in his own sexual and emotional makeup that he is forced to deny himself, and at the same time he constructs that figure as one connected to filth, degeneration, decay. James thereby explores his desires even in the act of renouncing them and suffuses them, in that act of renunciation, with the very qualities he feels compelled to expel from himself. Hence the curious effect by which the Jew is at once bound to and distanced from James himself, a boundary problem that is constitutive of anti-Semitic discourses: "The Jew becomes the feminine exalted to the point of mastery, the ambivalent, the border where exact limits between same and other, subject and object, and even beyond these, between inside and outside, and disappearing—hence an Object of fear and fascination" (184).

This model of Jamesian anti-Semitism is neat, perhaps too neat. For one thing, placing James against Céline (even Kristeva's Céline) reminds us of how much more sympathetic James allows himself to be to the qualities he would expel than was Céline. Perhaps more important, this juxtaposition reminds us of how much more open to the process of self-inquiry and self-renovation was James than his fellow artistic anti-Semite Céline—or, more relevantly, James's contemporary and friend, the French writer and rabid anti-Semite Paul Bourget; or, most relevantly of all perhaps, those gentry colleagues and contemporaries who helped effectuate the rise of the scientific discourse on race and the eugenics movement at the very time James was writing. James was, to put the matter simply, saner—more open and more generous on every level—than were figures like these, although, admittedly, Henry was undeniably less generous on the subject of Jews than his brother William, who was a committed Dreyfusard and an outspoken opponent of the rise of discrimination at the turn of the century.

Again, considering James under the sign of his anti-Semitism leads us to a measured, and somewhat ambiguous, response. But here, too, the very pattern of similarity and difference with Kristeva's model can help us position James's attitudes with a greater degree of precision. Kristeva writes, at one of her more dazzling and problematic moments—dazzling because it is so dialectically appropriate, problematic because it might seem to excuse anti-Semitic discourses—of the recuperative, cathartic function of the process of writing in and about abjection. The very putting into language of the responses to the abject "call[s] for a softening of the superego. Writing them imagines an ability to imagine the abject, that is, to see oneself in its place and to thrust it aside only by means of the displacements of verbal play." But, she continues, "it is only after his death, eventually, that the writer of abjection will escape his condition of waste, reject, abject" (16).

For James, however, this process of encountering the Jew in all that figure's uncanny similarity to and defensively drawn difference from himself performs the very psychic "softening" Kristeva writes about. To turn one last time to the passage from *The American Scene* that has served as our touchstone throughout this inquiry, what's perhaps most interesting about it is not only the lability of James's affect—his swinging from one polar extreme, that of slurring references to Jewish noses, to another, that of an idealization of the Jew as the privileged figure in an America governed by a homogenizing mass culture—but also the *rhythms* of his response. We watch James shifting about, testing, contesting, interrogating, and remaking his own responses to these Jews—emerging, in the end, with significantly different reactions, in which James, the alien outsider from the American scene, measures through the difference of the Jew from that scene and from himself the difference that difference itself will make. It is true that James's attitude at this moment is ambiguous, far more ambiguous than Posnock is willing to admit; James's final, and powerfully uncanny, image is that of the Jewish café whose

> fostered decencies and unprecedented accents took on thus, for the brooding critic, a likeness to that terrible modernized and civilized room in the Tower of London, haunted by the shade of Guy Fawkes, which had more than once formed part of the critic's taking tea there. In this chamber of the present urbanities, the wretched man had been stretched on the rack and the critic's ear (how else should it have been a critic's?) could still always catch, in pauses of talk, the faint groan of his ghost. (139)

Whatever else one may say about this passage, it brings to bear on James's relation with the Jew a powerfully moving reversal of the pattern we have seen Kristeva describing in Céline. In this passage it is not the Jew, but rather James, who reveals himself as the abject, and he so reveals himself in the very language of degeneration he had earlier used to position the Jew as arch-degenerate. It is James, rather than the Jew, who is revealed at this moment to be intrinsically connected to the past and passing values of art; he is the one who is set aside from the currents of modern, bustling New York; he is the one who is associated with ghosts and who alone is capable of hearing their groan of pain. Indeed, the famously loose Jamesian syntax here links the critic irrevocably to the ghost he alone is capable of perceiving; although the two are distinct enough early in the passage, by its end they appear nearly indistinguishable, linked indissolubly to one another by pronominal ambiguity.

In this passage, then, James the "incurable man of letters" positions himself as the irrevocably ghostly critic, the eternal outsider in the rapidly transforming world of culture—as that which is excrescential, unnecessary, waste, in the bustling world of the modern metropolis; and the age-old, if not eternal, Jew is positioned as the very embodiment of modernity. But what is most remarkable about this moment, it seems to me, is that James does not mourn—too much— this position; rather, he depicts it with a ruefulness and irony that allow both the Jew and James himself a certain degree of independence from the qualities associated with each other while seeing the ways in which they might be arranged in a loosely contiguous relation with one another. In this representational schema, in other words, the critic and the Jew serve not as metonymies masking as identities—the basic linguistic structure, as I have shown earlier, of racist discourse— but rather as metaphors in which both retain a certain independence from each other: whose tenors and vehicles gloss each other but are free of any but the most general injunction to accomplish the work of definition.

The passage—and, indeed, James's entire intercourse with the Jew throughout the period I have been discussing—can be understood, as Beverly Haviland has suggested of James's responses to the African Americans he encounters in the South, as a process of hermeneutic self-inquiry and re-vision.[34] To conclude on a slightly different note, what we are witnessing in the pulsions and compulsions of James's response to the Jew may be seen, rather, as something akin to the psychoanalytic process of working through—a process in which the sheer otherness of the Jew presents James with the chance to articulate and represent those conflicts within himself coming under cultural pressure at precisely this moment. Such a process may indeed, as I suggested early in this book, resemble the mechanism of scapegoating; at times, it certainly serves that function in James's career. But the shift in James's tone in *The American Scene* from abjection to appreciation, from demonization to a measured form of deference, it seems to me, indicate a process of psychic loosening, of decathexis, of psychic reworking undertaken on both a conscious and an unconscious level. "To worry or to smile, such is the choice when we are assailed by the strange; our decision depends on how familiar we are with our own ghosts," Kristeva writes elsewhere of the contemporary European's enactment of the highly Jamesian scenario of encountering an alien Other in one's newly strange homeland.[35] James's response to the Jew represents, I am arguing, this process when he moves from worrying to, if not smiling, at least accepting; and he makes the process work by confronting his own ghosts—or at least his own potential ghostliness.

Perhaps this response might guide the contemporary academic, as she or he decides whether to worry or to smile over James's response. That is, just as James's labile response to the Jew enacts a kind of working-through by means of a response to an abjected figure, so too the academy's treatment of James's anti-Semitism can be seen as a process of coming to terms with the problematic of modern anti-Semitism itself. From a period of repression—the period when James's anti-Semitism was the dirty little secret of academic Jamesianism of the 1940s and 1950s—through the response of Geismar, who abjects James as fully as James abjects the Jew, through Posnock's recuperative reading, James has served as an emblem of the Anglo-American academy's response to the scandal of fin-de-siècle and modernist anti-Semitism, a scandal affiliated with the rise, in the late nineteenth century, of scientific racism, eugenics, and anti-immigrant hysteria and one that threatens to return along with those pernicious forces at our own fin-de-siècle moment.[36] To face this scandal in a way that registers without demonizing the vicissitudes, specificities, and problematics of the various authors who contributed to it—whether enthusiastically (like Céline), ambivalently (like James), or somewhere in between (like Wharton, Cather, Eliot, Pound): this is the task to which, it seems to me, the encounter of the contemporary academic with James and the discourses of anti-Semitism might profitably next lead. And, it might be added, it might lead to the interrogation of the response of Jewish critics to this tradition of discourse—an interrogation that, like that I have attempted to perform of James, must bear in mind the specific social and cultural situation they faced, the vulnerabilities it created, and the opportunities it afforded. Here, as in our reading of the modernists, James's wrestlings with the Jew might guide us, for good *and* for ill, even as we interrogate with the utmost of care his recognitions and responses.

5

Henry James among the Jews

The truth of our little age is this: nowadays no one gives a damn about what Henry James knew. I dare say our "little age" not to denigrate (or not only to denigrate) but because we squat now over the remnant embers of the last diminishing decade of the dying twentieth century, possibly the rottenest of all centuries, and good riddance to it. . . . The victories over mass murder and mass delusion, are hardly permanent. "Never again" is a point- less slogan; old atrocities are models (they give permission) for new ones. The worst reproduces itself; the best is singular. Tyrants, it seems, can be spewed out by the dozens, and their atrocities by the thousands, as by a copy machine; but Kafka, tyranny's symbolist, is like a fingerprint, or like handwriting, not duplicatable. This is what Henry James knew: that civilization is not bred out of machines, whether the machines are tanks or missiles, or whether they are laser copiers. Civilization, like art its handmaid (read: hand-made), is custom built.

Cynthia Ozick

If you play the game, go to the right parties, talk to the right people and review books in the right way, then you get the patronage—the literary plums. . . . [Y]ou get $2000 for collect- ing the short novels of Henry James and pasting together an introduction from stuff somebody else has written. I don't want to collect the short novels of Henry James.

Paul Goodman, quoted by Victor Navasky

P<small>AUL</small> G<small>OODMAN</small>'<small>S</small> <small>COMMENT IS PERHAPS APOCRYPHAL</small>, but it sug- gests the kind of cultural authority Henry James had come to exert in Jewish intellectual circles by the 1950s—the circles we have learned to call, after Irving Howe, those of "the New York intellectuals."[1] Goodman reminds us that James, far more than any other such figure, might be seen as *the* central exemplar of literary culture for this group, and there is an abundance of reasons to reinforce his opinion. *Partisan Review*, the house organ of the New York intellectuals, was an early and vociferous advocate of James, publishing countless important essays on his life and work over the course of its first twenty years of publication. Lionel Trilling, the vital center of the group, wrote spectacular essays on James's fiction as well as highly Jamesian fiction of his own; in addition, he frequently invoked James at crucial points in his own criticism. Another powerful figure in this circle, Philip Rahv, edited an important early edition of James's stories and claimed credit for beginning the whole James revival—and then turned against James late in his career, denying the value of a writer he had been praising for the past thirty years.

James's power was not limited to this generation; he continued to occupy a central role for the New York intellectuals who followed. When Irving Howe sought to revise Trilling's understanding of the relation between literature and politics, he did so by writing an important essay on *The Princess Casamassima*. When Phillip Roth sought to find a formal structure to play out the conflict between the values of lived and artificed experience, he did so by rewriting *The Middle Years*. When Cynthia Ozick wanted to define a stance for herself as a Jewish-American writer who took the first side of that equation as seriously as the second, she did so by dismissing her attraction to James, only to evince the increasing sympathy that is reflected in the quotation I began with. And the most rebellious offspring of the New York intellectuals, Leslie Fiedler, may be said to have spent his entire career reacting to the hegemony of James he faced early in his academic career.

Nor, it might quickly be added, was the relation between Jewish critics and James uniquely a product of the hothouse New York scene. Jewish critics seemed especially drawn to the study of James from the time of Leon Edel, who began working on James in the 1940s, through the James boom in the 1950s and early 1960s and into the 1970s. Here are just a few: Charles Feidelson; Shoshana Felman (author of a powerful Lacanian rereading of *The Turn of the Screw* as well as a powerful theorist of Holocaust and trauma studies); and more recently Ross Posnock, author of some of the more extravagantly exculpatory narratives about James's anti-Semitism.

Why did James exert so powerful and so persistent an effect on Jewish critics and theorists for much of the twentieth century—some overtly self-identified as Jews, some wholly assimilated to non-Jewish norms and identities, some standing somewhere in between? Cynthia Ozick's coruscating response, in a volume of her essays published in 1993 and standing at the end of a long series of ambivalent responses to the Master, offers some hints. For Ozick (who discovered her vocation for letters in high school when reading *The Beast in the Jungle*, then wrote her master's thesis on James), James becomes the literal embodiment of civilization in an age of mechanical reproduction, rationalized brutality, and mass murder; in her hands, James is crafted into the figure he wished to be at certain moments in his writing, the very image of the artist as maker of life rather than its mere recorder. This is, to be sure, a bold if not entirely appropriate deployment of James—not that James would have disliked copier machines or liked mass murder, but he was, in some readings, more open to the pleasures as well as the pressures of modernity than were others in his genteel circle. But this identification performs for Ozick powerful work: it allows her to invoke as her own the experience of James as artist and then link it first to the great modernist paranoid Jew, Kafka, then to a Western civilization about which Ozick is elsewhere profoundly conflicted. "Pitchforked out of the Victorian and into the modern novel," Ozick writes in her James essay, "James could dare as Conrad dared, and as Kafka dared" (139). The verb is remarkable; so are the tenses, in which James seems as much as a belated addition as he is a crucial precursor to the modernist tradition of the Anglo-Pole Conrad and the European Jew Kafka—and the American Jew Cynthia Ozick. Indeed, in her essay on the unpublished tale *Hugh Morrow*, Ozick takes this act of affiliation one, slightly literalizing, step further, linking James's inability to finish that story to his discovery that the artist as such is a kind of woman—and hence, in some ways, a Cynthia Ozick of his (her?) moment: "Hugh Morrow demanded . . . that the artist become, through the visionary organization of his art, a mother. It equated the artist with the embryo-bearing woman—while at the same time urging the substitution of art for life" (140).

The pairing of Goodman and Ozick perhaps too neatly suggests the conflicting valences of James in Jewish New York intellectual circles: the rebellious son (leftist, gay, countercultural before there was such a thing) and the ambivalently but brilliantly faithful daughter play out their relation to the world of high intellectual discourse and culture by means of the genteel WASP whose relations to Jews were themselves so thoroughly overdetermined. In doing so, however, both demonstrate the contrasting roles James played for this culture, and indeed, as I argue further hereafter, for American Jewish intellectuals as a whole. Goodman's rebellious response reminds us of the ways that an investment in the nascent James industry could function: on the one hand, as providing access to cultural capital, in a sphere in which such capital could prove handy indeed; on the other, as a way of putting bread on the table, by bringing James to the attention of the larger audience that was at that precise moment burgeoning under the impact of postwar prosperity, expanding higher education, and the paperback revolution. Harold Rosenberg's nasty name for Rahv's James anthology, "the Henry James delicatessen," represents well this cultural work, at least when purged of its perverse snobbery. By packaging in the best American marketing tradition the taste treats of Jamesian prose and vending them to the new, booming middlebrow audience, Jewish intellectuals could augment their material sustenance and claim a new cultural authority for themselves. Ozick's response—more generous yet more conflicted than either Goodman's or Rosenberg's—suggests the complicated dialectics of literary influence and cultural inheritance that the response of these Jewish intellectuals invoked, and the richness of the effects they were able to achieve through their dialogue with James. The Henry James delicatessen, indeed, but the goods there are hardly chopped liver.

In the pages that follow, I am interested in both these responses to James on the part of Jewish intellectuals from the 1930s to the present day. The dialectics of literary affiliation and the grittier, down-to-earth realities of publication, hiring, and often just plain survival in American high culture between 1930 and the present day are both part of this story, as are changes in the ethnic composition and canonical compass of the high literary academy. In part, the story I have to tell is the familiar tale of assimilation: of how Jewish intellectuals used James to enter a world whose operative ideals and dominant style of response were white, Anglo-Saxon, Protestant, and centered on narratives of Anglo-Saxon cultural identity and authority. But in part the story I have to tell is one that suggests the complexity of such a process, the ways it is caught up with a certain kind of aggression against as well as accommodation to dominant ideals, the ways it transforms in unexpected ways the cultural field[2] in which it operates. Indeed, though their efforts were various, their results differing, and their responses divergent, the effect of the Jewish Jamesians was an ironic and impressive one indeed. Through their efforts, a double transformation occurred. They were remade into versions of Henry James, that ambivalent and conflicted embodiment of high-genteel culture; meanwhile, and, by the same logic, James was converted, in subtle but unmistakable ways, into a cosmopolitan Jew.

JEWS AND HIGH LITERARY CULTURE: 1880–1920

Literary criticism, as we now define it when we distinguish it from book reviewing, on the one hand, and literary exposition or literary scholarship, on the other, was obviously not born at Columbia. But it was born in New York City and it had its fine early flowering at Columbia in the years in which Lionel [Trilling] was an undergraduate. . . . That it appeared in New York is eas[y] to account for. We speak casually of the intellectual life of New York City as New York Jewish intellectual life. This is not because it lacked significant practitioners who were not Jews but because so many of its influential figures *were* Jews, not only self-conscious but self-advertised Jews whose parents had come to this country from East Europe to escape religious and political oppression. These first generation Americans were importantly concentrated in New York City and they gave its tone of significant contention to the intellectual life of America for several decades. One might conjecture, indeed, that one of the reasons why criticism as we knew it in earlier decades of this century has now disappeared . . . is that it is practiced by people reared at a generational remove from the contentious tradition of their European-bred forebears.

Diana Trilling

Diana Trilling's bold recasting[3] of the genealogy of American literary criticism— associating it with cosmopolitanism, modernity, and Jewishness (and hence with the notorious contentiousness that the New York intellectuals habitually brought to their interactions)—is no more accurate than most genealogies; but it is symp-tomatic of the way that first- and second-generation Jewish intellectuals thought about their world and its relation to the larger world of American literary culture. That world is utterly civilized, its criticism bellelettristic (her examples of possible genealogies for literary bellelettrists such as herself include the likes of Coleridge, Hazlitt, Carlyle, Ruskin, de Toqueville, Saint-Beuve, Emerson, and Henry Ad-ams). It is also resolutely *un*professionalized, taking place as much in journals, newspapers, and public discourse as in academic books and professional meet-ings. It resembles, in fact, nothing quite so much as the hothouse world of the eighteenth-century British coffeehouses that Habermas takes as a quintessential precursor of the bourgeois public sphere. And it is substantially, even defiantly, ethnically identified: the arrival of Jewish immigrants to America is linked causally to the full birth of the life of the mind in this country.

Trilling's narrative displays, in other words, the very chutzpah it celebrates.[4] But what I find most remarkable about it is the unquestioning linkage of the arrival of these Jews and *literary* culture, a linkage that makes this process of assimilation different in character and in consequences from any that had pre-ceded (or for that matter would follow) it. As I will suggest, matters are far more complicated than Trilling suggests, particularly as the first rumblings of Jewish immigration receded and the aftershocks started being felt in the cultural sphere—when the sons and daughters of these immigrants, joined by newer ones fleeing Nazi persecution, started to enter the professions in general, and the pro-fession of literary criticism in particular, as their way of joining a mildly, but nevertheless distinctly, anti-Semitic American culture. But the truth of her intu-ition is borne out in larger circles than those of the somewhat parochial and self-obsessed New York intellectuals. For what marks Jewish assimilation and differ-entiates it from that of other immigrant groups before or after is the crucial role that engagement with the canonical tradition of high Western literature—espe-cially the literature of England and America—played in this process.

At least initially, this prominence was due to the particular nature of the Jews who emigrated to these shores. There have been many distinct phases of Jewish immigration, each of which has played a prominent role in the making of American high culture in the past two centuries. The first focused on Sephardic merchants and itinerants, the second on German and Moravian commercial Jews, many of whom had by the late nineteenth century reached positions of economic prominence and thorough integration into the cultural mainstream.[5] Indeed, by the later years of the nineteenth century, many of the scions of the great German Jewish commercial families of New York had turned from money-making to culture-making: one son of the Guggenheim clan may have gone down on the *Titanic* after saving the life of his mistress, but another was a wealthy art collector who endowed a museum, and yet another bequeathed the foundation that partially funded this book.[6] One might leap ahead to add to this wave the roughly three hundred thousand middle-class German Jews who fled Hitler in the 1930s; included in this diaspora were (famously) professors, scholars, psychoanalysts, and scientists.[7] But even those less frequently celebrated brought with them a commitment to the Germanic ideal of enlightenment achieved through the cultivation of reason and ratified by the consummation of aesthetic taste—often to the irritation of Jews who had preceded them.[8]

But the greatest swell of immigration is of course the one that Trilling alludes to, the astonishing flood of immigration between 1880 and 1924, which was particularly concentrated in New York (by one estimate, the city was 30 percent Jewish by 1920) but extended to other large metropolises and then radiated out over the country at large. It is this wave that had the most profound and far-reaching effects on the American social imaginary and the greatest impact on American culture. That encounter, it is important to note, was shaped by the immigrants' European experience. The popular image of the Jewish immigrants of this period is that of poverty-stricken people fleeing the shtetl in the face of near-starvation and pogroms, presumably humming *Sunrise, Sunset* as they made their way off the boats and into the sweatshops. Historians of eastern and southern European immigration, however, paint a different picture. For most immigrants from Europe, John Bodnar writes,

> abundant evidence exists . . . to suggest that those departing were not coming from the depths of society but rather occupied positions somewhere between the middle and lower-middle levels of their social structures. Those too poor could seldom afford to go, and the very wealthiest usually had too much at stake in the homelands to depart.[9]

Bodnar adds the telling statistic that skilled workers composed 64 percent of the immigrants from the Pale of Settlement (the area in what is now western Russia and Ukraine to which Jews were confined) between 1899 and 1914.[10]

Many of those Jews who emigrated from the Pale of Settlement were already full participants in an urbanizing culture in which literary and dramatic expressions were often as sophisticated as among their European contemporaries. In

Lodz, Vilna, Odessa, Warsaw flourished a full-fledged Yiddish literary culture that was dispersed to places like New York along with the Jews who nurtured and supported it. Yiddish translations of British and American fiction circulated in both urban and rural quarters. A Yiddish *Uncle Tom's Cabin*, for example, created a tremendous stir in the 1870s (the slaves converted to Judaism at the end), as did Yiddish versions of the works of great eighteenth- and nineteenth-century novelists: Smollett and Dickens were particularly popular.[11] A flourishing Yiddish-speaking theater brought Shakespeare and Schiller, Goethe and Gorky, to a broad and riveted audience, especially in the cities. The result was a population that identified strongly with the cultural productions of the West. To cite but one example, Michael Gold records with heartbreaking humor the story of his father, an "uneducated manual worker" who had a photographic memory; on the ship over to America, he wrote down in Yiddish his favorite play, Schiller's *Robbers*, and then later talked his way into seeing the great Yiddish actor Moglescu, to introduce him to the play. Upon learning that it was already in Moglescu's repertory, he returned home heartbroken, muttering "always have I been too late." Gold concludes, in words that demonstrate the dimension of appropriation that accompanied this working-class appreciation: "I think my father got the feeling at times that he himself was the author of *The Robbers*, and that Moglescu had cheated him of his rights."[12]

Gold's narrative reminds us that, within the ghetto, numerous local factors enhanced the privilege given to the literary. Immigrants found themselves in the center of a burgeoning, fully modern urban culture that put literary expression front and center. I am thinking here of the prominence achieved by such culture-binding institutions as the *Jewish Daily Forward* (which reprinted reviews of and excerpts from Tolstoy, Turgenev, Hawthorne, Howells, and Henry James), the transplanted Yiddish theater (famous for its Shakespeare as well as sentimental melodramas), the literary cafés that Henry James visited and was much impressed by in his 1904 visit, as well as the poets and novelists and essayists and polemicists whom Hutchins Hapgood described in his 1902 *Spirit of the Ghetto*, led to them by his native informant (and one of their number), Abraham Cahan. There were even Yiddish "little magazines" conceived of on the model of the aesthete journals like the *Yellow Book*; Zisha Lindau, a Lower East Side poet, described himself in terms that unabashedly echoed the English decadents.[13]

In these and many more ways, cultural life on the Lower East Side seemed more fully advanced than elsewhere in a somewhat backward American culture; even if (as Malcolm Cowley claimed) Greenwich Village was the birthplace of literary modernism in America, the teeming streets of the Lower East Side stood as its unacknowledged predecessor a generation earlier:

While Broadway was giving Ibsen the cold shoulder, the East Side was acclaiming him with wild enthusiasm. I saw "Monna Vanna" on the Bowery before the Broadway type of theater-goer had ever heard the name of Maeterlinck. Many foreign writers—Hauptmann, Gorky, Andreiyev, Tolstoy—had their *premières* in the Ghetto. The same was true of actors: I saw Nazimova in "Ghosts" before she could speak English. And I made my first acquaintance with Greek tragedy when I had not yet learned to speak English.[14]

Further complicating this process were the efforts of the elites to Americanize these new immigrants. Crucial to the gentry elite who composed the school commissions or staffed public libraries—ideals shared by prosperous, established German Jews who rubbed shoulders with them on city commissions or at dinner parties—was the Arnoldian project of curing class conflict by cultural uplift, and as a result a number of cultural efforts to "Americanize" the influx of new Jews centered on the idea and ideals of literary culture in the high Arnoldian tradition. (Jane Addams's Hull House, to cite the quintessential effort of gentry intervention at its most sincere, offered instruction in Shakespeare and Ruskin as well as classes in domestic hygiene and the English language.) Exposure to literary culture was an explicit part of the efforts at Americanization sponsored by the Jewish community itself: lectures offered in the Educational Alliance, an organization largely sponsored by the Baron de Hirsch Fund and prominent German-born Jews in order to speed the assimilation of their embarrassing eastern European kin, centered frequently on cultural and literary topics as well as more practical fare; the alliance also sponsored George Eliot clubs for young women and put on English language performances of *As You Like It* and *The Tempest*.[15] The same Arnoldian precepts structured the official efforts at acculturation: the New York Public Schools Curriculum of 1905, to cite one example, sought to use culture conceived on this model as a means of bringing these new entrants to American society up to the fullest height of white, Anglo-Saxon civilization while at the same time preparing them for practical careers in the industrial economy. According to its authors, a curriculum should be marked by

> the predominance of the study of English—a most necessary provision in a city whose population is so largely foreign; the inculcation of a love of good literature . . . the requirement of handwork . . . in all grades—constructive work of many kinds for the younger children, and sewing and cooking for girls and carpenter work for boys; history, not as a mere chronicle of events but as an introduction to our "heritage" of institutions and as a reservoir of moral wealth. (quoted by Brumberg, 73)

One is struck in reading the curricular documents of this era by their reiterated emphasis on the co-equal importance of developing aesthetic faculties and inculcating practical workplace skills. Here is a description of the goals of the "Course of Study and Syllabus in Drawing and Constructive Arts"—itself a fairly significant presence in a curriculum designed to educate and socialize hordes of non-English-speaking immigrant children: "[t]he fostering of a love of order, neatness, and system in work, of a love of beauty, and of what contributes to that desirable attribute—taste" (quoted by Brumberg, 68).

To be sure, this Ruskinian/Arnoldian privileging of culture as a species of uplift had a built-in expectation of limited success; the education and socialization of "enormous alien population in our large cities . . . breeding crime and disease" (in the words of the Immigration Commissioner of the Port of New York) was intended by pro-immigrant gentry forces to provide a standing reserve army of workers for expanding American industries, precisely and not uncoincidentally at a time of increasing union activism and class warfare.[16] But such a strategy produced unexpected consequences. Rather than producing happy workers, socialization by high culture had the somewhat unexpected effect of multiplying the aspirants to the status of cultural authority. And as I show in more detail hereafter, it did so both within the ambit of traditional sites of culture-making—a career in the school system itself became a preferred vector of upward mobility for Jews, especially since other occupations (police, civil service) remained closed to them[17]—and in the creation of new sites entirely. If, as Diana Trilling suggests, the sons and daughters of eastern European Jews helped create a new literary culture centered in New York (but not limited to it), they did so because they were first prepared for Arnoldian culture and then barred from its precincts. The rich interplay of idealizations and hostilities that followed from this double bind is, in some sense, the subject of the rest of this book.

Merely to survey these facts is not fully to understand the dimensions of the process. Even the numerous retrospective accounts that have been provided by nostalgic memoirists of recent years fail to capture the full turbulence of life on the Lower East Side and other ghettos, the constant threat of violence posed by Irish and Italian street-gangs, the hostility of public authorities to these new immigrants (and their essential irrelevance to day-to-day life on the Lower East Side), the desperation that immigrants felt when they found their traditional learning or their literary tastes irrelevant to their new lives in sweatshops or light industry. (Tellingly, in one of the very first studies of the process of assimilation or adjustment to American life, that of University of Chicago sociologists Robert Park and Herbert Miller, the qualities of "Jewish learning" in Russia—of learning pursued as "a distinction, an artistic, religious occupation"—were seen as profoundly dysfunctional in adapting to an American society that, for all its rhetoric of Arnoldian uplift, demanded a more utilitarian, practical, business-oriented approach to education.)[18] Nor does it record the extensiveness of the immigrants' faith in education as providing a way for their children to escape their own fates, and the second generation's ambivalent reaction to their parents' plans.

This process had a number of ramifications. It led to a strain in the relations between immigrant parents and their children, the dissolution or at least attenuation of family bonds, the beginning of the process of Americanization, whose ends—secularization, intermarriage, and the like—rabbis and political conservatives have been decrying for the past fifty years. But most important for my purposes, the part of the process that I have called assimilation-by-culture (high-acculturation?) was accompanied by a powerfully complex set of affects, positive, negative, and somewhere in between. According to Hasia Diner, the primary distinguishing feeling of assimilating, second-generation American Jews, particularly those "passing" as they passed through elite educational institutions, was shame—the American version of the much-diagnosed European Jewish self-hatred: a persistent sense of inadequacy in the face of the cultures of the West and an earnest attempt to slough off immigrant garb and beliefs in order to pass as "real" Americans.[19] Diner may be right about Ivy League Jews of the 1930s and 1940s, but earlier accounts show a more complex affective pattern. Consider the following example from the *Jewish Daily Forward* of 1904:

> A thirteen-year-old girl returned two books [to the Public Library] and asked for others—a novel and something else. The novel must be a good one.
>
> "Do you want Dickens's *Dombey and Sons* [*sic*]?" asked the librarian.
>
> "I've read it," said the girl.
>
> "Have you read Thackeray's *Adventures of Philip?*"
>
> "Yes."
>
> The librarian mentioned several other novels by first-rate authors, but the girl had read them all. When she suggested a novel by F. Marion Crawford, the girl was insulted. "That's not for me! I won't read that!"
>
> Crawford is the most popular novelist in America today.
>
> The thirteen-year-old is not an exception. Stand by the takeout desk and you will be amazed at the good taste of the young readers.

This moment is far from unique, either in the *Forward* or among the memoirs of men and women growing up in American ghettos. (I think, for example, of numerous anecdotes, described with retrospective ruefulness, by Mary Antin: this young immigrant not only proudly wrote and recited an ode to George Washington, but strode into the office of the most high-toned of WASP publications, the *Boston Evening Transcript*, to submit it for publication. Antin here claimed for herself not only full identity as an American but also full access to its means of cultural production—although the *Transcript* turned down the neophyte's poem.)[20] And it suggests that the first and the young second generation of immigrants looked on their acquisition of cultural capital, of the tools of literacy and of literary and artistic sensibility and taste, with a sense of full equality with (if not superiority to) the American readers who saw them as ignorant aliens. Although the *Forward* story suggests just how fully they bought into the terms of the literary elite, especially the critique of mass culture that underlay their efforts of cultural improvement of the vulgar masses, it showed the other kind of cultural work that got done through literary taste. For by making these kinds of assertions, first- and second-generation immigrant Jews claimed against that anti-Semitic culture full rights to a tradition that they felt they already possessed and indeed in good measure had helped make.

A marvelous example of this admixture of affect is represented in an article entitled "Jew Babes at the Library" published in the *Evening Post* in October 1903.[21] The article notes the remarkable popularity of public libraries among Jewish children, who flocked to the Lower East Side branch and withdrew books at a rate of one thousand per week. And it observed the power of what it calls the "race sentiment" among these Jews, noting that the most popular withdrawals were the Bible, the inevitable *Uncle Tom's Cabin*, popular books about Jews, and works that took Jews as their chief subject like Sue's *The Wandering Jew* or Shakespeare's *Merchant of Venice*. Tellingly for my purposes, the author also notes that what distinguishes these Jewish readers is not only their "race sentiment" but also their tastes in reading. For although "the Jewish child has . . . an intellectual mania," an insatiable appetite for knowledge, Jews were noteworthy for their interest in novels. "No people reads so large a proportion of solid reading. In fact, the librarians say that no other race reads so much fiction as the Jew" (131). But the main point to be stressed here is that in so doing, young Jewish readers showed themselves to be more than empty vessels being filled with American virtues and Christian values. To the contrary, these readers exhibited a critical tendency that we today might gloss under the much-hyped heading of "resistance":

> Th[e] strong race bias in their reading vents itself in the opposite direction occasionally. Not long ago, the library put on its shelves a set of art and literature primers, beautiful little books exquisitely illustrated with reproductions of classic art. There is not a Madonna or Christ Child left undisfigured in those primers now. The faces have been marked with derisive crosses, blackened with stubby lead pencil points wet in contumelious little mouths, or eliminated entirely by scissors and penknives. The library has a bulletin board for the news of the day. One day an item concerning the death of a prominent church dignitary appeared among the others. Every boy of twelve or fourteen who stopped to read the notice deliberately spat upon it in the coolest and most matter-of-fact manner. (133)

The simultaneity of responses is what is most worth noting here. It is not as if the little Jewish children did not show proper reverence for the kind of cultural expression made available to them at the library—or to the librarians themselves. Indeed, the article is filled with anecdotes about the effusive regard with which the children treat the librarians, to and for whom they "write . . . fervid letters of adoration, make . . . presents, and run . . . errands" (131). But these children clearly recognized signs of Christian domination in the cultural milieu to which they were being exposed and responded to these petty pieces of pious socialization with acts of spontaneous and destructive counterviolence. "Stubby lead pencil points wet in contumelious little mouths" are the weapons of the weak indeed; but those weapons achieved greater force when they found less malicious but perhaps equally pointed uses in the hands of grownups. Although there was doubtless a good degree of "shame," name-changing, and conversion in the years that followed, these impulses were not lost by the assimilating generations. Indeed, as I will show, the two sets of feelings—chagrin and rage, inward- and outward-turning aggressivity—merged with, supplemented, and frequently reinforced each other.

But before turning to the complex admixture of assimilation of and aggression against dominant culture—the double-edged sword of the Jews' pencil point—it's necessary to thicken the cultural picture. Among second-generation Jews, new and different patterns obtained. First, it needs to be acknowledged (and all the more powerfully so in the face of the tendency to hold up Jews against other racial or immigrant groups as a model of successful assimilation)[22] just how destructive was the ghetto life in which these children were raised, and just how limited the efforts at assimilation via culture proved to be. What one participant called "our street existence, our sweet, lawless, personal, high-colored life" provided a kind of ironic Americanization complementary to that afforded in the schools and the settlement homes but highly subversive of its canons.[23] Its effects on the assimilation-by-culture scenario I have just outlined should not be underestimated, particularly in the Prohibition and Depression years. "The traditional Jewish passion for higher education . . . simply fell apart under the violent impact of street life," wrote one memoirist of his youth in Brownsville in the 1930s. "The lure of punchball, movies and 'working' proved stronger than parental authority or desire."[24] And indeed Jews made some of their most powerful contributions in such venues as mass entertainment—the film industry, vaudeville, and jazz music to name three—and sports, where Jewish boxers, baseball players, and college basketball players all rose to prominence in the 1930s and 1940s. One should add to this list crime. Celebratory narratives of Jewish contributions to America rarely include Bugsy Siegel's role in the making of Las Vegas; triumphalist narratives of Jewish assimilation to America never mention characters like Samuel "Red" Levine, the Orthodox hit man who wore a skullcap and refused to work on *Shabbat*.[25]

These triumphalist narratives, however, do obtain in the experience of a number of Jewish men, and to a lesser degree women, who followed the assimilation-by-culture route. A number of Jews did indeed find in the arena of the cultural a kind of middle ground between a hostile and seemingly anti-Semitic American society and their suffocating family and neighborhood—a place where they could stake their own fates, make their own futures, outside the constraints both within and without the Jewish community. Some found this world, as Alexander Bloom suggests, at CCNY, where literary and political radicalism alike shaped the experience of literati like Irving Howe and Alfred Kazin as well as more politically minded folk like Daniel Bell, Irving Kristol, and a host more.[26] Others, from more prosperous backgrounds, found it crosstown at Columbia, or at Harvard, Yale, and the University of Chicago—to name three highly prestigious schools in cities with large Jewish populations at a time when college admission was still open to any white male who could afford tuition. (All this changed, in large part because of the influx of Jews, later in the 1920s, when admissions quotas were imposed at the Ivy League schools—a sign of their increasing importance as gatekeeping mechanisms to the burgeoning professional-managerial classes.)[27] Many others simply leapt these barriers; despite the increasing importance of a college degree, there was still room enough in the culture industries for people who bypassed them altogether: Philip Rahv, to cite one illustrious example, was a self-taught immigrant from Russia and Palestine who, after setting off for New York to make his fortune, slept on park benches before landing a job with an advertising agency and, ultimately, as founding editor of *Partisan Review*.

Throughout the field of high culture, powerful barriers remained against Jews. Those who did graduate with college degrees in English found that, as Ludwig Lewisohn bitterly observed in 1922, the taboo against hiring Jews as college teachers "has not, to my knowledge, relented in a single instance in regard to the teaching of English. . . . [O]ur guardianship of the native tongue is far fiercer than it is in an, after all, racially homogenous state like Germany."[28] Lewisohn is being a bit hyperbolic here, as a handful of Jews was teaching in English departments— the eminent Shakespearean (and cofounder of the NAACP) Joel Springarn taught at Columbia in the 1920s, for example, where he came into frequent conflict with President Nicholas Murray Butler. But in general, Lewisohn's point remains well taken: Yale's William Lyon Phelps, to cite but one case of many, asserted that whatever their suitability for other academic tasks, Jews could not serve in English departments, for how could a Jew successfully teach Browning's *Easter-Day*?[29] Similarly, despite the experience of an isolated case like Rahv, most Madison Avenue advertising agencies were by and large closed to Jews until after the Second World War. And publishing (as I show in more detail hereafter) was dominated until the late 1920s by large WASP houses like Doubleday and Scribner's.

But, perhaps paradoxically, this crumbling but still powerful blockade against Jews in the centers of high literary culture had salutary effects for those Jews who wished to enter it—and ultimately for the culture at large. Precisely because they were discouraged from pursuing careers in English departments, blackballed from genteel publishing firms, and excluded from meetings of the most prestigious publishers and advertisers, they had to create alternative mechanisms of cultural expression and dissemination. Fascinated by "culture" but excluded from its study as a profession, these Jews entered into the high culture industries with a subversive force—changing, as I hope briefly to show with the following two case studies, the very nature of the literary field itself.

AT PLAY IN THE FIELD OF CULTURE I:
THE PUBLISHING INDUSTRY

One of the most fascinating but little-noted facets of Jewish assimilation to the American cultural sphere was the opening, after World War I, of the WASP-dominated publishing industry to Jews and the subsequent changes they made in the culture at large. As I suggested earlier, that world was so exclusionary that the first Jew was not employed in a major position until the 1910s, when Alfred Knopf, a bibliophile student of Springarn at Columbia, joined Doubleday, in the accounting department; he broke away and founded his own firm in 1915. A number of younger Jewish editors, many of them apprenticing at Knopf's house, followed his lead. Horace Liveright cofounded Boni and Liveright; Columbia graduates Richard Simon and Max Schuster began Simon and Schuster; Harold Guinzberg and George Oppenheimer moved from Simon and Schuster and Knopf, respectively, to form the Viking Press; even more memorable, Bennet Cerf moved from Boni and Liveright to form Random House, which soon assumed the Modern Library list and ultimately swallowed up Knopf as well. By 1937, Alfred Harcourt (as in Harcourt, Brace) described changes in the publishing scene that these new houses had made.

> While Boston publishers were bringing out sets of Emerson and Longfellow in new bindings, new publishers sprang up in New York, notably Huebsch, Knopf and Liveright, who began to publish translations of contemporary foreign authors and books by young American authors who had broken away from the Victorian point of view. . . . New York publishing became international and cosmopolitan.[30]

Harcourt's comments reflect as they enact the tenor of genteel anti-Semitism—associating Jewish publishers with internationalism and cosmopolitanism is a benign version of the slurs that Henry Ford was circulating at that precise moment in the *Dearborn Independent*. But his comments also point us to the cultural office performed by these Jewish houses. Because of the traditional ways of most American houses, these new competitors were forced—or enabled—to seek out new kinds of writing. Knopf brought out Mann and Conrad; Random House was of course the firm that imported and defended *Ulysses*; Heubsch was the American publisher of the works of Marx and Engels. (Simon and Schuster complicated this pattern by making their first fortune with crossword-puzzle books, which they followed up with middlebrow bestsellers ranging from Will Durant's *Story of Philosophy* to Norman Vincent Peale's *How to Win Friends and Influence Peo-*

ple.) It might be added that these Jewish houses also provided sustenance for Jewish writers, radicals, and bohemians seeking a paycheck, especially in the depths of the Depression—as well as a place for professional women to find work, albeit often at exploitative wages. Lillian Hellman, to cite one example of all of these categories, worked at Boni and Liveright after college and for many years thereafter.

But it needs to be stressed that the importance of these houses was not just in bringing new authors to the attention of a burgeoning American middle-class readership or giving jobs to editors of the *New Masses*. They also helped to create new markets for books and to shape new ways of reaching those markets. To cite one example of many, in 1927 Alfred Knopf founded the Publishers' Book Table to counter the preexisting Publishers' Lunch Club, a group that, in the wry words of noted historian of the industry John Tebbel, "was not notable in those days for the number of its Jewish members" and that met in men's clubs that barred Jews. At the Book Table, writes Tebbel, a shifting assortment of authors, publishers, distributors, advertisers, and designers all gathered to discuss how "to give books the widest attention," and did so in ways that transformed the marketing practices of the industry. A member of the Book Table, Michael Gross, founded a Book Publishers Cooperative Window Display Service, which (for a fee paid by the publisher) provided any retailer in the United States with a free set of book posters. Alfred Knopf was the first firm to use a sandwich board. Simon and Schuster pioneered the use of the mass media: in its campaign for Sigmund Spaeth's *Barber Shop Ballads* it staged local contests for barbershop quartets. Given the need faced by Knopf and his peers to reach markets beyond that controlled by dominant, WASP houses, it is no coincidence that (as Janice Radway has chronicled) when Harry Scherman, a literature-loving Jewish advertising man who was barred from moving onward with his studies at the University of Pennsylvania by the barriers against Jews in graduate school, took a job with Boni selling their Little Leather Library—a brand of low-priced hardcover editions of the classics centering on Shakespeare—he concentrated on developing new sites for selling these cheap classics: at drugstores and railway stations and by subscription. Boni took the idea of the Little Leather Library with him to Liveright, where it became the Modern Library; Scherman took the idea of the subscription and founded the Book-of-the-Month Club.[31]

The publishing industry as it grew in power before the Second World War and came to full articulation in the postwar boom, then, was revolutionized by these new, largely Jewish publishers seeking to bring modern business methods (advertising, marketing, expanded forms of distribution) to a dangerously hidebound business. In many ways, they can be compared to the moguls who seized control of the movie industry from the Edison Trust and remade that form of cultural expression, with a salient exception: publishers never achieved monopoly status and hence were continually forced to shift and transform their business, improvise new strategies, and forge new markets. But their effects on the remaking of American culture in the twentieth century were almost as great as that of the (frequently) lower-class, eastern European Jews who founded the Hollywood film industry. Indeed, I would rank one of the products of the publishing industry, the paperback book, just behind the movies and television and just ahead of radio in cultural significance, and this development was intimately tied to many of the firms that I have been describing—to Simon and Schuster, in particular, whose head, Richard Simon, was the biggest booster of Pocket Books.

The paperback revolution was given its greatest impetus in the 1920s by a figure I have not yet mentioned, although he soon came to be intimately connected with those I have discussed and in many ways embodies the cultural transition of second-generation Jews I have been tracing: Emmanuel Haldeman-Julius. The son of an immigrant tailor, Haldeman-Julius was forced to quit school at age thirteen in order to support his family; a young socialist, he drifted into the bohemian scene in Greenwich Village while working on a socialist paper, the *Daily Call.* In New York, he met, lived with, and married Jane Addams's niece, Marcet Haldeman (then and after their marriage a sex radical who preached the virtues of what they called "companionate marriage"—living together in a committed relationship, we call it today). The couple moved to Girard, Kansas, where they together ran a newspaper with her family money. Early in his career, Haldeman-Julius printed a series of editions of classic socialist texts at twenty-five cents apiece; he took the principle of cheap mass-produced texts and began to publish (at progressively cheaper prices, finally settling on five cents) a series of paperback books on social, cultural, and literary issues, which he called the Little Blue Books. The series began, interestingly enough, with the taboo *Ballad of Reading Gaol* by Oscar Wilde and continued with classics like the *Rubaiyat* of Omar Khayyam, and the works of Shakespeare, Balzac, Molière, Ibsen, and de Maupassant, all of which Haldeman-Julius freely amended, retitled, and edited. The Little Blue Book series expanded beyond imaginative expression to more classic middlebrow fare: guides to literature, music, and culture; freethinking critiques of every conceivable religion; and studies of sex, marriage, birth control (Margaret Sanger's writing in particular), and free love. The series succeeded beyond even Haldeman-Julius's quite grandiose dreams. Total sales for 1923 alone reached a staggering sixty million books; the average cost per copy (the books, it needs to be said, were poorly edited and typeset) was cut by Haldeman-Julius to one cent, so the profits were, to say the least, extraordinary.

Haldeman-Julius was not the first to issue these kinds of cheap editions, and he soon had competition, from Boni and Liveright's Little Leather Book series, for example. But what distinguished Haldeman-Julius from his competitors was his brilliance as a marketer. His appeal was blunt and populist, particularly in the upscaling 1920s. "BOOK PUBLISHING HAS BEEN 'FORDIZED'!" claimed one ad. "FOR THE FIRST TIME IN THE HISTORY OF PRINTING, MASS PRODUCTION ENABLES

THE SALES OF CLASSICS OF LITERATURE AT A PRICE THAT IS WITHIN THE REACH OF THE MASSES. THE DOOR TO LEARNING AND CULTURE HAS BEEN FORCED OPEN BY OUR PUBLISHING METHODS." In an era when college education had begun to become a ladder to upward mobility, Haldeman-Julius bluntly promised access to the kind of cultural capital available at colleges and universities to audiences that were excluded from them. "Would you spend 2.98 for a college education?" one advertisement blared; the promise was that sixty of Haldeman-Julius's books would more than amply provide the kind of knowledge on offer there.

More crucially, his advertisements did not appear in the genteel, middle-class, middlebrow periodicals like the *Atlantic* or on sandwich placards on the streets of New York; rather, they appeared in journals and newspapers appealing to every conceivable class and gender. He advertised in some of the better genteel journals, like the *Nation*, but also in rough-and-tumble tabloids like the *New York Daily Graphic*, in journals that appealed to a female audience, like *Good Housekeeping*, and in journals that appealed to a self-styled bohemian clientele, like the little magazine *Broom*. In so doing, Haldeman-Julius sought to construct works that would appeal broadly through and across lines of class, gender, race, and profession, without—and this is his crucial contribution—ignoring or invalidating those categories. His aim can be best gauged by the following test that he set for himself in thinking about adding new books to the Little Blue Book series.

> If I could have given myself, when I began the Little Blue Books, advice which I now might offer out of my nine years' experience, I would have said something like this: "Whenever you consider a book for publication, pick out twenty-five imaginary readers for it from all levels of life. Pick out a college professor, a scientist, a college student, a highschool boy and a highschool girl, a day laborer, a factory worker, a stenographer, a housewife, a school teacher, a hobo, a chorus girl, an editor, a doctor, a lawyer, a soda-fountain clerk, a waitress, a Pullman porter, a millionaire, a salesman, a bootblack, an undertaker, a grocery man, a preacher, and a tired businessman—and put yourself in the place of each one in turn, and ask yourself candidly whether such a person would buy the book for the price you are selling it if he had the chance. If fifteen out of the twenty-five would probably buy the book, then I would recommend putting it into the Little Blue Books. If less than fifteen would be likely to buy it at some time or other, its success as a Little Blue Book would be doubtful. If less than ten would buy it, its failure would be assured.[32]

Haldeman-Julius here does not, it should be noted, appeal to the universal subject of liberal-humanist aesthetic discourse—a subject, that is to say, freed from ethnic or racial or class affiliation by virtue of the faculty of taste. Nor does he appeal to a *mass* audience, in the sense of much of mass-culture theory or even the current theory of the middlebrow. Rather his is a vision of an audience very similar to that envisioned by current marketing practices, one composed of a number of distinct and quite different subgroups each of whose "lifestyle niches" is organized in complex differential relation to the others. Haldeman-Julius kept the segmented, multiclass, multiracial audience very much in mind in his products as well. None of the other middlebrow publishers created a list that varied so much in range, all the way from Maeterlinck and Ibsen to anthologies of Southern humor, or in racial and ethnic address. Little Blue Books were published by Russian and Italian authors, by immigrant writers, of African-American folktales and stories; there were guides to popular Italian operas as well as high art German ones, and there was an early handbook to "Negro jazz." The audience was multigendered as well. "Sex sells," Haldeman-Julius concluded (31), but to both sexes: he was an advocate of birth control, "companionate marriage," and sexual freedom, and his Little Blue Books included works by Margaret Sanger making arguments for birth control (it was illegal to *describe* contraceptive practices except while advocating their value); classic texts advocating free love; guides to male and female anatomy; and sympathetic accounts from lesbians and gay men coupled with pleas for social understanding (e.g., *Female Homosexuals, Lesbians, Tell Their Stories: The Truth Concerning Their Sexual Nature as Revealed by Courageous Women* [c. 1948]). These works sold, Haldeman-Julius proudly reported, to all classes as well as all sexes—hardly surprising, but not unimportant, at a time of intense sexual curiosity but also intense official repression.

The ironies proliferating around Haldeman-Julius are too delicious to pass over. This Jewish socialist applied to book publishing the principles of American industry then being pioneered by the anti-Semite Henry Ford—and on the Kansas plains, yet. And as an advertiser, he pioneered an understanding of the market as one composed of a reticulated, diverse set of audiences each possessing its own cultural politics: a vision of difference in unity that contrasted with the one-size-fits-all approach of contemporaries like Ford. And I would suggest that his political vision, his Jewish origins, and his marketing strategies were one. Haldeman-Julius's pan-class, pan-race, and pan-ethnic vision comported well with his own experience as a Jewish immigrant who found in a set of communities—whether Greenwich Village or the plains of Kansas—niches where he could thrive not despite but because of his manifest otherness; and his genius was to perceive that America was composed of countless such communities set in vibrant, dialectical relation to each other. Because of this perception of America as a set of separated ethno- and class spheres, he was able to construct a remarkably sophisticated set of products and marketing strategies, the end of which was to compose shifting alliances that cut across established communities and create new ones. His Jewishness fit well, moreover, with his politics. Although he abandoned his socialism after he made his first million, he adopted in its place a cranky and boid anti-clericalism. At a moment when Protestant revivals were sweeping the countryside—Billy Sunday was as important a cultural figure of the 1930s as Henry Ford or Walt Disney—and when those revivals were taking on an explicitly populist, anti-intellectual, anti-Jewish tinge, Haldeman-Julius delighted in publishing books that debunked Christian mysteries and pastoral practices.

To this list of activities inflected by his status as a second-generation immigrant freethinking radical Jew, we should add the institution of the Little Blue Book itself. By naming his series "Little Blue Books" at precisely the moment that universities were simultaneously becoming gatekeepers to the professional-managerial classes and closing themselves off to Jews, this high school dropout sought to establish a system of counter- or extra-education: one that was not limited to Jews but extended itself broadly over classes and culture.

Free of the condescension that marks the highbrow makers of middlebrow culture of his era, free of the insecurity that marks middlebrow audiences, and suffused with a set of radical, freethinking, anticensorship, antiauthoritarian, pro-sex attitudes, Haldeman-Julius intervened brilliantly in the cultural politics of his own era. Further, his cultural efforts were not idiosyncratic or isolated, even though, like him, they are missing from otherwise exemplary recent accounts of the making of middlebrow culture. I mean this in two distinct senses. Haldeman-Julius's example reminds us, first, of the ways in which Jews marginalized by race and class and excluded by economic necessity were able to leverage the culture industries of their time to their own advantage—not only, like Haldeman-Julius, by marrying a banker's daughter but also, as I have suggested earlier, by making their way into the Jewish-owned publishing houses in New York, gathering experience and connections there, and leaving to start their own. Bearing this in mind might change the ways in which (following critics like Lawrence Levine, Neil Harris, Joan Shelley Rubin, and Janice Radway) we have come to think about the social dissemination of high literary culture in the middle years of the twentieth century. The middlebrow, popularizing project looks one way when its cynosures are popularizing professors like William Lyon "Billy" Phelps or Henry Seidel Canby; it looks entirely different when its representatives are people who took a cathexis to culture formed in the immigrant Jewish community in the ways I have described earlier and used it to force their way into (or work their way around) Protestant-dominated literary institutions and communities.

And the example of this freethinking, midwestern Jewish socialist also complicates the narrative we have of the uses of high culture as a means of social control, the dominant narrative of the Levine/Rubin/Bourdieu/Radway approach. The dream of a culture remade by the availability of the best that has been thought and said may appear to be an effort at enforcing social hegemony as it is articulated by a Matthew Arnold, but it seems quite different when it is embodied by an anti-Klan activist who used his enterprise to acquaint Americans with the socialist-Marxist tradition, European philosophy, birth control, and freethinking critiques of Protestant and Catholic dogma. Indeed, Haldeman-Julius's example reminds us as well that this middlebrow enterprise was not merely an attempt by elites to gain and keep power in the public sphere, but also part of a political vision that we have regrettably lost sight of today. It reminds us that there are progressive as well as regressive dimensions to the making of middlebrow culture, and that these ideals functioned in complex ways across the cultural field.

These are most fully registered in the form that Haldeman-Julius both adumbrated and initiated, the paperback. (Haldeman-Julius provided more than just a pattern for subsequent publishers; he was also business partner with Simon and Schuster and was a technical consultant in the creation, in large measure by Richard Simon, of Pocket Books.) For, although the "paperbacking of America" had wildly uneven effects across the cultural spectrum, it changed the texture of middle-class American life in ways that comport themselves more to Haldeman-Julius's example than to Bennett Cerf's, and hence complicates the stories we tell about the hegemony-enforcing effects of middlebrow culture. To be sure, the project of disseminating high literary culture was enhanced by the paperback's alliance with high school and college English courses—the New American Library (NAL), founded by a European Jewish emigré, Kurt Enoch, and the gentile (and quite possibly anti-Semitic) Victor Weybright, was an example of particularly skilled marketing to this burgeoning postwar audience, spreading a traditional version of the literary canon broadly throughout American society: indeed, what more visible sign is there of the canon in its most exclusive aspects than Penguin Classics? But at the same time, the paperback industry also disseminated material that was taboo, forbidden, or otherwise problematic in ways that fulfilled Haldeman-Julius's dreams of subversion even as these publishers drove him out of business in the 1940s and 1950s. In a manner similar in its implications to Haldeman-Julius's rebellions against the gender orthodoxies of the 1920s, for example, the supreme bestseller of the 1950s was a strikingly enlightened guide, at a moment of high gender repression, to mothering—Dr. Spock's *Baby and Child Care*; what distinguished Dr. Spock was his equal concern for the psychological welfare of mother and child, a concern that caused an enormous stir and that caused him to be labeled by right-wing politicians as the cause of the youth rebellions of the sixties. Similarly, two enormous bestsellers of the 1950s and early 1960s were Simone de Beauvoir's *Second Sex* and Betty Friedan's *Feminine Mystique*, both of which eloquently spoke to the middle-class women who were a prime target for the paperback industry. That industry thus arguably did more to lead to the feminist movement of the 1970s than any other cultural form.

Nor should the complex relation of the paperback industry to newer ideas about race be obviated. From the first imprints of the New American Library, which included the works of Richard Wright (indeed, *Native Son* inaugurated the NAL series of longer, better-produced novels at the then unheard-of price of thirty-five cents), through the careers of Ralph Ellison and James Baldwin, through the 1960s publication of *The Autobiography of Malcolm X*, *Soul on Ice*, and *I Know Why the Caged Bird Sings*, the paperback industry provided African-American writers with access to the mass market, political notoriety, and financial success, and changed the ways that middle-class white and black Americans thought about race itself.

In many ways, I seem to have strayed from the question of Jews and their role in reshaping the field of letters, and in important ways I have consciously sought to do so. The *lack* of difference between a Victor Weybright and a Kurt Enoch is important to note, as is that between a Maxwell Perkins and a Bennett Cerf; that lack marks precisely what we call assimilation. (If there is a common denominator among these figures, linking Horace Liveright, Haldeman-Julius, Bennett Cerf, and later Jewish publishers like Barnet Rosset of Grove Press, it would be a strong antipathy to censorship and a questioning of authority over the dispersion of words, which has been a strong impulse in Jewish culture from the Haskalah forward.) Nor is the relation to their Jewishness of these Jews who dominated the book industry in general and paperback production in particular monolithic or simple; indeed, many of them had no relation to their Jewishness at all. What I find important in these figures and the cultural industries that they built, in fact, is not their Jewishness per se but what that Jewishness enabled them to do, and what transformations they wrought from the position in which they found themselves. For, I have been suggesting, through a series of historical accidents, these Jewish intellectuals were in a position—at a moment when a highly anti-Semitic culture began to break down its institutionalized barriers—to transform that culture in ways that would have a lasting impact. Precisely because they were positioned outside the cultural dominant and excluded from its traditional culture industries, precisely because they brought with them strong ties to the publishing industry in Europe, to the socialist and communist movements in the United States, and to modernist experimentation in lifestyle and literature, the figures I have been inventorying were able in subtle and not-so-subtle ways to change the substance of the industry they entered and, through it, the very texture of American culture itself.

AT PLAY IN THE FIELD OF CULTURE II: THE LITERARY ACADEMY

The same patterns obtain, but all the more powerfully, in the institution whose burgeoning growth paralleled and in many ways fed that of the publishing industry: the academy, particularly its literary wing. Indeed, many of the same patterns I have inventoried here—initial blockage on the part of genteel, anti-Semitic culture-makers; the creation of new institutions for the production of literary value; and the gradual transformation of the preexistent regime with implications that go well beyond the Jews who entered it—obtain as well in the literary academy. With a substantial lag time, it might be added, in comparison to the culture at large, especially at the most prestigious institutions. By and large, the Ivies tenured their first Jewish literature professors in the forties and fifties. (Indeed, when Harry Levin was tenured at Harvard in 1942, the matter was found so noteworthy that a special declaration in praise of Harvard's openmindedness was made at the Modern Language Association.) But the process of tenuring Jews had begun elsewhere, much earlier; more progressive universities in the Midwest, for example, were open to Jews as early as the 1920s (this is why Lionel Trilling began his postgraduate work at Wisconsin). The University of Michigan English Department was chaired by a Jew in the early thirties; Ruth Wallerstein was teaching at Wisconsin later in that decade; Morton Bloomfield did much of his most productive work at Ohio State before being called to Harvard in 1961. To be sure, Jews were very much the exception rather than the rule in these departments, too, but the pattern of greater openness to Jewish faculty and graduate students in these universities remained in place until the mid-1950s. At that time, the situation changed completely. First, of course, were the changes in attitudes toward Jews in the postwar era. Between the twenties and the forties, the kind of anti-Semitism I described in chapter 4 grew in power, supplemented by a Right that (correctly) associated Jews with labor unions, the Left, and the New Deal. After the war, the culture at large was bathed in a general aura of approbation for Jews, now officially installed in the status of world-historical Victim; in the fifties, the paranoid constructions that were affiliated with the figure of the Jew shifted—slightly—to such figures as communists, subversives, and homosexuals, all of whom were remodeled in the popular, populist image of the Jew. And at the same moment, the GI Bill sent thousands of white men to the universities, at exactly the same time that new state universities were being built and existing ones expanded. The result was a boom in English departments—all those freshman composition courses to teach!—and with it, an abundance of opportunities for newly minted Jewish Ph.D.s in previously forbidden territories.

The terrain these Jewish faculty entered was dominated by a new force whose example was not entirely friendly. To be sure, few if any of the Jewish professors of this era I have spoken with as I have been writing this book have reported direct discrimination in graduate school, although many have reported snubs or a lack of professional courtesy from their professors. One, for example, observed that a professor rumored to harbor anti-Semitic opinions gave the names of Jewish students a German pronunciation when calling on them. And many recorded their sense of dislocation at universities dominated by genteel social practices and institutions. But few reported any direct anti-Semitic responses, even from faculty rumored to dislike Jews, and some reported quiet support from politically advanced or liberal professors. F. O. Matthiessen supported his student Harry Levin for tenure, for example (which did not stop him from speaking with affectionate disparagement of Levin's intellectual aggression toward another Jewish protégé, Alfred Kazin). To cite another Harvard example, when Kenneth Murdock received a letter from the Duke English Department requesting the names of prospective professors and specifying that they be of the gentile persuasion, he pointedly responded by recommending his best student, a Jew. (The student heard nothing from Duke but was told about the event by Murdock.)[33]

Whatever difficulties or ease Jews might have felt on the personal level in literature departments, however, they confronted a far different set of barriers on the discursive or ideological level. The historical and philological criticism that had previously dominated in the elite universities was structurally antithetical to Jews, since it tended to associate the unfolding of the English literary tradition with the putative history of the so-called Anglo-Saxon "race" or people. I am not that old, but I can still remember a harp-strumming Anglo-Saxonist growling about the degenerative effects of the Norman invasion on the good, hearty, concrete diction of the Angles and the Saxons and proposing a theory of English literature based on the recovery of the bracingly specific Germanic noun from the debasingly abstract Latinate one. And composition courses put prejudice into practice. "Anglo-Saxon is a livelier tongue than Latin," William Strunk assured generations of college students in *The Elements of Style*, "so use Anglo-Saxon words."[34] Contesting the Anglo-Saxonist version of the historical/philological approach and moving into intellectual dominance over it was the so-called New Criticism, recommending the close reading of literary texts; underlying and inspiring all this ferment was T. S. Eliot, a figure whose dominance in the postwar literary field is as unrivaled by anything since as it was unanticipated by anything before, at least in the academic sphere (outside that sphere, figures like Arnold, Coleridge, and Dr. Johnson come to mind). As Karl Shapiro put it, in an unkindly but not too hyperbolic way, for this generation Eliot was "[m]odern literature incarnate and an institution unto himself . . . absolute monarch and Archbishop of Canterbury in one."[35] All these posed challenges to the Jews who sought to enter the literary field—particularly the newly dominant discourse of the New Criticism—challenges that were far more subtle than the overt anti-Semitism that Jews continued to face from some in the *derrière garde*, but nevertheless powerful and palpable.

The New Criticism, to begin with, was heavily loaded with an emphasis on "organic unity" that consorted with a complex (and highly Eliotic) High Church Episcopalianism or Anglo-Catholicism. It is important to note that formalism per se and Christianizing did not have to consort with each other to this extent. Formalism as a literary doctrine had been developing in Europe at precisely the same time that critics like John Crowe Ransom, Robert Penn Warren, Cleanth Brooks, and W. K. Wimsatt were announcing the autonomy of the text and privileging close reading as a methodology; writers in the so-called Prague Circle, for example, like René Wellek or Jan Murakovsky, brought together the work of

Russian formalists and post-Husserlian phenomenology to articulate an understanding of the literary act that remained immanent to the verbal texture of that work without invoking or necessarily even depending on a greater metaphysical apparatus. But in America a Coleridgean rather than phenomenological approach governed the rise of formalism, and with it came at its most sophisticated (as in the work of Wimsatt) the Coleridgean emphasis on the "concrete universal" and the self-ratifying powers of the imagination, an emphasis that (as I have shown in chapter 1) leads directly to a valorization of the Christian *logos*, the word made flesh, as the ultimate symbol of symbols, the universal of universals. No wonder that Wimsatt's *The Verbal Icon* concludes with a meditation on Christianity and criticism, one in which he directs Christian critics to the emphasis on language and symbol to be found in New Criticism. And no wonder that Brooks's last works turn explicitly to what was implicit in his *Well-Wrought Urn*, a Christianizing reading of poetry, imagination, and art as providing images of transcendence in an irrevocably fallen world.

In this latter key, I think, the Christianizing impulse of American New Criticism made itself felt most fully. For all its invocation of "the poem itself" and its insistence that (in Archibald MacLeish's words, which virtually every New Critic cited at one time or another) "a poem must not mean but be," in American New Criticism a powerful poetical-historical narrative obtained. This narrative came straight out of Eliot, especially his essays on Milton and the metaphysical poets. According to this account, with the English revolution, the unity of faith and reason had been riven; with the poetry of Milton, the eighteenth century, and the Romantics, a dissociation of sensibility, a sundering of thought and feeling, "set in" like a fog or a flu. Modern poetry, with its intellectual difficulty and use of metaphysical conceits, represents an attempt to return to that earlier tradition, albeit in a diminished, crabbed, ironic sense. It is difficult to remember now, but this rather fanciful narrative reigned supreme in academic criticism of the period. Again, to wax autobiographical, I remember being schooled in the difference between metaphysical conceits and mushy Romantic metaphors in an introduction to poetry as late as 1972. The canonical regimen enforced by Eliot's theorizing was mirrored by academic New Critics, who excavated the metaphysicals, condemned Milton, and abhorred the Romantics, then recharged the canon with Hopkins, Valéry, and of course Eliot, Auden, and Yeats. New Critical invocations of history, too, saw that history as a repeated catastrophe and linked poetry to a quest for unity with spiritual or metaphysical overtones. Here, for example, is a passage from one extraordinarily influential book, Louis Martz's *The Poetry of Meditation* (1947):

> It seems that in certain eras, under certain conditions of distress and disorder, some poets will inevitably be led to cultivate a unity of interior life through processes of thought that bear some degree of similarity to the

meditative exercises of the seventeenth century. In the poetry of Hopkins, and in the later poetry of Yeats or Eliot [as well as in that of Donne and Herbert], we may find that the individual ways of meditation are guided in part by traditional methods. (324)

And for all the anti-Romantic bias of the era, from here it is one small step back to the Coleridgean secondary imagination, now redefined in Wallace Stevens's terms as "the poem of the mind in the act of finding / What will suffice" (quoted by Martz, 324); except that this invocation of the mind's self-valorizing, self-authenticating power is launched through an explicit rather than an implicit linkage to Christian doctrines and devotional practices.

Even as Jews were increasingly accepted into doctoral programs and sent out into the world to populate burgeoning English departments, in other words, a fundamentally Christian narrative was installed at the center of their discipline: not so much as its subject matter, which is certainly understandable, but as the very essence of that subject matter—the "metaphysical essence . . . the principle analogous to phlogiston or the soporific virtue of opium," to adapt Sartre, that makes literature literature. But it was a single poem, I think, that did the most to promulgate this vision of literature: *The Waste Land*. This poem was perhaps the most frequently taught text of the crucial 1950s and early 1960s; it was a staple of the high school advanced placement class and the college introductory course as well as the Modern Poetry lecture or the advanced seminar. Its post–World War I vision of history was catastrophic enough to match the grim mood of the fifties and sixties; but its countervision was deeply shaped by a mythopoesis rooted in a Christian symbology and mid-nineteenth-century race theory. These links are implicit throughout the poem and perhaps so deeply ironical there (to invoke the favorite word of the New Criticism) that their proper critical application is impossible to decipher; nevertheless, particularly for the New Critics themselves, they are transparent throughout the poem. For Cleanth Brooks, in his influential chapter on Eliot in *Modern Poetry and the Tradition*, the poem is to be read as a quest to rescue a specifically Christian faith from the sterility to which it had been consigned in the world of modernity, and Eliot's transhistorical allusiveness is the means by which he does so. "The Christian material is at the center, but the poet never deals with it directly," Brooks assures us. Instead, he attempts to limn the crisis of faith and its possible solution by playing out a repeated Christian paradox, that "life devoid of meaning is death; sacrifice, even the sacrificial death, may be life-giving, an awakening to life."[36] And the persistent allusions to the Grail narrative are read, via Jesse Weston and Frazer, as linking this story to "primitive" fertility rites in a way that accretes to itself distinct racial overtones. When describing the wastedness of the waste land, for example, Brooks notes that "the hordes" in "The Fire Sermon" represent "the general waste land of the modern world with a special application to the breakup of eastern Europe, the region with which the fertility cults were especially connected and in which today the traditional values are thoroughly discredited." (Bolshevism is on his mind of course, but so are any number of contemporary ideologies subversive of "traditional values," as is indicated by his next sentence: "The cities, Jerusalem, Athens, Alexandria, Vienna, like the London of the first section of the poem, are 'unreal,' and for the same reason"—I assume cosmopolitanism, race- and culture-mixing, and psychoanalysis are three of the manifold suspects for Brooks's Eliot here [160].) And when he turns to the other side of the Christian paradox, a more specific racial symbology is invoked. In his commentary on the apocalyptic "What the Thunder Said," Brooks traces the prehistory of these cults to their putative racial origins:

> As Miss Weston has shown, the fertility cults go back to a very early period and are recorded in Sanscrit legends. Eliot has been continually, in the poem, linking up the Christian doctrine with the beliefs of as many people as he can. Here he goes back to the beginnings of Aryan culture, and tells the rest of the story of the rain's coming, not in terms of the setting already developed but in its earliest form. (162)

Published in 1939 and obviously written before the war (but well after the rise of Nazism), Brooks's invocation of Eliot's invocation of the "beginnings of Aryan culture" is stunning in its historical tone-deafness. But the matter is more problematic still. The so-called Aryan peoples were—in the school of thought that underwrote Weston, entered into Eliot's poem, and became the keystone of Brooks's influential explication—taken to be the origins of either the primitive *Volk* of Europe or in another context, the Anglo-Saxon peoples themselves. This identification explains, according not only to Weston but to the so-called Cambridge School of comparative (i.e., armchair) anthropology, the similarity among the vegetative rituals based on the seasonal cycle to be found in the Vedas, the Greek Attis and the Egyptian Osiris narratives, the Christian religion, and the European folk rituals still on display in peasant cultures in northern and eastern Europe. Such assertions were steeped in, as they led directly to, that stew of philological-historical-anthropological assertions that, as English critic David Richards reminds us, informed "doctrines of racial superiority and the biologizing of history—in other words . . . fascist myths of heredity."[37] Particularly powerful among them was the claim of the nineteenth-century linguist Max Müller, which resonated throughout philology and anthropology alike, that Sanskrit was the ur-language, the fount of all Western idioms, and contained within its resonant words an organic, intrinsic value greater than the debased, demotic jargon of modernity. When the thunder speaks in Eliot's poem it does so in a language that is culturally inscribed in a position of an originary power vis-à-vis the languages, and cultures, of "the West": the language of the so-called Aryan peoples.

I need to be clear about what I am and am not suggesting here. My position is not that Frazer, Eliot, and Brooks (or even for that matter Müller) are anti-Semites or that they are covertly complicit with racialism of a Nazi hue. Rather, I am pointing to the presence, at the imaginative center of Eliot's influential poem and Brooks's canonizing response, of the circuit of thought I described in chapter 1: the telling of narratives of the cultural identity of the West in such a way as to exclude Jews from the mainsprings of a civilization that they had much to do with creating in the first place. I traced a literary-philosophical genealogy for that narrative, from Hegel and the German Romantics to Arnold and hence to Eliot; we can now trace another branch of that same family tree, leading from Fichte and Herder to Müller into the nineteenth-century disciplines of philology, anthropology, and mythology. In the nineteenth century this branch made up an Anglophonic variant of the formation that Martin Bernal has controversially, but not inaccurately, called Aryanism: the disposition in philological narrative that traces the linguistically encoded transmission of culture and value from India to Greece (bypassing the Hebrews, Phoenecians, Egyptians, and so on) and hence to the Teutonic peoples and their progeny the Angles and the Saxons.[38] In its most malign guise, this narrative combined with other discourses circulating around European and specifically German romanticism—nationalism, primitivism, racism—to craft the essential ideology of National Socialism. In its more benign form, it merges with Romanticism—the theorizing of Coleridge, the privileging of art in the later years of the nineteenth century—to suture the literary in particular, and the aesthetic in general, to an Aryanist model of the translation of poetic and linguistic value.

One place the latter tendency ends up, I have been arguing, is in the 1940s and 1950s cult of *The Waste Land* and of Christianizing readings of that text. Another place it eventuates is the 1940s and 1950s school of "myth criticism," a broad interdisciplinary tendency that united Frazer and Jung with the speculations of Joseph Campbell on the metamorphosis of the hero and, especially in literary studies, the work of the Canadian polymath Northrop Frye. In such influential texts as *The Anatomy of Criticism*, Frye spun Frazer, Spenser, Blake, Milton, and Jung into a brilliant theory of "the structure of literature," a fourfold anatomy based on the seasonal cycle, to explicate the various modes of literary expression; in such later works as *The Secular Scripture* and *The Great Code* Frye turned to the Bible as the basis for reading Western literature (and sometimes world literature itself) as a unified structure based on typological principles. Frye was never as famous or influential as Eliot in either the academic or the non-academic arena, although his example has in many respects proved longer lasting. Frye's refusal to distinguish between levels of literary value anticipated by thirty years the ways in which we have come to think about the literary canon, and his focus on the previously marginalized forms of romance and allegory has proved equally influential for critics of genre, gender, and ideology. For example, Frye's emphasis on the collective nature of imaginary expression and his privileging of romance laid the groundwork for Frederic Jameson's magisterial *Political Unconscious*, a book that was as important to criticism in the 1980s and 1990s as was Frye's work to the work of a previous generation. For all its beneficial effects, however, one powerful effect of Frye and myth criticism was to elevate the Christian myth or the typological method of reading into the essence of literary criticism itself. Western literature, as in the New Criticism, is read not so much as a product of Christian culture, with all the virtues and vices of that culture, but as the playing out of archetypal patterns or the embodiment of typological structures that tell a profoundly Christian narrative. Whatever the virtues of this criticism, it posed ideological as well as cultural barriers to the Jews who sought to study, teach, and articulate a mythopoeic vision of literature.

What, indeed, did the new Jewish professors of literature entering the academy in tidal waves in the 1950s make of this literary terrain? To be sure, many were drawn into new programs in comparative literature that opened under the inspiration of such emigré figures as (the Jewish) Erich Auerbach and Leo Spitzer or (the gentile) Ernst Curtius and that were instanced by such figures as (the gentile) René Wellek. Here, the world-historical perspective of these philologically trained scholars, sensitive (as many of their American philological kin were not) to literary nuance, provided an alternative vision to the insular, Anglo-Saxonist historicism reigning in the English departments. And their work subtly revised monolithic or Christological versions of the Christian and the New Critical hierarchy of value and taste that accompanied it. To cite but one example, Auerbach's emphasis on *figura*, on reading texts in medieval literature as engaged with rereading the world in Christian terms exactly as Christian hermeneutics reread the Old Testament as adumbrating the New Testament's dispensation, had the effect of both historicizing Christian readings of the world and reminding the reader of the ways in which they sublated (or even engulfed) other cultures and experiences.[39] Similarly, Leo Spitzer's rereadings of the lyric tradition often brought medieval Hispanic and Jewish perspectives to bear on works that were treated by the New Critics as exclusively British in nature; after his bravura account of Donne's *Canonization* in terms of medieval Jewish and Christian erotic poetry, it is impossible to read Cleanth Brooks's hifalutin' account of the poem as a lyric about metaphor and art seriously again.[40]

No wonder that bright Jewish students, many themselves emigrés, flocked to comparative literature and romance language programs at Yale and Hopkins, thence to be farmed out to an America where these programs, too, were burgeoning: a new comparative literature program at the University of Iowa, for example, attracted Geoffrey Hartman before his return to the Ivies and ultimately Yale; a few years later, Marc Shell followed a similar path from Hopkins to Buffalo to Harvard; and many of their contemporaries remained to build lives in Irvine,

California, Bloomington, Illinois, and the countless other outposts of the academic world that sprang up.

Slightly different attractions were exerted by the new field of American studies; here methodological interdisciplinarity provided an alternative to the hieratic formalism reigning in the English departments. Particularly important for students of literature was the so-called myth-and-symbol school—a method that, although akin to the mythological criticism of a Frye or (the overtly anti-Semitic) Joseph Campbell, sought to ground myths in specific cultural determinants and social facts. Charles Feidelson—the first Jew tenured in the Yale English Department— reread post-Puritan American literature under the sign of a Continental notion of symbolism, thereby subtly revising both the tendency of Frye or Eliot to expand the symbol to metaphysical proportions and narratives of American literature that grounded the American self in Puritan identities and hence Christian practices.[41] In a more overtly political vein, Leslie Fiedler used the mythic method to bring to the fore questions of anti-Semitism, sexuality, and racism that other Americanists had long swept under the rug, and he continued to do so even amidst an unabashed swerve back to Jewishness late in his career.[42] And Leo Marx adapted the notion of dominant myths to reread American culture as a battle between industrialism and pastoralism in *The Machine and the Garden*. Given the interest in culture, it is no wonder that here too a number of bright Jewish graduate students, many of them possessing strong political commitment, were drawn to the study of American literature by these powerful figures, often taking their work in an even more explicitly leftist direction: one thinks here of critics like Alan Trachtenberg, Myra Jehlen, Sacvan Bercovitch, and Paul Lauter.

The experience of Jews in building comparative literature and American studies programs has been partially but not fully acknowledged.[43] But it is more important, at least for my purposes, to focus on the experience of those Jewish academics who sought to make their way into or through English departments of the 1950s and 1960s. For in an era of widespread (if not wildfire) expansion, these departments were centers of institutional power, drawing positions, budgets, and esteem in greater proportion than (say) the new programs I have just outlined in no small measure through their monopoly over freshman writing and humanities courses. As they entered these English departments in the 1950s, many younger Jewish critics entered precisely the terrain I have been describing in a fairly reverent way, producing in an unqualified manner the standard critical essays on organic form or devotional poetry, often changing their names or even converting to Episcopalianism. But, particularly later in the fifties, many Jewish critics also started seeking out new venues of criticism, ones that would change first the notion of what was to count as literature, then the way that it was studied; in many ways this is the crucial link between the two generations I have described. A crucial figure here is M. H. Abrams, whose *Mirror and the Lamp* (1953) essentially resuscitated Romanticism as a critical idiom and whose *Natural Supernaturalism* (1972) dealt a deathblow to the anti-Milton model of the dissociation-of-sensibility school by returning *Paradise Lost* and Protestantism to the center of Romanticism and even beyond, to Proust, Eliot, and the moderns as well. Similarly, Robert Langbaum's *The Poetry of Experience* (1954) offered the similarly counter-Eliotic claim that Romanticism was modernism, not its antithesis. And Langbaum extended the anti-Eliot campaign by arguing for the power of a period Eliot despised—the Victorian era—by showing that its central form, the dramatic monologue, was one that Eliot himself practiced and promulgated.

What was important about the work of this generation, further, was not only the canon revision it effected, although this was undeniably important (and one extended by critics of a slightly later age, like Richard Ellmann, who brought Oscar Wilde and Irish literature firmly into the mainstream). What was also crucial were the doors they opened to a subsequent generation. Sometimes, this function was performed directly: Abrams sent his most brilliant undergraduate student, Harold Bloom, to graduate school in the heart of the New Criticism, then watched as Bloom took Abrams's critical reorientation one step further. In *Shelley's Mythmaking*, Bloom took on two of the most central shibboleths of his time—Eliot's anti-Romanticism and Frye's mythopoesis—and complicated each by rereading them in terms of Martin Buber's *I and Thou*. Bloom followed with a similar engagement in his *Visionary Company*, a massive synoptic rereading of the Romantic canon in terms that sought to introduce it, and its imaginative principles, to the center of literary esteem and value, before turning later in his career to rereadings of the canon itself in a Freud-and-Nietzsche-based theorization of influence as Oedipal struggle. But the more indirect intellectual door-opening accomplished by this generation of critics was important, too. If, as I have suggested, they varied the canonical preferences of the New Critical generation that preceded them, they also expanded the ways that literature could be thought about. If, as I argued earlier, the New Criticism fetishized, out of its persistent bias toward the "symbol," the literary object, the generation of Jewish critics that followed turned beyond the object to other forces and powers—the reader, the interplay of literary influences, the play of language itself—in such a way as to explode or at least expand the metaphysics of the symbol and the fetishization of the text.

Their goal, it is important to stress, was not revolutionary but evolutionary; their agenda seemed to be a way to continue the formalist project without adhering to the particular onto-theological predispositions of high Yale formalism at its high Anglican best. Such seems to me to have explicitly become the project of Geoffrey Hartman, at least in his Derridean phase. *Saving the Text* (1981), for example, turns quite self-consciously on its very first page from quoting Coleridge to citing Derrida, as if to draw clear lines of communication between them, and concludes with a revisionary close reading of that chestnut of the New Criticism, Donne's *Valediction: Forbidding Mourning*. Hartman's attempt throughout would seem to be to continue the New Critical project of close reading while reveling in the freedom provided by Derrida's critique of the metaphysics of presence that New Criticism embodied so faithfully. Or, to cite a much earlier example, Stanley Fish's *Surprised by Sin* (1965) not only daringly turns to Milton at a moment before that great schismatic had fully been revived but also challenges text-based hermeneutics by suggesting that the text works by tricking or playing with the expectations of the reader, which become an important ingredient in its meaning.

The work of these critics would seem to comport to the pattern described by Susanne Klingenstein, who has recently written that "the history of Jews in English and American literature since 1930" can be described in "terms of a clear generational pattern of consent and dissent, assimilation and dissimilation." The first generation, she argues, "confined their work to main currents in American and English literature" despite their infatuation with the European moderns; the second "started out writing conventional books," but "once tenure was achieved in the 1960s and early 1970s, this generation set out to rediscover other aspects of their identity."[44] The career trajectories of Abrams or Langbaum, or Hartman or Fish or Bloom, do indeed comport to the major outlines Klingenstein describes; but she misses I think, the subtleties of the process. The so-called assimilating generation was, I would argue, much more complex in its engagements with traditional high culture than Klingenstein's bald summary would suggest; their accommodation to the norms of Anglo-American high culture, involved fluxes and refluxes of assertion as well as assimilation, even if (as sometimes doubtless happened) those energies were turned against themselves or exerted in the enterprise of "passing" as much as they were directed against the high-cultural order. And the second generation, which allegedly rebelled by rediscovering its Jewishness, is haunted, as well, by the same cathexis to high culture, the same idealizations of the Western literary tradition, that its predecessors demonstrated and exemplified.

Indeed, this last aspect of these two generations is what I find most affecting and problematic for both of them. For all their revisionary efforts contra Eliot, Wimsatt, and Brooks (the latter two were, after all, the teachers of many of the critics I have just cited, and responded to their students with a certain degree of asperity), the first and the second generation kept the formalist project alive well after its time, and adhered to the canonical dispensation it enforced well after a number of their contemporaries had challenged that dispensation. Tellingly, many of these challenges were launched by Jewish or half-Jewish women who had entered the academy at the same time as, or a little later than, their male peers and who resuscitated women's literature and promulgated feminist challenges to a male-dominated canon: Patricia Meyer Spacks, Elaine Showalter, Elaine Marks, Eve Sedgwick. In this context, as I discuss in the coda, Bloom's turn to the Western canon or Geoffrey Hartman's recent rethinking of the Arnoldian idiom of culture achieve a certain pathos, as aged rebels defend the terrain that they seized in the glory days of the revolution from the next generations who have attacked it.

As this formulation suggests, the dialectics of canon formation and careerism as they functioned up to about 1975 had complex internal as well as external determinants—were driven by, and eventuate in, a maze of cathexes and countercathexes that unfold variously over time: aggressions against, and accommodations to, a literary world populated by people who, from Chaucer on, have had notorious difficulties dealing with people unlike themselves. Alfred Kazin puts the matter with rueful wit:

> We cannot let [the anti-Semitic writers] go nor can they let us go, for they imitate us, they are obviously fascinated by us. . . . We do not turn to the humanists, nor the truly Christian, like Bernanos and Mauriac, but precisely to the nasty ones, the clever modern ones—a Dostoevsky, a Henry James, a Henry Adams, an André Gide, a Santayana, a Cummings, a Céline, an Eliot, a Pound. How we love them, tho they love us not. How we squirm and strain to get into Eliot's City of God . . . tho he has barred us from it in advance![45]

Kazin's diagnosis, which also stands as a brilliant piece of self-analysis, could well serve as an epigraph to the critical work I have surveyed, which does indeed return repeatedly, for whatever reason, to the work of writers who foregrounded their anti-Semitism. To turn to my prime example, this diagnosis certainly guides us to the fascination of these critics (including Kazin himself) with Henry James. Of all the writers Kazin mentions, James was the one most fully bonded to the experience and example of culture-loving Jews as both a positive and a negative example. For in both the venues in which Jews "made it," to quote the notorious phrase of Norman Podhoretz, in the 1950s and early 1960s—the academy and the world of upper-middlebrow fiction—Henry James was at once an embodiment of traditional high culture and a figure from it with whom they wrestled as they made their way into its precincts. With good reason, since, as I have shown in chapter 4, James himself constructed the figure of the Jew in a resolutely double manner, as a way of both responding to his own ghosts and embodying his own aspirations. The interplay between James and Jewish critics of the past fifty years thus provides a powerful example of the complexities of the project of assimilation-by-culture, transforming both those who would so assimilate and the canonical figures whom they used to facilitate their entry into the temple of culture.

THE EXAMPLE OF JAMES

Jacques Barzun has written, in a narrative of origins no more accurate and no less self-serving than Diana Trilling's account of the birth of criticism in America:

> In the prehistory of the James revival, I played by chance a small and unexpected role of a go-between. Despite a dwindling reputation towards the end of his life, James had always kept his hold on a small band of readers here and in England and when I first became acquainted with American literature I was introduced to his works. . . . I thus became a Jamesian in youth, before the boom, and even before the lowest ebb of James's renown, which lasted from Vernon Parrington's "liberal" on-slaught to the Marxist denunciation in the nineteen thirties.
>
> It was some time later that I casually tried to interest a friend and colleague, now a famous critic, to read a little Henry James. He had once come across the story "Glasses": and on the strength of its weakness was now a declared enemy of its author. I persevered and made him read, first, *The Pupil* and then, I think, *The Spoils of Poynton*. My friend was soon converted and shortly became a propagandist in turn. It was he who convinced two very influential writers to reconsider their hostile views, and they, through revivals and anthologies, led the great revival.[46]

Whatever its accuracy—as far as I can see, F. O. Matthiessen and Leon Edel have just as great a claim to be founders of the modern James industry—Barzun's account is also deeply revelatory of the literary and cultural politics of the great Henry James revival that occurred in the 1940s and 1950s. The "friend and colleague" who became converted to the cause of James was none other than Lionel Trilling; and the "influential writers" that he interested in James were *Partisan Review* editor Philip Rahv and Modern Library factotum and middlebrow icon (host of the quiz show *Information Please*) Clifton Fadiman. Barzun's narrative thus suggests two noteworthy qualities to the James boom, at least in the context of the issues I have described in this chapter. First, it calls on all the cultural developments I have delineated here. This revival was, that is to say, a matter of highbrow culture; the *Kenyon Review* or *Partisan Review*—Rahv was a founding member of the latter—were not only highbrow periodicals but journals that staked their identities on opposition to the rise of mass and middlebrow culture. But the revival also accompanied the burgeoning of academic culture, which included Barzun himself, as well as Lionel Trilling, and even the great unacknowledged figure in Barzun's account (of whom more hereafter), Leon Edel. And it was, more telling still, a matter of middlebrow culture itself: what better embodiment of the middlebrow could there be than Clifton Fadiman, what better vehicle than the Modern Library?

Second, and not uncoincidentally, Barzun implicitly reminds us that the James revival was the first major effort at canon revision undertaken in American cultural life in which Jews participated on a fully equal footing with gentiles. The elegant, if not reverberant, *Partisan Review* essays of the Russian-born and accented Philip Rahv were as crucial in this process as the orotund essays of F. O. Matthiessen; the biographical and bibliographical endeavors of Edel were as crucial as those of Fadiman in bringing James back to the attention of the broader audience for literature.

And Barzun's account of the conversion of the Jews—or, more specifically, of Lionel Trilling—to the cause of Henry James suggests a third thing as well: by just what complex inner rearrangements this integration was wrought, and how fully the reading of James registered as it conduced to that process. For the story he cites as leading to Lionel's disapproval, "Glasses," as I have suggested in chapter 4, represents the apogee of the anti-Semitic note in James's work; a Jewish critic like Trilling would be more than entitled to dislike James if that were his sole experience of his writing. But the other stories Barzun mentions present interesting counterexamples. Both possess thoroughly admirable protagonists—Morgan Moreen in *The Pupil*, Fleda Vetch in *Spoils*—who distinguish themselves from other characters (the exploitative Moreen family in the first tale, the appalling fiancée Mona Brigstock in the latter) on the basis of their aesthetic and moral judgment alike. They are tales whose central message would seem to be the Arnoldian one that even among the appallingly vulgar classes, the upper crust, or the middle classes (the barbarians and the philistines) can be found a few with greater powers of moral judgment that exercise themselves in the greater extent of their taste. And they are tales that promise what they enact: that those who appreciate them are aesthetically and morally fitter than those who surround them in the aggressively banal world of the social everyday.

These lessons, I think, were what all three of the Jewish critics I have here named—Rahv, Trilling, and Edel—took from the writing of Henry James and applied in their own writing. Indeed, to look more closely at each of them is to see how fascinatingly intertwined their entry into the cultural mainstream was with the example of James—to witness how fully all of these very different figures modeled themselves, their personae, and their arguments on the example of James and used that model to gain entrance into a closed or hostile literary or cultural world.

I turn first to Rahv, not only because he is a relatively neglected figure among the New York intellectuals but also because he is such a powerful test case of the assimilation-by-high-culture path I traced earlier and the complexities it leaves in its wake. Born in Poland, Rahv's parents moved to Palestine, then sent the young Philip to join his brother in Providence, Rhode Island; he never lost his accent or sense of foreignness. Mary McCarthy noted in her obituary that Rahv "went to grade school still dressed in the old-fashioned European style, in long black trousers and black stockings, looking like a somber little man among American kids"; his friend-turned-enemy William Phillips wrote that "in his person, Rahv always struck me as having the physical traits and psychology of an immigrant. He reminded me of my father in his awkwardness and detachment from his body. . . . He could not throw or catch a ball, ride a bike, play any game, or swim."[47] Rahv may not have mastered the fine points of all-American game-playing (and Phillips's comparison of Rahv to his own immigrant father, most distinctly not originally named Phillips, may explain some of the tension between the two); but he rapidly mastered the game of literary and cultural politics in this brave new American world. After dropping out of high school and making his way to New York in the 1930s, he found sustenance in the advertising industry and a home in the cultural wing of the Communist Party until 1937, when he publicly and vociferously abandoned the Party. He mastered, as well, the rough-and-tumble style of the true New York intellectual: Rahv was nothing if not a gifted polemicist, even if he changed his opinions at various times (swinging back to an old-style leftism in the 1960s, for example, at the precise moment when it went out of fashion); and all his friends record the sting and pith of his arguments with them, and the increasing sense of anger, paranoia, and isolation that he brought to his life and work alike.

It is therefore all the more surprising that Rahv should have written with such elegance and flair on the unlikely subject of Henry James. Rahv's *Partisan Review* essays on James, which date to the late thirties and early forties—to his immediate post-Party period—are masterpieces of sweet reason. "The Heiress of All Ages" takes up the question of James's heroines in a commandingly sympathetic way, reading the representation of these women as the key to James's own self-representation. Another, "Attitudes towards Henry James," is more polemical, since it takes on the stuffy academic criticism of James (which it brilliantly associates with the figure of James's pestiferous aesthete Gilbert Osmond) as well as the leftist critiques of James so common in the late thirties. But Rahv steers a very interesting middle course here between critique and celebration; his own attitude towards Henry James is one that prizes him for his inconsistencies, his contradictions. Undue celebration of James, Rahv writes,

> contributes . . . to the misunderstanding of James, in that it is so impeccable, one might even say transcendent, that it all but eliminates the contradictions in him—and in modern literature, which bristles with anxieties and ideas of isolation, it is above all the creativity, the depth and quality of the contradictions that a writer unties within himself, that gives us the truest measure of his achievement. And this is not primarily a matter of the solutions, if any, provided by the writer . . . but of his force and integrity in reproducing these contradictions as felt experience. Very few of us would be able to appreciate Dostoevski, for example, if we had first to

accept his answer to the problem of the Christian man, or Proust if we first had to accept his answer to the problem of the artist. We appreciate these novelists because they employ imaginative means that convince us of the reality of their problems which are not *necessarily* ours.[48]

Influentially, Rahv redefines James not as an Anglo-American novelist of great achievement but limited effect—this is how he was read by virtually all the critics of the 1930s and 1940s—or, as Matthiessen did, as an Anglo-American aestheticist in the tradition of Eliot, but as a psychological realist in the tradition of Dostoyevski or a high modernist in the tradition of Proust, to whom he then goes on further to compare James. Even more crucial, I think, is the emphasis on the contradiction in James. For this focus registers the sophistication of Rahv's own critical method. The concept of contradiction itself of course was originally embedded in Marxist critique; but here, Rahv translates it into the register of cultural response. In so doing, he breaks down an impasse of his own, one that bedeviled cultural criticism in his own time (and that seems, *mutatis mutandis*, to afflict our own as well): the binary between political criticism, with its emphasis on reading the class backgrounds of a writer into the response to his work, and Formalist criticism, in which a Matthiessen (for all his political sympathies) would read James's work as a purely aesthetic phenomenon. The dialectical quality of Rahv's critique is evident in the ways in which he deploys that prime quality of thirties criticism, "realism." With respect to James, Rahv's use of the notion is closer, in fact, to that of his (then untranslated) contemporary Lukacs than to that of, say, Granville Hicks; the fidelity to experience that is of prime value is one that faithfully mirrors an experience that is irrevocably multiple, divided—contradictory. Further to heighten the comparison to European critics in the Marxist tradition, Rahv's very criteria of judgment remain throughout as contradictory—as dialectical—as the aesthetic example of James that he takes as his warrant. Indeed, Rahv's own dialectical temperament is revealed most thoroughly in his responses *to* James, which are always embedded within a complex array of judgments—always played off against other writers, traditions, and values. Thus James is frequently invoked as a term in comparison with another figure: in "Paleface and Redskin" James is played off against Whitman, for example; in "Attitudes towards Henry James" he is contrasted with Proust; or, to cite a more positive example, in an essay on Kafka, James and Kafka are cited together as examples of the modern spirit in literature.

In his dialectical treatment of James, Rahv breaks down another binary as well, one that bedeviled and continues to bedevil the act of criticism: that between European and American. Throughout his essays on James in particular, and American literature in general, Rahv foregrounds James's expatriation but doesn't read it—as did Van Wyck Brooks or Vernon Parrington—as a sign of his effeteness or aestheticism. Rather, to Rahv, James is to be read as an exile; and this quality renders him not the last Bostonian, as Brooks would have it, but the first cosmopolitan modernist, the American Joyce.

> These contradictions in James . . . are chiefly to be accounted for in terms of his situation as an American writer who experienced his nationality and the social class to which he belonged as at once an ordeal and as an inspiration. The "great world" is corrupt, yet it represents an irresistible goal. . . . History and culture are the supreme ideal, but why not make of them a strictly private possession? Europe is romance and reality and civilization, but the spirit resides in America. (85)

This last term—America—suggests one final dialectical dimension to Rahv's maneuvering; that in writing about James, he is really writing about himself—or, more accurately, writing himself, creating a genealogy for the role that he is to occupy, that of the freelance cultural critic in an American context. Like Lewisohn before him, Rahv searches for a model who might stand both within and without a culture from which Rahv feels profoundly alienated; Rahv here finds such an example not in Lewisohn's ideal, Arnold, but in a figure thoroughly reviled by most of the leftist-leaning criticism of his time, Henry James. In so doing, Rahv also creates a space for himself in the American scene. The question of residence on which he focuses his comments on James, after all, is one that resonates in Rahv's own rootless experience; and James's similar rootlessness (the source of much of the criticism of the Brooks/Parrington/Hicks generation that preceded Rahv) becomes the ground of his value. Indeed, James would seem to be transformed here into something of an image of Rahv—and his entire generation. As a member of the gentry class who emigrated to Europe but never lost touch with the forces that drove him there, as a man devoted to European high culture yet still fascinated with a booming, bustling, materialist America, James becomes a mirror in which Rahv can measure his own experience as an emigré.

But what about James's own snobbishness, his ostentatious (if, as I have argued earlier, second-order) anti-Semitism? For all James's odd identification with the figure of the alien, he would, I think, have had nothing but problems identifying with a *real* alien like Rahv. And the converse is also true: Rahv never fully identified with a figure like James, for all the imaginative sympathy he clearly feels for him. There remain nuances, reservations, even in the earlier criticism; later in his career, as Leon Edel's biography poured forth and James was canonized in the academy ("showing," Rahv sniffs, "its usual lack of discrimination" [Porter and Dvosin, p. 95]), Rahv turned on James and denounced him for his nastiness, snobbery, and upper-class elitism—all the qualities that Rahv had attempted to explain away in his earlier work. He reverses his early judgment of James as the great modernist by claiming that "if James is a great writer—and I believe he is one—it is strictly on a national scale that he can be most highly appreciated. In the literature of the world he is not a figure of the first order." He then goes on to compare James to obscure figures like "the Russian novelist and storyteller Nikolai Leskov, the Austrian novelist Adalbert Stifter, and the Swiss Gottfried Keller" (97).

The ironies here are multiple. James the expatriate is ironically condemned to a fate that would have horrified him—a provincial American, indeed!—while Rahv the American adopts the position of the worldly critic, the critic unbounded by the constraints of the merely "Anglo-Saxon." In short, Rahv becomes James—speaks in a demonstrably Jamesian voice—even in or precisely through his denunciation of James. Indeed, his mimicry of James is yet more precise, for James himself makes exactly the same dismissive moves as Rahv in his own account of a problematic literary precursor, *Hawthorne* (1878). There, James dismisses the importance of his predecessor by consigning him to the status of an American provincial, and then goes on to compare his masterpiece, *The Scarlet Letter*, unfavorably to a lesser work of a minor English contemporary, John Gibson Lockhart's *Adam Blair*. Whatever else one may say about it, Rahv's most stunning move—the damning comparison of James to minor European writers—turns out to be his most Jamesian.

What we witness in Rahv's career-long engagement with the works of James, in other words, is an excellent example of the complexities of the assimilation-by-high-culture path I have been describing in this chapter. James for Rahv is at once the occasion for his own dialectical self-positioning vis-à-vis a culturally regressive America; vis-à-vis the cultural politics of the Left; and, late in his own career, vis-à-vis the academic establishment that lionized James, the literary establishment that was becoming increasingly conservative, and himself. That the Jewish emigré Rahv helped construct the terms by which James was rescued from his WASP detractors—as a modernist exile—suggests how powerful this intervention proved to be. That he learned from James the very terms by which he denounced James suggests just how thorough this process of self-fashioning on the Jamesian model actually was, how deep down it went.

A similar set of dialectics marks the experience of Rahv's contemporary Lionel Trilling. Far more gentlemanly than the willfully uncouth Rahv, and far more influential, Trilling came to symbolize for an entire generation the cathexis to traditional Anglo-European high culture in all its nuanced complexity—and demonstrated as well the unstable amalgam of affect that marked this legitimating move. For all his fastidious elegance, Trilling, like Rahv, possessed an unusual amount of aggression against, even as he registered an internal accommodation to, the discipline of high culture; and both were registered, as was the case with Rahv, by means of an odd identification with the figure of Henry James.

To be sure, unlike Rahv, Trilling's acquaintance with Anglo-European high culture seemed his by birthright. Indeed, his family is a perfect example of the ways in which, as I showed in the first half of this chapter, immigrant Jews often considered themselves superior to the bustling commercial world of America even as they tried to fit into it. Trilling was raised by a Dickens-reading mother with severe delusions of gentility (his biographer, Mark Krupnick, was embarrassed to learn after the publication of his biography that Lionel's mother had inflated her cultural status by falsely claiming to be an opera singer in her youth) and by a manufacturer father who went broke when he decided that the rise of the Model T meant that drivers would require fur-lined gloves. Trilling's involvement with traditional high culture continued at Columbia University, which he entered at a time when the administration worried explicitly about the overabundance of hypercompetitive Jews in the college and imposed new admissions tests with the explicit goal, as Susanne Klingenstein reminds us, of restricting the number of "the lowest grade of applicant," which was disproportionately composed of "New York City Jews."[49] What is remarkable about Trilling is that this increasingly anti-Semitic climate had little or no effect on his studies or self-conception. At Columbia, first as an undergraduate, then a graduate student and assistant professor, Trilling consistently, one might even say blithely, ignored the ethnic currents around him as he forged a vibrant connection to an Arnoldian model of culture; indeed, his thesis was a nuanced and balanced (which is to say willfully Arnoldian) study of Arnold. And with the exception of a year of graduate study at the University of Wisconsin, Trilling never left the Upper West Side; he was a creature of Columbia from his entrance there until his death in 1975.

But of what Columbia? Although it was finally his institutional home, it was not really, I think, the English Department that constituted Trilling's idea of the university: although that department changed radically in his time there, it started out as a very traditional, philologically and historically oriented place, and Trilling's interests ranged across the entire orbit of European and American culture and civilization. If there was one model he found at Columbia that best summarized—that quite conceivably sparked—his own humanistic temper, it was, Trilling later claimed, the undergraduate program in which he was enrolled, the Course on General Study.

Words that Trilling spoke in a late memoir of his time at Columbia may serve as the best gloss on this educational experiment:

> The Columbia mystique [embodied in this program] was directed to showing young men how they might escape from the limitations of their middle-class or lower-middle-class upbringings by putting before them great models of thought, feeling, and imagination, and great issues which suggested the close interrelation of the private and personal life with the public life, with life in society.[50]

Founded in 1920 by the popularizing professor John Erskine and based on his course of instruction for soldiers during the First World War, the Course on General Study (which later mutated into Columbia's Humanities Division) had

as its explicit goal the promulgation of the Western classics to a newly heterogeneous student body. Judging from the success of Trilling's class (which included
not only him but also Barzun) and the subsequent expansion of Erskine's program into a curriculum for Columbia undergraduates, the program succeeded
brilliantly in its task.[51]

What is crucial about Erskine's own understanding of this program was that
it aimed at the shaping of sensibilities as well as the imparting of information.
And insofar as it succeeded, it had psychic as well as educational or vocational
dimensions, effects that are enacted in the twists and turns of Trilling's sinuous
prose. The Western literary tradition was to provide the young men who entered
it, according to Trilling, with what he calls "great *models* of thought, feeling and
imagination"; their cognition, affect, and imagination were to be remodeled on
the pattern provided by *literary* protoypes. In the great tradition of *bildung*-
building, those faculties are themselves to be nurtured by acquaintance with the
works that argue for the power of these texts: becoming steeped in them remakes
the self by exposing it to what Arnold called the best that has been thought and
said. But the end of this enterprise is the remystification of the social project with
which it began. Having detoured to a remodeling job on the self performed by
the literary—to in some sense the creation of a new self *through* the literary—
Trilling ends with a euphemizing restatement of the original goal, life in society,
stripped of its original class agenda. Indeed, "less grandiose" as the original statement of the matter may have been, Trilling ends on a tellingly grandiose note.
The goal of the acquaintance with the literary is to learn to connect the private
and public spheres, to enter into "life in society." The cultural and the class
project have become so interfused with each other that one can't tell the difference between them any more; and the mission at the center of both, upward
mobility and an improvement of the social fabric alike, has been accomplished
precisely through its own erasure, paved over rather than enabled by the royal
road of the literary.

There is room in Trilling's elegant, indeed quite reverberant language to admit
of the project of class mobility through literary education. But, and this is a
crucial point, this admission conceals another silence: one about the fraught issue
of ethnic assimilation. This erasure is itself accomplished by a selective understanding of social context. Trilling may praise historical specificity and a complex
awareness of "the public life" that he found at Columbia, but when it comes to
the two sides of elite responses to the presence of Jews in traditionally WASP-
dominated institutions—Butler's impulse toward exclusion, Erskine's toward re-
education—Trilling is interestingly silent. And such silence is the most striking
aspect of Trilling's response to overt anti-Semitism. Early in his career, he wrote
an essay for the *Menorah Journal* on the complicity of English literature with
anti-Semitism, but he ended up dismissing it as a serious issue, and he never
addressed it again. Later in his career he faced the issue more concretely, with

similar results. When told that he was to be dismissed, "as a Jew, a Marxist, and a Freudian," Trilling's first response was to (in his own words) "explode" with intense politicking and work so brilliant that it convinced his colleagues to grant him tenure, and even Nicholas Murray Butler to approve it. But his experience with genteel anti-Semitism was just beginning. According to Diana's account (it is, tellingly, the only one we have, since Lionel himself never spoke about the episode), his dissertation advisor, Emery Neff, dropped by their house one day to tell them "now that Lionel was a member of the department, he hoped he would not use it as a wedge to open the English department to more Jews.... Lionel and I just sat and stared. Neither of us spoke."[52]

This silence is of course easily explicable: in response to a visit like *that*, what can one say? Yet anger followed by silence persisted as Lionel's response to institutional anti-Semitism. Although he seemed to have no difficulty with his own Jewishness, the question of ethnic prejudice that he himself faced was persistently met by him with a stiff upper lip, a gentlemanly reserve, an elegant silence. Which is, I think, the key to that response. Trilling was determined, it would seem, to prove himself on the terrain on which he was judged by the likes of Neff, an enterprise that concealed, barely, the aggression by which it was accomplished even as it enacted the very assimilation that Neff feared. The best revenge for Trilling, it would seem, was to perform the equanimity that Jews, stereotyped as being passionate and overemotional, were accused of lacking. No wonder, as Diana's autobiography reveals for the first time, that he was to suffer periodic bouts of severe depression for the rest of his time at Columbia.[53]

And, I want to suggest, the full range of these responses—rage, creativity, acquiescence—is most fully present and worked through most capably by Trilling's response to that cynosure of high genteel culture, Henry James. As Robert Boyers has noted, the spirit of James hangs over Trilling's fiction, in particular his fine novel *The Middle of the Journey*: like *The Princess Casamassima*, this novel registers political choice at a revolutionary moment through the register of refined consciousness, and ends in a resolute inconclusiveness that privileges—if it privileges anything—consciousness. And James's example hovers over Trilling's frequent exaltation of the fineness of consciousness as the prime means of registering, and responding to, the real. Boyers puts it nicely: "Though he was ambivalent about everything ... Trilling felt he knew with some certainty what was real and what was not, and he felt in James the presence of a sensibility that knew reality as Trilling wanted all of us eventually to know it."[54] But, as Mark Krupnick has observed, Trilling's greatest engagement with James came in what was his most influential work of criticism, *The Liberal Imagination*, a compendium of essays he wrote in the crucial decade between 1940 and 1950. There are thirteen essays in the book, and James figures in nine of them. And these are not just offhand quotations. One of these deals explicitly with James—a justifiably famous essay on *The Princess Casamassima*; one, "The Sense of the Past," takes its title from

James's novel and Eliot's comment about James's not having the sense but rather the sense of the sense of the past; another, "Art and Neurosis," turns on the reminder that, while James was undeniably an arch-neurotic, not every neurotic is a Henry James; most important of all, perhaps, in "Manners, Morals, and the Novel" James is cited as the American novelist who "was alone in knowing that to scale the moral and aesthetic heights in the novel one had to use the ladder of social observation." And Trilling goes on to cite, more or less verbatim, James's famous denunciation from *Hawthorne* of all the things that Hawthorne's America was missing—omitting, tellingly, James's own distancing of himself from this indictment, his recognition that "the American knows that while a good deal is left out, a good deal remains."[55]

In each of these cases, James serves Trilling as what another great exemplar, Matthew Arnold, would call a touchstone: the embodiment of the ideal against which more transitory notions are to be assessed; in each of these cases, a central problematic of modernist thought—the persistence of the political, the power of the unconscious, the insistence of history—is weighed against the example of James. More important, Trilling invokes James the critic of the American scene. Not only is James the only American deemed fit to join Arnold, Freud, Nietzsche, and Austen in Trilling's unlikely pantheon of heroes, he is the one Trilling uses to bring the tragic knowledge of historical contingency to bear on the American, that is to say, the liberal imagination. Indeed, in a move I have more to say about hereafter, Trilling rescripts that eminently Jamesian scenario in such a way as to make James even more of a detached observer of the American scene than he in fact was.

But what about James's palpable, if genteel, anti-Semitism? As should not surprise us, Trilling preserves a discreet silence. This silence is in strong contrast to his willingness to call a Jew-hater by his proper name in other venues, sometimes even in the same passage in which he is praising James. Here is one powerful example, drawn from the crucial essay "Reality in America." Trilling is tracing what he calls "the dark and bloody crossroads where literature and politics meet" and staging there a battle royal between Dreiser and James, representatives respectively of the politics and the art camps of literary judgment (11). "The liberal judgment of Dreiser and James goes back of politics, goes back of the cultural assumptions that politics makes," Trilling writes, then adds:

> It is a judgment on the proper nature of mind, rather than any actual political meaning that might be drawn from the works of the two men, which accounts for the unequal justice they have received from the progressive critics [i.e., Vernon Parrington and Granville Hicks]. If it could be conclusively demonstrated—by, say, documents in James's handwriting—that James explicitly intended his books to be understood as pleas for co-operatives, labor unions, better housing, and more equitable taxa-

tion, the American critic in his liberal and progressive character would still be worried by James because his work shows so many of the electric qualities of mind. And if something of the opposite were proved of Dreiser, it would be brushed aside—as his doctrinaire anti-Semitism has in fact been brushed aside—because his books have the awkwardness, the chaos, the heaviness, we associate with "reality." (12–3)

Given the dialectics of literary affiliation in the thirties, this maneuver smacks of a tactical genius, albeit of a sneaky sort. Along with Dreiser, Trilling dumps on Parrington and Hicks the full weight of the anti-Semitism that freights the Marxist tradition itself, particularly in the aftermath of the purges and the assassination of Trotsky. But the move has an even greater suppleness. Trilling's comments about Dreiser's programmatic anti-Semitism raise, by contrast if nothing else, the specter of a nonprogrammatic anti-Semitism, an anti-Semitism like, say, James's—one that finally just doesn't have to be worried about. This anti-Semitism, one could infer from Trilling's silence about it, is trivial or second order, its ethnic awareness and agenda as easily elided by the magisterial critic as the efforts at social engineering represented by the Course on General Study. Indeed, if all we have to worry about is a *programmatic* anti-Semitism, then we can afford to be blasé about the rest: the sneers of Trilling's genteel colleagues, or the collusion of the Western literary tradition itself with the kind of prejudice that would ostracize people like Trilling, can be responded to with an urbane shrug of the shoulders—a shrug that performs, well, many things: the inclusion of Trilling in the very circles that would ostracize him by his mimicry of their behavior; an assertion of the irrelevance of their prejudice; an implicit assertion of their own lack of gentility in contrast with his more surpassing kind.*

But this performed urbanity should not conceal the considerable reserves of aggression that persistently surround the whole vexed question of anti-Semitism for Trilling. If he mimics a genteel silence on these issues when he speaks about James, he does so in order to preserve James for other purposes. For when Trilling turns to the condition of American culture, he does so in terms that ventriloquize James's bemused responses to his native land. We have seen one example of this in "Manners, Morals, and the Novel," where Trilling not only echoes James's criticism of Hawthorne but heightens his European hauteur by ignoring James's qualifications of his own stance and his openness to America as a space of pos-

---

*Trilling's tactic of exculpating James for his anti-Semitism but inculpating one of James's peers seems to have been habitual. After I gave a talk based on this material at the Henry James Sesquicentennial in 1992, the prominent Israeli critic Hana Wirth-Nesher spoke from the audience about her experience as a graduate student with Trilling. When she told Trilling that she wished to write a dissertation on Virginia Woolf, he replied: "Why work on that anti-Semite? Why not work on someone more sympathetic, like Henry James?"

sibility. And when Trilling goes on in that essay to detail his own sense of what is missing in American life—"implication, modulation, personal idiosyncrasy" and "awareness of social forms, both great and small"—he is virtually paraphrasing James's lament of the complex fate of being an exile from America (216). Indeed, one might even go so far as to say that the persona Trilling crafts for himself throughout his work—his tone, his range of reference, his enactment of the free play of supple consciousness for which he argues—is profoundly Jamesian: that of the sympathetic but distanced figure invoking a more capacious sense of consciousness and a cosmopolitan perspective to critique the lacunae of the American scene. Indeed, by means of his persistent references to James and of the selective nature of those references, Trilling defines both himself and James in resonant common terms: as aliens.

This final trope suggests how complex is the work that Trilling is accomplishing here. It suggests that he is not merely claiming James as a warrant for his own authority and insights but instead is retrospectively reconstructing James as a proleptic version of himself. By his explicit claim of kinship with James, Trilling implicitly represents himself here as a Henry James who did not leave home; as the urbane insider-outsider fully at home neither in the university nor the general culture, located not in the political arena or among the apathetic polity but able to bring the electric qualities of his own intelligence to bear on all of them. But in so detaching James from the realities of his class position and obviating the force of his prejudices, Trilling reconstructs James—as a Jew. For as I have been showing, Trilling's representation of James stresses precisely those aspects of James's experience that were most fully like his own. An American in England, an Englishman in America, a detached moral witness bearing knowledge of the horrors of history and social life, an alien wherever he stands, but one who erects from that alienation a stance that endures, this James reflects with uncanny accuracy the tragic experience of the middle-class, culture-loving Jews like Trilling. No wonder that in one of Trilling's few comments on the Holocaust, he invokes as a key to understanding that horrific experience not a Jewish theologian or even a European philosopher but . . . Henry James: "Henry James in the eighties understood what we have painfully learned from our own grim glossary of wars and concentration camps. . . . 'I have the imagination of disaster—and see life as ferocious and sinister.' Nowadays we know that such an imagination is one of the keys to truth" (92). In some weird sense, this passage suggests that the Holocaust validates James, his descendent Trilling, and by extension, high culture itself. All these are tied together under the sign of the tragic recognition of historical process in a booming, bustling, materialist America. At precisely the moment, in other words, that Theodor Adorno was arguing that the Holocaust called into question the viability of culture, Trilling was turning to precisely that high culture, and its priest, Henry James, for consolation: for Trilling, it is James and culture understood on the Jamesian model that brings us *true* knowledge of the meaning of the Holocaust, rather than the Holocaust in general, and the question of Jewishness in particular, that forces us to confront the complicity of high culture in racism, anti-Semitism, and mass murder.

In all these ways, what Trilling did, finally, was not only successfully to create a genealogy and a position for himself by invoking a remodeled version of Henry James; but also thereby to make "culture," as an idiom, and the pursuit of literary high culture, as a practice, safe for postwar Jewish intellectuals. He did so by performing a number of remarkable reversals: by turning himself into a James, James into a Jew, and culture itself into a solution to the problem of anti-Semitism rather than a powerful instantiation of it. And as I will soon show, the fact that Henry James has remained at the center of critical esteem for the next fifty years is due in no small measure precisely to Trilling's example.

A third Jewish figure who had an equally powerful influence on the course of James studies for the next twenty years was Leon Edel, although, for reasons I discuss hereafter, he served as less of a role model than Trilling. Like Rahv a Russian-born immigrant—indeed, Edel's mother returned *to* Russia for a brief period of time between arriving in America and settling in Saskatchewan—Edel, like Trilling, entered a major Northeastern university, McGill, and like Trilling initially entered Jewish literary circles in the face of a bristling anti-Semitism.[56] But Edel found another way to maneuver in the world he was entering, which was to do precisely that. He relocated himself to Paris, to do a dissertation on James at the Sorbonne, as a way to cope with the lack of job prospects in Canada for a bright young Jewish man with an English degree during the Depression; in subsequent years, his Jamesian interests and eye for the main chance merged with one another to such an extent that they became inseparable. Edel produced, especially at the beginning of the James boom, a startling number of anthologies of James's writing (including the *Complete Tales*) as well as of critical writing, in addition to a massive five-volume biography and, later in life, a four-volume selection of the letters.

But in addition to an almost preternatural energy, Edel showed a somewhat problematic opportunism. Having won the confidence of the James family and established himself in the public eye as *the* prime exponent of Henry James, Edel proceeded to establish a monopoly on the prime biographical record, the literally tens of thousands of letters that James wrote during his life, many of which are collected at Harvard's Houghton Library (and many of which were added to that collection through Edel's indefatigable efforts). Edel quite proudly reported that he had withheld the publication of some, and facilitated the printing of others, in order to support the needs of his own unfolding biography—to accentuate some points and presumably draw attention away from others. And he was quite ruthless at limiting the access of both hostile and competing scholars to the James archive at Harvard, demonstrating along the way an amazing shamelessness about his own mercenary motives. As Edel told an interviewer for the *Paris Review,* "[i]n simple business terms I wasn't going to tolerate trespassers. There were plenty of other subjects in the world open to them; the old frontier spirit of my childhood asserted itself. I had established my territory. I didn't see why I shouldn't exercise my rights."[57] In 1956, *Time* magazine published a review of the fourth volume of the James biography with a portrait of Edel posing in front of a portrait of James, dressed in the same garb as the Master; its caption was "Who Owns Henry James?" As far as the beaming entrepreneur was concerned, the answer was obvious.

Of all the ways that Edel responded to the works of Henry James, it is this last one—standing before a representation of the Master dressed in the same clothes and striking the same stance as the subject of his biography, at once portrait-subject and portrait-painter—that resonates in the experience of American Jews entering the academy. But few Jewish academics adopted Edel's overt entrepreneurialism, and only Leslie Fiedler made explicit the kind of Jewish triumphalism over the canon that Edel, for all his idealization, exemplified. Rather, it was the cosmopolitan urbanity of James—and Trilling—that many academic Jews of the fifties adopted as they made their way down the tweed path into shabby academic gentility. "Here I was in graduate school," writes Theodore Solataroff, soon to become an editor at the New American Library,

> studying American and English literature from an Aristotelean point of view and writing a dissertation on *The Bostonians*. I'd fallen into a kind of fascination with gentile literary culture, with that elegant *otherness*— trying to relate to it, even to become part of it. I was particularly interested in Lionel Trilling, who functioned as a guide, for young Jews like myself, to the Anglo-American literary tradition and to the higher style of criticism. . . . Trilling could show you the way to Henry James; he came to seem like the best model for the academic I was becoming; a Jewish Matthew Arnold, full of graceful energy and high public concerns.[58]

But if, as Solataroff notes, "many good Jewish boys of the fifties" were working on James, they were not just at the University of Chicago, and many were not boys. Jewish Jamesians of the period between 1950 and 1970—the heyday of the academy—include Charles Feidelson, Leo Levy, Naomi Lebovitz, Ora Segal, Sallie Rabinovitz Sears, Dorothea Krook, and Fred Kaplan; Jamesians of the next decades include Shoshana Felman, Mark Seltzer, Ross Posnock, Julie Rivkin, and me. To this list one needs to add a number of Jewish-born (if not -identified) critics who have written authoritatively on James, including Eve Sedgwick, Philip Weinstein, Alan Trachtenberg, and Joseph Litvak.

To be sure, Henry James was not the only figure to whom Jewish academics of the 1950s were drawn—Henry Adams, to name an even more notoriously anti-Semitic writer, was also prominently studied in the postwar era and, like James, found a Jew as his biographer (Ernest Samuels).[59] And, obviously, not only Jews wrote about Henry James. But what is striking about this list is that so many of them did; and what is also important about it is that, until recently, only one, Leo Levy, responded to or wrote about James's own problematic relations with the figure of the Jew.

Indeed, one could trace the ebb and flow of Jewish self-representation by watching the different Henry Jameses that emerge in the works of these writers. From the idolatry of the early years (with the exception of Levy) to the critique in the later ones, James becomes the proof-text for these intellectuals of their own Jewishness or the lack thereof. Between Levy and Posnock, there is no major sustained account of James's response to Jewishness in the critical canon; it is as if the passages on *The American Scene* that I noted earlier, much less the Jews who proliferate in James's fin-de-siècle writing, didn't exist at all. (Tellingly, WASP critics found it necessary to notice or decry these—and not only Geismar but also, in an important passage, Matthiessen.) While this omission might be more understandable in the era of the New Criticism, when social and political contexts were thoroughly rejected and passing muster with Mr. Eliot reigned supreme, it remained in place even for a later, more politically vigilant generation of Jewish critics in the academy. To cite but one example, in his 1984 *Henry James and the Art of Power*, Mark Seltzer announces that he "wants to radically redirect the traditional course of Jamesian criticism, to expose the ruses that have maintained an opposition between the art of the novel and the subject of power, to change the rules by which we speak of politics and the novel." But despite the direct allusion to Irving Howe (whose *Politics and the Novel* [1957] contains his famous essay on *The Princess Casamassima*, a text Seltzer also takes up), Seltzer correlates James's putatively authoritarian authority with virtually every other tactic of power on display in fin-de-siècle America *except* the ones that gentile culture uses with its Jews. Or perhaps it would be better to say that his silence about Jews is a direct corollary of his agon with Howe: that if Seltzer wishes to distinguish his own Foucauldian politics from an ancien régime socialism, he must also banish any reference to the Jewish questions that were so important for Howe and his generation's cultural politics.

This omission, and it is hardly unique to Seltzer, reminds us of the continuities between academic generations of assimilating Jews and their difference from those who stood at a more skeptical distance from academic professionalization. It reminds us that whether they were disciples of Trilling or Foucault, those generations of Jews who entered the academy as Jamesians didn't consider their Jewishness an integral part of their identity: that, if anything, they may have been vaguely ashamed of it, for motives ranging from the lack of gentility associated with Jews in the fifties to the political incorrectness associated with them in the 1960s and 1970s. It is also important to note that, by contrast, these concerns were not far from the surface of Jewish-American critics who were *not* in the academy or whose relation to the academy was more tenuous than the card-carrying professors I have named. The self-doubt of an Alfred Kazin, his pervasive sense of guilt at his cathexis to high culture at the moment of the Holocaust and his simultaneous allegiance to a high culture he saw as part of the problem, gets brilliantly negotiated through his responses to James. Early on in his collected journals, for example, Kazin records his sense of cognitive dissonance at hearing F. O. Matthiessen lecture at the Salzburg Seminar on James and then visiting a DP camp full of starving concentration-camp survivors; but that volume ends with Kazin comparing himself to the figure on whom his friend "Matty" had so genteelly lectured:

> The beast in the jungle only *seems* to threaten us, being outside in its jungle. The final act, when it comes, will be to show us where the failure of our expectation lies. . . .
>
> But that is a marvelous fable, isn't it, coming from a writer virgin, who acted in life only by writing, writing, who had left his own country behind while hardly finding one in England's upper classes, who became part of England only by changing his citizenship when England went to war in 1914? Yet Henry James manages now to make his reader feel like an accomplice. He proved that whatever his withdrawals as a man, his valor as a writer was enough—and overreaching.

Kazin concludes with a poignant quotation from James: "The starting point of my life has been loneliness."[60]

Or, to cite a case with which I began, Cynthia Ozick consistently negotiates her own sense of herself as a Jewish writer with a career-long obsession with the example of James. As I suggested earlier, Ozick discovered her vocation for letters after a high school reading of *The Beast in the Jungle*, and when it came time to go to college, she naturally attended a campus right on Henry James's Washington Square before doing postgraduate work at the most un-Jamesian campus of Ohio State, where she wrote a master's thesis on James and did research for a professor on James's correspondence. Her earliest novel, *Trust*, is dominated by James; written in the voice of an upper-crust gentile, the novel, like Philip Roth's *When She Was Good*, is in many ways a retread of James's *Portrait of a Lady*. In a 1963 essay on *The Sacred Fount* clearly drawn from her master's thesis, Ozick even begins the cultural process I have been limning throughout this chapter, that of grafting herself and her tradition onto a Western tradition of letters by rereading James's parabolic method "in the Talmudic or Chassidic class of the parable."[61] But she soon rebelled against his authority on precisely these grounds; looking back from the perspective of 1983, Ozick writes that she had to reject most of what she had originally learned from the writer who was most crucial to her.

> From [high school] forward, gradually but compellingly . . . I became Henry James. . . . When I say I "became" Henry James, you must under-

stand this: although I was a near-sighted twenty-two-year-old woman infected with the commonplace intention of writing a novel, I was *also* the
elderly bald-headed Henry James. Even without close examination, you
could see the light glancing off my pate; you could see my heavy chin, my
watch chain, my heavy paunch.[62]

Like Trilling, who adopted James's stance vis-à-vis the American scene, or
Edel, who quite literally dressed himself in the garb of the Master while imitating
Ralph Pendrell, the publishing scoundrel of *The Aspern Papers*, Ozick became
what she perceived in the guise of James, which in her case was a matter of cross-
dressing literary Mastery. But in donning this particular garb, she later came to
realize, she was abandoning the "life" side of James's art-makes-life injunction;
she yearned prematurely after an authority that James struggled his whole life to
affirm and attain. In consequence she urges on the young writer a certain modesty
in the place of mastery—and to disavow the kind of high ambition she associates
with James: "Influence and homage are not the way. Influence is perdition" (278).

As Ozick charts her own course as a Jew and a writer (not to mention a Jewish
writer), she continues to define herself against the example of James, well aware
of the paradoxical homage that such self-fashioning pays. Thus, in another quite
moving essay from this period, she compares the experience of her own mother
painstakingly learning English via Tennyson's *Lady of Shalott* with James's snooty
declarations on the subject of proper diction in his address to the ladies of Deer-
field Summer School, *The Question of Our Speech*. But, in an assimilative move
analogous to the ones I have been describing throughout this chapter, by the
end of the essay, both her mother and James are made into representatives of a
dying print culture, assaulted by media and mediocrity in the age of a postmod-
ernity that Ozick associates with the rejection of the medium of print and its
"spooky"—ghost-filled, presence-ridden, uncannily alive—vehicle, the book. As
Ozick's career continues, and as she becomes more confident in asserting her
own Jewish identity, the identification with James paradoxically accelerates. Thus
to return to the essay whose quotation begins this chapter, by the 1993 publication
of *What Henry James Knew* in the neoconservative pages of the *New Criterion*,
all ambivalence has passed away. Ozick identifies herself fully with the tradition
of James and the culture of letters that she has attached to him.

Ozick's trajectory reveals just how much remains at stake for Jewish intellectuals in their investment in James—how fully they have defined and continue to
define their own projects and identities in shifting relation to the authority of
the Master. In so doing, much has been gained, both for the intellectuals who
have appropriated James and for those who, seeking to distance themselves from
the entire process, have done so through their critical rereadings of James. And
much has been gained for James as well. Indeed, through the efforts of Rahv,
Trilling, Edel, and Howe, not to mention the countless academic Jamesians pro

and con, James has been granted an immortality that has escaped many of the contemporaries with whom he quarreled and whose success he envied. Neither Wharton nor Howells—much less Robert Louis Stevenson or Owen Wister, two writers whom James particularly envied—have endured so many twists and turns of critical fashion to emerge quite so triumphant. But something is lost as well in this parade of cultural reverence and revision. If James has received some of his most powerful rereadings from these figures, he has also been consistently treated by them in such a way as to ignore his own position as an uncertain and varying historical agent (a process that has only been enhanced by his recent apotheosis in another branch of the culture industry, Hollywood).

One of the ironies of this canonization at the hands of assimilating Jewish critics is that James's own most anxious moments led to his own spates of anti-Semitism, to the construction of the figure of the Jew as a false double for the perverse artist. This side of James—the side that feared the identification of his art with voyeurism, homosexuality, sadomasochism, and the social disease of degeneracy—is conspicuously absent from the accounts of either the James-philes or the James critics I have been inventorying, and for good reason, as acculturating Jews sought to slough off all the charges of perversion and deviancy that anti-Semitic American culture brought against them. But there is one powerful Jewish artist who straddles the worlds of high- and middlebrow fiction and frequently invokes James, who does not ignore this side of the Master's mastery, and who connects it to the complexities not only of his work but also of his identity as a Jewish writer: Philip Roth. And I want to conclude this chapter with a work that brings into sharp focus all the issues I have been dealing with here and suggests an entirely different purchase on them: his 1979 story *The Ghost Writer*.

Roth's fiction is an apt conclusion to the tales of literary genealogy I have been attempting to tell here, because, despite its "hook"—the story of a young woman who may well be impersonating Anne Frank—it is a story of recoiling, fallible fathers, literary and otherwise. Roth's Nathan Zuckerman, twenty-three years old and just escaped from a relationship with a ballet dancer upon whom he had been systematically cheating for two years, arrives in the Berkshire home of E. I. Lonoff, "the region's most original storyteller since Melville and Hawthorne," a cross between J. D. Salinger and Bernard Malamud.[63] Zuckerman is locked in Oedipal struggle with his own father, who, having been offended by Zuckerman's use of family anecdotes in his fiction, has asked a local luminary, Judge Leopold Wapter, to intercede with his son. Judge Wapter sends Zuckerman a pompous letter and a questionnaire whose queries parody the concern with anti-Semitism that marked Kazin and Trilling's generation and that may well have led to Trilling's notorious silence: "If you had been living in Nazi Germany in the thirties would you have written such a story?" and "Do you believe Shakespeare's Shylock and Dickens's Fagin have been of no use to anti-Semites?" are representative examples (102–3). No wonder Zuckerman goes scrambling off to visit a reclusive short story writer whose rueful tales of passion overcome by prudence, of "a bemused isolate who steels himself to be carried away, only to discover that his meticulous thoughtfulness has caused him to wait too long to do anyone any good" (13), putatively redefined the possibilities of Jewish fiction for the mid-fifties. But this fifty-six-year-old author proves no wiser than Zuckerman's other father figures. His marriage is strained by the presence in his household of the Frank impersonator, one Amy Bellette, with respect to whom Lonoff seems not to have observed the caution exhibited by his protagonists. As the story ends, the tensions between Amy and Mrs. Lonoff rise to the surface and they go scattering off in different directions; Lonoff chooses to follow the latter, leaving Zuckerman to weave Lonoff's tale into the rude tapestry of his own art.

Written in 1979 but set twenty-five years earlier, *The Ghost Writer* commemorates the world of Jewish intellectuals at their apogee. Mailer, Malamud, Bellow, Delmore Schwartz, the young Roth, and the aging Singer all make their presences felt over the course of the fiction, in either Lonoff or Zuckerman or another, crazy, writer named Abravanel. It should come as no surprise, then, that the figure who obsessed Jewish writers of this generation, Henry James, should put in an appearance, too. There is more than a small touch of James in Lonoff's stories: their protagonists closely resemble Lambert Strether in *The Ambassadors*, whose great action in that novel, we may remember, is his supreme refusal to act; a less heroic Jamesian analogue might be the protagonist of the story that turned Cynthia Ozick's life around, *The Beast in the Jungle*. The form of *The Ghost Writer*, too, is deeply Jamesian. The narrative is, technically speaking, a *nouvelle*, that is, an elongated short story or foreshortened novel, a form that James pioneered and that has more recently found in Roth its most faithful exponent. Most important, the story pays direct homage to James in its very center, in which the following events transpire. Zuckerman is placed in Lonoff's study, where he tries to write a letter explaining himself to his father, then guiltily masturbates (he is after all a Roth hero). He cannot sleep and instead reads James's nouvelle, *The Middle Years*. Its story, of course, chimes with the one that Nathan is telling: a dying artist in quest of a late style by the name of Dencombe is confronted by an eager fan, Dr. Hugh, who ultimately has to choose between attending to him or marrying a rich widow. To Dencombe's consternation, Hugh abandons a fortune in order to care for him; just before dying, Dencombe speaks to Hugh a phrase that Lonoff has typed and pinned to his wall: "We work in the dark—we do what we can—we give what we have. Our doubt is our passion and our passion is our task. The rest is the madness of art." But James's book proves to have other uses than explicating these lines, for, hearing voices above him, Zuckerman stands on it to eavesdrop. What he hears is a conversation between Amy, who is at that moment baring her breasts, and Lonoff, who, at least at this particular juncture, is asking her to cover up. "Ah, the unreckoned consequences, the unaccountable uses of art!" Nathan wisecracks as he stands on the volume. "Dencombe would understand. James would understand. But would Lonoff?" (117).

The moment is brilliantly sedimented and culturally precise; it captures the uses to which an entire generation of intellectuals put Henry James, the work they made him perform. Briefly to parse its multiplicities, the image of Zuckerman standing on James reminds us of the ways that this generation of Jewish intellectuals literally stood on James: made of James a footing, a material ground for itself in the brave new world of the postwar literary marketplace. Indeed, *The Middle Years* was one of the James stories that both Rahv and Edel anthologized and annotated; it is the title, as well, of Ozick's meditations on James and mastery. Thinking less materially but no less pragmatically, it is precisely the James represented in Lonoff's quotation that Trilling and the New York intellectuals celebrated: a James who combined reverence for the powers of art (the James who was not Dreiser) with a resolute and highly intellectual skepticism—a James for whom "our doubt is our passion" and who then leaves the rest for "the madness of art." Indeed, Zuckerman recapitulates precisely their tone of reverence for James in his most magisterial cultural incarnation; he reads the tale "twice through," thinking that "[it] was canon law to me then, ready to write a thousand words on 'What does Henry James mean by "the madness of art"'" if the question should happen to turn up on my paper napkin at breakfast" (77). Given this canonization, it is all the more crucial that in this tale of lost faiths—faith in Judaism, faith in the law, faith in fathers—only James does not disappoint Nathan. Every other authority, from his father to Judge Wapter to Lonoff, proves inadequate; only his faith in James is sustained.

But for all these allusions, Roth is also reminding us of a different James than Lionel Trilling's. The eavesdropping Zuckerman, after all, is not just balancing himself on a James volume but could have come out of one: he is literally standing in an overtly Jamesian position, albeit a different one from that of idealized artist or alienated cultural critic. For at this moment he quite literally embodies the Jamesian topos of narrator or artist as vicarious voyeur: a topos that runs from *Roderick Hudson* forward but reaches its creative apogee in the 1901–1902 doublet of *The Sacred Fount* and *The Ambassadors*. Indeed, this scene echoes as it inverts the famous scene in *The Ambassadors* in which Strether stumbles upon Chad and Madame de Vionnet on a country excursion and realizes, by witnessing unobserved their gestures of easy familiarity with each other, the "deep, deep truth of intimacy revealed"; it also reminds us of the scenes in *The Sacred Fount* where the nameless narrator peeps in on various couples of assorted ages at a country house in order to measure who is draining whom of life force. Roth here recasts these Jamesian dramas in his own distinctive idiom of masturbation and exhibitionism just as thoroughly as Trilling recast them in his distinctive idiom of cultural identity and alienation. More to the point, Roth is bringing out for his own purposes a potential lurking just barely beneath the surface of James's prose by employing an idiom where the latent is made blatant, the sexual is returned from the repressed and made the explicit object of the text itself.

In so doing, Roth is performing multiple cultural work. On the one hand, he is registering his difference from Trilling and from the New York intellectual Jamesians by invoking his own image of the Master against their idealized version of him. Particularly as an author attacked by the New York Jewish establishment for his lasciviousness—Irving Howe and Norman Podhoretz were in rare agreement on their distaste for Roth's *Portnoy*, a critique that made no distinction between the sex-obsessed hero and his author[64]—Roth is reminding his critics of the profound linkage between a sexual imagination they despised and that of the author they most idolized. Just as Trilling invokes James the international Master to out-WASP the Columbia WASPs, Roth invokes the perverse aspects of James to claim a genealogy for himself against the disavowals of a Jewish literary establishment that had founded itself in Trilling's image of high seriousness and moral complexity.

And it is important to note that in so doing, Roth also engages himself directly with James, and James's own problematic anti-Semitism. What Roth does here is to return precisely to those texts of James that grapple most fully with the topos of the artist as degenerate; indeed there is no better example than *The Middle Years*, the central focus of which is a homoerotic bond between a young fan (who abandons the chance at a great heterosexual union) and a dying artist who hymns the "madness of art." Roth's gesture is revisionary, but also recuperative. It is as if he connects his neurotic Jewish protagonists fully to the degenerate moments in James to redeem James from his own deeply defensive anti-Semitism. Roth's Jews and the Jamesian artist can be one, finally, not because they are fellow aliens, à la Trilling, but because they are fellow perverts.

With *this* commonality, it seems to me, we are in a position to close off the narrative of Henry James and the Jews and return it to the larger story that I have been telling through it, the story of the multiple work that Jews have historically done through their encounter with the sphere of high culture that Henry James represented. As far as the first of these narratives is concerned, we are in a position to see both James and the generations that canonized him as engaged in analogous acts of self-positioning, fraught with intensities of cathexis and countercathexis for that very reason. Just as Rahv and Trilling were able to read Henry James as an archetypal Jew—an exile, a cosmopolite, an internationalist—so too we might be able to read these generations of Jewish intellectuals as versions of Henry James, as engaged in the complex enterprise of negotiating new literary and cultural institutions that they were able to use to their advantage to craft an authoritative position for themselves. For in a manner directly analogous to James's ability to create a space for himself in the new literary marketplace of the turn of the century these Jewish writers, critics, and intellectuals were able to use the bends and folds of the Arnoldian idiom of "culture" as a way of making their way into a decreasingly anti-Semitic society—and not at its margins but at its very center of cultural value. And just as James created new forms as his response to this process, forms like the *nouvelle* or, more powerfully, the novel conceived on the model of high art as well as popular entertainment, so too these Jewish writers, critics, and intellectuals crafted new means of production and reception in the literary world that they were entering.

Second, Roth's reminder of the other Henry James, the artist as pervert, can serve to remind us of the limitations as well as the virtues of this endeavor. Assimilation-by-culture is a project that, to say the least, can produce a number of unfortunate consequences: an idealization of the cultural project, a measure of self-alienation, the introjection of the most severe models of cultural authority. Although many of the writers and critics who sponsored the James revival began as Greenwich Village bohemians, their passage into uptown respectability and their canonization of James proceeded in tandem with each other, with the effect of reinforcing both the most genteel models of self-understanding *and* the most genteel understanding of Henry James himself. Roth's reminder of the other Henry James—of the self-divided "degenerate" who was fascinated by the sexual, drawn to voyeurism, obsessed with desire even as he struggled to assert a mag-isterially Olympian calm—can serve to remind us of what is lost in this project. And on both sides. Even as Roth impishly brings the perverse back to a high-cultural icon of the New York Jewish intellectuals, he also points to a more expansive construction of Jewish cultural identity itself, one that can envision the possibility of playful, varying, and perverse models of being Jewish in a diasporic, postmodern world.

If this means the supersession of the culture-Jew, of the figure of the Jew who embodies the best that has been thought and said in a culture that founded itself on marginalizing that very figure, then so be it (although, unlike many, I must confess that I feel more than a small twinge of nostalgia for that character). For in that figure's place might come a new, more commodious way of thinking about the relations between ethnicity, identity, and cultural value, one that opens up new, less paranoid or grumpy ways of thinking through the questions that have come, largely through the efforts of Jewish intellectuals both inside and outside the academy, to define the cultural agenda. And with that way of thinking might also come a more commodious approach on the part of a cultural Left that has taken on many of the same rigidities of its neoconservative antagonists vis-à-vis high culture. Reminding ourselves that Henry James was both Master and degenerate, and that he constructed a way of thinking about Jews out of his own deepest fears, which they then seized upon to make their way into the very temple of culture that he was helping to build, is a way of reminding ourselves, at the very least, of the multifaceted social work that high culture can do and forestalling us from launching premature polemics against that social work. It might open us, I will suggest next, to the vibrant possibilities that exist in and around texts of all sorts—high, middle, low, and all places in between.

Coda

Beyond the Battle of the Blooms

In 1987, ALLAN BLOOM, then an obscure University of Chicago professor best known for his translation of Plato's *Republic*, published *The Closing of the American Mind*. The book denounced the effects of historicism, relativism, and mass culture on the teachers and students at American universities in the 1960s and hence on the tenor of American life. It was an instant sensation. Praised by reviewers in the middlebrow press (the *New York Times* assigned the review to *New Criterion* contributor Roger Kimball, guaranteeing a rave), *The Closing of the American Mind* shot to the top of the bestseller list, sold more than four hundred thousand copies in hardcover, and helped Bloom attain that most American of fates, celebrity, until his death seven years later.

In 1994, a not-so-obscure professor at Yale and New York University, Harold Bloom, ventured into the same terrain with less remunerative, though still impressive, results. This Bloom's entry into the Jeremiad market was called *The Western Canon*, and it offers both a description and a defense of the masterpieces of Western literature from Hesiod to James Merrill and indeed well beyond. Along the way, Bloom provides a powerful defense of close reading and an often quite funny critique of the politicization of literary criticism by the groups he calls "the school of resentment"—the work of Marxists, feminists, new historicists, and indeed just about anyone who doubts the value of the "best that has been thought and said."[1] The book concludes with what was obviously one of its major selling points: an eccentric list of what constitutes the properly canonical, in which Shakespeare and Dante are supplemented by less well-known components of the traditional canon (Euripides's *Medea* in Rex Warner's translation), underappreciated inclusions (Basil Bunting's *Collected Poems*), and wildly campy additions (Frederick Tuckerman's *The Cricket and Other Poems*). Like its predecessor, *The Western Canon* climbed the bestseller lists; in addition, it was named a notable book of the year by the *New York Times* and nominated for a National Book Critics' Circle Award.

Numerous ironies attend both of these performances—a term I use advisedly. As far as the first is concerned, there is no more self-refuting project than a mass-market diatribe against the current conditions of the American mind; the more successful such a project, the less valid its arguments would seem to be. Similarly, *The Western Canon* is caught between two utterly contradictory positions—one decrying the social conditions that have led to the decline of reading (political correctness, poor public schools, MTV), the other arguing that reading takes place in existential "solitude" that would seem to transcend such conditions. Bloom simultaneously endorses the Emersonian notion that geniuses stand beyond the texture of their historical circumstances—indeed, they shape them—and articulates a Viconian narrative of decline that never explains why we have so few geniuses around to remake the tenor of our times.

It would, however, be carping to impose the hobgoblin of a foolish consistency on either of these Blooms, neither of whom exactly aspires to logical argumentation. But what would be productive, I think, is to note how these projects extend all the concerns I have been treating in this book, and inject those concerns into the cultural politics of our own moment, in ways that I find both disturbing and poignant.

Both Blooms, for example, instantiate the labile dynamics of the middlebrow project in terms that remind us of those we saw circulating in *Trilby*. In the case of Allan Bloom, Svengali appears as Nietzsche, whose pernicious doctrines of relativism seduced "the young" in the sixties and have continued to debase American culture thereafter. And, as in *Trilby*, there is a musical origin to cultural decline. Here not opera but rock-and-roll and jazz are the villains, and, while the argument is Platonic (music educates or debases the soul), the effects of this debased music are described in a language of mind control that is immediately recognizable from *Trilby*-mania. One particularly striking example—singled out by reviewers and noted as well by students to whom I have taught the book—is the passage in which Bloom decries, in a kind of delirium of his own, the social conditions in which the most productive culture in the history of the world, forged in adversity and "consecrated by the blood of martyrs," eventuates in a thirteen-year-old listening to rock on his headphones: "a pubescent child whose body throbs with orgasmic rhythms; whose feelings are made articulate in hymns to the joys of onanism or the killing of parents, whose ambition is to win fame and wealth in imitating the drag-queen who makes the music."[2] As in *Trilby*-mania, merely to witness a musical performance is to be doubly seduced, first into a set of emotions that normal life and experience repress, then into an imitative frenzy with overtones of sexual deviance. Hypnotized by MTV, the thirteen-year-old hears nothing but Alice Cooper, Alice Cooper, Alice Cooper.

Despite Allan Bloom's explicit disavowal of the middlebrow project (he is contemptuous of the Great Books program that was also housed at Chicago under the guidance of Mortimer Adler and Robert Maynard Hutchins), his success in this very arena suggests just how much power the tactics of fin-de-siècle middle-brow culture-makers continue to exert a century later. Like du Maurier, Bloom exploited as he managed the mass audiences's cultural ambivalence—the positive and negative cathexes to high culture that make the middlebrow a middlebrow—by furnishing them with objects to idealize and to revile in the cultural field, then redirecting their attention from the authority of his cultural competitors (chiefly, academics not of a conservative bent) to his own. The results speak for themselves; *Closing* made Bloom a fortune exactly as *Trilby* did du Maurier, even though, like du Maurier, Bloom didn't live long enough to enjoy fully the fruits of his success. There is a further affinity: just as *Trilby*-mania encouraged a spate of imitations, so *Closing* has spawned crossover books by academics attacking multiculturalism, seeking to renew Victorian standards, or defending the soon-to-be-lost art of close reading. It is not surprising to learn that many of these writers are drawn from the warring sects of New York intellectuals who, despite their political differences, nevertheless make common cause in the defense of the Western cultural tradition: *Commentary* contributor Gertrude Himmelfarb meets *Dissent* contributor David Bromwich on this ground and no other.

One particularly inspired contribution to this discourse, however, has come from a resolutely apolitical figure, Harold Bloom. To be sure, unlike Allan Bloom, *this* Bloom is an unabashed Freud and Nietzsche worshiper, and his great defense of literature is not that it contains great thoughts or makes us better people but rather that it brings us into contact with great writing, which he common-sensically defines as "mastery of figurative language, originality, cognitive power, knowledge, exuberance of diction" (27–8). But Harold Bloom deploys many of the same demonizing tactics as Allan Bloom, critiquing the hidden conspiracy between popular culture and the forces of political correctness, denouncing with special fervor "professors of hip-hop, clones of Gallic-German theory . . . multi-culturalists unlimited"—anyone who politicizes literary response and fails to love literature at least half as much as he does (76).

As such, Bloom's enterprise recalls a different nest of tensions from those that I have been attempting, throughout, to stress in the making of culture from the Victorian era to our own: the paradoxical position of the intellectual who both decries the effects of a market culture and seeks to profit from it. For like a Trollope or an Eliot (or his own role model, Dr. Johnson) Bloom is well aware that he is writing in a market economy that, by the logic of the market, produces precisely the mass culture whose leveling effects he disparages. Unlike these fig-ures, he does not waste any time in decrying the results; instead he resembles Emmanuel Haldeman-Julius in seeking to make a fine profit off the cultural aspirations that underlie this market culture. For all its hifalutin' rhetoric, the promise of *The Western Canon* is that any reader with $22.95 will be able to get as much or even more knowledge than that provided by colleges and universities. The list of the properly canonical provided at the end of the book is thus not a throwaway, as Bloom disingenuously suggests, but an essential ingredient in the book's success (doubtless it has been better read than the chapters on Portuguese poets). This list makes *The Western Canon* into a pure product of middlebrow culture, a "cultural how-to kit," in Bourdieu's phrase, one whose very success in the marketplace is authenticated by its author's claim to stand outside the hurly-burly market in a realm of purely poetic struggle and strength.

Both these Blooms, in other words, instantiate as they update the central contradictions of the remaking of the field of letters from the nineteenth century to our day. The mutual, interlocking interplay of a zone of "high culture" that defines itself against a mass culture but constructs instead a tense relation to a conflicted middlebrow public; the positioning of the intellectual within and without a marketplace society at one and the same time; the use of a rhetoric of high cultural authority to delegitimate other would-be authorities and claim the exclusive attention of a common reader interpellated by that very address—these dynamics are as fully on display here as they were a century ago. But something important has changed. Were I writing about the 1890s or even the 1930s, I would point to the use of the Jew as a way of managing these double investments, of curing cultural contradictions by embodying them. But the conditions I described in chapter 5 are indeed different: instead of being anxious gentiles deploying the Jew to position themselves in the shifting cultural scene of the fin de siècle—a scene that, in so many ways, our own moment resembles—these figures *are* Jews, and have mastered the very rhetoric of cultural decline and social anarchy that, as I have shown throughout, was originally used to measure and control people just like *them*. "The rabblement, the barbarians, have taken over the academy," Harold Bloom told an interviewer, putting into melodramatic words Nicholas Murray Butler's worst nightmares about people just like him.[3]

Indeed, when reading either or both of the Blooms, one encounters a sense of *déja vu* all over again, to quote one of my own favorite cultural players, Yogi Berra. That is, one doesn't merely have a sense of throwback to the cultural polemics of the fin de siècle in Allan Bloom's denunciations of the sexual perversity of the young or Harold Bloom's Arnoldian canon-construction; one feels in addition thrust back into the cultural polemics of the 1890s, in which, as I argued, Jewish critics like Max Nordau debated with their philistine peers over whether Jews or artists were the prime vector of social degeneration. Except that now, at least in the hands of these critics, the warring parties have reached an uneasy truce and agreed to assign the role of prime degenerate to multiculturalists and academics. And in this process, something quite remarkable has happened. The very rhetoric of alien influence, racial hysteria, and sexual perversity that originally circulated at the fin-de-siècle to describe and decry the presence of Jews in the great centers of Western culture gets projected onto the putatively multi-cultural academy, which becomes metaphorically Jewified—treated in precisely the terms that the anxious gentry elite of the nineteenth and twentieth century used to decry the arrival of alien, aggressive Jews in the colleges and universities, the publishing houses, and the law and medical schools.

Consider, for example, Harold Bloom's denunciation of "professors of hip-hop, clones of Gallic-German theory . . . multiculturalists unlimited." The language here is quite funny in its hyperbolic specificity—indeed, at moments like this, Bloom's writing reminds one of the elephants in Walt Disney's *Fantasia* pirouetting *en pointe* to the *Dance of the Hours*. But even more disturbingly than Allan Bloom, who at least is open about his paleolithic politics, Harold here resonates with unwitting appeals to racial and nativist hysterias that have been with us from the moment of the fin de siècle and that, as I have argued, were persistently invoked in Europe, England, and America when eastern European Jews started to enter the professions, the universities, and the career of writing. Why, for example, decry "professors of hip-hop" rather than, say, *Seinfeld* studies? Why invoke the putative foreignness of Franco-German theory when the huge gaps, if not outright quarrels, between a Derrida and a Habermas, a Foucault and a Heidegger, are utterly elided? Why the emphasis on unnatural or unchecked reproduction—"clones" of theory, "multiculturalists unlimited"? At a moment like this, one feels uncomfortably thrust back into the most disturbing moment of *The Golden Bowl*, that passage when the translation of the cultural goods of the West is put in the hands of the greasy Gutermann-Seuss and his large and dirty family, except now it is the professoriate who are portrayed as a potential threat to the very treasures it is their duty to revere. In other words, one feels at moments like these that Jewish critics are portraying the multicultural, feminist-inclined, members of the putative cultural left in exactly the language previously used to revile dirty, culturally debased, disease-bearing Jews.

My point here is not to accuse Harold or Allan Bloom of harboring an unconscious anti-Semitism, or invoke that most thoroughly clichéd category "Jewish self-hatred" to describe them. Nor is it to accuse them of racism, xenophobia, homophobia, sexism, and so on: *ad hominem* attacks are all too frequent in the academy these days, and even if Bloom and Bloom stoop to such arguments, that is no reason to follow them. Instead, it is important here to see their invocation of this rhetoric of cultural decline in its full historical situatedness, which is also to say its deep pathos. For we need to read these two Blooms, whatever their differences, as participating in that process I have been tracing throughout this book, the process of assimilation-by-culture. Both were second-generation Jews (Allan Bloom the child of social workers in Indianapolis, Harold Bloom the child of a garment worker from the Bronx) and were nurtured by such acculturating institutions as excellent public schools or the public library, where an eight-year old Harold Bloom was intoxicated by Hart Crane and Whitman. Both then attended and made careers at fine academic institutions—Allan Bloom at Chicago and Cornell, Harold Bloom at Cornell and Yale—which both have credited as nurturing their best selves. As Allan Bloom wrote, "When I was fifteen years old,

I saw the University of Chicago for the first time and sensed that I had some-how discovered my life" (243). This mingling of humility and pride, the articu-lation of a process in which a literary education produces an entirely new order of selfhood—these are reminiscent of the similar structures of feeling we saw among the second-generation immigrants I described in chapter 5; indeed, these closely replicate the experience of a Brooklyn glove manufacturer's son, Lionel Trilling.

This similarity is no accident; each Bloom bears a significant personal relation to the first generation of Jews to find careers in the academy. Indeed, Trilling strikes me as Harold Bloom's true precursor, all the more powerful an influence because he is so rarely acknowledged. (This has been true, I might stress, through-out Harold Bloom's career; Trilling's essay "Freud and Literature" anticipates Bloom's tropological reading of Freud by a generation, just as "Wordsworth and the Rabbis" foreshadowed the ways in which Bloom has attempted, throughout his career, to bring together English Romantic poetry and Jewish theology.) Sim-ilarly, even more obviously in the case of Allan Bloom, stands the example of the great emigré scholar Leo Strauss. In both these cases, the critic's spoken or un-spoken precursor is both fully a Jew *and* an American, credentialed authoritatively by institutions whose Gothic architecture testifies to an academic and intellectual past that had marginalized or barred people just like them. But having made a place for themselves in these cathedrals of culture in exactly the same way as did their own precursors, Bloom and Bloom face a disturbing recognition: that the paths their role models blazed for them no longer exists, that the faith in the Western literary canon or the philosophic tradition as a way of interpreting and so entering "America" can longer stand unquestioned or unquestionable. Having mastered their mentors or role models, having in their own way exceeded them, at least in material terms, the Blooms discover that the model of authority and professional success they attained is no longer regarded as dominant, even in the institutions where they achieved their success.

Their horrified reaction is the direct result of this professional predicament. But such responses, it is important to stress, are not merely career- or vocation-driven. Indeed, the powerful cathexis to culture, the "passion for reading" (Har-old Bloom), the love of literature or philosophy that both Blooms manifest and praise strikes me as not only genuine but the most important gift that they bring to the cultural table, particularly at this moment of high professionalism in the academy and cheap cynicism in the culture at large. But love, as we all know, is not an easy or a simple thing—particularly the kind of passionate, romantic love these two Blooms evidence. *Pace* Allan Bloom's Platonizing reading, romantic love overinvests in its object and sets the lover up for a perpetual disappointment when the object is discovered to be just another person, no matter how wonderful he or she might be. And love, moreover, often involves a good bit of aggression against this object: there is always a dimension of rage involved in this experience, even when that rage is involved in the recovery of a primal narcissistic wound (loss of plenitude, loss of the mother, discovery of the solitude of the self) that the later affection is supposed to make up for, but inevitably cannot.

And there is aggression aplenty in both Blooms, some of it obviously directed outward toward anyone who challenges their overinvested ideal, much of it covertly directed at that ideal itself. My one-and-a-half-year-old son has just discovered the possessive pronoun: he walks up to me and his mother, almost knocking us over with his hugs and repeating over and over again "*My* daddy" and "*My* mommy." One hears very much the same tone in Harold Bloom on canonicity or Allan Bloom on Plato: an appreciation that verges into appropriation, that insists that *this* canon, and this reading of the canon, is the only one— a rather dubious proposition to anyone who wonders why we once read Longfellow and no longer do or why Allan Bloom's Plato looks so different from, say, that of Gregory Vlastos. There is, of course, a social aggression at the heart of this process as well; one is reminded again of Trilling, both in his out-WASPing the WASP establishment by invoking Henry James against it and in his performatively urbane response to the anti-Semitism of traditional literary studies and canonical literature. For these Blooms, literary and philosophic traditions that have had problems with anti-Semitism are apotheosized as universal, transcendent of historical circumstance—as if that problem did not exist, or were trivial at best. What better way to triumph for people who were traditionally excluded from the Great Tradition than to define themselves as its only remaining faithful priests? As the Israeli critic Haim Chertok put it,

> it is delectable that, just two generations after Northwestern University would not hire the young Saul Bellow on the grounds that a Jew could not adequately respond to the Western tradition, the contemporary critic with the range and ambition and sheer audacity to bestride the Western canon and serve as its knight-errant and arbiter should be the son of a Bronx garment worker.[4]

Chertok's tone of retrospective triumph, and his mingled imagery of Bloom as a knight-errant serving the Western canon and a parfit, gentil knight mounting it, captures the admixture of assimilation and aggression I have been foregrounding throughout my account of this generation of culture-loving Jews.

The reader has no doubt sensed that, despite my ideological differences with these two, I regard the passing of the model they advocate with no small degree of ambivalence. Much of value has been contributed by men and women working within (and sometimes against) its constraints; much of value continues to be produced by them. And, as I said before, I severely doubt either that students a generation hence will stop reading Plato or Shakespeare or even Henry James or that the Plato or Shakespeare or James they read will be the same as ours. But to confront the proclaimed, if not *willed*, supersession of these figures is to face another question, one I want briefly to address here: what about the future? Specifically, what roles can both inscriptions of Jewishness and those figures I referred to in chapter 1 as real, live Jews play in the cultural dispensations of the next millennium? I want briefly to suggest that even if the model of the assimilated culture-Jew is proving to be increasingly less cogent as "culture" continues its century-long transformation, the experience of Jews *in* Western culture is not. Indeed, the kinds of issues I have been thinking through over the course of this book—clearly facing the new ethnic and racial minorities whose presence in the centers of the arenas of traditional culture-making poses such difficulties to the Blooms—may be glossed, if not solved, by the experience of Jews in the epistemic and cultural regimes of Europe and America.

To understand this point, we need briefly to note the current situation of the project we call multiculturalism. For while African-American and ethnic studies were marked by a tendency toward polarizing identity politics in the 1980s, both have shown in the 1990s a greater emphasis on racial and ethnic heterogeneity, cultural "ambivalence," and hybridity (none dare call it cultural pluralism). And, it is important to stress, this new postidentity politics in the academy is based on changing realities on the ground, evident in both the cities and suburbs of the United States. To cite one example: historian George Sanchez has powerfully argued that the Los Angeles "riots" or "insurrection" of the early 1990s were widely misperceived as an African-American rebellion on the model of the Watts conflagration of the 1960s. For, as Sanchez observes, arrest records and surveillance cameras reveal that this insurrection was also an affair of Latinos, Asians, and poor whites; the media, however, had no conceptual language beyond that of the black-white binary and so portrayed the event as a replay of the Watts riots of the 1960s.[5] Sanchez reminds us that our social imaginary, the very categories we use to organize racial identities and parse social action, is at least two generations behind realities on the ground. And this is true not just of Chicanos in California but of numerous other social groups in the cities and suburbs of America: of Haitians and Dominicans in New York; Koreans in Los Angeles; Hmong in San Francisco; Japanese in Scarsdale or Pakistanis in Evanston, Illinois; Cubans in Miami; Salvadorans in Washington, D.C., et (in my view, quite wonderfully) al.

This extraordinary burst of immigration, legal and illegal, and the continuing ferment among African Americans (the generation of a black middle class, the accelerating immiseration of an urban subaltern class left behind) have led to reactions familiar from the last fin de siècle: nativist immigration legislation, a tightening of the gatekeeping mechanisms into the professional-managerial classes, a sense that the hallowed masterpieces of Western culture are being challenged. But it has also led to a new way of thinking about race and ethnicity similarly based on models of racial admixture rather than identity, of relationality rather than essence.

In such a new social situation, producing new forms of interchange, the experience of Jews takes on a new—and different—salience.[6] Jews, after all, are nothing if not a spectacular example of the ways that members of racial or ethnic groups can interact, intersect, and intermarry outside their own community and still seek to retain a distinctive group identity: Jews are walking hybrids and hence vivid illustrations of the powers and limitations of that category. And more: the sheer lability of the Jew as a conceptual category—that figure's simultaneous salience to idioms of race, of religion, of culture, and of ethnicity and failure to be encompassed by any one of these classifications—allows us to see just what is at stake in those classifications even as it allows us to assess the limitations of those categories. The experience of real live Jews in the cultures of the West, too, throws into sharp relief the experience of other minorities at the present time. The problematics of entering into a culture that constructs you as Other yet depends on you for its own self-understanding; the quest to gain social acceptance through entry into the professional-managerial classes that are closed off at the moment you start knocking on their doors; the difficulties of being or becoming a "model minority" while the less successful members of your group are ignored by this ascription: these issues currently face a number of ethnic and racial minorities in the United States, and they are responding with versions of the admixture of assimilation to and aggression against the dominant norms of their cultures in ways analogous, but not identical, to those followed by Jews in the later years of the nineteenth and the earlier years of the twentieth centuries.

It is true that there are powerful reasons *not* to bring the experience of the Jew to bear on ethnic and racial minorities, some testimony to the tensions too long concealed at the heart of the New Deal coalition, some resulting from the sense among ethnic and racial scholars of color that Jews are fully assimilated into a dominant Caucasian majority. Sander Gilman has written of hearing from a young Asian-American scholar of the irrelevance of the Jewish example (along with white women and postcolonial intellectuals) to the ethnic studies project; Jews, Gilman learned, are "lite" and ethnic studies is directed at those who are not. I myself was similarly bewildered when colleagues at the University of Michigan refused to allow a course in Jewish-American literature to count for credit in an ethnic studies concentration on the grounds that "ethnicity" as a category referred to writers of color, one that self-evidently did not include Jews. Intellectually, I found this position wacky (if Jews are fully credentialed members of a white elite, this has been true for only twenty years out of the last two thousand; moreover, to learn that they are white will be news to many Sephardic Jews, particularly those of Latin American and North African descent). But I also recognize that, at least in the academy, this position achieves its credibility because of many of the developments I have traced here and in chapter 5. For, as Karen Brodkin reminds us, African Americans and Latinos were not fully included in the effects of the GI Bill, that great broadening mechanism that led so many white ethnics into the middle class: GIs of color were by and large excluded from the universities that white ethnics were using as a springboard to the professional-managerial classes.[7] Second, and not unrelated, is the way that assimilating Jews in the 1940s and 1950s and their intellectual progeny in the 1970s and 1980s interacted with the established literary culture so as to seem to congeal that culture in the most glacial of guises, if not to use it as a battering ram against scholars, students, and subjects with different experiences and agendas.

But this story is not the only one we need to tell about the participation of American Jews in the cultural life; indeed it is largely to dispel, or at least complicate, this accepted narrative that I have been trying to tell the story of assimilation-by-culture in terms that are analogous to those at the center of contemporary ethnic studies (without, I hope, appropriating them unduly): resistance, performativity, "mimicry," in Homi Bhabha's sense of the word. The result, I hope, has been not to render the category "Jew" safe for ethnic studies or vice versa but to suggest to all parties in this quarrel that there are moments at which productive contact can be made between traditions and experiences that seem, disturbingly but understandably, all too distant.

Whether or not these hopes are realized, I hope at the very least that I have been able to historicize the encounter between the Jew and the idioms of culture and hence to make each term seem less inevitable and hence invariable. Vis-à-vis high culture, my hope has been to remind us not only that "culture" has a history but that this history contains a variety of impulses that we would do well not fully to reify as either "the Canon" or "the Tradition" (hence all that is good) or "the Canon" and "the Tradition" (hence all that is bad). Rather, I have argued that the set of texts and understandings that—from the German philosophers forward—has served to structure a discursive regime organized by the term "culture" that has created possibilities both progressive and regressive, critical and complicit, emancipatory and enchaining, in a variety of different situations over time. Nowhere can this better be seen than in the experience of Western Jews, who have been variously the limit-case and the embodiment, the subject and the object, of this cultural idiom, and who both have been constructed by it and have seized upon it as the means of their emancipation with results tragic (as in Germany), triumphant (as in the American academy of the 1950s), and everything in between.

By the same token, I have tried to historicize and so complicate that fraught category "Jew" and, more important, the uses to which it is put. As I suggested in chapter 1, one of the problems afflicting Jews in a Christian-dominated culture is the tendency of that culture to read symbolically or typologically: to see facts and events as resonating with meanings that are ultimately assimilable to a Christian narrative. That tendency, obviously antithetical to Jews, endures in the secularized culture discourse of the Enlightenment, in which the sign "Jew" was first made to take on a coherence that the course of Jewish history was increasingly denying and then made to stand for many things, ranging from villain to victim, cultural degenerate to culture hero, and stopping numerous places in between. One payoff of historicizing that figure, and historicizing its construction in the context of the idiom of culture, is that we might desymbolize, demetaphorize the Jew: to see "the Jew" not as a symbol of Culture or Anarchy, of historical victimization or historical progressivism, but as a descriptor for a group of people who are defined only by their incessant and unsatisfactory attempts to describe themselves. And when we do *that*, the process of bringing that figure to bear on the cultural and social situations of other minorities and ethnicities is enhanced. To think in a de-essentialized and historicized way about the relation between ethnic and racial others and the Jew is not to suggest that the experience of this or that group can be glossed by that of Jews qua Jews or Jews qua participants in the drama of Western "culture," with either the implicit understanding that Jewish assimilation provides a model for other forms of entry into the dominant culture or the angry rebellion against such an understanding. Rather, it would be to suggest that there are important points of contact in the play of similarities and differences that govern the experience of this people and those of other Others, themselves composed by their own contingent histories and varying experiences that defy a facile politics of identity.

Thinking this way might help us avoid a number of significant political problems at our own cultural moment, and opens up a new opportunity. Chief among these problems—and deserving a book to itself—is the fraught question of relations between American Jews and African Americans. In the past, particularly in America, these two have been grouped under the heading of a common victimization, in ways that led to both solidarity and tension; recently, this tendency of thought has conduced to the horrifying spectacle of comparing victimizations each of which is uniquely horrific and hence incommensurable. Speaking only from the Jewish side of the dialogue—the sole contribution, I think, I ought to be trying to make—we can address the problem only by removing from Jews the burden of victimization, returning to Jews the property of being different from themselves as well as others. For to do so is to begin to be able to specify closely and clearly the ways in which the experience of Jews in America (as elsewhere) is and is *not* like that of African Americans, and to use the similarities among their experiences as points of contact amidst a play of similarities and differences, not appropriating predications of common identity or claims of utter divergence. And there are signs that, in the hands of both Jewish and gentile critics, this process is underway. Certainly, the work of Jonathan Boyarin on the Jewish side and Paul Gilroy on that of diaspora studies has created a set of careful articulations of the relations between the Jewish experience as Other within and the Afro-Caribbean experience of exile, enslavement, and cultural resistance. Similarly, to extend from the African-American or Afro-Caribbean to the postcolonial, the work of Bryan Cheyette and Homi Bhabha has created in England a dialogue between Jewish and postcolonial critics. What I look forward to in the next generation of American studies and ethnic studies is a similar move, perhaps profitably beyond the barrier of the Jew's putative whiteness and toward an articulation of the commonalities and the divergences between the experience of Jews and the new predications of nation, of culture, of identity that are emerging within ethnic studies.

For this is what is finally at stake: whether intellectuals, Jews, and Jewish intellectuals (three different entities that I have been attempting to disarticulate from each other) have any contribution to make to the new cultural dispensations that are emerging in the new, more complex, more diverse America, as they are throughout a globalizing world. Freed from the baggage of bearing witness to Western culture as the best that has been thought and said but no longer impelled by the necessity of rejecting these possibilities and predications out of hand, freed as well from the burdens of an essentializing racial and ethnic idiom, Jews and intellectuals alike may participate in the production of both new modes of ethnic and racial address and new, more inclusive cultural formations to go along with them. Having opened up the canon and deconstructed racial and ethnic essentialisms, intellectuals of the Jewish and non-Jewish persuasion alike may now be freer to create new combinations of high and low, new assortments of identity and vectors of relationality that cut across, while they do not seek to annul, older orders of culture and communities of ethnicity and race. But whether intellectuals do or do not accomplish these tasks, and the jury is very much out, such new awarenesses are breaking out all around us in mass or popular culture.[8] As I suggested earlier, it is in popular music rather than literature or criticism that the new cultural and ethnic possibilities I refer to are beginning to emerge; here, too, there is an increasingly creative interchange between the traditional art music of Europe and the vernacular jazz and rock-and-roll traditions of America. I take a certain pleasant satisfaction in this fact; as we have seen, from the nineteenth century forward, the battle between high- and lowbrow musical canons has been one of the most significant contests in which both the middlebrow and the figure of the Jew have been constructed. Hence it is particularly welcome to be able to conclude with one example of an artist who juggles all the terms I have been trying to play with throughout this book and who suggests new ways of articulating their interrelation.

The artist in question is Don Byron, an African-American clarinettist trained at the New England Conservatory (where he was told by one of his teachers that he could never succeed, as the shape of his lips would produce the wrong embouchure). While at the conservatory, Byron played in a klezmer band which later became the Conservatory Klezmer Orchestra, one of the first and one of the best of the groups to bring about the revival of eastern European Jewish popular music—itself already a synthesis of sacred and secular musics, of Jewish and European traditions, and of European and American jazz instrumentations, rhythms, and melodies. His recordings have continued this syncretism and have brought it into even more explicit contact with the American and African-American traditions. One, *Tuskegee Meditations*, is a brooding set of improvisations organized by the experience of the poor black men in the South who were left to die of syphilis as part of a government experiment. Another, *Don Byron Plays Mickey Katz*, revives the delightful parodies of a Yiddish-speaking comedian/musician who learned as much from the anarchic parodies of Spike Jones (in whose band Katz briefly played) as from his klezmer peers; included here are delightful versions of Katz tunes like *Haim Afen Range*, in which Yiddish-speaking cowboys sing, to the tune of *Home on the Range*, of their desire to emigrate from the ranch to the mythical city of Oy Vegas. Byron performs these straight—or at least as straight as one can be with a figure like Katz—but, like the klezmer musicians themselves, adds to them riffs and tunes drawn from great African-American jazz artists; the fantastical *Haim Afen Range*, for example, ends with a tag from Duke Ellington's *Black and Tan Fantasy*. Byron's most recent album, *Bug Music*, continues this syncretism with respect to high and low cultures as well as to Yiddish and African-American ones: it includes a number of jaunty musical selections by white and black jazz orchestras, many of which draw parodically and yet reverently on the classics of the European musical tradition: Ellington's elfin but swinging version of the *Dance of the Sugar Plum Fairies*, for example.

Byron's syncreticism vis-à-vis race, ethnicity, and the canon is a delightful alternative to the all-or-nothing paradigms that dominate thinking on all sides of these questions at the current moment. But this is not to say that his works are innocent bagatelles; rather, he draws meaning from his juxtapositions that problematizes all the positions he is addressing. Consider the Ellington tag at the end of *Haim Afen Range*: not only does it remind us that native-born African Americans like Ellington were not as easily able to find a home in America as Jews (even the gangster Jews who founded Las Vegas), it also reminds us of the inevitable fantasmatic nature of all these racialized narratives: the black (and *tan*, "colored," race-mixed) fantasies that surround and construct the Cotton Club, Ellington, Byron himself. There are similar moments of interplay that suggest the *lack* of identity between the Jewish tradition and its African-American exponent; when Byron himself sings in the *Mechaya Love Call*, for example, the Yiddish-speaking lead singer reminds him in English to sing in Yiddish, as if to suggest that this tradition is properly not fully any more Byron's than the jazz tradition is Katz's. And with respect to the third term I have been juggling throughout this book, "culture," Byron is equally sophisticated. He concludes *Tuskegee Meditations* with a gorgeous melody from Schumann's Clarinet Sonata; plangent to the point of heartbreak, this clarinet solo serves as both an appropriation of the ability of European culture to pay tribute to people whose humanity it would not recognize and an acknowledgment of the aesthetic powers that that culture organized and deployed.

Byron's work, it seems to me, reminds us that in the blooming, buzzing world outside the academic hothouse, more generous models of the interaction among high and middle and low cultures, and between Jewish and non-Jewish cultures, are not only possible but easily available. Certainly, not only a Don Byron but an Emmanuel Haldeman-Julius suggest that there are, and always have been, more combinations of ethnic and cultural possibility than have been dreamed of in our cultural and literary studies. Perhaps without knowing it, I have written this book in the hope that we might follow in the footsteps of writers, artists, publishers, and musicians like these, as we build or renovate or raze and renew that temple of which we are such ambivalent votaries, the temple of culture.

Notes

Introduction

1. Dan Oren, *Joining the Club: A History of Jews and Yale* (New Haven: Yale University Press, 1985), p. 76.

2. There are two other constructions of "culture" circling around those that I am using in this paragraph, and it is important to mention them here. The first is the anthropological sense, the Malinowskian "culture concept" brought to its highest pitch by Clifford Geertz; the second is the dialectical theory of cultural criticism advanced by critics of the so-called Frankfurt School, most notably Walter Benjamin and (especially) Theodor Adorno. But for all their differences, both of these have undergone serious skeptical attack on more or less the same grounds: that is, that they hypostasize "culture" as a monolithic ideal rather than a shifting, eddying process shaped by competing political powers and social interests; and that for all their enlightened political aspirations, they end up placing the critic outside the hurly-burly of social life and change.

3. See, for example, Jonathan and Daniel Boyarin, eds., *Jews and Other Differences: The New Jewish Cultural Studies* (Minneapolis: University of Minnesota Press, 1997).

4. Some of the works tracing this development are: John Henry Raleigh, *Matthew Arnold and American Culture* (Berkeley: University of California Press, 1957); T. J. Jackson Lears, *No Place of Grace: Antimodernism and the Transformation of American Culture, 1880–1920* (New York: Pantheon, 1981); Alan Trachtenberg, *The Incorporation of America: Culture and Society in the Gilded Age* (New York: Hill and Wang, 1982); Jonathan Freedman, *Professions of Taste: Henry James, British Aestheticism, and Commodity Culture* (Stanford: Stanford University Press, 1990).

5. For a full sense of American resistance to high culture, see Richard Hofstadter, *Anti-Intellectualism in American Life* (New York: Knopf, 1963). Just to underscore the relevance of these concerns to the Jewish intellectuals I discuss hereafter, Hofstadter was an old friend of Alfred Kazin's (they worked together in the New York Public Library when the latter was writing *On Native Grounds*) and of many other New York intellectuals. He was also half Jewish—a fact that perhaps explains his simultaneous curiosity about and detachment from the American culture whose study was his life work; as Kazin puts it, he "was secret in many things, in some strange no man's land between his Yiddish-speaking

Polish father and his dead Lutheran mother." *New York Jew* (New York: Knopf, 1978), p. 14.

The failure to give proper weight to the anti-intellectual, anti–high culture impulse in American civic and cultural life strikes me as the great failing of arguments like those of Lawrence Levine, which seem to me to exaggerate the social power of highbrow culture and to underestimate the relations of anti-highbrow sentiments not only to insurgent or politically progressive impulses but also to reactionary ones. Babbittry and Pecksniffery, to give them their literary names, have been and remain as powerful impulses in the making of American culture as, say, subversion and resistance.

6. For a critique of current intellectual culture that makes this predisposition into the prime vector of critique, see Russell Jacoby, *The Last Intellectuals* (New York: Free Press, 1985).

7. In Jeffrey Rubin-Dorsky and Shelley Fisher Fishkin, *People of the Book: Thirty Scholars Reflect on Their Jewish Identity* (Madison: University of Wisconsin Press, 1996), p. 45.

8. For an argument about the relation of Judaism to early Christianity, for example, that seeks to complicate a facile identity politics based on either, see Daniel Boyarin, *A Radical Jew: Paul and the Politics of Identity* (Berkeley: University of California Press, 1994).

1. The Jew in the Museum

1. "Eliot v. Julius," *New Yorker* 72 (May 20, 1996), pp. 29–30.

2. Two recent books have reminded us of the powerful hold exerted by the figure of the Jew over the Victorian (and modernist) British imagination: Bryan Cheyette, *Constructions of the Jew in English Literature and Society: Racial Representations, 1875–1945* (Cambridge: Cambridge University Press, 1993), and Michael Ragussis, *Figures of Conversion: "The Jewish Question" and English National Identity* (Durham: Duke University Press, 1995). Both provide powerful readings of the intersection between the figure of the Jew and the figure of Matthew Arnold, represented in Cheyette's case in Arnold's creation of "semitic discourse," in Ragussis's in his responses to Disraeli. For my own reading of Arnold and its differences from these powerful accounts, see the last section of this chapter.

As for the question of Jews and modernism, the literature is equally vast, and again I confine my citations to recent work. With regard to Eliot (in addition to Julius's *T. S. Eliot, Anti-Semitism, and Literary Form* (Cambridge: Cambridge University Press, 1995), is Christopher Ricks's casuistical *T. S. Eliot and Prejudice* (London: Faber and Faber, 1988) and, with regard to Pound, Robert Casillo, *The Genealogy of Demons: Anti-Semitism, Fascism, and the Myths of Ezra Pound* (Evanston, Ill.: Northwestern University Press, 1988). One of the most intelligent responses to both Eliot and Pound is Maud Ellmann, "The Imaginary Jew: T. S. Eliot and Ezra Pound," in *Between "Race" and Culture: Representations of "the Jew" in English and American Literature*, ed. Bryan Cheyette (Stanford: Stanford University Press, 1996). I have more to say about Ellmann, in particular, in chapter 4. Concerning Joyce, see Ira Nadel, *Joyce and the Jews* (Iowa City: University of Iowa Press, 1989), and Marylin Reizbaum, "A Nightmare of History: Ireland's Jews and Joyce's Ulysses," in Cheyette, *Between "Race" and Culture.*

The question of Jews and the formation of "culture" in the 1920s has been provocatively raised by Walter Michaels in a context entirely different from mine. For Michaels, an idiom of "culture" (as in cultural pluralism or the anthropological culture concept) emerges in the twenties to contest racist and nativist idioms; yet this idiom ends up, according to Michaels's ingenious analyses, replicating the racist discourse it seeks to dismantle. As I try to show later in this chapter, the notion of race and the idea of culture were so fundamentally intertwined with each other from the moment of their first appearance as to be if not isomorphic, at least interrelated to a degree almost incestuous. See Michaels, *Our America: Nativism, Modernism, and Pluralism* (Durham: Duke University Press, 1995).

3. For this history, see Chris Baldick, *The Social Mission of English Criticism, 1860–1930* (Oxford: Clarendon Press, 1983) and Terry Eagleton's sprightly chapter (much indebted to Baldick, Eagleton's student), "The Rise of English," in *Literary Theory: An Introduction* (Minneapolis: University of Minnesota Press, 1983). The professionalization of literary studies on the Germanic model accompanied the rise of philology as a dominant method of literary studies in the English and American academies alike, and with the philological model came a narrative of literary origins that got conflated with a narrative of national origins. For this, see Gerald Graff's interesting but often superficial account in *Professing Literature: An Institutional History* (Chicago: University of Chicago Press, 1987) and the revealing documents that Graff and Michael Warner have collected in *The Origins of Literary Study in America: A Documentary Anthology* (New York: Routledge, 1989). For the role of Anglo-Saxon in this process, see Allen Frantzen's nuanced account in *Desire for Origins: New Language, Old English, and Teaching the Tradition* (New Brunswick: Rutgers University Press, 1990).

I want to be clear here about an argument I make more fully in chapter 5. The links between philological method, Germanic origins of "English," and Aryanism were not necessarily in force throughout this period nor felt with equal intensity by people entering into the profession of literary study (indeed, as with all forms of literary study, many powerful exponents of the philological perspective were Jewish, the most eminent being Morton Bloomfield). But these links were deeply rooted in the discipline and felt by many Jews entering into the terrain of literary study, as Julius's study and the accounts of many Jewish scholars offered in *People of the Book* suggest.

4. Again, this development is traced, inter alia, by Graff, Eagleton, Graff and Warner, and others. I again want to put on the record at this point, before arguing for them more fully in chapter 5, two things (at least) that need to be added to their quite partial accounts. First, there is no reason why New Criticism had to take this explicitly Christian, organicist, and conservative turn—one represented by writers like Cleanth Brooks and W. K. Wimsatt, whose valorization of the poetic object as such was fully coextensive with their Anglicanism. A powerful tradition of intrinsic literary criticism growing out of phenomenology and Prague School formalism is untouched by this ontological agenda. This tradition was imported to the United States by emigré scholars like the late René Wellek at roughly the same time and was embedded at the center of literary studies by such crucial texts as Wellek and Austin Warren's *Theory of Literature* (1958). So too were the works of great Jewish emigré philologists like Erich Auerbach and Leo Spitzer, whose ventures into literary history and *explication de texte* appeared at the same time and even alongside many of the most influential works of the New Criticism (many of the chapters of *Mimesis*, for example, appeared in *Kenyon Review*, which also printed the theoretical musings of Ransom, Warren, and Brooks). So the by-now-clichéd identification of formalism with organicism, Christian dogmatics, and even, in the hands of Eagleton, slavery (!), overstates the historical record quite considerably.

5. For an example of this process, see Jeffrey Rubin-Dorsky and Shelley Fisher Fishkin, *People of the Book: Thirty Scholars Reflect on their Jewish Identity* (Madison: University of Wisconsin Press, 1996), a collection of personal narratives by Jewish academics reflecting on their Jewishness, which also suggests many of the problems with this process. For Jews, it is important to remember, have been and continue to be many things: people of faith, people of the gun (Meyer Lansky, after all, was a Jew), people of labor, and so on. The identification of the essence of Jewish identity with intellectual matters and pursuits is one of the things my book attempts to historicize and hence critique.

6. Cheyette, *Constructions of "the Jew" in English Literature and Society*, p. 36.

7. See Jonathan, Boyarin, "The Other Without and the Other Within," in *The Storm from Paradise* (Minneapolis: University of Minnesota Press, 1992).

8. The term is from Fritz Ringer, *The Decline of the German Mandarins: The German Academic Community, 1890–1933* (Cambridge: Harvard University Press, 1969).

9. There is much work under way on the long-neglected question of Jewish women in both traditional and assimilated culture. For the purposes of my argument, the most important is Marion Kaplan, *The Making of the Jewish Middle Class: Women, Family and Identity in Imperial Germany* (New York: Oxford University Press, 1991), and Paula Hyman, *Gender and Assimilation in Modern Jewish History: The Roles and Representation of Women* (Seattle: University of Washington Press, 1995).

10. See Deborah Hertz, *Jewish High Society in Old Regime Berlin* (New Haven: Yale University Press, 1988), and Hannah Arendt, *Rahel Varnhagen: The Life of a Jewess*, tr. Richard and Clara Winston (Baltimore: Johns Hopkins University Press, 1997).

11. The list of books produced by this heterogeneous group is too long to give here; but I do want to indicate the texts from this recent flourishing of scholarly activity that have proven most useful in this project. I have learned much from and been most influenced by Daniel Boyarin, *A Radical Jew: Paul and the Politics of Identity* (Berkeley: University of California Press, 1994); Jonathan Boyarin, *The Storm From Paradise*; Cheyette, *Constructions of "the Jew" in English Literature and Society*; Sander Gilman, *The Case of Sigmund Freud: Medicine and Identity at the Fin de Siècle* (Baltimore: Johns Hopkins University Press, 1993) and *Freud, Race, and Gender* (Princeton: Princeton University Press, 1993); Ragussis, *Figures of Conversion*. Two things, I think, distinguish this extraordinary burst of scholarship from its predecessors: first, an increasing willingness to affirm a distinctively Jewish identity politics vis-à-vis predications of identity; second, a willingness to critique or challenge normative ideas of Jewishness from the perspective of gender theory, critical race theory, and so-called cultural studies. The effects both on the theorizations of Jewishness and on "cultural studies" itself have been, in my view, thoroughly salutary.

12. The term is Daniel Boyarin's; see *A Radical Jew*.

13. Gilroy, *The Black Atlantic* (Cambridge: Harvard University Press, 1993).

14. Goldberg and Krausz, *Jewish Identity* (Philadelphia: Temple University Press, 1993). Citations in the text refer to this edition.

15. In making this argument, I am conflating de Man, "The Rhetoric of Temporality," in *Blindness and Insight: Essays in the Rhetoric of Contemporary Criticism*, 2nd edition, pp. 187–228 (Minneapolis: University of Minnesota Press, 1983), with Derrida, *Of Grammatology*, tr. Gayatri Spivak (Baltimore: Johns Hopkins University Press, 1976). De Man quotes Coleridge, *The Statesman's Manual*, ed. W. G. T. Shedd (New York: Harper and Brothers, 1875); exemplifying the chain of deferred meaning that is the true nature of "symbol" for de Man (that is, allegory), de Man cites Angus Fletcher's *Allegory: The*

Theory of a Symbolic Mode (Ithaca: Cornell University Press, 1964), p. 16, as the source for his citation of Coleridge.

16. Lionel Gossman, "Philhellenism and Antisemitism: Matthew Arnold and his German Models," *Comparative Literature* 46 (Winter 1994), pp. 8–9.

17. Sorkin, *The Transformation of German Jewry, 1780–1840* (New York: Oxford University Press, 1987), p. 36.

18. Roth, *Operation Shylock: A Confession* (New York: Simon and Schuster, 1993), p. 332. Smilesburger, in addition to being a transparently fictional creation of the "real" Philip Roth, is a member of the Israeli Secret Service whose plot enmeshes the "fictional" (real only for the purposes of the fiction) Philip Roth and who attempts, at the end of the novel, to bribe him not to publish it. He is, in short, the voice that cries for "authentic" Jewish identity—the Jewish thought police. It is entirely in keeping with this tendency of thought that, as such, he is also the voice for the *heterogeneity* of Jewish identity, for its inauthenticity: the lesson he cynically enforces is that precisely out of this multiplicity of identities arises the need to form a unitary model of Jewishness, else chaos comes again.

19. All the figures I name here are doubtless familiar to the reader, with the possible exception of Edward Burnett Tylor. Author, most famously, of *Primitive Culture* (London: 1871), Tylor is generally credited as the originator of the anthropological use of the concept of culture. In an important essay, "Matthew Arnold, E. B. Tylor, and the Uses of Invention," George Stocking has argued that Tylor's seemingly descriptive sense of the term "culture," and hence the anthropological culture-concept that flows from it, is actually congruent with Arnold's more prescriptive use of the term in *Culture and Anarchy*, and that both grow from common roots in German philosophy. The essay can be found in Stocking, *Race, Culture, and Evolution: Essays in the History of Anthropology* (New York: Free Press, 1968).

20. Williams, *Keywords: A Vocabulary of Culture and Society* (New York: Oxford University Press, 1976), pp. 76–82. Culture, Williams writes there, "is one of the two or three most complicated words in the English language"; he then proceeds to give a bravura reading of its many inflections and complications from the time of Milton to the present day.

21. Finkielkraut, *The Imaginary Jew*, tr. David Suchoff (Lincoln: University of Nebraska Press, 1994), p. 164.

22. Bauman, *Life in Fragments: Essays in Postmodern Morality* (London: Blackwell, 1995), pp. 214–5.

23. The literature on German-Jewish relations is vast; in addition to the work of George Mosse I use here, I have learned the most from Michael Meyer, *The Origins of the Modern Jew: Jewish Identity and European Culture in Germany, 1749–1824* (Detroit: Wayne State University Press, 1967), Werner Mosse, "From 'Schutzjuden' to 'Deutsche Staatsbürger Jüdischen Glaubens': The Long and Bumpy Road of Jewish Emancipation in Germany," in Pierre Birnbaum and Ira Katznelson, eds., *Paths of Emancipation: Jews, States and Citizenship* (Princeton: Princeton University Press, 1995), pp. 59–93; Werner Mosse cites and to a certain extent complicates the work of Reinhard Rürup, "Jewish Emancipation and Bourgeois Society," *Leo Baeck Institute Yearbook* 14 (1969), pp. 78–86.

Also quite useful to me have been, for the earlier periods, Sorkin, *The Transformation of German Jewry*, and, for the later ones, Uriel Tal, *Christians and Jews in Germany: Religion, Politics, and Ideology in the Second Reich, 1870–1914*, tr. Noah Jacobs (Ithaca: Cornell University Press, 1975). The best theoretical treatment of the various options available to—

and followed by—Jews in this period is Zygmunt Bauman, "Exit Visas and Entry Tickets: Paradoxes of Jewish Assimilation," *Telos* 77 (1988), pp. 45–72.

24. Mosse distills much of his work on German Jews in "Jewish Emancipation: Between *Bildung* and Respectability," in *Confronting the Nation: Jewish and Western Nationalism* (Hanover, N.H.: University Press of New England, 1993); this quotation is from p. 132. I have also consulted and learned much from *German Jews beyond Judaism* (Cincinnati: Hebrew Union College Press, 1985) and *Toward the Final Solution: A History of European Racism* (New York: Harper and Row, 1980).

25. This work has been translated as *Concerning the Amelioration of the Civil Status of the Jews* (Cincinnati: Hebrew Union College, 1957).

26. Mosse, "Culture, Civilization, and German Anti-Semitism," in *German Jews*, p. 40.

27. Arendt, *The Origins of Totalitarianism* (New York: Harcourt Brace, 1950), p. 52. Needless to say, Arendt herself embodies the consummation of this process.

28. See *The Jews of Vienna, 1867–1914: Assimilation and Identity* (Albany: State University of New York Press, 1983), p. 99. Rozenblit stresses that these Jews were already the children of the bourgeoisie, who sought for their children the cultural capital that they themselves lacked (and this was as true of women as men; Viennese Jews were as concerned with the education and hence acculturation of their daughters as of sons). This situation differs considerably, she continues, from that of other immigrants, who by and large sent their children to trade schools. But the Jews who entered Gymnasia did not interact with their gentile peers; they attended school, by and large, with other Jews.

29. Pulzer, *The Rise of Political Anti-Semitism in Germany and Austria* (New York: Wiley, 1964), p. 76.

30. Julius Braunthal, *In Search of the Millennium* (London: V. Gollancz, 1945), p. 17, quoted in Pulzer, *The Rise of Political Anti-Semitism*, p. 13. For more on the fascinating experience of Viennese Jewry in the at once culturally most advanced and racially most prejudiced city in Europe, see Carl Schorske, *Fin-de-Siècle Vienna: Politics and Culture* (New York: Knopf, 1980) and Steven Beller, *Vienna and the Jews, 1867–1938: A Cultural History* (New York: Cambridge University Press, 1989).

For the experience of two truly assimilated Jews in this context, Sigmund Freud and Ludwig Wittgenstein, see Peter Gay, *A Godless Jew: Freud, Atheism, and the Making of Psychoanalysis* (New Haven: Yale University Press, 1987), and Schorske's magisterial chapter on Freud's *Interpretation of Dreams*; for Wittgenstein, see Allan Janik and Stephen Toulmin, *Wittgenstein's Vienna* (New York: Simon and Schuster, 1973).

31. It needs to be stressed here, of course, that urban, middle-class Jews were by no means the norm even in fin-de-siècle Austria and Germany. Pulzer startlingly reminds us that even while cultured Jews flocked into the professions in the cities, five to six thousand Jews died *annually* of starvation in Galicia and Bukovina, the provinces where Jewish peasants were concentrated.

32. Emil Fackenheim, *The Jewish Thought of Emil Fackenheim* (Detroit: Wayne State University Press, 1987), p. 350. In this memoir, Fackenheim makes an offhand comment that summarizes for me the issues I am trying to confront here: "You must remember," he says, "that the Jews were murdered by the people they went to school with." As if, as of course on some level we all believe, going to school with people teaches you that you should not kill them.

33. Scholem, *From Berlin to Jerusalem: Memories of My Youth*, tr. Harry Zohn (New York: Schocken Books, 1980), p. 31. Adorno's classic statement can be found in "Cultural

Criticism and Society," reprinted in *Prisms*, tr. Samuel Weber and Sherry Weber (Cambridge: MIT Press, 1981), p. 21. Marcuse's most explicit invocation of the aesthetic as a redemptive sphere of value can be found in his late *The Aesthetic Dimension: Toward a Critique of Marxist Aesthetics* (Boston: Beacon Press, 1978).

34. This may be changing; after I wrote these words in 1995, Butler joined Rogin, Cheyfitz, and Sedgwick as explicit musers on their Jewish identity. None of these figures, however, seems easy or comfortable with affirming their Jewish birth or background. Rogin and Cheyfitz introduce their Jewishness in qualified and complicated ways in relation to other, less privileged, Others—African and Native Americans; Butler and Sedgwick do so in the context of their concern with the delineation of a queer identity, which for Butler is continuous with her Jewishness and for Sedgwick is less so. See Butler's as yet untitled contribution to Daniel Boyarin, Daniel Itzkovitz, and Anne Pelligrini, eds., *Jewish Responses to Queer Theory* (New York: Columbia University Press, forthcoming); Cheyfitz, *The Poetics of Imperialism: Translation and Colonization from the Tempest to Tarzan* (New York: Oxford University Press, 1991); Rogin, *Blackface, White Noise: Jewish Immigrants in the Hollywood Melting Pot* (Berkeley: University of California Press, 1995); Sedgwick, *Epistemology of the Closet* (Berkeley: University of California Press, 1990).

35. See Paul Rose, *Revolutionary Anti-Semitism in Germany from Kant to Wagner* (Princeton: Princeton University Press, 1990), pp. 117–32. My account here is much indebted to Rose's magisterial (and depressing) survey of the power of anti-Semitism in the German philosophical tradition, although I have somewhat more sympathetic views (as will become clear hereafter) than Rose's toward Kant and Hegel and less sympathetic ones toward Fichte and Herder.

36. For a summary of Herder's writings on Jews, see Rose, *Revolutionary Anti-Semitism*, pp. 97–109. For Gilman's argument, see *Jewish Self-Hatred: Anti-Semitism and the Hidden Language of the Jews* (Baltimore: Johns Hopkins University Press, 1986). And for a somewhat overstated but nevertheless powerful critique of Herder, and a defense of the Enlightenment, from a Jewish perspective, see Alain Finkielkraut, *The Defeat of the Mind*, tr. Judith Friedlander (New York: Columbia University Press, 1995).

37. See Fackenheim, *The Religious Dimensions in Hegel's Thought* (Bloomington: Indiana University Press, 1968), p. 36. A fine recent study by Yirmiyahu Yovel treats Hegel's response to Jews in tones somewhere between Fackenheim's and the ones I use hereafter. For Yovel, as for Fackenheim, Hegel's early theological writings are of less importance than the relatively benign later treatment of the Jews, particularly in the *Philosophy of History* and the *Lectures on the Philosophy of Religion*. But Yovel ends with a recognition that goes beyond Fackenheim's—and jibes with the critique I sketch: that rather than being a small problem with Hegel's system, his career-long treatment of the Jews consistently underlines how powerfully his "implicit Christocentric standpoint is . . . at work at both the beginning and the end of his philosophy"; *Dark Riddle: Hegel, Nietzsche, and the Jews* (University Park, Pa.: Pennsylvania State University Press, 1998), p. 101. Indeed, Yovel goes so far as to conclude that "the [Christocentric] flaws and limitations of Hegelianism cannot be remedied by offering particular, eclectic local corrections (as in the Jewish issue) but only, I think, through a bolder and more comprehensive move—by renouncing the claim to absolute knowledge in one critical stroke"—a move Yovel associates with Nietzsche (p. 101).

38. Hegel, *Early Theological Writings*, tr. T. M. Knox (Philadelphia: University of Pennsylvania Press, 1948), p. 186. Further citations refer to this edition.

39. Kant, *Religion within the Limits of Reason Alone* (New York: Harper and Row, 1960), p. 249.

40. Katz, *Philo-Semitism and the Readmission of Jews to England, 1603–1655* (Oxford: Clarendon Press, 1982). See also Katz's invaluable recent work, *The Jews in the History of England, 1485–1850* (Oxford: Clarendon Press, 1994).

41. Howard Weinbrot, *Britannia's Issue: The Rise of British Literature from Dryden to Ossian* (Cambridge: Cambridge University Press, 1993), p. 558.

42. Frank Felsenstein, *Anti-Semitic Stereotypes: A Paradigm of Otherness in English Popular Culture, 1600–1830* (Baltimore: Johns Hopkins University Press, 1995).

43. Matthew Arnold, *Culture and Anarchy*, ed. R. W. Super (Ann Arbor: University of Michigan Press, 1968), pp. 173–4. Further citations in the text refer to this edition.

44. Michael Ragussis, *Figures of Conversion: "The Jewish Question" and English National Identity*, p. 47.

45. "Spinoza and the Bible," in *Lectures and Essays in Criticism*, ed. R. W. Super (Ann Arbor: University of Michigan Press, 1962), p. 188.

46. *Love and Theft* (New York: Oxford University Press, 1993).

47. *The Poetry of Matthew Arnold*, ed. Kenneth Allott (London: Longman's, 1965), pp. 483–5. Further citations in the text refer to this edition. For an excellent biography of Rachel, and a fine reading of Arnold's responses to her, see Rachel Brownstein, *Tragic Muse: Rachel of the Comédie Française* (New York: Knopf, 1993).

48. The classic text here is Jacob Katz, *Out of the Ghetto: The Social Background of Jewish Emancipation, 1770–1870* (Cambridge: Harvard University Press, 1973); also very useful is Jonathan Israel, *European Jewry in the Age of Mercantilism, 1550–1750* (Oxford: Clarendon Press, 1985).

49. Joseph Jacobs, *Jewish Statistics: Social, Vital, and Anthropometric* (London, 1891), p. vii, as quoted in John Efron, *Defenders of the Faith: Jewish Doctors and Race Science in Fin-de-Siècle Europe* (New Haven: Yale University Press, 1994), p. 195.

50. Lewisohn, *Up Stream: An American Chronicle* (New York: Boni and Liveright, 1922), p. 94.

51. Lewisohn, "Matthew Arnold: December 24, 1822–December 24, 1922," *Nation*, December 27, 1922, p. 708.

52. *Creative Intelligence: Essays in the Pragmatic Attitude* (New York: Holt, 1917), p. 9. Further citations refer to this edition.

2. The Temple of Culture and the Market for Letters

1. Much attention has recently been paid to the literary marketplace as a factor in the making and unmaking of social and cultural value and literary lives; Regenia Gagnier, *Idylls of the Marketplace* (Stanford: Stanford University Press, 1986) and my *Professions of Taste* (Stanford: Stanford University Press, 1990), for example. But the classic texts here remain Richard Altick, *The English Common Reader* (Columbus: Ohio State University Press, 1957), and, especially, Raymond Williams, *The Long Revolution* (London: Chatto and Windus, 1961). Indeed, of all these works, the reader should consult Williams first and return to him most frequently; his analysis of the making of literary markets is the broadest, subtlest, and most multidimensional.

2. "George Eliot and *Daniel Deronda*: The Prostitute and the Jewish Question," in

Sex, Politics, and Science in the Nineteenth Century Novel, ed. Ruth Yeazell (Baltimore: Johns Hopkins University Press, 1986), pp. 42–3.

3. Trollope, *The Prime Minister*, ed. David Skilton (London: Penguin, 1994), pp. 35, 75. Further citations in the text refer to this edition.

4. A Foreign Resident [T. H. S. Escott], *Society in London* (London, 1885), pp. 86–7, quoted in David Feldman, *Englishmen and Jews: Social Relations and Political Culture, 1840–1914* (New Haven: Yale University Press, 1994), pp. 80–1. Escott, to underscore just how small and self-contained was the London literary world he was writing about, was a good friend of Trollope and wrote a biography of him.

5. See Michael Ragussis, "Israel in England: English Culture and the 'Hebrew Premier,'" in *Figures of Conversion: "The Jewish Question" and the English National Identity* (Durham: Duke University Press, 1995), pp. 174–233, for an excellent analysis of anti-Semitic responses to Disraeli and their role in the articulation of a distinct English national identity.

6. Poliakov, *The History of Anti-Semitism*, vol. 3, *From Voltaire to Wagner*, tr. Miriam Kochan (London: Routledge and Kegan Paul, 1975), p. 397.

7. Zizek, "Enjoy Your Nation as Yourself," in *Tarrying with the Negative: Kant, Hegel, and the Critique of Ideology* (Durham: Duke University Press, 1993), p. 206.

8. The classic analysis of the former is Ernest Mandel, *Late Capitalism* (London: NLB, 1975; first published as *Die Spätkapitalismus* [Frankfurt: Suhrkamp Verlag, 1972]). For the latter, see Scott Lash and John Urry, *The End of Organized Capitalism* (Cambridge: Polity Press, 1987). The ability of capitalism to evolve more quickly than the explanatory paradigms that have arisen to encompass its changes can be registered by wondering what critic will attempt to encompass the economic changes of our moment, exactly none of which Mandel's extraordinary synthesis or Lash and Urry's less satisfying one anticipate.

9. Schumpeter derives the term "animal spirits" from John Maynard Keynes, who himself seems to have derived it from his reading of Descartes and Hume. In Keynes's *General Theory*, Robin Matthews has observed, the term denotes that affective, irrational leap of faith that drives investment: "if human nature felt no temptation to take a chance, no satisfaction (profit apart), in constructing a factory, a railway, a mine or a farm, there might not be much investment merely as a result of cold calculation." As such, the term provides at least a supplement to, if not a critique of, the utilitarian logic prevailing in Keynes's time, and a potent reminder to the rational expectations school that prevails in our own. See Matthews, "Animal Spirits," in *Thoughtful Economic Man: Essays on Rationality, Moral Rules, and Benevolence*, ed. J. Gay Tulip Meeks (Cambridge: Cambridge University Press, 1991), pp. 103–25. This and other citations from Keynes can be found on p. 103.

10. *The Philosophy of Money*, tr. Tom Bottomore and David Frisby (London: Routledge and Kegan Paul, 1978).

11. Löwy, *George Lukacs—From Romanticism to Bolshevism*, tr. Patrick Camiller (London: NLB, 1979).

12. "The Use of Knowledge in Society," in *The Essence of Hayek* (Stanford: Hoover Institution Press, 1984), pp. 218–9.

13. Dimock, *Residues of Justice: Literature, Law, Philosophy* (Berkeley: University of California Press, 1996), p. 140. The classic example of Becker's application of economics to

cultural and social phenomena is *The Economic Approach to Human Behavior* (Chicago: University of Chicago Press, 1976).

14. For an excellent historical analysis of the more manic moves of the market and an account of their causes and consequences, see Charles Kindleberger, *Manias, Panics, and Crashes: A History of Financial Crises* (New York: Basic Books, 1978).

15. Hirschman, *The Passions and the Interests: Political Arguments for Capitalism before Its Triumph* (Princeton: Princeton University Press, 1977).

16. Martin Wiener, "Market Culture, Reckless Passion, and the Victorian Reconstruction of Punishment," in *The Culture of the Market: Historical Essays*, ed. Thomas Haskell and Richard Teichgraebner III (Cambridge: Cambridge University Press, 1993), p. 139.

17. For a study of this new arena of economics, see Miriam Bensman, "Putting the Market on the Couch," *Institutional Investor* 31 (January 1997), pp. 133–4. Interestingly, the study of marketplace behavior grew out of cognitive psychology, and so its focus remains not emotion but rather "cognitive error or factors beyond greed that motivate investors to explain the underpinnings of market anomalies." Its study, in other words, focuses on effect rather than affect—poor decisions caused by warps in thinking. One notes as well that, as in all economic thought post–Adam Smith, greed is the one emotion that is understood to be profoundly rational, or at least excluded from the category of the irrational.

18. In *The Marx-Engels Reader*, ed. Robert Tucker (New York: Norton, 1978), p. 49. Further citations refer to this edition.

19. Zundi al-Fatih, *The Jews* (Detroit: privately printed, 1972). Further citations in the text refer to this edition.

20. Quoted in Selzer, *"Kike!"* (New York: New World, 1972), pp. 50–1. Further citations refer to this edition.

21. For a theoretical account of this "transcoding"—the sliding of categories of demonization from one out-group to the other—see Peter Stallybrass and Allon White, *The Politics and Poetics of Transgression* (Ithaca: Cornell University Press, 1983). What Stallybrass and White miss in their lively if somewhat superficial account, the crucial role that racial categories play in the establishment of this process, is provided by Anne Stoler, *Race and the Education of Desire* (Durham: Duke University Press, 1995), especially pp. 123–36, in which Stoler demonstrates how fully the language of class that Stallybrass and White deploy is drenched with racial categories and shaped by colonial experiences. And Stoler completely and interestingly ignores the ways that categories of Jewish otherness shaped this language and these assumptions: for example, the topos of "the other within."

22. One needs to be very careful here, because each of these two linkages has historically been used to demonize Jews (the latter most recently by Louis Farrakhan's Nation of Islam, which has argued that Jews were indispensable to the slave trade). The slippery slope from thinking about the economic role played by Jews to anti-Semitism can be best attested to by the career of Werner Sombart; before writing *Luxury and Capitalism*, Sombart wrote *The Jews and Modern Capitalism*, in which he made an argument very similar to Weber's— that capitalism was indispensably shaped by religious practices—but ascribed those practices to the Jews. Thanks to the legalism, restraint, and rationality preached by their religion, Jews became bankers and moneylenders and opened stock exchanges and so made themselves an indispensable part of the new capitalist order. To a large extent, Sombart

is sympathetic with Jews—and he certainly differentiated himself from the Jew-as-passionate-lecher stereotypes that surrounded him. But there are strong anti-Semitic currents that course through his thought, largely by implication: seeing Jews qua Jews as occupying by virtue of their religion rather than by their social positioning a crucial role in the making of capitalism is a very long step down the slippery slope toward reviling Jews as the source of all the more problematic aspects of capitalism, as variously do Marx, Hitler, and Farrakhan. Late in his career, just to confirm these difficulties, Sombart expressed sympathies with National Socialism.

23. These famous lines from act 4 of the *Merchant* can also serve to remind us how complex the issue of anti-Semitism and Shakespeare's responses to it have been in critical history. For an excellent recent treatment of these issues, see James Shapiro, *Shakespeare and the Jews* (New York: Columbia University Press, 1996).

24. *Spectacles of Strangeness: Imperialism, Alienation, and Marlowe* (Philadelphia: University of Pennsylvania Press, 1993), p. 98.

25. Marlowe, *The Jew of Malta*, ed. Richard W. Van Fossen (Lincoln: University of Nebraska Press, 1982), p. 6, emphasis mine. Further citations give line number, not page number, from this edition.

26. Lopez's Jewishness in the text, like that of many of Trollope's Jews, is veiled in a certain amount of mystery, leading critics like Robert Tracy to suggest that Lopez may well not be a Jew. (See *Trollope's Later Novels* [Berkeley: University of California Press, 1978, p. 48].) To a degree that ascription is a product of the profoundly jealous Mr. Everett, who does not know for a fact that Lopez is Jewish (Lopez refuses to give him any accounting of his background) but constantly refers to him in bitingly anti-Semitic terms anyway. But Lopez's background (son of a peddler), occupation (speculator), and appearance (swarthy, hook-nosed) are all properly to be associated with Jews in Victorian England, the majority of whom were Sephardic and hence dark-skinned. Finally, although Jews, like Lopez père, were stereotypically associated with peddling earlier in the century (see Mayhew, for example, for whom the words "Jew" and "pedlar" are virtual synonyms) they were popularly associated with high finance throughout the later years of the century, particularly with investment houses that speculated abroad with British capital. (Tellingly, all of Lopez's speculations—Spanish bonds, guano futures—have to do with foreign locales.) And Lopez identifies himself as a Jew by quoting Shylock's famous "hath not a Jew" speech to his father-in-law. As I will argue, he conforms explicitly to the anti-Semitic model of the passionate, economically driven, sexually perverse Jew I have been describing in the first half of this chapter.

27. Anthony Trollope, *An Autobiography* (London: Oxford University Press, 1950), pp. 335–6.

28. See Herbert, *Trollope and Comic Pleasure* (Chicago: University of Chicago Press, 1987), p. 217.

29. Henry James, *Letters*, ed. Leon Edel (Cambridge: Harvard University Press, 1974), 3:376. James adds: "He has a gross and repulsive face and manner, but appears *bon enfant* when you talk to him. But he is the dullest Briton of them all." James's posthumous comments on Trollope, recorded in a fine essay reprinted in *Partial Portraits* (London: Macmillan, 1888), pp. 325–72, are, appropriately enough, far more generous.

30. Anthony Trollope, *The Way We Live Now* (London: Penguin, 1994), p. 19. All further citations in the text refer to this edition.

31. For reminding me of this, I am grateful to John Kucich.

32. These plans are reprinted in John Sutherland, "Trollope at Work on *The Way We Live Now*," *Nineteenth-Century Fiction* 36 (1982), pp. 472–93.

3. The Mania of the Middlebrow

1. See I. A. Richards (who builds a theory of literature quite directly out of the analysis of readers' responses), *Practical Criticism: A Study of Literary Judgment* (New York: Harcourt, Brace 1956); Norman Holland, *Five Readers Reading* (New Haven: Yale University Press, 1975); Janice Radway, *Reading the Romance: Women, Patriarchy, and Popular Literature* (Chapel Hill: University of North Carolina Press, 1984); Altick, *The English Common Reader: A Social History of the Mass Reading Public, 1800–1900* (Chicago: University of Chicago Press, 1957); Vicinius, *The Industrial Muse: A Study of Nineteenth-Century British Working-Class Literature* (New York: Barnes and Noble, 1974); Gagnier, *Subjectivities: A History of Self-Representation in Britain, 1832–1920* (New York: Oxford University Press, 1991).

2. For the classic account of these, see Lawrence Levine, *Highbrow/Lowbrow: The Making of Cultural Hierarchy in America* (New York: Basic Books, 1986). Although I argue with Levine over the course of this chapter, it's difficult to overstate the importance of this sprightly and polemical work.

3. The quotation is from E. C. Stedman and can be found in William Peterson, *Interrogating the Oracle* (Athens: Ohio University Press, 1969), p. 36.

4. For more on these literary societies, see Peterson, *Interrogating the Oracle*.

5. For a fuller examination of these groups and the cultural work done in and through them, see Anne Gere's fine recent study, *Intimate Practices: Literacy and Cultural Work in U.S. Women's Clubs, 1880–1920* (Urbana: University of Illinois Press, 1997).

6. *The Notebooks of Henry James*, ed. F. O. Matthiessen and Kenneth Murdock (New York: Oxford University Press, 1947), p. 97. Du Maurier's recollection of this incident can be found in *Trilbyana: The Rise and Progress of a Popular Novel* (New York: Critic Company, 1895), p. 3. Further citations in the text refer to these editions.

7. *Trilbyana*, pp. 18, 21, 26. The novel was published first in America by Harper, subsequently in England by Longman. The figures for sales are from, respectively, *Trilbyana*, p. 13, and Hart, *The Popular Book*, p. 167.

8. Woolf, "Middlebrow," in *Collected Essays* (London: Hogarth Press, 1966), 2:196–203.

9. See Smith, *Democracy and the Novel: Popular Resistance to Classic American Writers* (New York: Oxford University Press, 1978); Rubin, *The Making of Middlebrow Culture* (Chapel Hill: University of North Carolina Press, 1992); and Radway, *A Feeling for Books: The Book-of-the-Month Club, Literary Taste, and Middle-Class Desire* (Chapel Hill: University of North Carolina Press, 1997).

10. For more on the rise of this segment and its attempt to negotiate class status through judgments of taste, see my *Professions of Taste: Henry James, British Aestheticism, and Commodity Culture* (Stanford: Stanford University Press, 1990).

11. *Distinction: A Social Critique of the Judgment of Taste*, tr. Richard Nice (Cambridge: Harvard University Press, 1984), p. 323. Further citations in the text refer to this edition. I need to complicate and qualify Bourdieu's terms even as I use them, and the intrepid reader, if interested, will find my methodological caveats here. I have been writing as if

Bourdieu's middlebrow were indeed a distinct and coherent social fragment and as if Bourdieu's delightfully circular argument about the relation of taste to class—that we have the tastes we have because they are given us by our social position and we are ensconced in our social position because of the tastes that we are given—were indeed fully tenable. Neither is necessarily the case. For example, Bourdieu writes as if his categorizations were unitary and discrete social reifications—as if, in fact, they were fully self-contained taste-systems having little or no contact with each other. However accurate this may be with respect to the French sociocultural scene—and I have my doubts—empirical experience alone suggests that it would be an oversimplification of the American. One could easily imagine, for example, even the most thoroughly middle class–mired American middlebrow shuttling giddily between an abundance of "symbolic expressions of class positions" over the course of a single day: eating breakfast to *Good Morning America* (lowbrow?), driving to work while listening to Mozart on a Classical-Lite radio station (high middlebrow?), driving home to rap music on the local soul station (brow classification, significantly, breaks down altogether when inflected by questions of race), eating a steak for dinner (classic middlebrow) while drinking a fine Merlot (highbrow?), then watching a baseball game (potentially everybrow) before retiring to bed, there to read a chapter of Dostoevsky (utter highbrow), Tom Wolfe (utter middlebrow), or John MacDonald (again, brow classification impossible). Rather than see this lability as a sign of muddiness or confusion, I would like to take it as a variety of specificity. For it would seem to be the defining characteristic of the middlebrow that such a figure is able to shift and slide between various taste-positions at different moments of experience; that this figure possesses on the one hand the grounding in the popular or lowbrow culture and on the other at least the potential access to highbrow culture to allow for the potential experience of all aspects of the cultural spectrum; and that finally, the rise of brow positions is made possible by—is a consequence of—mass culture.

The middlebrow, in short, is an inherently complex and multiply-identified figure, one who embodies, far more than does any other taste-fragment, the full ramifications of cultural experience itself in a postmodern, polycultural, media-saturated world in which at least exposure to a manifold of cultural experiences is widely available, if not uniformly accessible. Matters become yet more complicated when one interrogates further the properties of that taste-fragment I have been calling the middlebrow. What seems to define most compellingly Bourdieu's middlebrow—what distinguishes his version of that figure from other accounts of the middlebrow—is not the middlebrow's project of upward mobility through cultural attainment but rather the middlebrow's conflicted affect vis-à-vis high culture. And who among us, even the highest of high American highbrows, is not capable of a similar amalgam of sentiments—particularly, to pick a not entirely random example, when brought face to face with one of Bourdieu's grand-bourgeois highbrows:

> [He] remembers "wines drunk three years ago, a bouquet, a Port, a rather special Saint-Estèphe from a particular year. . . . I still have ten bottles of wine from 1923 here. And four bottles of liqueur dated 1870." A good bottle "isn't to be drunk with just anyone." . . . It requires a certain liturgy, a liturgy to get the temperature right, a liturgy to drink it. It's a "communion" to be celebrated "only with certain people who are capable of enjoying it in the same way. . . . I'd rather drink it on my own than with people who don't appreciate it." (p. 278)

Writing from the American perspective, at least, it would seem that *le middlebrow, c'est nous*. If we understand middlebrow-hood, as I have earlier tried to suggest we must, not as a discrete and unvarying class position but as an affect, an attitude, a stance toward multiply available cultural experiences, then anyone socialized by our cultural system will find moments of middlebrow response inevitable, if not uniformly understood and experienced. And these problems are enhanced by Bourdieu's habit of combining (unacknowledged) cultural specificity with poststructuralist atemporality. Bourdieu offers a knowledge that is not only thoroughly local ("I have every reason to fear this book will strike the reader as very French," he writes [p. xi], with good reason) but resolutely ahistorical (the survey to which many of his analyses refer, for example, was conducted in 1967, before some rather remarkable changes in the French social and cultural order, a fact nowhere commented on in the book). Any attempt directly, unironically, uninflectedly to "apply" Bourdieu to American cultural experience would present, it would seem, insuperable difficulties.

I nevertheless seek in this book to make use of Bourdieu's theoretical endeavor because his terms of inquiry get at two phenomena I consider crucial to the social determination of taste in the America of the nineteenth and twentieth fins de siècle alike. The first is his diagnosis of the conflicted nature of middlebrow experience. It is precisely the admixture of intense admiration for and a correlative—and consequent—anxiety from high culture that Bourdieu describes in his ideal-type of the middlebrow that produces the labile response at work first in the American 1890s and then in the American 1990s: a hyperbolized and idealized vision of the products and possibilities of high culture that leads, by its very intensity, to a rebellious countervision of that culture as sinister and malevolent, if equally authoritative. The second is the distinction Bourdieu makes between the middlebrow qua middlebrow and those organs of middlebrow culture that are chartered by that figure's particular cultural needs. For the organs of middlebrow culture generate this dual response as they guide the middlebrow audience in its cultural experience—as they *act* to enhance both the positive and the negative visions of the cultural in order to assert their own role as definers of what can and cannot be included in legitimate culture. Indeed, it is precisely the interplay between these three terms—an eager but conflicted middlebrow public, a high culture that condescends to them when it is not ignoring them, and a middlebrow culture that acts to aggrandize itself as it seeks to mediate the clash of taste—that I see operative in recent controversies over avant-garde art and politics in the academy; and I hope to trace this interplay to the origins of the middlebrow as a full-blown cultural consumer and of middlebrow culture as a fully articulated cultural formation in the late nineteenth century. We can see both these emergences most fully, and their problematics most clearly, I argue hereafter, in the fin-de-siècle rise of *Trilby*-mania.

12. George du Maurier, *Trilby* (London: Dent, 1931, 1978), p. 35. Further citations in the text refer to this edition.

13. Charles Dudley Warner, "Editor's Study," *Harper's Magazine* 89 (September 1894), p. 636. Further citations in the text refer to this publication.

14. See Levine, *Highbrow/Lowbrow*, pp. 83–168. Most of the conductors and many of the phenomena that Levine anatomizes in the American fin de siècle were evident in England at the same time; see, for example, the comments on English audiences for music from the highbrow press that I quote hereafter. The full study of the making of "highbrow" culture in English cultural life remains to be written, although in many ways the work of

Raymond Williams (which has been quite influential for Levine) is constantly engaged with this process.

15. Quoted in John Mueller, *The American Symphony Orchestra*, pp. 132–3, 356–7, quoted in Levine, *Highbrow/Lowbrow*, p. 192.

16. Rosenberg, *From Shylock to Svengali: Jewish Stereotypes in English Fiction* (Stanford: Stanford University Press, 1960), p. 261. Further citations in the text refer to this edition.

17. "Du Maurier appartient à une époque où l'antisemitisme acquèrit ses lettres de noblesse scientifiques. . . . La diffusion des théories racistes, qui concluent à la supériorité de la race germanique, va donner bonne conscience aux antisémites viscéraux." "Si Svengali était parvenu à consommer son union charnelle avec Trilby, ce n'est plus du crime de sorcellerie dont il aurait été coupable, mais de celui de *Rassenschande*." *Le regard de l'autre: Le juif dans le roman anglais 1800–1900* (Nancy: Presses Universitaires de Nancy, 1994), pp. 107, 108 (my translations).

18. Benjamin Disraeli, *Coningsby, or The New Generation* (Oxford: Oxford University Press, 1982), p. 222.

19. Jacobs, quoted in John Efron, *Defenders of the Faith: Jewish Doctors and Race Science in Fin-de-Siècle Europe* (New Haven: Yale University Press, 1994).

20. Thackeray, "Codlingsby," in *Contributions to "Punch,"* in *Complete Works*, vol. 8 (New York: Harper and Brothers, 1910), p. 31.

21. *Contemporary Review* 7 (January 1868), pp. 36–54.

22. *Saturday Review* 47 (May 1879), p. 804.

23. Wagner, *Judaism in Music*, in *Richard Wagner's Prose Works*, vol. 3, tr. William Ashton Ellis (London: Routledge and Kegan Paul, 1894), p. 96. Further citations in the text refer to this edition.

24. *Punch* 15 (1847), p 145.

25. Norman Lebrecht, *The Maestro Myth: Great Conductors in the Pursuit of Power* (London: Simon and Schuster, 1991), p. 191.

4. Henry James and the Discourses of Anti-Semitism

1. See, for example, Christopher Ricks's recent *T. S. Eliot and Prejudice* (London: Faber and Faber, 1988). I forbear citing the spate of commentary from the 1940s to the present day on the anti-Semitism of Ezra Pound.

2. For more on this matter, see Elizabeth Ammons, *Edith Wharton's Argument with America* (Athens: University of Georgia Press, 1980).

3. James, *The American Scene* (Bloomington: Indiana University Press, 1968), p. 111. Further citations in the text refer to this edition.

4. Recent work in genetics has complicated considerably the question of "race," nowhere more so than in the question of the so-called racial identity of "the Jew." It is clear that both Ashkenazic (largely lighter complected eastern and northern European) Jews and Sephardic (largely darker complected Middle Eastern, North African, and Mediterranean) Jews share significant genetic affinities both with each other and with the populations among whom they lived; see T. Livsitz, R. P. Sokal, and E. Kobliansky, "Genetic Affinities of Jewish Populations," *American Journal of Human Genetics* 49 (1991), p. 131. For some genetic affinities between Sephardic and Ashkenazic Jews, see Gerard Lucotte, "Y-chromosome specific haplotype diversity in Ashkenazic and Sephardic Jews," *Human Bi-*

ology 65 (1993), p. 835. It also is clear from work underway on Tay-Sachs disease that there was a high degree of interbreeding among Ashkenazic Jews—that most contemporary Ashkenazis (the vast majority of Jews living today) are descended from a relatively small community of quite prolific breeders (see N. Risch et al., "Genetic Analysis of Idiopathic Torsion Dystonia in Ashkenazi Jews and Their Recent Descent from a Small Founder Population," *Nature Genetics* 9 [1995], pp. 152–59).

But does this mean that Jews are a "race"? After all, the same body of data that shows genetic similarity among Jews (Lucotte tells us that Ashkenazic and Yemenite Jews share more genetic similarities than any other two groups of Jews, for what that's worth) also shows a significant degree of overlap between Jewish and non-Jewish populations. And what is a race, anyway? Is it defined by genetic similarities? If so, which genes?—especially since those that control the prime markers of race, skin color and physical appearance, are monumentally insignificant when placed in the full panoply of genetic material. (This argument was brilliantly made in another racial context by Anthony Appiah, "The Uncompleted Argument: Du Bois and the Illusion of Race," in Gates, ed., *"Race," Writing, and Difference* [Chicago: University of Chicago Press, 1986], pp. 30–32.) The persistent identification of Jews as a "race," in my view, is more a case of the irrational appeal of the notion of race than a description of anything particularly salient in Jewish identity.

For classic examinations of these issues from a non- (or at least less) genetically inflected approach, see Raphael Patai and Jennifer Patai Wing, *The Myth of the Jewish Race* (New York: Scribner's, 1975), and Ashley Montagu, "Are the Jews a 'Race?'" in *Man's Most Dangerous Myth: The Fallacy of Race*, 4th ed. (Cleveland: World, 1964), pp. 317–38.

5. Both this example and a larger treatment of the tendency of thought underlying it are provided by George Stocking, "Lamarckianism in American Social Science, 1890–1925," in *Race, Culture, and Evolution* (Chicago: University of Chicago Press, 1968, 1982), p. 244. Stocking adds that any other Jewish "racial" characteristics were often cited by American neo-Lamarckians as examples of acquired traits: William Z. Ripley explained Jewish "deficiency" in lung capacity as "an acquired characteristic, the effect of long subjection to an unfavourable sanitary and social environment . . . [which] has nevertheless become a hereditary trait" (p. 244). For more on the Enlightenment origins of the Jewish nose, see George Mosse, *Toward the Final Solution: A History of European Racism* (New York: Harper and Row, 1980), p. 29.

6. Jean-Paul Sartre, *Anti-Semite and Jew*, tr. George Becker (New York: Schocken, 1948, reprinted 1965), pp. 38–9. For these matters, the classic texts remain John Higham, *Strangers in the Land: Patterns of American Nativism, 1860–1925* (New York: Atheneum, 1968), and "Social Discrimination against Jews, 1830–1930," in *Send These to Me: Jews and Other Immigrants in Urban America* (New York: Atheneum, 1975). But I also have reference hereafter to a "revisionist" or nonmainstream body of historiography on this issue, including Michael Dobkowski, *The Tarnished Dream* (Westport, Conn.: Greenwood Press, 1968), and Robert Singerman's very useful essay, "The Jew as Racial Alien" in *Anti-Semitism in American History*, ed. David Gerber (Urbana: University of Illinois Press, 1986). This scholarship differs from Higham on a number of crucial specifics, including his stressing of objective grounds for anti-Semitic prejudices (economic strains, parvenu behavior) and his understatement of the extensiveness of racial stereotyping in American popular culture and consciousness. But this scholarship differs more powerfully in its being

explicitly informed by a sense of ethnic identity and political urgency that is lacking not only in Higham but also in the "mainstream" history he represents. For a fine survey of the historiographical issues involved in this matter, see Gerber's introduction to his own volume, "Anti-Semitism and Jewish-Gentile Relations in American Historiography and the American Past," in *Anti-Semitism in American History*, pp. 3–56. In recent years, a new generation of Americanists has returned to the question of Jewish immigration in the period between 1880 and 1920 in a comparative context and with special attention to the racialization of Jewish (and other white) ethnicities. Particularly important has been the work of Matthew Jacobson, *Special Sorrows: The Diasporic Imagination of Irish, Polish, and Jewish Immigrants in the United States* (Cambridge: Harvard University Press, 1995) and *Whiteness of a Different Color: European Immigrants and the Alchemy of Race* (Cambridge: Harvard University Press, 1998).

7. Paul Leland Haworth, *America in Ferment* (Indianapolis, 1915), quoted in Singerman, "The Jew as Useful Alien," pp. 108–9. Note that Jews from northern and eastern Europe— the Pale of Settlement in Russia is not exactly a Mediterranean clime—are conflated with immigrants from southern Europe, especially Italy. The common element here seems to be double: an insistence on the ubiquitously Levantine nature of Ashkenazic Jews, despite quite literally centuries of intermarriage in Germany, Russia, and the rest of western Europe; and an insistence (especially powerful in America) that races originally from the South had to possess darker countenances than those originally from Northern climes and hence were, in the racial theory of the time, irrevocably of lower intelligence and lesser moral fiber.

8. To cite but one example of the latter, in 1892 *Frank Leslie's Weekly* described the Lower East Side in language startlingly similar to James's:

> There exists on the east side of this town a great and coherent population of foreigners of a low order or intelligence, speaking their own languages, following their own customs, and absolutely blind or utterly indifferent to our ideals, moral, social, and political.... Go and see them swarm in the stores and the houses of the east side if you have any doubt on the subject and form your own conclusions as to the availability of the material for manufacturing into the sort of citizen the founders and fathers of the republic had in mind. (February 27, 1892, p. 57)

9. Geismar, *Henry James and the Jacobites* (New York: Hill and Wang, 1962), pp. 349–50.

10. One who did was Leo Levy, author of a fine 1956 book on Jamesian melodrama, which was published, tellingly, in *Commentary* in 1958. (*Versions of Melodrama: A Study of the Fiction and Drama of Henry James, 1865–1897* [Berkeley: University of California Press, 1957].) But the very specialized audience of that journal, and the fact that Levy's work was not published in an academic venue that was, at that precise time, admitting Jews like Levy to its precincts, is telling of the social dynamics of academic Jamesianism. See Levy, "Henry James and the Jews," *Commentary* 26 (September 1958), pp. 243–9. For more on Levy and Jewish academic Jamesians, see chapter 5.

11. In Higham's *Send These to Me*, for example, James's shadowy presence in the terrain of anti-Semitism is acknowledged by a footnote to the passage I have been discussing in *The American Scene*; and Michael Dobkowski includes James on the roster of elite anti-

Semites, even though he spends the majority of his time discussing Edith Wharton, Vance Thompson, and the Adams family. See Dobkowski, *The Tarnished Dream.*

12. See Posnock, *The Trial of Curiosity: Henry James, William James, and the Challenge of Modernity* (New York: Oxford University Press, 1991).

13. Indeed, it can be argued that "Western civilization" as a discursive category from Juvenal through Gibbon through Allan Bloom is composed largely of warnings about the decline and fall of itself. See, *inter alia*, Patrick Brantlinger, *Bread and Circuses* (Ithaca: Cornell University Press, 1984), pp. 38–46.

14. Nietzsche continues: "The Jews are the counterparts of the *décadents*: they have been compelled to *act* as *décadents* to the point of illusion." Nietzsche, *Twilight of the Idols and The Anti-Christ,* tr. R. J. Hollingdale (Baltimore: Penguin Books, 1968), p. 149. I first encountered this quotation in Eve Sedgwick, *Epistemology of the Closet* (Berkeley: University of California Press, 1990), p. 177.

15. Gilman, *Difference and Pathology: Stereotypes of Sexuality, Race, and Madness* (Ithaca: Cornell University Press, 1985), especially pp. 150–63 and 191–217. Further citations in the text refer to this edition.

16. On inbreeding, see Patai and Wing, *The Myth of the Jewish Race,* pp. 99–118.

17. The notion of "mongrelization" and its implicit delineation of the lower classes or demonized races as less than human is built into racist discourse by Gobineau and recurs throughout racist discourses of all varieties. Indeed, it is central to Lombroso's theory of degeneration, in which criminals and other deviants as well as "lesser" races are seen as literally members of another, less evolved species. To his credit, this is one of the aspects of Lombroso that Nordau does not echo in his own writings on degeneration.

18. Reprinted in Paul Popenoe and Roswell Johnson, *Applied Eugenics* (New York, 1918), p. 133, quoted in Singerman, "The Jew as Racial Alien," p. 113.

19. Henry Suksdorf, *Our Race Problems* (New York: Shakespeare Press, 1911; reprint, Miami: Mnemosyne, 1969), p. 8.

20. To quote again from the egregious Suksdorf: "There are only two solutions of the irritating problems [posed by the Jew]: either a complete fusion of the heterogeneous ethnic elements into heterogeneity, or extermination or expulsion of the weaker race by the stronger." (p. 8)

21. In a powerful and controversial essay, Edmund Shorter argues that the higher incidence of manic depression among Ashkenazic Jews gives medical support to the hypotheses of Freud and Lombroso. Shorter's essay is a reminder of strict constructionism in our analysis of race (although I have serious problems with the coherence of the category "Ashkenazic Jew"; see note 4). But the most problematic step here would seem to be cultural: the move from registering higher rates of a certain mental disorder among Western Jews to perceiving the Jew as bearer of mental disease *tout court.* See Shorter, "Women and Jews in a Private Nervous Clinic in Nineteenth-Century Vienna," *Medical History* 33 (1989), pp. 149–83.

22. Nordau, *Degeneration* (New York: Appleton's, 1895), p. 19. Further citations in the text refer to this edition.

23. The 1937 Munich exhibition of "degenerate art" (*entarte kunst*), organized at the behest of Goebbels himself, was reassembled at the Los Angeles County Museum of Art; the catalogue-cum-commentary is entitled *"Degenerate Art": The Fate of the Avant-Garde in Nazi Germany* (Los Angeles: Los Angeles County Museum of Art, 1991).

24. Edwin Cady, ed., *W. D. Howells as Critic* (London: Routledge and Kegan Paul, 1973), p. 165.

25. *Complete Tales of Henry James* (Philadelphia: Lippincott, 1964), vol. 9, p. 317.

26. In *The Two Magics* (London: Macmillan, 1899), pp. 390–1.

27. James, *The Tragic Muse* (London: Penguin, 1979), p. 323. This edition reprints the original 1890 version of the text, not the later New York Edition revised version.

28. "Calchas," "Will England Last the Century?" *Fortnightly Review* 2 (n.s.) (March 1901), pp. 20–34; W. J. Corbet, "What Should England Do to Be Saved?" *Westminster Review* 155 (June 1901), pp. 604–13; "Musings without Method: The Degeneracy of the English People," *Blackwood's Edinburgh Magazine* 176 (August 1904), pp. 271–80.

29. John Randolph Dos Passos, *The Anglo-Saxon Century and the Unification of the English-Speaking Peoples* (New York: Putnam's, 1903); "Will the Anglo-Saxon Be the Dominant Race a Century Hence?" *Harper's Weekly* 86 (March 14, 1903), pp. 439–45. Charles Beresford, "The Future of the Anglo-Saxon Race," *North American Review* 171 (December 1900), p. 803. For the arguments in favor of race-mixing, see Mark Haller, *Eugenics: Hereditarian Attitudes in American Thought* (New Brunswick: Rutgers University Press, 1963), p. 53.

30. Henry James, *The Golden Bowl*, the New York Edition, vols. 23 and 24 (New York: Scribner's, 1908), p. 10. Further citations to this edition identify volume then page number.

31. In this respect, Maggie must become more like Charlotte too, whose multiple racial lineage is stressed by the pedigree-obsessed Prince. Charlotte is a strange amalgam of Anglo-American and European identities; her parents, "already of a corrupt generation, demoralized falsified polyglot before her," raised her in Florence but educated her in Paris (along with Maggie), and she speaks Italian so convincingly that the Prince fantasizes her as possessing Italian "blood": he "insist[s that] some strictly civil ancestor—generations back, and from the Tuscan hills if she would—made himself felt ineffaceably in her blood and her tone" (23:79). This mixed or multiple identity—and the capacity to manipulate and adjust appearances that go along with the Italianate side of things—is, I argue hereafter, what Maggie must attain over the course of the novel: only it is one that she learns rather than one that is given her by racial birthright.

32. Ellmann, "The Imaginary Jew: T. S. Eliot and Ezra Pound," in *Between "Race" and Culture: Representations of "the Jew" in English and American Literature*, ed. Bryan Cheyette (Stanford: Stanford University Press, 1996), pp. 84–101.

33. Kristeva, *Powers of Horror: An Essay on Abjection*, tr. Leon Roudiez (New York: Columbia University Press, 1982), p. 1. Further citations in the text refer to this edition.

34. Haviland, *Henry James's Last Romance* (Cambridge, U.K.: Cambridge University Press, 1997), pp. 108–34.

35. Kristeva, *Strangers to Ourselves*, tr. Leon Roudiez (New York: Columbia University Press, 1991), p. 191.

36. Consider the recrudescence of arguments about the genetic basis of I.Q. and the racial endowments thereof in Charles Murray and Richard Herrnstein's *The Bell Curve* (New York: Free Press, 1994). At first sight, these arguments would seem to be exempt from the charge of anti-Semitism (at least), since Herrnstein and Murray include "Ashkenazi Jews" in their lists of the genetically equipped elite. But to the contrary, these arguments are a perfect expression of Murray and Herrnstein's quite amazing, if quite unconscious, incoherence on the subject of race. For any sustained reflection on the difference between Ashkenazic and Sephardic Jews would question Herrnstein and Murray's

astonishingly naive sense of racial identity, since that very difference would have to be constructed by the interpenetration of genetic materials between people living in the same geographical terrain (or how else could we distinguish between Ashkenazic and Sephardic?). If, to the contrary, the distinction between Ashkenazic and Sephardic is to be seen as a cultural one, then the genetic basis of Murray and Herrnstein's argument is dealt a quite significant blow. In either case, one is called upon to wonder why Murray and Herrnstein are compelled to make the distinction in the first place. The answers, while not attractive, are revealing: for Murray and Herrnstein, despite their arguments to the contrary, skin color and proximity to Europe seem to be the chief determining factors of cognitive intelligence and social success in contemporary culture.

5. Henry James among the Jews

1. Ozick, *What Henry James Knew and Other Essays on Writers* (London: Jonathan Cape, 1993), p. 5. Further citations in my text refer to this edition. Goodman quoted in Alexander Bloom, *Prodigal Sons: The New York Intellectuals and Their World* (New York: Oxford University Press, 1986), p. 315.

2. A terminological note: my use of the term "field" here chimes with Pierre Bourdieu's sense of the term. For Bourdieu, the cultural field (like the academic "field") is not merely a taxonomic term but a field of play or even combat, where individuals and groups struggle with each other for social leverage. Bourdieu's players on this field are always, however, defined only in terms of class; I seek here to add ethnicity to the conceptual mix.

3. *The Beginning of the Journey: The Marriage of Diana and Lionel Trilling* (New York: Harcourt Brace, 1993), pp. 80–1.

4. Although, as David Hollinger has observed, a similar spirit animates the work of a number of WASP writers in the 1920s and 1930s; he delightfully cites figures like Floyd Dell and Alvin Johnson, from Iowa and Nebraska, who found in Jews there or in New York exciting versions of a life devoted to secular, intellectual pursuits. See his crucial essay, "Ethnic Diversity, Cosmopolitanism, and the Emergence of the American Liberal Intelligentsia," *In the American Province: Studies in the History and Historiography of Ideas* (Bloomington: Indiana University Press, 1985), pp. 58–73. Although my account of these intellectuals varies from Hollinger at many points, his work is indispensable.

5. There is an abundance of writing about Jews in America; I have drawn my account here largely from Arthur Hertzberg, *The Jews in America: Four Centuries of an Uneasy Encounter: A History* (New York: Simon and Schuster, 1989), and from Ira Katznelson, "Between Separation and Disappearance: Jews on the Margins of American Liberalism," in *Paths of Emancipation: Jews, States, and Citizenship*, ed. Pierre Birnbaum and Ira Katznelson (Princeton: Princeton University Press, 1995), pp. 157–205. (*Pace* Katznelson, one of the fascinating stories that has not yet been told is the role of Jews on the American Right, especially its libertarian side: Milton Freidman, after all, was not a gentile.) For the period I am focusing on here, the most helpful account is provided by Gerald Sorin, *A Time for Building: The Third Migration, 1880–1920* (Baltimore: Johns Hopkins University Press, 1992).

This is perhaps the place to sketch the relation of my concerns with the ways assimilation has been studied for the past thirty years. Milton Gordon's classic *Assimilation in American Life: The Role of Race, Religion, and National Origins* (New York: Oxford University Press, 1964) implicitly takes the experience of eastern European Jews as its baseline for assessing the experiences of immigrants *tout court*; as such, it is symptomatic but limited, particularly when it attempts to apply its categories to racial categorizations. Scholars of what we might want to call the new ethnic studies—especially of Latino and Asian immigrant groups—have turned away from this model to ones that stress the differences between patterns of adaptation adopted by ethnic groups of color and European ones, the latter of whom are assimilable into a white identity in ways that the former are not. It might be added that conceptual paradigms of these scholars, too, have been developed in tandem with idioms of subversion and of resistance that owe much to those scholars involved in British cultural studies who have treated race as seriously as their predecessors did class: Stuart Hall and Paul Gilroy in particular. Equally important has been the Gramsci-inflected work of African-American historian Robin Kelly and American anthropologist James Scott, which stresses the ways in which the experiences of ordinary people can create patterns of resistance that are just as powerful in their effects as events in larger political arenas.

Like many of these latter scholars, I am as interested in dissent as in consent, to play with Werner Sollers's terms, and I try to suggest hereafter some of the ways in which events and experiences generally taken to be signs of Jewish assimilation to American life encode or enclose patterns of resistance and express forms of aggressivity that are generally thought to be incompatible with the project of cultural assimilation. In doing so, however, I have tried to use these as general guides rather than specific, point-by-point analogues. For the point of many of the scholars of color I have just noted is well taken: via their engagement with culture, Jews did end up making a symbolic compact at least with dominant culture, ratified by their accession to cultural power in a number of specific and limited guises. (This is not to say, I might add, that scholars of color have been as attentive as they might be to the Christian privilege—the assumption of a normative Christian identity—that frequently cuts across lines of racial division and excludes Jews).

Indeed, if there is an analogy between my thinking about Jews and high culture and the work of contemporary critics, it is probably more accurately drawn in the arena of postcolonial studies, particularly those centering on rereadings of colonial India. For among the Indian colonial elite, too, we witness an engagement with the powers of the West consummated under the sign of culture as filled with ambivalent admixtures of idealization and contempt on either side as was that evinced by Jews and traditional Anglo-Saxon elites in the nineteenth and the early years of the twentieth centuries. For a brilliant exposition of these problematics, see Sara Suleri, *The Rhetoric of English India* (Chicago: University of Chicago Press, 1992).

6. These sons were Daniel (who is said to have helped women and children into the lifeboats and is credited by his mistress with sacrificing his life for her own); Solomon, who endowed the Guggenheim Museum to house his own collection; and Simon, who endowed the Guggenheim Foundation in memory of his son, John Simon. Their niece, Peggy, was also a noted art collector and benefactor. For a gossipy and entertaining account of the family, see John Davis, *The Guggenheims: An American Epic* (New York: Morrow, 1978). For an equally gossipy account of the other German-Jewish philanthropists, see Stephen Birmingham, *"Our Crowd": The Great Jewish Families of New York* (New York: Harper and Row, 1967).

7. The literature on this wave of immigrants is almost as vast as the work that they produced. As an overview, the most useful work is Anthony Heilbut, *Exiled in Paradise:*

German Refugee Artists and Intellectuals in America, from the 1930s to the Present (New York: Viking, 1983).

8. These German Jews arrived, it might be added, with a sense of cultural superiority that cut across lines of American and Jewish identity alike. "When I arrived . . . in New York and went to register at George Washington High School," writes one of these refugees,

> the last thing on my mind was how to nurture my Jewish legacy. What did reassert itself, with a vengeance I might say, was that very "classical" education we had so gladly left behind. . . . We had little doubt that we were the bearers of a venerable European tradition of true intellectual knowledge that put us way ahead of the greedy commercialism that surrounded us. In that respect also, our future was very clear to us: as writers, artists, and professionals would we make our mark in this crassly materialistic culture. In principle we were not different from any other immigrant youths who had come before us, wanting to make something of themselves, shedding their ties to the old culture and become "Americanized." Only we were steeped in the chauvinistic intellectualism of *Mitteleuropa*, and the characterization *er amerikaniseret sich* (he is becoming American) was reserved for those who had lost their intellectual *Drang* (fervor). Herbert Pierre Secher, "*Bildung* and the Dilemma of Hyphenation," in *The German Jewish Legacy in America, 1938–1988: From Bildung to the Bill of Rights*, ed. Abraham Peck (Detroit: Wayne State University Press, 1989), pp. 66–67.

His account is hardly unique: although we are properly reminded that not all German Jews were of the sort who sent their children to the Gymnasium, and not all the 250,000 German Jews who came to America were upper middle class, nevertheless this group had a powerful effect on the construction of American literary culture.

9. *The Transplanted: A History of Immigrants in Urban America* (Bloomington: Indiana University Press, 1985), p. 20.

10. See also Moses Rischin, *The Promised City: New York's Jews, 1870–1914* (Cambridge: Harvard University Press, 1962), p. 26. Rischin reminds us that Jewish immigration from rural to urban locales was massive in 1870s and 1880s Russia and Poland, so much so that Jews composed 21 percent of the factory hands in the Pale of Settlement and 28 percent in Poland. Along with this movement came not only the highly advanced secular culture I have been outlining here, but also fairly advanced unionization—an activity that Jews brought with them to American factories. The relation between this experience and the formation of community on the Lower East Side is a crucial subject for historians of first-generation immigrants, particularly over the last decade; its relation to the sense of community among women is also the subject of Susan Glenn, *Daughters of the Shtetl: Life and Labor in the Immigrant Generation* (Ithaca: Cornell University Press, 1990).

11. Stephen Brumberg, *Going to America, Going to School: The Jewish Immigrant Public School Encounter in Turn-of-the-Century New York City* (New York: Praeger, 1986), p. 38.

12. Gold, *Jews without Money* (New York: Liveright, 1930). For more on Liveright, one of the first Jewish publishing firms in New York, see hereafter.

13. See Howe, *World of Our Fathers* (New York: Simon and Schuster, 1976), p. 370.

14. M. E. Ravage, *An American in the Making: The Life Story of an Immigrant* (New York: Harper, 1917; reprint, New York: Dover, 1971), p. 76.

15. For these activities, see Rischin, *The Promised City*, pp. 91–2. For the Baron de Hirsch Fund, see Samuel Joseph, *History of the Baron de Hirsch Fund: The Americanization of the Jewish Immigrant* (Philadelphia: Jewish Publication Society for the Baron de Hirsch Fund, 1935). Sociologists distinguish between "acculturation" and "assimilation": the first is a stage in the second, which eventuates, as Paula Hyman puts it, in a third category: "integration." According to Hyman, the "first steps, often called acculturation, include the acquisition of the basic markers of the larger society, such as language, dress, and the more amorphous category of 'values'" and are defined by the mutual willingness of the assimilating group and the dominant society to be open to each other (Hyman, *Gender and Assimilation: The Roles and Representation of Women in Modern Jewish History* [Seattle: University of Washington Press, 1995], p. 13). In what follows, I try to trace two variants of this process. First, I stress the ways in which traditional high culture of WASP America became the means of acculturation—this is what I mean by the term "assimilation-by-culture." Second, I suggest that, while Jews and dominant white Americans were indeed willing to engage in productive negotiations with each other, this traditional culture became as much of a battleground as a meeting-place.

16. "Commissioner Sargent Cuts Immigration Perils," *New York Times*, January 29, 1905, quoted in *Portal to America: The Lower East Side, 1870–1925*, ed. Allon Schoener (New York: Holt, Rinehart, and Winston, 1967), p. 27.

17. This despite the intense efforts of the school authorities to keep Jews out of the teaching profession, including the notorious oral examination for prospective schoolteachers. In a memoir, Grace Paley gives us an example of how normative English was used to weed out Jewish immigrants and their children—and the effects this had on the self-disciplining, via language, of the Jews:

> I remember their language being corrupted by those exams. . . . These difficult oral exams were meant to keep immigrants out, to keep the Irish and other English-speaking people in. They didn't want "greenhorns and mockies" coming around, right? . . . I'll never forget my poor sister and her friends sitting around and practicing all those goddamned words! "Ig-no-MIN-y, "Ig-NO-min-y" they said. Then "Ig-no-MIN-y, ig-no-MIN-y." I'll never forget how to pronounce *that* word! Those of us who were contemptuous of the whole thing used to call it the establishment of Hunter College English, and the wreckage, as far as I could tell, of our New York tongue. A couple of women in my family still talk like that.

Quoted in Bernard Rosenberg and Ernest Goldstein, *Creators and Disturbers: Reminiscences by Jewish Intellectuals of New York* (New York: Columbia University Press, 1982), p. 296.

18. In William Thomas, ed., *Old World Traits Transplanted* (Chicago, 1925), p. 17.

19. "Ethnicity and Emotions in America: Dimensions of the Unexplored," in Peter Stearns and Jan Lewis, eds., *An Emotional History of the United States* (New York: New York University Press, 1997), pp. 197–217.

20. *Jewish Daily Forward*, quoted in Irving Howe and Kenneth Libo, *How We Lived: A Documentary History of Immigrant Jews in America, 1880–1930* (New York: Richard Marek, 1979), p. 204. Mary Antin tells this story with irony and gusto in *The Promised Land* (Boston: Houghton Mifflin, 1912), pp. 233–8. The poem was ultimately published in the much less tony *Boston Herald*.

21. Quoted in Schoener, *Portal to America*, pp. 133–5. Further citations in the text refer to this edition.

22. This tendency of thought mars the thinking of a number of Jewish neoconservative critics of the 1970s and 1980s; it is pronounced in even the most thoughtful of them, like Nathan Glazer, who has recently proclaimed, *We Are All Multiculturalists Now* (Cambridge: Harvard University Press, 1997). For an application of this model to recent immigrant groups, see Peter Salins, *Immigration American-style* (New York: Basic Books, 1997). "American-style" means, it will not surprise the reader to learn, like the immigrants at the turn of the century; and it will also not surprise the reader to learn that Salins's sociological model for immigration is derived from Milton Gordon's, which is itself based on the experience of Jews.

23. Samuel Ornitz, *Haunch, Paunch, and Jowl* (New York: Boni and Liveright, 1923), pp. 30–1, quoted in Brumberg, *Going to America, Going to School*, p. 124.

24. William Poster, quoted in Deborah Dash Moore, *At Home in America: Second Generation New York Jews* (New York: Columbia University Press, 1981), p. 94.

25. For more on Jewish gangsters, see Albert Fried, *The Rise and Fall of the Jewish Gangster in America* (New York: Holt, Rinehart, and Winston, 1980), and Jenna Weissman Joselit, *Our Gang: Jewish Crime and the New York Jewish Community, 1900–1940* (Bloomington: Indiana University Press, 1983). The lack of popular success enjoyed by two excellent films that centered on the experience of the Jewish mob (Sergio Leone's *Once Upon a Time in America* and Warren Beatty's *Bugsy*) compared to films that centered on the Italian mob (Coppola's *Godfather* series, whose subtext, at least in *Godfather II*, is the battle between Sicilian and Jewish gangsters) suggests how images of the Jew have marched into social respectability along with Jews themselves.

26. Alexander Bloom, *Prodigal Sons: The New York Intellectuals and Their World* (New York: Oxford University Press, 1984). Bloom has been criticized by Alan Wald for his focus on the Jewishness of the so-called New York intellectuals in contrast to other possible vectors of mutual affiliation and concern—especially radical politics. Wald's meticulously detailed and marvelously researched *The New York Intellectuals: The Rise and Decline of the Anti-Stalinist Left from the 1930s to the 1980s* (Chapel Hill: University of North Carolina Press, 1987) makes the case for reading the New York intellectuals with politics front and center; so too does Michael Denning's panegyric *The Cultural Front* (New York: Verso, 1996).

27. See Burton Bledstein, *The Culture of Professionalism: The Middle Class and the Development of Higher Education in America* (New York: Norton, 1976). Although more than twenty years old, Bledstein's account of the rise of professionalism, the invention of credentialing, and the role of both in creating gatekeeping mechanisms for the middle class remains indispensable.

28. Lewisohn, *Up Stream: An American Chronicle* (New York: Boni and Liveright, 1922), p. 94.

29. See Dan Oren, *Joining the Club: A History of Jews at Yale* (New Haven: Yale University Press, 1985), p. 76. Herbert Tucker has reminded me of the delicious irony that rumors circulated throughout his life that Robert Browning was, in fact, Jewish.

30. As quoted in Charles Madison, *Jewish Publishing in America* (New York: Sandherin Press, 1976), p. 78.

31. John Tebbel, *A History of Book Publishing in the United States,* vol. 3, *The Golden Age between the Two Wars 1919–1940* (New York: Bowker, 1978), p. 130. Janice Radway in

A Feeling for Books: The Book-of-the-Month Club, Literary Taste, and Middle-Class Desire (Chapel Hill: University of North Carolina, 1997). Although Radway doesn't develop the links between Scherman's experience at Penn and his subsequent career as a popularizer of literature via the Book-of-the-Month Club, she at least notices them, which is more than one can say for her (frequently Jewish) peers in this form of critique.

32. Haldeman-Julius, *The First Hundred Million* (New York: Simon and Schuster, 1928), pp. 195–6.

33. This anecdote was related to me by the student in question, David Levin.

34. *The Elements of Style* (New York: Harcourt Brace, 1952), p. 76. Similar lessons were taught in Otto Jespersen's widely assigned history of the English language, where students were assured that the essentially democratic and "manly" quality of the English people was best conveyed by the hearty tongue of the Anglo-Saxons rather than by the effete aristocratic locutions of the French or the dauntingly abstract and interminably long-winded languages of the Greeks and the Romans. See Jespersen, *The Growth and Structure of the English Language*, 5th ed. (Leipzig: Teubner, 1926), especially pp. 78–138.

35. *In Defense of Ignorance* (New York: Vintage, 1965), p. 84. I am indebted for this quotation to Laurence Goldstein's excellent chapter on Shapiro in *The American Poet at the Movies: A Critical History* (Ann Arbor: University of Michigan Press, 1994).

36. Brooks, *Modern Poetry and the Tradition* (Chapel Hill: University of North Carolina Press, 1939), p. 130. Further citations in the text refer to this edition.

37. In Robert Frazer, ed., *Sir James Frazer and the Literary Imagination: Essays in Affinity and Influence* (London: Macmillan, 1990), p. 84.

38. See Bernal, *Black Athena: The Afroasiatic Roots of Classical Civilization*, vol. 2 (New Brunswick: Rutgers University Press, 1991). Bernal's work has been tremendously controversial, and it is not my intention here utterly to endorse it. But one of its great benefits has been its critical rereading of the anti-Semitism (not to mention racisms of other sorts) of the German philological establishment, especially but not exclusively in the nineteenth century. As Sarah Morris has observed, Bernal's meditations on the anti-Semitism that permeated German classical *Wissenschaft* are neither original nor the most subtle and penetrating; nonetheless, he had a considerable degree of success in bringing that matrix to the attention of critics and scholars who might otherwise have overlooked it; see Morris, "The Problem of *Black Athena*," in *Black Athena Revisited*, ed. Mary Lefkowitz and Guy MacLean Rogers (Chapel Hill: University of North Carolina Press, 1996). For a similar inquiry into the effects of anti-Semitic religious theorizing on a different discipline, sociology, and a different nation-state, France, see Ivan Strenski, *Durkheim and the Jews of France* (Chicago: University of Chicago Press, 1997).

39. This aspect of Auerbach's Jewishness escapes Foucauldian and deconstructive critics like Paul Bové (*Intellectuals in Power: A Genealogy of Critical Humanism* [New York: Columbia University Press, 1985]) and Vassilis Lambropoulos (*The Rise of Eurocentrism: Anatomy of Interpretation* [Princeton: Princeton University Press, 1993]). Bové notes Auerbach's Jewishness in the context of his famous exile in Istanbul (a post which Spitzer preceded him) but sees this narrative as an essential element in the rise of a myth of heroic critical power in the postwar American academy. Lambropoulos acknowledges Auerbach's Jewishness but sees his work as positing a unified Judeo-Christian narrative that marginalizes Greek (hence other non-Judeo-Christian) influences in the making of a narrative of European culture. Although each pays lip service to history, neither historicizes Auerbach's condition as a Jew in a rabidly anti-Semitic German academy, a fact that I think is crucial

to understanding his work. Not only is Auerbach's emphasis on *figura* a powerful inter-vention indeed, as the Nazi party attracted numerous adherents in the academy, but his whole work stands as a rebuke to a Rankian historicism that read the progression of European history as eventuating in the nation-state of Germany. One has only to compare Auerbach as classical philologist (as in the earlier chapters of *Mimesis*) to the notorious anti-Semite Wilamowitz-Müllendorf to note the ways in which Auerbach was intervening in a field that was notorious for its hostility to Jews.

40. "Three Poems on Ecstasy (John Donne, St. John of the Cross, Richard Wagner)," in *A Method of Interpreting Literature* (New York: Russell and Russell, 1974), pp. 1–63.

41. Feidelson, *Symbolism and American Literature* (Chicago: University of Chicago Press, 1948). Despite his overt interest in symbolism, Feidelson is not usually included in the myth-and-symbol school of American literature; rather, following an influential article by Barbara Foley, he has been read as instantiating a New Critical hegemony in American literature. But because, like so many ideologically minded Americanists, Foley is insensitive to Jewish issues and hence the revisionary efforts of a Jew at Yale like Feidelson, she ignores the ways in which he revises even as he adapts the New Critical topoi of the times. For Foley's argument, see "From New Criticism to Deconstruction: The Example of Charles Feidelson's 'Symbolism and American Literature,' " *American Quarterly* 36 (1984), pp. 44–70.

42. It is one of my regrets that considerations of time and space prevent me from writing more about Fiedler. Of all the Jewish critics of his generation, he is the one who rebelled most productively against the New Critical orthodoxy; and his treatment of pop-ular literature and women's writing (a long chapter in *Love and Death in the American Novel* is devoted to fiction by women, thirty years before it became fashionable), his homoerotic readings of classic texts, and his critique of the canon all anticipate directions in which the academy was to go. One of his most recent books, *Fiedler on the Roof* (Boston: Godine, 1991), collects many of his essays on Jewish writers and literary identity that bear closely on the concerns of this chapter. To single out one of particular interest: in "The Jewish Writer in America," Fiedler accounts for his interest in Whitman and Twain by suggesting (rather incredibly, with regard to the latter) that they, rather than moderns like James or Eliot, were free from the anti-Semitism that afflicted the genteel tradition in American writing. But elsewhere in that essay he echoes James almost precisely: uncom-fortable as a Jew in America and an American in Israel, Fiedler writes, it is only in Italy that he feels comfortably alienated from both. Having started his career writing stories in the mode of James (or so he tells us there) he ends it recapitulating the Jamesian stance of finding a productive alienation as an American in Europe.

43. As far as American studies is concerned, one finds a reference or two to the pro-gram-building role of Jews in histories like Gerald Graff, *Professing Literature* (Chicago: University of Chicago Press, 1987), but no real interrogation of this fact. That Graff belongs to the generation of Jews who were less than proud of their Jewishness is not irrelevant here. To cite an even more egregious example of some of the ideological effects of this omission, consider Elaine Tyler May's 1995 presidential address to the American Studies Association, "The Radical Roots of American Studies" (reprinted in *American Quarterly* 48 [June 1996], pp. 179–200). Here, May wittily divides the history of American Studies into three periods—the period of Karl, Leo, and Groucho Marx—without ever coming to terms with what it means to think about a discipline in which many Jews found a home in terms drawn from the careers of three different kinds of Jews. As a result of this

omission, May does a serious injustice to many of the Jewish academics of the 1950s and 1960s who took the myth-and-symbol school (which she rather awkwardly conflates with the consensus ideology) to open up the study of texts that focus on racial and sexual difference: Leslie Fiedler is never mentioned here, for example.

May's lacuna reminds us that revisionary students of American literature have been remarkably inattentive to the obstacles faced by Jewish scholars of the 1930s, 1940s, and 1950s. Thus, as Rael Meyerowitz observes, the Jewishness of such critics as Howe, Kazin, Trilling, and so on, goes virtually unremarked in such criticism as Randall Reising's *The Unusable Past: Theory and Study of American Literature* (New York: Methuen, 1986), where these writers are lambasted for idealizing a racist, sexist, classist ideal of "America" without any attention to their motives for such an idealization or the revisionary work they accomplished through it. See Meyerowitz, *Transferring to America: Jewish Interpretations of American Dreams* (Albany: State University of New York Press, 1995).

44. "Stranger in Paradise: Encounters with American Jews," in *People of the Book: Thirty Scholars Reflect on their Jewish Identity*, ed. Jeffrey Rubin-Dorsky and Shelley Fisher Fishkin (Madison: University of Wisconsin Press, 1996), p. 200.

45. "The Jewish Writer and the English Literary Tradition 2: A Symposium," *Commentary* 26 (September 1949), p. 367. The two-part symposium was sparked by an essay by Leslie Fiedler, "What Can We Do about Fagin?" and contained responses from Diana Trilling, William Phillips, Isaac Rosenfeld, and others, as well as Kazin.

46. Barzun, *The Energies of Art* (New York: Harper, 1956), p. 228.

47. McCarthy, in Rahv, *Essays on Literature and Politics, 1932–1972*, ed. Arabel Porter and Andrew Dvosin (Boston: Houghton Mifflin, 1978), p. 7; Phillips, in *A Partisan View: Five Decades of the Literary Life* (New York: Stein and Day, 1983), pp. 278–9.

48. Rahv, *Image and Idea: Twenty Essays on Literary Themes*, 2nd ed. (New York: New Directions, 1957), pp. 83–4. Further citations in the text refer to this edition.

49. The quotation is from Herbert Hawkes, dean of Columbia College, writing in 1922, and is included in Susanne Klingenstein, *Jews in the American Academy, 1900–1940: The Dynamics of Intellectual Assimilation* (New Haven: Yale University Press, 1991), p. 146. Klingenstein's accounts of Columbia and of Trilling's work are exemplary, but in my opinion, she overestimates the importance of Jewish theological thinking in Trilling's work and underestimates the degree to which the process of assimilation-by-high-culture I have been detailing here worked to create a new model of selfhood for Lionel. I attempt to detail this process hereafter. Klingenstein's study of Jewish literary scholars from the Depression to the present day has appeared too recently to be incorporated into the account I give here; the reader wishing further information about the figures I treat, and more besides, should consult *Enlarging America: The Cultural Work of Jewish Literary Scholars, 1930–1990* (Syracuse: Syracuse University Press, 1998).

50. "Some Notes for an Autobiographical Lecture," in *The Last Decade: Essays and Reviews, 1965–1975*, ed. Diana Trilling (New York: Harcourt Brace Jovanovich, 1979), p. 234.

51. For more on Erskine, see Joan Shelley Rubin, *The Making of Middlebrow Culture* (Chapel Hill: University of North Carolina Press, 1992), pp. 36–95.

52. "Lionel Trilling: A Jew at Columbia," in Trilling, *Speaking of Literature and Society* (New York: Harcourt Brace Jovanovich, 1979), p. 422. Diana Trilling gives a more extended, but less pointed, account of this episode in *The Beginning of the Journey*, pp. 266–81. She excerpts liberally from his journals of the time; these were also published in (naturally) *Partisan Review* 51 (1984), pp. 498–503.

53. Although Diana explicitly denies that Lionel felt any psychic aftereffects of his encounter with anti-Semitism, it seems impossible not to link the psychic process she describes with the prevailing anti-Semitic attitudes in the workplace.

54. Boyers, *Lionel Trilling: Negative Capability and the Wisdom of Avoidance* (Columbia: University Press of Missouri, 1977), p. 24.

55. Trilling, *The Liberal Imagination: Essays on Literature and Society* (New York: Viking Press, 1950) pp. 212–13. Further citations in the text refer to this edition. Trilling is playing off the famous enumeration of the things missing in American life offered by James in his *Hawthorne* (1879): "No State, in the European sense of the word, and indeed barely a specific national name. No sovereign, no court, no personal loyalty, no aristocracy, no church, no clergy, no army, no diplomatic service, no country gentlemen, no palaces, no castles, nor manors, nor old country-houses, nor parsonages, nor thatched cottages, nor ivied ruins; no cathedrals, nor abbeys, nor little Norman churches; no great Universities nor public schools—no Oxford, nor Eton, nor Harrow; no literature, no novels, no pictures, no political society, no sporting class—no Epsom nor Ascot." This passage, and the following claim that "what remains" is the American's "secret, his joke, one might say," can be found in *Hawthorne* (Ithaca: Cornell University Press, 1956), pp. 34–5.

56. Edel wrote in a 1930 essay on a contemporary Canadian poet, Abraham Klein, words that clearly bear on his own situation:

> Abraham Moses Klein—need we say it?—is a Jew. That means that in the Dominion of Canada, whether he be true to his race, or try to emulate his Christian brethren, most doors will be shut against him. Let him carry twenty degrees (honorary included) and our universities would as little consider him fit to teach as they would an insurance agent; they would invariably prefer a man with an Oxford third. . . . Canada as a whole does not accept Jews, for the simple reason that they are Jews. . . . Fortunately Mr. Klein has an ivory tower into which he can withdraw.

The philistinism of Canadian society meant that Klein would be, at least, left alone in his chosen vocation. Edel, "Canadian Writing of Today—Abraham M. Klein," *Canadian Forum* 12 (March 1938), p. 300.

57. As quoted in Lyall Powers, "Leon Edel: The Life of a Biographer," *American Scholar* 66 (1997), p. 605. My account of Edel is also based on the following: Edel, "How I Came to Henry James," *Henry James Review* 3 (Spring 1982), pp. 160–4; Daniel Mark Fogel, "Leon Edel and James Studies: A Survey and Evaluation," *Henry James Review* 4 (Fall 1982), pp. 3–30; and Geoffrey T. Hellman, "Chairman of the Board," *New Yorker*, March 13, 1971, pp. 44–86.

58. Quoted in Rosenberg and Goldstein, *Creators and Disturbers*, p. 408.

59. Ernest Samuels, *The Young Henry Adams* (Cambridge: Harvard University Press, 1948); *Henry Adams: The Middle Years* (Cambridge: Harvard University Press, 1958); and *Henry Adams: The Major Phase* (Cambridge: Harvard University Press, 1964). The alert reader will note that the subtitles of the last two volumes not only are drawn from the work of Henry James, but were also used by Edel as subtitles for his own massive biography. Samuels's treatment of Adams's anti-Semitism, his response to Jews, and his reactions to other racial and ethnic minorities is quite extensive. This contrasts with the treatment of Adams's anti-Semitism in another important book on Adams by another Jewish critic of the period, J. C. Levenson, *The Mind and Art of Henry Adams* (Boston:

Houghton-Mifflin, 1957). Levenson (the editor of Adams's *Collected Letters*, 6 vols. [Cambridge: Harvard University Press, 1982–1988]) devotes three pages to the topic, and concludes with the following:

> His virulence began to taper off [after the Dreyfus affair], partly because it had run its course, partly because he was harnessing his intellectual energies to hard constructive work. The latter is the one hopeful aspect of a story which is disagreeable in itself and necessarily alarming to a world that has witnessed anti-semitism as a catastrophic social event rather than as, in Adams's case, a datum of personal psychology like insomnia or addiction to privacy. One consequence of the episode is the occasional obscure use of the word "Jew" which disfigures, albeit inessentially, his late masterpieces—pockmarks of a disease that can be fatal. (254)

Adams exerted a powerful fascination on other Jewish intellectuals of the era, particularly those who were affiliated with Harvard or associated with F. O. Matthiessen and Kenneth Murdock, Harvard's nineteenth-century Americanists. Alfred Kazin, who taught there under the auspices of Matthiessen, returns over and over again in his many memoirs to the question of Adams, never so amusingly as in the following passage from *New York Jew*:

> [Richard] Hofstadter and I were in quest of, forever fascinated by . . . the years of crude expansion and technical innovation in which *our* America had settled into shape. . . . The background was America the powerhouse and our own fear of it. Hofstadter, the half-Jew and once-Lutheran choirboy, liked to mock my fascination with Henry Adams by quoting Adams's insane hatred of Jews, particularly immigrant Jews: "God tried drowning out the world once, but it did no good, and there are said to be Four-hundred-and-fifty-thousand Jews now doing Kosher in New York alone. God himself owned failure." (14)

60. Seltzer, *Henry James and the Art of Power* (Ithaca: Cornell University Press, 1985), p. 24. *A Lifetime Burning in Every Moment: From the Journals of Alfred Kazin* (New York: Harper Collins, 1996), pp. 340–1. For the anecdotes about Matthiessen and Kazin's experiences in Salzburg, see pp. 81–90.

61. "A Jamesian Parable: *The Sacred Fount*," *Bucknell Review* 11 (1963), pp. 55–71.

62. "The Lesson of the Master," in *The Cynthia Ozick Reader*, ed. Elaine Kauvar (Bloomington: Indiana University Press, 1993), p. 274. Further citations in the text refer to this edition.

63. *The Ghost Writer* (New York: Farrar, Strauss and Giroux, 1979), p 4. Further citations in the text refer to this edition.

64. In one of the most famous one-two punches in American literary criticism, Podhoretz and Howe both slammed *Portnoy* in the same issue of *Commentary* (54, December 1972). Podhoretz's brief attack was called "Laureate of the New Class" (p. 4) and denounced Roth for his belief that "Americans are disgusting people." Howe's more elaborate but no less negative critique ("Philip Roth Reconsidered," pp. 69–77) reread all of Roth's work from the perspective of *Portnoy*, denigrating him for an abiding but increasing "vulgarity."

Coda

1. Harold Bloom, *The Western Canon: The Books and School of the Ages* (New York: Harcourt Brace, 1994), p. 7. Further citations refer to this edition.

2. Allan Bloom, *The Closing of the American Mind: How Higher Education Has Failed Democracy and Impoverished the Souls of Today's Students* (New York: Simon and Schuster, 1987), pp. 74–5. Further citations refer to this edition.

3. Quoted in Adam Begley, "A Colossus among Critics: Harold Bloom," *New York Times Magazine*, September 25, 1994, p. 13.

4. Haim Chertok, "Antidote to Resentment," *Jerusalem Post*, December 8, 1995, p. 16. I cannot resist adding that Chertok notices the singular lack of interest in Henry James in Bloom's account of the canon.

5. George Sanchez, "Reading Reginald Denny: The Politics of Whiteness in the Late Twentieth Century," *American Quarterly* 47 (1994), pp. 280–94. Just to add to Sanchez's observations, things look even more complicated on the ground in 1999. I recently had occasion to visit the flashpoint of the riots, the corner of Florence and Normandie. My wife took ill on a trip from Los Angeles International Airport to suburban Pasadena, where we lived; so that I might get her some water, our van driver pulled off the expressway and into a Burger King located at this infamous corner. While he circled the parking lot to prevent carjacking, I ventured inside, to a scene superficially similar to fast-food joints I have visited in New York and Chicago: inch-thick plate glass protecting the workers; little slots, ironically reminiscent of Horn and Hardart automats of my middle-class youth, through which food was passed. But the crowd there was utterly different from any I had encountered in Harlem or the South Side. It was about one-quarter African-American (mixed age as well as class); one-quarter Latino; one-quarter Asian; and one-quarter white. If I felt out of place there, and I did, it was largely because of signs of my class (and mindset?), not my white skin.

That same week, I read stories in the local alternative weekly lamenting the demise of black Los Angeles—the African-American community is apparently decamping from places like South Central Los Angeles and Compton for the suburbs of Orange County or for Riverside and San Bernardino (the "Inland Empire"). Whatever new social, racial, and ethnic arrangements emerge in Southern California—where, one has read recently, there are more Filipinos than any one locale besides Manila; where the traditional white enclaves of Glendale (identified by urban legend as the home of the Klan in the 1950s and 1960s) and San Marino are becoming increasingly Latino- and Asian-dominated—this extraordinary demographic churning foretells, I think, the new racial and ethnic arrangements that will define American society at large. Both as a student of the past turn of the century and a participant in this one, I find the prospect enthralling.

6. A recent anthology explores many of these issues: *Insider/Outsider: American Jews and Multiculturalism*, ed. David Biale, Michael Galchinsky, and Susannah Heschel (Berkeley: University of California Press, 1998).

7. Karen Brodkin, *How Jews Became White Folks and What That Says About Race in America* (New Brunswick: Rutgers University Press, 1998). For a more nuanced, comparative, and historicized account of this process, see Matthew Jacobson, *Whiteness of a Different Color: European Immigrants and the Alchemy of Race* (Cambridge, Mass.: Harvard University Press, 1998). Gilman's observation may be found in *PMLA* 113 (Jan. 1998), p. 23.

8. My position here is a variant of that advocated by David Hollinger in his *Postethnic America: Beyond Multiculturalism* (New York: Basic Books, 1995). Hollinger correctly notes that the changing racial and ethnic mix of America is challenging the predications of the first generations of multiculturalists as fully as those who advocate unitary models of Americanization. The increasing diversity of these newer immigrants; their frequent inter-

nalization of middle-class norms; their increasing political power; their disinclination to be folded into political programs of the multicultural Left: these have borne out Hollinger's insights. (As I write these words, a majority of Latino voters in California has voted to reject multilingual education; just to complicate the situation further, the conservative Republican candidate for governor vocally opposed this initiative, in order to court the Latino vote that his predecessor had alienated.) But unlike Hollinger, I think that we are likely to witness not a new postethnic dispensation but rather more of the same: that is, uneven developments of ethnic assimilation, reticulated by class and complicated by geography. And in this process, I think, the important common denominator is going to be provided not by official culture or universities, both of which I see as increasingly irrelevant to changes in social awareness, but rather by mass culture, especially popular music.

Index